George Harris, William Jewett Tucker

**Hymns of the Faith With Psalms**

For the Use of Congregations

George Harris, William Jewett Tucker

**Hymns of the Faith With Psalms**
*For the Use of Congregations*

ISBN/EAN: 9783744783798

Printed in Europe, USA, Canada, Australia, Japan

Cover: Foto ©Lupo / pixelio.de

More available books at **www.hansebooks.com**

FROM THE LIBRARY OF

REV. LOUIS FITZ GERALD BENSON, D. D.

BEQUEATHED BY HIM TO

THE LIBRARY OF

PRINCETON THEOLOGICAL SEMINARY

*POPULAR EDITION*

# HYMNS OF THE FAITH

## With Psalms

### FOR THE USE OF CONGREGATIONS

EDITED BY

GEORGE HARRIS, D. D.

AND

WILLIAM JEWETT TUCKER, D. D.

PROFESSORS IN ANDOVER THEOLOGICAL SEMINARY

AND

EDWARD K. GLEZEN, A. M.

OF PROVIDENCE, R. I.

BOSTON AND NEW YORK
HOUGHTON, MIFFLIN AND COMPANY
The Riverside Press, Cambridge

*The Riverside Press*, *Cambridge*, *Mass.*, *U. S. A.*
Electrotyped and Printed by H. O. Houghton & Company.

# PREFACE.

The edition of "Hymns of the Faith" which is now put before the churches is not an abridgment of the original edition, but an entirely new arrangement of hymns and tunes. It fitly retains, however, the same title with its predecessor, as like that it is based upon and follows the order of the Apostles' Creed. The number of hymns has been reduced to less than five hundred, the more popular tunes have been frequently repeated, and second tunes added in many cases where old hymns have been set to new tunes.

Of the 472 hymns, about 150 are set to tunes which are familiar in all churches, such as Olmutz, Laban, Italian Hymn, and Silver Street. Nearly fifty more are set to modern music which is quite generally known and can be sung in almost any congregation or prayer-meeting, such as "Abide with me" to Eventide, "Holy, holy, holy, Lord God Almighty" to Nicæa, "Jerusalem the golden" to Ewing, and "Onward Christian soldiers" to St. Gertrude. Nearly half the tunes, therefore, are at once available in almost any church. The new tunes which are offered have been chosen for their melody, sweetness, plaintiveness, vivacity, force, or dignity, according to the character of the various hymns to which they are set. The following are a few examples of the character of the new music: Beatitude, 11, 66, 249; Marshall, 15, 74; Mirfield, 20; Coronæ, 26, 112; Humility, 8, 9, 327; St. Saviour, 44, 108, 109; Manger, 53; St. Denys, 87; Koenig, 123; Alleluia, 126; Dismission, 180, 187; Amerton, 192; Ellacombe, 195; Greenland, 199; Munus, 201, 322; Service, 209, 250; Waltham, 217, 316; St. Edith, 245, 376; Invitation, 264; Vox Dilecti, 285; Lachrymæ, 266; Emmaus, 286, 421; Tristitia, 291; Eagley, 305, 306; St. Andrew of Crete, 311; Armes, 320; Castle Rising, 395; and nearly all of the tunes under "Evening" and "The Life Everlasting."

The utmost care has been taken to adapt the music to the sentiment and rhythm of the hymns. Some hymns which have heretofore been set to unsuitable tunes have been recovered by appropriate adaptations, and some have been given a new tune when the old has been retained, such as "Rock of Ages, cleft for me" to Rock of Ages, "There is a fountain filled with blood" to St. Agnes, "Stand up, stand up for Jesus" to Greenland, "Nearer my God to Thee" to Kedron, "Just as I am, without one plea" to Penitence, "O holy Saviour, Friend unseen" to Pascal, "Majestic sweetness sits enthroned" to St. Leonard, and "Soldiers of Christ, arise" to Amerton. The best tunes have been repeated as frequently as practicable. Many of the tunes, without being trivial or secular, are admirably adapted to meetings of evangelistic preaching and religious revival. There are also under some of the topics hymns and tunes for children, besides the choral and animated music which children love and in which the book abounds.

The Amen is given at the end of every hymn, and the musical notes for singing it

## PREFACE.

with every tune. It should become an invariable practice to use the Amen, as the singing thus becomes more significant as worship, and does not end abruptly.

In order to give the proper movement the number of quarter notes to be sung in a minute is indicated at the beginning of each tune. This is of great service to organists and leaders, as a given mark, 65, 90, 112, shows at a glance the time which should be taken, whether slow or fast or moderate. The effectiveness of many tunes, especially those which require a quick movement, is lost if the rate is taken slowly, and stately, solid, choral tunes may be spoiled by too rapid singing.

In making a popular edition of "Hymns of the Faith," the compilers have not allowed themselves to lower the standard of hymnology or of church music which they at the first adopted. The present book is not designed to be inclusive of such hymns and tunes as have simply a transient popularity. Neither is it designed to compete with books which have a special object, like well known collections of Revival Melodies, or Sunday-school Hymnals, or the books of particular societies, like the Society of Christian Endeavor. Any or all of these may be used to supplement the working hymn-book of the church, but they cannot take the place of it. That book, as the compilers believe, has a distinct office to fulfill, which cannot be met if it is constructed with a view to satisfy every special use and to cater to every taste. The hymn-book of the church, it is assumed, should represent the church in its entire life, its faith, its experience, its devotion, and its work, but it should represent it consistently. There seems to be no reason why the hymns or the music of the church should be on a lower grade or have less educating and stimulating power than the sermon, or the instructions of the Sunday-school, or the devotions of the prayer-meeting. And it is believed that the church has in its possession hymns and tunes which are full of inspiration and freedom, of tenderness and persuasion, of incitement and awakening; and that there is no occasion to resort to the more doubtful secular music or to imitations of it.

It has been the aim of the compilers to prepare a book which may be used in all departments of the life and activity of the church, and which may minister to its spiritual growth and enlargement.

# AUTHORS OF HYMNS.

Adams, Mrs. Sarah F. (*d.* 1848), 13.
Addison, Joseph (*d.* 1719), 351.
Alexander, Mrs. Cecil F., 54, 73, 88, 89, 110, 268, 395.
Alford, Rev. Henry (*d.* 1871), 200, 393, 461.
Allen, Rev. James (*d.* 1804), 93.
Allen, Oswald, 261.
Ambrose of Milan (*d.* 397), 430.
Anatolius of Constantinople (*d.* 458), 69, 441.
Andrew of Crete (*d.* 732), 311.
Anstice, Joseph (*d.* 1836), 66.
Aquinas, Thomas (*d.* 1274), 182.
Auber, Harriet (*d.* 1862), 140, 416.

Bacon, Rev. Leonard (*d.* 1881), 221, 470.
Baker, Francis (*d.* 16th cent.), 400.
Baker, Sir Henry W. (*d.* 1877), 17.
Bakewell, John (*d.* 1819), 124.
Bancroft, Mrs. Charitie L. S., 246.
Barbauld, Mrs. Anna L. (*d.* 1825), 250, 459.
Baring-Gould, Rev. Sabine, 191, 240, 449.
Barton, Bernard (*d.* 1849), 156, 370.
Bathurst, Rev. William H. B. (*d.* 1877), 338.
Baxter, Rev. Richard (*d.* 1691), 1, 357.
Beddome, Rev. Benjamin (*d.* 1795), 255.
Bernard of Clairvaux (*d.* 1153), 20, 88, 187, 307.
Bernard of Cluny (*d.* 12th cent.). 401, 403, 404, 405.
Bethune, Rev. George W. (*d.* 1862), 380.
Bickersteth, Rev. Edward H., 40, 186, 333.
Blew, William J., 439.
Bode, John E., 194.
Boden, Rev. James (*d.* 1841), 114.
Bonar, Rev. Horatius, 47, 131, 162, 211, 270, 279, 282, 285, 286, 334, 342, 372, 377, 406, 455.
Borthwick, Jane, 135, 263.
Bowring, Sir John (*d.* 1872), 64, 90, 352.
Bridges, Matthew (*d.* 1847), 125.
Brooks, Rev. Charles T. (*d.* 1883), 472.
Brooks, Rev. Phillips, 56.
Brown, Mrs. Phebe H. (*d.* 1861), 437.
Browne, Mrs. Jane E., 150.
Buckoll, Henry J. (*d.* 1871), 431.
Burns, Rev. James D. (*d.* 1864), 15.

Campbell, Robert, 102.
Carlyle, Rev. Joseph D. (*d.* 1804), 7.
Cary, Phœbe (*d.* 1871), 387.
Caswall, Rev. Edward (*d.* 1878), 4, 20, 42, 307, 432, 436.
Cennick, Rev. John (*d.* 1755), 136, 230, 309.
Chandler, Rev. John (*d.* 1876), 61, 419, 430.

Clement of Alexandria (*d.* 3d cent.), 173.
Clephane, Elizabeth C. (*d.* 1868), 280.
Collins, Rev. Henry. 291.
Conder, Josiah (*d.* 1855), 34, 181.
Cooper, Rev. Edward (*d.* 1833), 271.
Cowper, William (*d.* 1800), 8, 38, 78, 94, 154, 257, 369, 467.
Cox, Frances E., 103.
Coxe, Rev. Arthur C., 65, 163.
Cross, Mrs. A. C., 410.
Crossman, Rev. Samuel (*d.* 1683), 402.
Crosswell, Rev. William (*d.* 1851), 206.

Dana, Mrs. Mary S. B., 289.
Dayman, Rev. Edwin A., 133, 378, 465.
Deck, James G., 304.
Denny, Sir Edward, 63, 130, 317.
Dexter, Rev. Henry M., 173.
Dix, William C., 58.
Doane, Rev. George W. (*d.* 1859), 217, 435.
Dobell, John (*d.* 1840), 260.
Doddridge, Rev. Philip (*d.* 1751), 5, 44, 115, 164, 171, 188, 205, 244, 288, 305, 312, 354, 412, 458.
Draper, Rev. Bourne H. (*d.* 1843), 214, 215.
Duffield, Rev. George, 199.
Duncan, Mary L., 451.
Dunn, Rev. Robinson P. (*d.* 1867), 381.
Dwight, Rev. John S., 472.
Dwight, Rev. Timothy (*d.* 1817), 159.

Edmeston, James (*d.* 1867), 336, 443.
Ellerton, Rev. John, 105, 383, 414, 438, 440.
Elliott, Charlotte (*d.* 1871), 267, 320, 328, 340, 365.
Elliott, Emily E. S., 53.
Evans, Rev. James H. (*d.* 1849), 322.
Evans, Rev. Jonathan (*d.* 1809), 95.

Faber, Rev. Frederick W. (*d.* 1863), 35, 85, 151, 210, 249, 251, 284, 353, 391, 392, 434, 450.
Fabin, 203.
Fawcett, Rev. John (*d.* 1817), 155, 231, 424, 427.
Fortunatus, Venantius (*d.* 609), 105.
Fulbert of Chartres (*d.* 1028), 102.

Ganse, Rev. Hervey D., 77.
Gellert, Christian F. (*d.* 1769), 103.
Gerhardt, Rev. Paul (*d.* 1676), 32, 51, 80, 337.
Gill, Thomas H., 62, 67, 142, 152, 293.
Gilmore, Rev. Joseph H., 327.
Gladden, Rev. Washington, 76.

# AUTHORS OF HYMNS

Goethe, J. W. von (*d.* 1832), 371.
Grant, Sir Robert (*d.* 1838), 25.
Greek Hymn, 31.
Grigg, Rev. Joseph (*d.* 1768), 180, 262.
Guion, Jeanne M. B. (*d.* 1717), 467.

Hammond, Rev. William (*d.* 1783), 116.
Hardenberg, Friedrich von (*d.* 1801), 99.
Hart, Rev. Joseph (*d.* 1768), 145.
Hastings, Thomas (*d.* 1872), 252, 253, 349.
Haweis, Rev. Thomas (*d.* 1820), 243, 350, 397.
Hawks, Mrs. Annie S. (*d.* 1872), 344.
Hayward, J. (?), 407.
Heath, Rev. George (*d.* about 1800), 321.
Heber, Rev. Reginald (*d.* 1826), 3, 59, 81, 170, 185, 224, 228, 272, 447, 464.
Hedge, Rev. Frederic H. (*d.* 1890), 364.
Hemans, Mrs. Felicia D. (*d.* 1835), 389.
Herbert, Rev. George (*d.* 1632), 208.
Holmes, Oliver W., 30, 330.
How, Rev. William W., 153, 204, 233, 245, 469.
Humphrey, Rev. Joseph (*d.* about 1770), 295.
Hupton, Job (*d.* 1849), 18.
Hyde, Mrs. Abigail B. (*d.* 1872), 256.

Ingemann, Bernhardt S. (*d.* 1862), 240.
Irons, Rev. William J. (*d.* 1883), 343.

John of Damascus (*d.* 8th cent.), 100.
Johns, Rev. John (*d.* 1847), 216, 218.
Johnson, Rev. Samuel (*d.* 1882), 160.
Joseph of the Studium (*d.* 9th cent.), 197, 229.
Julian, J., 43, 123.

Keble, Rev. John (*d.* 1866), 26, 141, 429, 452.
Keith, George (*d.* about 1800), 325.
Kelly, Rev. Thomas (*d.* 1855), 97, 109, 112, 118, 220, 300.
Ken, Rev. Thomas (*d.* 1711), 428, 444.
Kennedy, Rev. Benjamin H., 91.
King, Rev. John (*d.* 1858), 82.

Langford, Rev. John (*d.* 1790), 296.
Laurenti, Laurentius (*d.* 1722), 135.
Leeson, Jane E., 362.
Lockwood, Amelia De F., 239.
Longfellow, Rev. Samuel, 161, 209, 212.
Luke, Mrs. Jemima, 71.
Luther, Rev. Martin (*d.* 1546), 52, 364.
Lynch, Rev. Thomas T. (*d.* 1871), 68.
Lyte, Rev. Henry F. (*d.* 1847), 19, 36, 283, 345, 386, 417, 453, 462.

Mackay, Mrs. Margaret, 379.
Malan, Rev. Cæsar H. A. (*d.* 1864), 380, 381.
Mant, Rev. Richard (*d.* 1848), 237.
Marchant, John (*d.* about 1590), 278.
Mason, Rev. John (*d.* 1694), 413.
Maude, Mrs. Mary F., 358.
McCheyne, Rev. Robert M. (*d.* 1843), 138.
Medley, Rev. Samuel (*d.* 1799), 298, 303.
Millard, Rev. James E., 23.

Milman, Rev. Henry H. (*d.* 1868), 79, 331.
Monsell, Rev. John S. B. (*d.* 1875), 12, 193, 213, 323, 376.
Montgomery, James (*d.* 1854), 21, 60, 169, 179, 184, 207, 223, 238, 346, 366, 367, 382, 385, 422, 426.
Muhlenberg, Rev. William A. (*d.* 1877), 172, 178.

Neale, Rev. John M. (*d.* 1866), 18, 69, 83, 100, 134, 165, 197, 229, 247, 311, 355, 401, 403, 404, 405, 441.
Nelson, Earl, 234.
Nevin, Rev. Edwin H., 335.
Newman, Rev. John H. (*d.* 1890), 347.
Newton, Rev. John (*d.* 1807), 6, 10, 120, 158, 273, 308, 408, 454.
Noel, Caroline M., 127.

Oakeley, Rev. Frederic (*d.* 1880), 55.
Old Latin Hymns by unknown authors, 4, 42, 55, 104, 111, 165, 166, 419, 436.
Onderdonk, Rev. Henry U. (*d.* 1858), 258, 259.

Palgrave, Francis T., 74.
Palmer, Rev. Ray (*d.* 1887), 14, 146, 175, 182, 187, 306.
Perronnett, Rev. Edward (*d.* 1792), 113.
Pierpont, F. S., 360.
Plumptre, Rev. Edward H., 70.
Pott, Rev. Francis, 28, 104.
Potter, Rev. Thomas J., 202.
Prentiss, Mrs. Elizabeth P. (*d.* 1878), 348.
Procter, Adelaide A. (*d.* 1864), 359.
Prynne, George R., 274.
Pusey, Philip, 166.

Rawson, George, 148, 183, 448.
Reed, Rev. Andrew (*d.* 1862), 46, 421.
Robert II. of France (*d.* 1031), 146.
Robinson, Rev. Robert (*d.* 1790), 126, 310.
Russell, Rev. Arthur T. (*d.* 1874), 80.

Santolius, Maglorianus (*d.* 1684), 87.
Seagrave, Rev. Robert, (*d.* 1764), 157.
Sears, Rev. Edmund H. (*d.* 1876), 49, 50.
Shepherd, Anne, 306.
Shepherd, Rev. Thomas (*d.* 1739), 318.
Shirley, Rev. Walter (*d.* 1786), 93.
Shurtleff, Rev. Ernest W., 196.
Smith, Mrs. Caroline S., 442.
Smith, Rev. Samuel F., 222, 445, 468.
Steele, Anne (*d.* 1778), 108, 149, 248, 341.
Stennett, Rev. Samuel (*d.* 1795), 121, 299.
Stone, Rev. Samuel J., 157, 265.
Stowell, Rev. Hugh (*d.* 1865), 9.
Swain, Joseph, 232.
Swain, Rev. Leonard (*d.* 1869), 314, 315.

Tappan, Rev. William B. (*d.* 1849), 84, 388.
Taylor, Rev. Thomas R. (*d.* 1835), 384.
Tersteegen, Gerhard (*d.* 1769), 176, 263.
Thomson, John (*d.* 1818), 466.
Thring, Rev. Godfrey, 57, 128, 301, 446.
Thrupp, Dorothy A. (*d.* 1847), 361.

## AUTHORS OF HYMNS

Toplady, Rev. Augustus M. (d. 1778), 269, 332, 356.
Tuttiett, Rev. Laurence, 137, 195.
Twells, Henry, 433.
Unknown Authorship, 111, 281, 292, 368, 399.
Upham, Rev. Thomas C. (d. 1872), 190.

Voke, Mrs. (d. about 1825), 227.
Von Canitz, Friedrich R. (d. 1699), 431.

Wardlaw, Rev. Ralph (d. 1853), 216.
Ware, Rev. Henry, Jr. (d. 1843), 33.
Waring, Anna L., 363.
Watts, Rev. Isaac (d. 1748), 16, 22, 24, 29, 30, 37, 45, 75, 86, 92, 117, 119, 143, 144, 167, 168, 177, 225, 226, 236, 242, 313, 316, 324, 329, 339, 373, 390, 398, 411, 415, 418, 420, 423, 425, 471.
Weissel, Rev. George (d. 1635), 290.
Wesley, Rev. Charles (d. 1788), 2, 11, 48, 98, 106, 107, 122, 129, 132, 136, 189, 192, 235, 239, 254, 276, 277, 294, 297, 302, 326, 375, 456.
Wesley, Rev. John (d. 1791), 139, 208, 337.
Whately, Rev. Richard (d. 1363), 447.
Whitfield, Rev. Frederic, 275.
Whiting, William (d. 1878), 463, 607.
Whittemore, J., 362.
Whittier, John G., 72.
Whytehead, T. W., 96.
Wigner, John M., 264.
Williams, Helen M. (d. 1827), 374.
Williams, Rev. Isaac (d. 1865), 201, 266.
Williams, Rev. William (d. 1791), 41, 219.
Winkworth, Catherine (d. 1878), 51, 99, 290.
Wolcott, Rev. Samuel (d. 1886), 198.
Wordsworth, Rev. Christopher (d. 1885), 101, 147, 174, 241, 394, 409, 460.
Wreford, Rev. John R. (d. 1881), 287.

Young, J., 27.

Zinzendorf, Nikolaus L. (d. 1760), 139.

# INDEX

## OF COMPOSERS, ARRANGEMENTS, AND SOURCES OF TUNES.

Ahle, Johann R. (*d.* 1673), 98, 221, 296, 459.
Allen, George N. (*d.* 1877), 319.
Armes, Philip, 320.

Baker, F. G., 44, 108.
Baker, Rev. Sir Henry W. (*d.* 1877), 180, 187, 247.
Barber's Psalm Tunes, 273.
Barkworth, Rev. S. M., 372.
Barnby, Joseph, 12, 43, 70, 80, 106, 123, 166, 172, 178, 206, 233, 235, 291, 342, 378, 391, 404, 432, 449, 450, 477, 480.
Bartholemon, François H. (*d.* 1808), 428.
Beethoven, Ludwig von (*d.* 1827), 139, 373, 398, 458, 474.
Bennett, E., 173.
Blumenthal, Jacques, 254.
Bonner, Robert, 409.
Boyce, William, 478.
Bradbury, William B. (*d.* 1868), 84, 379, 429.
Brown, Arthur H., 176, 289, 334.
Burgmüller, Friedrich (*d.* 1824), 400.

Caldeck, G. F., 333.
Calkin, J. Baptiste, 201, 217, 260, 316, 322, 370.
Carey, Henry (*d.* 1743), 468.
Chard, W., 475.
Chope, Richard R., 208.
Church Psalm and Hymn Book, 174.
Cobb, Gerard, 111.
Conkey, Ithamar, 90.
Cottman, Arthur (*d.* 1879), 20, 152, 160.
Crasselius, Rev. Bartholomäus (*d.* 1724), 61.
Croft, William (*d.* 1727), 27, 37, 56, 163, 167, 339, 406, 486.
Crosbie, Rev. H. A., 32, 127, 317.
Cuff, C. R., 71.
Cutler, Henry S., 228.

Darwall, Rev. John (*d.* 1789), 33, 121.
Daye's Psalter, pub. 1563 (?), 188, 237, 314.
Deane, W. H., 131.
Dykes, Rev. John B. (*d.* 1876), 3, 11, 17, 66, 72, 79, 81, 85, 90, 94, 137, 140, 143, 194, 249, 257, 261, 268, 285, 311, 318, 326, 331, 346, 347, 357, 365, 369, 371, 383, 393, 394, 441, 442, 460, 463.

Elliott, James W., 34, 105, 115.
Elvey, Sir George J., 47, 125, 417, 461, 479.
English Air, 396.
Estes' Psalter, pub. 1592, 141.
Ewing, Rt. Rev. Alexander, 405.

Felton, W., 485.
Flemming, Friedrich F. (*d.* 1813), 328.

Gardner, William (*d.* 1853), 119, 205, 297.
Garrett, George M., 133, 379.
Gaul, Albert R., 68, 253.
Gauntlett, Henry J. (*d.* 1876), 54, 78, 102, 103, 147, 212, 241, 338, 352, 401, 424, 438.
Geer, Rev. G. J., 15, 74, 377.
Geneva Psalter, pub. 1551, 24.
German, 18, 195, 220, 229.
Giardini, Felice (*d.* 1796), 2, 114, 198, 448.
Glezen, Edward K., 64, 69, 89, 203, 332, 367, 380, 381, 455, 482, 487.
Goss, Sir John (*d.* 1880), 19, 46, 128.
Gould, John E. (*d.* 1875), 50, 263.
Gould, N. D., 388.
Gounod, Charles, 134, 362.
Greatorex, Henry W. (*d.* 1857), 39, 168, 385.
Greek Melody, 397.

Haking, Rev. R., 148, 272.
Händel, George Frederick (*d.* 1759), 45, 145, 207, 218, 293, 312.
Hasler, H. Leonhard (*d.* 1612), 88.
Hastings, Thomas (*d.* 1872), 219, 269, 437.
Hatton, John (*d.* 1793), 21, 109.
Havergal, Frances R. (*d.* 1879), 57, 193.
Havergal, Rev. William H. (*d.* 1870), 122, 155, 232, 419, 431.
Haydn, Franz Joseph (*d.* 1809), 158, 431.
Haydn, Johann M. (*d.* 1806), 25, 165, 200, 336.
Hayes, P., 484.
Hayne, Rev. Leighton G., 279.
Haynes, William, 97, 186, 192.
Hermann, N., 16, 375.
Hervey, Rev. Frederick A. J., 395.
Hews, George, 445.
Hiles, Henry, 7, 299.
Hodges, Rev. John S. B., 185.
Holden, Oliver (*d.* 1831), 113.
Hopkins, Edward J., 328, 436, 440.
Howard, Samuel (*d.* 1782), 177, 236.
Hummel, Johann N. (*d.* 1837), 162, 382.
Husband, Rev. E., 182, 245, 376.

Irons, Herbert S., 399.

Jackson, R., 469.
Jewson, James P., 184, 350.
Jones, J., 483.
Jones, William (*d.* 1800), 154, 161, 274.

## COMPOSERS, ARRANGEMENTS, ETC.

Kettle, C. E., 389.
Kingsley, George (d. 1884), 248, 307.
Kirbye, George (d. about 1700), 35.
Knapp, William (d. 1768), 52, 412, 470.
Kocher, Conrad (d. about 1835), 58, 360, 462.

Lahee, Henry, 45, 210, 238.
Langran, James, 265.
Lausanne Psalter, 135, 199, 213.
Lee, W., 481.
Lomas, George, 387.
Lowe, Albert, 73, 126.
Luther, Rev. Martin (d. 1546), 364.

Maker, F. C., 51, 183, 264, 280, 340, 359, 446.
Malan, Rev. Cæsar H. A. (d. 1864), 91, 295.
Marsh, Simeon B. (d. 1875), 326.
Mason, Lowell (d. 1872), 10, 13, 14, 31, 45, 75, 94, 118, 146, 149, 151, 189, 211, 223, 224, 231, 252, 259, 267, 303, 316, 321, 324, 351, 356, 408, 409, 472.
Mendelssohn-Bartholdy, J. L. F. (d. 1847), 48, 77, 179, 209, 250, 270, 300, 310.
Miller, Edward (d. 1807), 92, 175.
Monk, William H., 23, 26, 87, 98, 107, 112, 132, 281, 422, 434, 452, 453.
Mornington, Lord Garret W. (d. 1781), 216, 244, 416.
Mozart, Wolfgang A. (d. 1791), 164, 283, 323.

Nägeli, Hans G. (d. 1836), 341, 354.
Nares, James (d. 1783), 457.

Oakeley, Sir Herbert S., 414.
Oliver, Henry K. (d. 1885), 86, 262.
Ouseley, Rev. Sir Frederick A. G., 304.

Palestrina, Giovanni P. (d. 1594), 104.
Pigou, Rev. F., 343.
Pleyel, Ignace (d. 1831), 4, 62, 230, 358, 374, 415.

Read, Daniel (d. 1836), 288.
Reading, John (d. 1692), 55, 325.
Redhead, Richard, 42, 95, 96, 117, 136, 269, 277, 290, 353, 466.
Reinagle Alexander R. (d. 1877), 353, 374.
Reinecke, Carl, 53.
Roe, J. E. (d. 1871), 294.
Root, George F. (d. 1882), 398.
Rossini, Giachino A., 292.
Rousseau, Jean J. (d. 1778), 349, 427.
Russell, W., 476.

St. Albans' Tune Book, pub. 1865, 170, 267, 276.
St. Gall. Cath. Gesangbuch, 197, 403.
Sachsen Choralbuch, 181, 243.
Sacred Mus. Cabinet, 451.
Scheffler, Johann G. W., 76, 330, 433.
Schein, Johann H. (d. 1630), 271.
Schumann, Robert (d. 1856), 204.
Scotch Psalter, pub. 1615, 30, 84, 411, 465.
Shrubsole, Rev. William (d. 1806) (?), 113.
Sleeman, P. R., 344.
Smart, Henry (d. 1879), 41, 60, 100, 240, 251, 283, 392.
Smith, Isaac (d. 1800), 110, 192, 337, 423.
Spark, William, 59.
Spratt, A. B., 13, 348.
Stainer, John, 40, 99, 275, 282.
Stanley, Samuel (d. 1822), 239.
Steggall, Charles, 1, 302, 402, 447.
Störl, Johann G. C. (d. 1743), 352, 424.
Sullivan, Sir Arthur, 28, 101, 124, 191, 202, 266, 384, 464.

Tallis, Thomas (d. 1585), 36, 284, 368, 444, 474.
Tansur, William, 471.
Taylor, V. C., 39, 467.
Teschner, Melchior (d. about 1600), 83, 234.
Tours, Berthold, 82.
Troyte, Arthur H. D. (d. 1857), 453.
Tuckerman, Samuel P., 8, 327, 366.
Turle, James, 63, 144, 156.
Tye's Psalter, pub. 1621, 278.

Venua, Frederick M. A., 418.
Vincent, C. J., Jr., 22, 242.

Walch, J., 130, 305.
Wallace, William V. (d. 1865), 72.
Wartensee, X. von, 250.
Webb, George J., 222.
Webbe, Samuel (d. 1816), 390, 413, 454, 456.
Weber, Carl Maria von (d. 1826), 6, 120, 129, 335, 435.
Wesley, Samuel S. (d. 1876), 138, 150, 153, 157, 363.
Willcox, John H. (d. 1875), 361.
Williams, Aaron (d. 1776), 116, 309, 329, 425.
Wilkes, John P., 255, 386.
Willis, Richard S., 49.
Wilson, Hugh (d. about 1820), 345.
Woodbury, Isaac B. (d. 1858), 73, 171.
Woodman, Jonathan C., 5, 159, 190.

Zeuner, Charles (d. 1857), 29, 102, 214, 225.

# ALPHABETICAL INDEX OF TUNES.

The asterisk indicates that the tune has been named by the editors.

Abridge, 110.
Adeste Fideles, 55.
Adoration, 122, 419.
Albans, 200.
Alford, 393.
All Saints, 228.
Alleluia,* 126.
Alma Lux,* 57, 193.
Almsgiving, 365, 460.
America, 468.
Amerton, 192.
Amsterdam, 457.
Angel Guards,* 447.
Angel Voices, 28.
Angelus, 76, 330, 433.
Antioch, 45.
Ariel, 303.
Armagh, 63, 144, 156.
Armes.* 320.
Arthur's Seat, 46.
Ascension, 107.
Aubrey, 22, 242.
Audi Nos,* 274.
Aurelia, 153, 157, 363.
Austria, 158.
Avon, 345.

Babylon's Streams, 84.
Beatitude, 11, 66, 249.
Belmont, 300, 413.
Benedic Anima, 19, 128.
Benevento, 454.
Bera, 262.
Bethany, 13.
Bethany (Eng.), 251, 283.
Bishopsgate, 298.
Blessed Saviour,* 301.
Blumenthal, 254.
Bonner, 409.
Boylston, 231.
Brattle Street, 374.

Carol, 49.
Castle Rising, 395.
Chalvey, 279.
Children's Praises,* 396.
Children's Prayer, 451.
Children's Service, 203.
Christ Church. 1, 302, 402.
Christmas, 312.
Church Triumphant, 34, 115.
Cloisters, 106.

Coronæ, 26, 112.
Coronation, 113.
Cowper, 94.

Dalehurst, 152.
Darwall, 33, 121.
Dedham, 119, 205, 297.
Deliverance, 70.
Dennis, 354.
Diademata, 125.
Dismission, 180, 187.
Dix, 58, 360, 462.
Domenica, 414.
Dominus regit me, 17.
Dorrnance, 73.
Dort, 472.
Downs, 351.
Downton, 150.
Duke Street, 21, 169.
Dulce Carmen, 165, 336.
Dundee, 30, 465.
Dunn, 381.

Eagley, 130, 305.
Easter Hymn, 98.
Ein Feste Burg, 364.
Eisenach, 271.
Ellacombe, 195.
Ellers, 440.
Ellesdie, 283.
Elvet, 357.
Emmanuel, 373, 398.
Emmaus, 286, 421.
Eucharistic Hymn, 185.
Euroclydon, 69.
Evan. 155, 232.
Eventide, 453.
Eversley, 105.
Every Hour,* 344.
Ewing, 405.

Faith, 72, 318.
Faithful, 366.
Federal Street, 86, 262.
Filius Dei, 68.
Flavian, 273.
Flemming, 328.
Frederika, 89.
Freude,* 436.

Galilee,* 73.
Gennesaret,* 464.

Germany, 139, 458.
Gould, 50.
Gounod,* 362.
Grace Church, 4, 62, 415.
Greenland, 135, 199, 213.
Greenville, 349, 427.
Grostete, 39.
Guildford, 186.
Guter Hirt,* 172.

Hamburg, 75, 267.
Harwell, 118.
Haskell, 64.
Haydn, 431.
Heber, 248, 307.
Hebron, 149.
Hendon, 91.
Hermann, 16, 375.
Hermon, 151.
Himmel,* 384.
Holley, 445.
Hollingside, 326.
Holy Cross, 99.
Holy Trinity, 206, 235, 450.
Homeland, 397.
Horton, 250.
Hosanna, 81.
Humility, 8, 327.
Hummel, 29, 102.
Hursley, 452.

Ignatius, 438.
Illo, 31.
In Christo,* 379.
In Memoriam, 183, 340, 446.
Innocents, 23, 422.
Invitation, 264.
Irby, 54.
Islington, 133.
Italian Hymn, 2, 114, 198, 448.

Jesus Bone Pastor, 361.
Jesus Magister Bone, 194, 261.

Kedron, 13, 348.
Kirby Bedon, 173.
Knight, 455.
Koenig,* 106, 123.

Laban, 321.
Lachrymæ, 266.

## ALPHABETICAL INDEX OF TUNES

Lancashire, 100.
Lancaster, 177, 236.
Langdale, 42.
Langran, 265.
Lauda Zion, 300.
Laudes Domini, 432.
Laus Deo, 43.
Leighton, 108, 385.
Lisbon, 288.
London, 167.
Louvan, 39, 467.
Lux Benigna, 347.
Lux Eoi, 101, 124.
Lyons, 25.
Lyte, 255, 386.

Magdalena, 40, 275, 282.
Magdalen College, 97.
Maitland, 319.
Manger, 53.
Manoah, 292.
Marshall, 15, 74, 377.
Martyn, 326.
Mary Magdalene, 346, 371.
Mason, 332, 367.
Mear, 309, 329.
Melita, 137, 463.
Mendebras, 409.
Mendelssohn, 48.
Mendon, 211, 316, 324.
Merrial, 449.
Merton, 184, 350.
Miles Lane, 113.
Mirfield, 20, 160.
Missionary Chant, 214, 225.
Missionary Hymn, 224.
Morning Hymn, 428.
Mornington, 216, 244, 416.
Moultrie, 111.
Mozart, 164, 323.
Munus,* 201, 322.

Naomi, 341.
Nativity, 45, 210, 238.
Nativity, New, 51.
New Year's Hymn, 456.
Nicæa, 3.
Nox Præcessit, 370.
Nuremberg, 98, 221, 296, 459.

Oblations,* 59.
Old Hundredth, 24.
Old 148th, 27, 406.
Olive's Brow, 84.
Olivet, 14, 146.
Olmutz, 10, 189, 356.
Olney, 259.
Ouseley, 304.

Palestrina, 104.
Paradise, 391.
Park Street, 418.
Pascal, 328.
Passion Chorale, 88.
Pax Tecum, 333.
Pearsall, 197, 403.

Penitence, 267, 276.
Peregrinus, 253.
Peterborough, 174.
Pilgrims, 392.
Pleyel's Hymn, 230, 358.
Portuguese Hymn, 325.
Promise, 240.

Rathbun, 90.
Ratisbon, 181, 243.
Ravenscroft,* 95, 136.
Regent Square, 41, 60.
Renovation, 162, 382.
Requiem, 378.
Requiescat, 383.
Rest, 379.
Rest (Eng.), 277.
Resurrection, 18, 220.
Rhine, 400.
Risenholme, 241.
Rock of Ages, 96, 269.
Rockingham (Eng.), 92, 175.
Rodbourne, 148, 272.
Rosefield, 295.
Rosslyn, 71.

St. Agnes, 94, 143, 268, 331, 369.
St. Alban, 208.
St. Albinus, 103.
St. Alphege, 401.
St. Ambrose, 147.
St. Anatolius, 441.
St. Andrew, 12, 178.
St. Andrew of Crete, 311.
St. Ann's, 37, 163, 339.
St. Anselm, 80, 404.
St. Anstell, 289.
St. Bees, 257.
St. Cephas, 127.
St. Christopher, 280.
St. Cross, 85.
St. Cuthbert, 140.
St. Denys, 87.
St. Drosdane, 79.
St. Edith, 182, 245, 376.
St. Fulbert, 102.
St. George's Chapel, 47, 417, 461.
St. Gertrude, 191.
St. Leonard, 7, 299.
St. Mabyn, 176, 334.
St. Mark, 78, 212, 338.
St. Martins, 471.
St. Mary, 278.
St. Matthew, 56.
St. Matthias, 434.
St. Michael, 188, 237, 314.
St. Paul's College, 387.
St. Peter's, Oxford, 353, 374.
St. Saviour, 44, 108.
St. Sebastian, 138.
St. Stephen, 154, 161.
St. Sylvester, 442.
St. Theodulph, 83, 234.
St. Theresa, 202.

St. Thomas, 116, 425.
Sabbath, 408.
Sanctuary, 394.
Sarum, 233.
Sawley, 343.
Schumann, 204.
Serenity, 72.
Service,* 179, 209, 250, 270.
Seymour, 6, 435.
Sicilian Mariner's Hymn, 93, 310.
Sienna, 131.
Siloam, 170, 171.
Silver Street, 192, 337, 423.
Southwell, 390.
State Street, 5, 159, 190.
Stephanos, 247.
Stuttgard, 352, 424.
Summons,* 260.
Supplication, 132, 281.
Sychar, 90.

Tallis' Canon, 444.
Tallis' Ordinal, 36, 284, 368.
Thatcher, 145, 207, 218, 293.
The Saviour's Call, 252.
Toplady, 269.
Tours, 82.
Tristitia, 291.
Troyte's Chant, 453.
Trust, 77, 310.
Tunbridge, 117, 290.

Unser Herrscher, 229.

Varina, 398.
Veni Immanuel, 134.
Via,* 342.
Via Crucis, 372.
Victor, 380.
Vox Dilecti, 285.

Waltham, 217, 316.
Wareham, 52, 412, 470.
Warwick, 230.
Waveney, 355, 466.
Waverton, 469.
Webb, 222.
Welfield, 32, 317.
Wentworth, 359.
Weston, 294.
Wickliffe, 437.
Wilmot, 120, 129, 335.
Winchester, New, 61.
Winchester, Old, 141.
Windsor, 35.
Woodland, 388.
Woolwich, 389.

Yarmouth, 223.
York, 411.

Zephyr, 429.
Zion, 219.

# METRICAL INDEX OF TUNES.

### COMMON METRE.

| | |
|---|---|
| Abridge | 110 |
| All Saints, D | 228 |
| Armagh | 63, 144, 156 |
| Antioch | 45 |
| Aubrey | 22, 242 |
| Avon | 345 |
| Beatitude | 11, 66, 249 |
| Belmont | 390, 413 |
| Brattle Street | 374 |
| Carol | 49 |
| Castle Rising, D | 395 |
| Children's Praises, with Chorus | 386 |
| Christmas | 312 |
| Coronation | 113 |
| Cowper | 94 |
| Dalehurst | 152 |
| Dedham | 119, 205, 297 |
| Deliverance, D | 70 |
| Downs | 351 |
| Downton | 150 |
| Dundee | 30, 465 |
| Eagley | 130, 305 |
| Elvet | 357 |
| Emmanuel | 373, 398 |
| Emmaus | 286, 421 |
| Evan | 155, 232 |
| Faith | 72, 318 |
| Faithful | 366 |
| Filius Dei, D | 68 |
| Flavian | 273 |
| Frederika, D | 89 |
| Gould | 50 |
| Heber | 248, 307 |
| Hermann | 16, 375 |
| Hermon | 151 |
| Holy Cross | 99 |
| Holy Trinity | 206, 235, 450 |
| Hummel | 20, 102 |
| Lancaster | 177, 236 |
| Loudon | 167 |
| Maitland | 319 |
| Manoah | 292 |
| Mear | 309, 329 |
| Merton | 184, 350 |
| Miles Lane | 113 |
| Mirfield | 20, 160 |
| Naomi | 341 |
| Nativity | 45, 210, 238 |
| Nox Præcessit | 370 |
| Paradise, D | 391 |
| Rhine | 400 |
| St. Agnes | 94, 143, 268, 331, 363 |
| St. Ann's | 37, 163, 339 |
| St. Fulbert | 102 |
| St. Leonard, D | 7, 230 |
| St. Mark | 78, 212, 338 |
| St. Martin's | 471 |
| St. Mary | 278 |
| St. Matthew, D | 56 |
| St. Peter's, Oxford | 353, 374 |
| St. Saviour | 44, 108 |
| St. Stephen | 154, 161 |
| Sawley | 343 |
| Serenity | 72 |
| Siloam | 170 |
| Southwell | 399 |
| Tallis' Ordinal | 36, 284, 368 |
| Varina | 398 |
| Vox Dilecti, D | 285 |
| Warwick | 239 |
| Waveney | 355, 406 |
| Wickliffe | 437 |
| Winchester, Old | 141 |
| Windsor | 35 |
| York | 411 |

### LONG METRE.

| | |
|---|---|
| Angelus | 76, 330, 433 |
| Babylon's Streams | 84 |
| Bera | 262 |
| Bishopsgate | 298 |
| Church Triumphant | 34, 115 |
| Dismission | 186, 187 |
| Duke Street | 21, 169 |
| Eisenach | 271 |
| Federal Street | 86, 262 |
| Germany | 139, 458 |
| Grace Church | 4, 62, 415 |
| Grostete | 39 |
| Hamburg | 75, 267 |
| Haskell | 64 |
| Hebron | 149 |
| Hosanna, with Chorus | 81 |
| Humility | 8, 327 |
| Hursley | 452 |
| Illo | 31 |
| In Christo | 379 |
| Koenig, D | 106, 123 |
| Louvan | 39, 467 |
| Melita, 6l | 137, 463 |
| Mendon | 211, 316, 324 |
| Missionary Chant | 214, 225 |
| Morning Hymn | 428 |
| Mozart | 164, 323 |
| Old Hundredth | 24 |
| Olive's Brow | 84 |

# METRICAL INDEX OF TUNES

Park Street, 51. . . . . . . . . . . . . . . . . . . . . . . .418
Penitence. . . . . . . . . . . . . . . . . . . . . . . . .267, 276
Peterborough, D. . . . . . . . . . . . . . . . . . . . . .174
Rest . . . . . . . . . . . . . . . . . . . . . . . . . . . . . . .379
Rockingham (Eng.) . . . . . . . . . . . . . . . . .92, 175
St. Cross. . . . . . . . . . . . . . . . . . . . . . . . . . . . .85
St. Drosdane. . . . . . . . . . . . . . . . . . . . . . . . .79
St. Matthias, 6l. . . . . . . . . . . . . . . . . . . . . . .434
Tallis' Canon. . . . . . . . . . . . . . . . . . . . . . . . .444
Tristitia, 6l. . . . . . . . . . . . . . . . . . . . . . . . . . .291
Tmbridge . . . . . . . . . . . . . . . . . . . . . . .117, 290
Veni Immanuel, 6l. . . . . . . . . . . . . . . . . . . .134
Waltham . . . . . . . . . . . . . . . . . . . . . . . .217, 316
Wareham . . . . . . . . . . . . . . . . . . . .52, 412, 470
Winchester, New. . . . . . . . . . . . . . . . . . . . . .61
Zephyr. . . . . . . . . . . . . . . . . . . . . . . . . . . . . .429

## SHORT METRE.

Amerton. . . . . . . . . . . . . . . . . . . . . . . . . . . .192
Boylston . . . . . . . . . . . . . . . . . . . . . . . . . . . .231
Chalvey, D. . . . . . . . . . . . . . . . . . . . . . . . . .279
Dennis . . . . . . . . . . . . . . . . . . . . . . . . . . . . .354
Diademata, D. . . . . . . . . . . . . . . . . . . . . . . .125
Domenica. . . . . . . . . . . . . . . . . . . . . . . . . . .414
Ignatius. . . . . . . . . . . . . . . . . . . . . . . . . . . . .438
Knight, D. . . . . . . . . . . . . . . . . . . . . . . . . . .455
Laban . . . . . . . . . . . . . . . . . . . . . . . . . . . . . .321
Leighton. . . . . . . . . . . . . . . . . . . . . . . .168, 385
Lisbon . . . . . . . . . . . . . . . . . . . . . . . . . . . . .288
Lyte. . . . . . . . . . . . . . . . . . . . . . . . . . . .255, 386
Marshall. . . . . . . . . . . . . . . . . . . . .15, 74, 377
Mason . . . . . . . . . . . . . . . . . . . . . . . . . .332, 367
Mornington . . . . . . . . . . . . . . . .216, 244, 416
Olmutz. . . . . . . . . . . . . . . . . . . . . . .10, 189, 356
Olney. . . . . . . . . . . . . . . . . . . . . . . . . . . . . . .259
Renovation . . . . . . . . . . . . . . . . . . . . . .162, 382
St. Alban . . . . . . . . . . . . . . . . . . . . . . . . . . .208
St. Andrew. . . . . . . . . . . . . . . . . . . . . .12, 176
St. Michael. . . . . . . . . . . . . . . . .188, 237, 314
St. Paul's College. . . . . . . . . . . . . . . . . . . . .387
St. Thomas . . . . . . . . . . . . . . . . . . . . . .116, 425
Schumann . . . . . . . . . . . . . . . . . . . . . . . . . .204
Sienna. . . . . . . . . . . . . . . . . . . . . . . . . . . . . .131
Silver Street. . . . . . . . . . . . . . . . .192, 337, 423
State Street. . . . . . . . . . . . . . . . . . . .5, 159, 190
Simmons. . . . . . . . . . . . . . . . . . . . . . . . . . . .260
Thatcher. . . . . . . . . . . . . . . .145, 207, 218, 293
Victor . . . . . . . . . . . . . . . . . . . . . . . . . . . . . .380
Woolwich. . . . . . . . . . . . . . . . . . . . . . . . . . .389

## 4s & 6s.
Requiem, D. . . . . . . . . . . . . . . . . . . . . . . . .378

## 6s.
Landes Domini, 6l. . . . . . . . . . . . . . . . . . . .432
Via . . . . . . . . . . . . . . . . . . . . . . . . . . . . . . . .342
Via Crucis . . . . . . . . . . . . . . . . . . . . . . . . . .372

## 6s & 3.
Invitation. . . . . . . . . . . . . . . . . . . . . . . . . . .264

## 6s & 4s.
Euroclydon. . . . . . . . . . . . . . . . . . . . . . . . . . .69
Every Hour. . . . . . . . . . . . . . . . . . . . . . . . .344
Freude. . . . . . . . . . . . . . . . . . . . . . . . . . . . . .436
The Saviour's Call. . . . . . . . . . . . . . . . . . . .252

## 6, 4, 6, 4, 6, 6, 4.
Bethany . . . . . . . . . . . . . . . . . . . . . . . . . . . . .13
Himmel. . . . . . . . . . . . . . . . . . . . . . . . . . . .384
Kedron . . . . . . . . . . . . . . . . . . . . . . . . .13, 348

## 6s & 5s.
Albans, 121. . . . . . . . . . . . . . . . . . . . . . . . .200
Alma Lux, D with Chorus. . . . . . . . . . .57, 193
Andi Nos. . . . . . . . . . . . . . . . . . . . . . . . . . .274
Blessed Saviour, D . . . . . . . . . . . . . . . . . . .301
Eversley, D . . . . . . . . . . . . . . . . . . . . . . . . .105
Laus Deo, 12l. . . . . . . . . . . . . . . . . . . . . . . .43
Mary Magdalene, D . . . . . . . . . . . . . .346, 371
Merrial. . . . . . . . . . . . . . . . . . . . . . . . . . . . .449
St. Andrew of Crete, D. . . . . . . . . . . . . . . .311
St. Cephas, D. . . . . . . . . . . . . . . . . . . . . . .127
St. Gertrude, D. . . . . . . . . . . . . . . . . . . . . .191
St. Theresa, D with Chorus. . . . . . . . . . . . .202

## 6, 6, 4, 6, 6, 6, 4.
America . . . . . . . . . . . . . . . . . . . . . . . . . . .468
Dort . . . . . . . . . . . . . . . . . . . . . . . . . . . . . . .472
Italian Hymn. . . . . . . . . . . . . .2, 114, 198, 448
Kirby Bedon. . . . . . . . . . . . . . . . . . . . . . . . .173
Olivet . . . . . . . . . . . . . . . . . . . . . . . . . .14, 146
Ouseley . . . . . . . . . . . . . . . . . . . . . . . . . . . .304

## 6, 6, 6, 6, 8, 7, 8, 7.
Islington. . . . . . . . . . . . . . . . . . . . . . . . . . . .133

## 6, 6, 6, 6, 8, 8.
Adoration. . . . . . . . . . . . . . . . . . . . . . .122, 419
Arthur's Seat . . . . . . . . . . . . . . . . . . . . . . . . .46
Christ Church . . . . . . . . . . . . . . . .1, 302, 402
Darwall. . . . . . . . . . . . . . . . . . . . . . . . .35, 121
Old Hundred Forty-eighth. . . . . . . . . .27, 406
Waverton. . . . . . . . . . . . . . . . . . . . . . . . . . .469

## 7s.
Ascension, with Alleluia. . . . . . . . . . . . . . .107
Benevento, D. . . . . . . . . . . . . . . . . . . . . . . .454
Blumenthal, D . . . . . . . . . . . . . . . . . . . . . . .254
Dix, 6l . . . . . . . . . . . . . . . . . . . . .58, 360, 462
Easter Hymn, with Alleluia. . . . . . . . . . . . . .98
Guildford, 6l. . . . . . . . . . . . . . . . . . . . . . . .186
Hendon, 5l . . . . . . . . . . . . . . . . . . . . . . . . . .91
Holley . . . . . . . . . . . . . . . . . . . . . . . . . . . . .445
Hollingside, D. . . . . . . . . . . . . . . . . . . . . . .326
Horton. . . . . . . . . . . . . . . . . . . . . . . . . . . . .250
Innocents. . . . . . . . . . . . . . . . . . . . . . . .23, 422
Lachrymae, 3l . . . . . . . . . . . . . . . . . . . . . . .266
Martyn, D. . . . . . . . . . . . . . . . . . . . . . . . . .326
Mendelssohn, 10l . . . . . . . . . . . . . . . . . . . . .48
Munus. . . . . . . . . . . . . . . . . . . . . . . . . .201, 322
Nuremberg. . . . . . . . . . . . . . . .98, 221, 296, 459
Pleyel's Hymn. . . . . . . . . . . . . . . . . . . .230, 358
Ratisbon. 6l. . . . . . . . . . . . . . . . . . . . .181, 243
Rest (Eng.). . . . . . . . . . . . . . . . . . . . . . . . . .277
Rock of Ages, 6l. . . . . . . . . . . . . . . . . .96, 269
Rosefield, 6l. . . . . . . . . . . . . . . . . . . . . . . . .295
St. Austell. . . . . . . . . . . . . . . . . . . . . . . . . .289
St. Bees. . . . . . . . . . . . . . . . . . . . . . . . . . . .257
St. George's Chapel, D. . . . . . . . . .47, 417, 461
St. Sebastian, 6l. . . . . . . . . . . . . . . . . . . . . .138
Sabbath, 6l. . . . . . . . . . . . . . . . . . . . . . . . . .408
Service . . . . . . . . . . . . . . . . . .179, 209, 250, 270
Seymour. . . . . . . . . . . . . . . . . . . . . . . . .6, 435
Toplady, 6l. . . . . . . . . . . . . . . . . . . . . . . . . .269

# METRICAL INDEX OF TUNES

### 7s & 6s.
Amsterdam, D .......................457
Aurelia, D ....................153, 157, 363
Bonner, D ...........................409
Ellacombe, D ........................195
Ewing, D ............................405
Greenland, D ................135, 199, 213
Homeland, D ........................397
Jesus Magister Bone, D ..........194, 261
Lancashire, D .......................100
Magdalena, D ..............40, 275, 282
Mendebras, D .......................409
Missionary Hymn, D ................224
Passion Chorale, D ..................88
Pearsall, D .....................197, 403
St. Alphege .........................401
St. Anselm, D ...................80, 404
St. Edith, D ..................182, 245, 376
St. Theodulph, D .................83, 234
Tours, D .............................82
Unser Herrscher, D ................229
Webb, D .............................222
Yarmouth, D ........................223

### 7, 6, 7, 6, 8, 8.
St. Anatolius .......................441

### 7, 6, 7, 7, 6.
Dunn ................................381

### 7, 6, 8, 6.
Alford, D ............................393

### 7, 6, 8, 6, 8, 6, 8, 6.
St. Christopher .....................280

### 7, 6, 8, 8, 6.
Children's Service ..................203

### 7, 7, 7, 5.
Armes ...............................320
Rodbourne ......................148, 272
St. Ambrose ........................147

### 7, 7, 7, 7, 8, 8.
Requiescat .........................383

### 7, 8, 7, 8.
St. Albinus, with Alleluia ..........103

### 8, 4, 7, 8, 4, 7.
Haydn ..............................431

### 8, 4, 8, 4, 8, 4.
Wentworth .........................359

### 8, 4, 8, 4, 8, 8, 8, 4.
Angel Guards ......................447

### 8, 5, 8, 3.
Stephanos ..........................247

### 8, 5, 8, 5, 8, 7.
Angel Voices .......................28

### 8, 6, 6, 8, 6, 6.
Nativity, New .......................51

### 8, 6, 8, 4.
St. Cuthbert .......................140

### 8, 6, 8, 6, 4.
Peregrinus .........................253

### 8, 6, 8, 8, 6.
Woodland ..........................388

### 8s & 7s.
Alleluia, with Alleluia ..............126
Austria, D ..........................158
Benedic Anima, 6l ..............19, 128
Bethany (Eng.), D ..............251, 283
Children's Prayer ..................451
Dominus regit me ..................17
Dormance ...........................73
Dulce Carmen, 6l ..............165, 336
Ellesdie ............................283
Galilee .............................73
Gounod, 6l .........................362
Greenville, D ..................349, 427
Guter Hirt .........................172
Langdale ...........................42
Lux Eoi, D .....................101, 124
Moultrie, D ........................111
Promise, D ........................240
Rathbun .............................90
Regent Square, 6l ..............41, 60
Resurrection, 6l ...............18, 220
St. Denys, 6l .......................87
St. Mabyn ......................176, 334
St. Sylvester ......................442
Sanctuary, D ......................394
Sicilian Mariner's Hymn ......93, 310
Stuttgard ......................352, 424
Supplication, D ................132, 281
Sychar ..............................90
Trust ...........................77, 310
Weston, D .........................294
Wilmot ....................120, 129, 335

### 8s, 7s, & 4.
Coronæ ........................26, 112
Jesus Bone Pastor ................361
Ravenscroft ....................95, 136
Resurrection ......................220
Zion ................................219

### 8, 7, 8, 7, 7, 7.
Irby .................................54

### 8, 7, 8, 7, 7, 7, 8, 6.
Harwell .............................118

### 8, 8, 6, 8, 8, 6.
Ariel ................................303
Magdalen College ...................97
Welfield ........................32, 317

### 8, 8, 8, 4.
Almsgiving ....................365, 460
In Memoriam .............183, 340, 446
Palestrina ..........................104
Risenholme ........................241

### 8, 8, 8, 5.
Lauda Zion ........................300

# METRICAL INDEX OF TUNES

**8, 8, 8, 6.**
Flemming..................................328
Pascal....................................328

**9, 8, 9, 8.**
Eucharistic Hymn..........................185

**10s.**
Ellers....................................440
Eventide..................................453
Langran...................................265
Pax Tecum, 21.............................333
Sarum, 31, with Alleluia..................233

**10, 4, 10, 4, 10, 10.**
Lux Benigna...............................347

**10, 10, 11, 11.**
Lyons......................................25

**11s.**
Alma Lux............................57, 193
Portuguese Hymn...........................325

**11s & 10s.**
Oblations..................................59

**11, 10, 11, 10, 9, 11.**
Pilgrims..................................392

**11, 11, 11, 5.**
Cloisters.................................166

**11s & 12s.**
Nicæa.......................................3

**12s.**
Gennesaret................................464

**IRREGULAR, ETC.**
Adeste Fideles.............................55
Ein Feste Burg............................364
Manger.....................................53
New Year's Hymn...........................456
Rosslyn....................................71
Troyte's Chant............................453

# SELECTIONS FROM THE PSALMS

FOR

## RESPONSIVE READING

TOGETHER WITH

# THE COMMANDMENTS, THE LITANY, AND THE APOSTLES' CREED.

The arrangement of the Psalms for reading corresponds with the arrangement for Chanting in the original edition of Hymns of the Faith. The music of the Gloria for use at the close of each selection is appended to the first selection.

## Selection 1

*Psalm I*

BLESSED is the man that walketh not in the counsel of the ungodly, nor standeth in the way of sinners, nor sitteth in the seat of the scornful.

2 But his delight is in the law of the Lord; and in his law doth he meditate day and night.

3 And he shall be like a tree planted by the rivers of water, that bringeth forth his fruit in his season; his leaf also shall not wither; and whatsoever he doeth shall prosper.

4 The ungodly are not so: but are like the chaff which the wind driveth away.

5 Therefore the ungodly shall not stand in the judgment, nor sinners in the congregation of the righteous.

6 For the Lord knoweth the way of the righteous: but the way of the ungodly shall perish.

*Psalm II*

7 Why do the heathen rage, and the people imagine a vain thing?

8 The kings of the earth set themselves, and the rulers take counsel together, against the Lord, and against his Anointed, saying,

9 Let us break their bands asunder, and cast away their cords from us.

10 He that sitteth in the heavens shall laugh: the Lord shall have them in derision.

11 Then shall he speak unto them in his wrath, and vex them in his sore displeasure.

12 Yet have I set my King upon my holy hill of Zion.

13 I will declare the decree: the Lord hath said unto me, Thou art my Son; this day have I begotten thee.

14 Ask of me, and I shall give thee the heathen for thine inheritance, and the uttermost parts of the earth for thy possession.

15 Thou shalt break them with a rod of iron; thou shalt dash them in pieces like a potter's vessel.

16 Be wise now therefore, O ye kings: be instructed, ye judges of the earth.

17 Serve the Lord with fear, and rejoice with trembling.

18 Kiss the Son, lest he be angry, and ye perish from the way, when his wrath is kindled but a little. Blessed are all they that put their trust in him.

## SELECTIONS FROM THE PSALMS

*Psalm IV*

19 Hear me when I call, O God of my righteousness : thou hast enlarged me when I was in distress ; have mercy upon me, and hear my prayer.

20 O ye sons of men, how long will ye turn my glory into shame ? how long will ye love vanity, and seek after leasing ?

21 But know that the Lord hath set apart him that is godly for himself : the Lord will hear when I call unto him.

22 Stand in awe, and sin not : commune with your own heart upon your bed, and be still.

23 Offer the sacrifices of righteousness, and put your trust in the Lord.

24 There be many that say, Who will shew us any good ? Lord, lift thou up the light of thy countenance upon us.

25 Thou hast put gladness in my heart, more than in the time that their corn and their wine increased.

26 I will both lay me down in peace, and sleep : for thou, Lord, only makest me dwell in safety.

T. TALLIS.

Glory be to the *Fa*ther | and · to the | Son ‖ *and* | to · the | Ho · ly | Ghost.

As it was in the beginning, is *now* and | ev · er | shall be ‖ *World* without | end · — | A · — | men.

## Selection 2

*Psalm V*

GIVE ear to my words, O Lord, consider my meditation.

2 Hearken unto the voice of my cry, my King, and my God : for unto thee will I pray.

3 My voice shalt thou hear in the morning, O Lord ; in the morning will I direct my prayer unto thee, and will look up.

4 For thou art not a God that hath pleasure in wickedness : neither shall evil dwell with thee.

5 The foolish shall not stand in thy sight : thou hatest all workers of iniquity.

6 Thou shalt destroy them that speak leasing : the Lord will abhor the bloody and deceitful man.

7 But as for me, I will come into thy house in the multitude of thy mercy : and in thy fear will I worship toward thy holy temple.

8 Lead me, O Lord, in thy righteousness because of mine enemies ; make thy way straight before my face.

9 For there is no faithfulness in their mouth ; their inward part is very wickedness ; their throat is an open sepulchre ; they flatter with their tongue.

10 Destroy thou them, O God ; let them fall by their own counsels ; cast them out in the multitude of their transgressions ; for they have rebelled against thee.

11 But let all those that put their trust in thee rejoice : let them ever shout for joy, because thou defendest them : let them also that love thy name be joyful in thee.

12 For thou, Lord, wilt bless the righteous ; w.th favour wilt thou compass him as with a shield.

*Psalm VIII*

13 O Lord our Lord, how excellent is thy name in all the earth ! who hast set thy glory above the heavens.

14 Out of the mouth of babes and sucklings hast thou ordained strength

because of thine enemies, that thou mightest still the enemy and the avenger.

15 When I consider thy heavens, the work of thy fingers, the moon and the stars, which thou hast ordained;

16 What is man, that thou art mindful of him? and the son of man, that thou visitest him?

17 For thou hast made him a little lower than the angels, and hast crowned him with glory and honour.

18 Thou madest him to have dominion over the works of thy hands; thou hast put all things under his feet:

19 All sheep and oxen, yea, and the beasts of the field;

20 The fowl of the air, and the fish of the sea, and whatsoever passeth through the paths of the seas.

21 O Lord our Lord, how excellent is thy name in all the earth!

*Psalm XV*

22 Lord, who shall abide in thy tabernacle? who shall dwell in thy holy hill?

23 He that walketh uprightly, and worketh righteousness, and speaketh the truth in his heart.

24 He that backbiteth not with his tongue, nor doeth evil to his neighbour, nor taketh up a reproach against his neighbour.

25 In whose eyes a vile person is contemned; but he honoureth them that fear the Lord.

26 He that sweareth to his own hurt, and changeth not.

27 He that putteth not out his money to usury, nor taketh reward against the innocent. He that doeth these things shall never be moved.

Glory be to the Father, and to the Son, and to the Holy Ghost.

As it was in the beginning, is now, and ever shall be, world without end. Amen.

## Selection 3

*Psalm XVI*

PRESERVE me, O God: for in thee do I put my trust.

2 O my soul, thou hast said unto the Lord, Thou art my Lord: my goodness extendeth not to thee;

3 But to the saints that are in the earth, and to the excellent, in whom is all my delight.

4 Their sorrows shall be multiplied that hasten after another god: their drink-offerings of blood will I not offer, nor take up their names into my lips.

5 The Lord is the portion of mine inheritance and of my cup: thou maintainest my lot.

6 The lines are fallen unto me in pleasant places; yea, I have a goodly heritage.

7 I will bless the Lord, who hath given me counsel: my reins also instruct me in the night seasons.

8 I have set the Lord always before me: because he is at my right hand, I shall not be moved.

9 Therefore my heart is glad, and my glory rejoiceth: my flesh also shall rest in hope.

10 For thou wilt not leave my soul in hell; neither wilt thou suffer thine Holy One to see corruption.

11 Thou wilt shew me the path of life: in thy presence is fulness of joy; at thy right hand there are pleasures for evermore.

*Psalm XVII*

12 Hear the right, O Lord, attend unto my cry, give ear unto my prayer, that goeth not out of feigned lips.

13 Let my sentence come forth from thy presence; let thine eyes behold the things that are equal.

14 Thou hast proved mine heart; thou

hast visited me in the night; thou hast tried me, and shalt find nothing: I am purposed that my mouth shall not transgress.

15 Concerning the works of men, by the word of thy lips I have kept me from the paths of the destroyer.

16 Hold up my goings in thy paths, that my footsteps slip not.

17 I have called upon thee, for thou wilt hear me, O God: incline thine ear unto me, and hear my speech.

18 Shew thy marvellous loving-kindness, O thou that savest by thy right hand them which put their trust in thee from those that rise up against them.

19 Keep me as the apple of the eye, hide me under the shadow of thy wings,

20 From the wicked that oppress me, from my deadly enemies, who compass me about.

21 They are inclosed in their own fat: with their mouth they speak proudly.

22 They have now compassed us in our steps: they have set their eyes bowing down to the earth;

23 Like as a lion that is greedy of his prey, and as it were a young lion lurking in secret places.

24 Arise, O Lord, disappoint him, cast him down: deliver my soul from the wicked, which is thy sword:

25 From men which are thy hand, O Lord, from men of the world, which have their portion in this life, and whose belly thou fillest with thy hid treasure: they are full of children, and leave the rest of their substance to their babes.

26 As for me, I will behold thy face in righteousness: I shall be satisfied, when I awake, with thy likeness.

Glory be to the Father, and to the Son, and to the Holy Ghost.

As it was in the beginning, is now, and ever shall be, world without end. Amen.

## Selection 4

*Psalm XVIII: 1-24*

I WILL love thee, O Lord, my strength.

2 The Lord is my rock, and my fortress, and my deliverer; my God, my strength, in whom I will trust; my buckler, and the horn of my salvation, and my high tower.

3 I will call upon the Lord, who is worthy to be praised: so shall I be saved from mine enemies.

4 The sorrows of death compassed me, and the floods of ungodly men made me afraid.

5 The sorrows of hell compassed me about: the snares of death prevented me.

6 In my distress I called upon the Lord, and cried unto my God: he heard my voice out of his temple, and my cry came before him, even into his ears.

7 Then the earth shook and trembled; the foundations also of the hills moved and were shaken, because he was wroth.

8 There went up a smoke out of his nostrils, and fire out of his mouth devoured: coals were kindled by it.

9 He bowed the heavens also, and came down: and darkness was under his feet.

10 And he rode upon a cherub and did fly: yea, he did fly upon the wings of the wind.

11 He made darkness his secret place; his pavilion round about him were dark waters and thick clouds of the skies.

12 At the brightness that was before him his thick clouds passed, hail-stones and coals of fire.

13 The Lord also thundered in the heavens, and the Highest gave his voice; hail-stones and coals of fire.

14 Yea, he sent out his arrows, and scattered them; and he shot out lightnings, and discomfited them.

SELECTIONS FROM THE PSALMS

15 Then the channels of waters were seen, and the foundations of the world were discovered at thy rebuke, O Lord, at the blast of the breath of thy nostrils.

16 He sent from above, he took me, he drew me out of many waters.

17 He delivered me from my strong enemy, and from them which hated me: for they were too strong for me.

18 They prevented me in the day of my calamity: but the Lord was my stay.

19 He brought me forth also into a large place: he delivered me, because he delighted in me.

20 The Lord rewarded me according to my righteousness; according to the cleanness of my hands hath he recompensed me.

21 For I have kept the ways of the Lord, and have not wickedly departed from my God.

22 For all his judgments were before me, and I did not put away his statutes from me.

23 I was also upright before him, and I kept myself from mine iniquity.

24 Therefore hath the Lord recompensed me according to my righteousness, according to the cleanness of my hands in his eyesight.

Glory be to the Father, and to the Son, and to the holy Ghost.

As it was in the beginning, is now, and ever shall be, world without end. Amen.

## Selection 5

*Psalm XVIII: 25-50*

WITH the merciful thou wilt shew thyself merciful; with an upright man thou wilt shew thyself upright;

2 With the pure thou wilt shew thyself pure; and with the froward thou wilt shew thyself froward.

3 For thou wilt save the afflicted people; but wilt bring down high looks.

4 For thou wilt light my candle: the Lord my God will enlighten my darkness.

5 For by thee I have run through a troop; and by my God have I leaped over a wall.

6 As for God, his way is perfect: the word of the Lord is tried: he is a buckler to all those that trust in him.

7 For who is God save the Lord? or who is a rock save our God?

8 It is God that girdeth me with strength, and maketh my way perfect.

9 He maketh my feet like hinds' feet, and setteth me upon my high places.

10 He teacheth my hands to war, so that a bow of steel is broken by mine arms.

11 Thou hast also given me the shield of thy salvation: and thy right hand hath holden me up, and thy gentleness hath made me great.

12 Thou hast enlarged my steps under me, that my feet did not slip.

13 I have pursued mine enemies, and overtaken them: neither did I turn again till they were consumed.

14 I have wounded them that they were not able to rise: they are fallen under my feet.

15 For thou hast girded me with strength unto the battle: thou hast subdued under me those that rose up against me.

16 Thou hast also given me the necks of mine enemies; that I might destroy them that hate me.

17 They cried, but there was none to save them: even unto the Lord, but he answered them not.

18 Then did I beat them small as the dust before the wind: I did cast them out as the dirt in the streets.

19 Thou hast delivered me from the

strivings of the people: and thou hast made me the head of the heathen: a people whom I have not known shall serve me.

20 As soon as they hear of me, they shall obey me: the strangers shall submit themselves unto me.

21 The strangers shall fade away, and be afraid out of their close places.

22 The Lord liveth; and blessed be my Rock; and let the God of my salvation be exalted.

23 It is God that avengeth me, and subdueth the people under me.

24 He delivereth me from mine enemies: yea, thou liftest me up above those that rise up against me: thou hast delivered me from the violent man.

25 Therefore will I give thanks unto thee, O Lord, among the heathen, and sing praises unto thy name.

26 Great deliverance giveth he to his king; and sheweth mercy to his anointed, to David, and to his seed for evermore.

Glory be to the Father, and to the Son, and to the Holy Ghost.

As it was in the beginning, is now, and ever shall be, world without end. Amen.

## Selection 6

*Psalm XIX*

THE heavens declare the glory of God; and the firmament showeth his handywork.

2 Day unto day uttereth speech, and night unto night sheweth knowledge.

3 There is no speech nor language, where their voice is not heard.

4 Their line is gone out through all the earth, and their words to the end of the world. In them hath he set a tabernacle for the sun,

5 Which is as a bridegroom coming out of his chamber, and rejoiceth as a strong man to run a race.

6 His going forth is from the end of the heaven, and his circuit unto the ends of it: and there is nothing hid from the heat thereof.

7 The law of the Lord is perfect, converting the soul: the testimony of the Lord is sure, making wise the simple.

8 The statutes of the Lord are right, rejoicing the heart: the commandment of the Lord is pure, enlightening the eyes.

9 The fear of the Lord is clean, enduring for ever: the judgments of the Lord are true and righteous altogether.

10 More to be desired are they than gold, yea, than much fine gold: sweeter also than honey and the honeycomb.

11 Moreover by them is thy servant warned: and in keeping of them there is great reward.

12 Who can understand his errors? cleanse thou me from secret faults.

13 Keep back thy servant also from presumptuous sins; let them not have dominion over me: then shall I be upright, and I shall be innocent from the great transgression.

14 Let the words of my mouth, and the meditation of my heart, be acceptable in thy sight, O Lord, my strength, and my redeemer.

*Psalm XX*

15 The Lord hear thee in the day of trouble; the name of the God of Jacob defend thee.

16 Send thee help from the sanctuary, and strengthen thee out of Zion.

17 Remember all thy offerings, and accept thy burnt-sacrifice.

18 Grant thee according to thine own heart, and fulfil all thy counsel.

19 We will rejoice in thy salvation, and in the name of our God we will set

up our banners: the Lord fulfil all thy petitions.

20 Now know I that the Lord saveth his anointed; he will hear him from his holy heaven with the saving strength of his right hand.

21 Some trust in chariots, and some in horses: but we will remember the name of the Lord our God.

22 They are brought down and fallen: but we are risen, and stand upright.

23 Save, Lord: let the king hear us when we call.

Glory be to the Father, and to the Son, and to the Holy Ghost.

As it was in the beginning, is now, and ever shall be, world without end. Amen.

## Selection 7

### Psalm XXIII

THE Lord is my shepherd; I shall not want.

2 He maketh me to lie down in green pastures: he leadeth me beside the still waters.

3 He restoreth my soul: he leadeth me in the paths of righteousness for his name's sake.

4 Yea, though I walk through the valley of the shadow of death, I will fear no evil: for thou art with me; thy rod and thy staff they comfort me.

5 Thou preparest a table before me in the presence of mine enemies: thou anointest my head with oil; my cup runneth over.

6 Surely goodness and mercy shall follow me all the days of my life: and I will dwell in the house of the Lord forever.

### Psalm XXIV

7 The earth is the Lord's, and the fulness thereof; the world, and they that dwell therein.

8 For he hath founded it upon the seas, and established it upon the floods.

9 Who shall ascend into the hill of the Lord? or who shall stand in his holy place?

10 He that hath clean hands, and a pure heart; who hath not lifted up his soul unto vanity, nor sworn deceitfully.

11 He shall receive the blessing from the Lord, and righteousness from the God of his salvation.

12 This is the generation of them that seek him, that seek thy face, O Jacob.

13 Lift up your heads, O ye gates; and be ye lift up, ye everlasting doors; and the King of glory shall come in.

14 Who is this King of glory? the Lord strong and mighty, the Lord mighty in battle.

15 Lift up your heads, O ye gates; even lift them up, ye everlasting doors; and the King of glory shall come in.

16 Who is this King of glory? the Lord of hosts, he is the King of glory.

### Psalm XXV: 1-9

17 Unto thee, O Lord, do I lift up my soul.

18 O my God, I trust in thee: let me not be ashamed, let not mine enemies triumph over me.

19 Yea, let none that wait on thee be ashamed: let them be ashamed which transgress without cause.

20 Shew me thy ways, O Lord; teach me thy paths.

21 Lead me in thy truth, and teach me: for thou art the God of my salvation; on thee do I wait all the day.

22 Remember, O Lord, thy tender mercies and thy lovingkindnesses; for they have been ever of old.

23 Remember not the sins of my youth, nor my transgressions: according

to thy mercy remember thou me, for thy goodness' sake, O Lord.

24 Good and upright is the Lord: therefore will he teach sinners in the way.

25 The meek will he guide in judgment: and the meek will he teach his way.

Glory be to the Father, and to the Son, and to the Holy Ghost.

As it was in the beginning, is now, and ever shall be, world without end. Amen.

## Selection 8

*Psalm XXV: 10-22*

ALL the paths of the LORD are mercy and truth unto such as keep his covenant and his testimonies.

2 For thy name's sake, O Lord, pardon mine iniquity; for it is great.

3 What man is he that feareth the Lord? him shall he teach in the way that he shall choose.

4 His soul shall dwell at ease; and his seed shall inherit the earth.

5 The secret of the Lord is with them that fear him; and he will shew them his covenant.

6 Mine eyes are ever toward the Lord; for he shall pluck my feet out of the net.

7 Turn thee unto me, and have mercy upon me; for I am desolate and afflicted.

8 The troubles of my heart are enlarged: O bring thou me out of my distresses.

9 Look upon mine affliction and my pain; and forgive all my sins.

10 Consider mine enemies; for they are many; and they hate me with cruel hatred.

11 O keep my soul, and deliver me: let me not be ashamed; for I put my trust in thee.

12 Let integrity and uprightness preserve me; for I wait on thee.

13 Redeem Israel, O God, out of all his troubles.

*Psalm XXVII*

14 The Lord is my light and my salvation; whom shall I fear? the Lord is the strength of my life; of whom shall I be afraid?

15 When the wicked, even mine enemies and my foes, came upon me to eat up my flesh, they stumbled and fell.

16 Though an host should encamp against me, my heart shall not fear: though war should rise against me, in this will I be confident.

17 One thing have I desired of the Lord, that will I seek after; that I may dwell in the house of the Lord all the days of my life, to behold the beauty of the Lord, and to inquire in his temple.

18 For in the time of trouble he shall hide me in his pavilion: in the secret of his tabernacle shall he hide me; he shall set me up upon a rock.

19 And now shall mine head be lifted up above mine enemies round about me: therefore will I offer in his tabernacle sacrifices of joy; I will sing, yea, I will sing praises unto the Lord.

20 Hear, O Lord, when I cry with my voice: have mercy also upon me, and answer me.

21 When thou saidst, Seek ye my face; my heart said unto thee, Thy face, Lord, will I seek.

22 Hide not thy face far from me; put not thy servant away in anger: thou hast been my help; leave me not, neither forsake me, O God of my salvation.

23 When my father and my mother forsake me, then the Lord will take me up.

24 Teach me thy way, O Lord, and

lead me in a plain path, because of mine enemies.

25 Deliver me not over unto the will of mine enemies: for false witnesses are risen up against me, and such as breathe out cruelty.

26 I had fainted, unless I had believed to see the goodness of the Lord in the land of the living.

27 Wait on the Lord: be of good courage, and he shall strengthen thine heart: wait, I say, on the Lord.

Glory be to the Father, and to the Son, and to the Holy Ghost.

As it was in the beginning, is now, and ever shall be, world without end. Amen.

## Selection 9

### Psalm XXIX

GIVE unto the Lord, O ye mighty, give unto the Lord glory and strength.

2 Give unto the Lord the glory due unto his name; worship the Lord in the beauty of holiness.

3 The voice of the Lord is upon the waters: the God of glory thundereth: the Lord is upon many waters.

4 The voice of the Lord is powerful; the voice of the Lord is full of majesty.

5 The voice of the Lord breaketh the cedars; yea, the Lord breaketh the cedars of Lebanon.

6 He maketh them also to skip like a calf; Lebanon and Sirion like a young unicorn.

7 The voice of the Lord divideth the flames of fire.

8 The voice of the Lord shaketh the wilderness; the Lord shaketh the wilderness of Kadesh.

9 The voice of the Lord maketh the hinds to calve, and discovereth the forests: and in his temple doth every one speak of his glory.

10 The Lord sitteth upon the flood; yea, the Lord sitteth King for ever.

11 The Lord will give strength unto his people; the Lord will bless his people with peace.

### Psalm XXX

12 I will extol thee, O Lord; for thou hast lifted me up, and hast not made my foes to rejoice over me.

13 O Lord my God, I cried unto thee, and thou hast healed me.

14 O Lord, thou hast brought up my soul from the grave: thou hast kept me alive, that I should not go down to the pit.

15 Sing unto the Lord, O ye saints of his, and give thanks at the remembrance of his holiness.

16 For his anger endureth but a moment; in his favour is life: weeping may endure for a night, but joy cometh in the morning.

17 And in my prosperity I said, I shall never be moved.

18 Lord, by thy favour thou hast made my mountain to stand strong: thou didst hide thy face, and I was troubled.

19 I cried to thee, O Lord; and unto the Lord I made supplication.

20 What profit is there in my blood, when I go down to the pit? Shall the dust praise thee? shall it declare thy truth?

21 Hear, O Lord, and have mercy upon me: Lord, be thou my helper.

22 Thou hast turned for me my mourning into dancing: thou hast put off my sackcloth, and girded me with gladness;

23 To the end that my glory may sing praise to thee, and not be silent. O Lord my God, I will give thanks unto thee for ever.

Glory be to the Father, and to the Son, and to the Holy Ghost.

As it was in the beginning, is now, and ever shall be, world without end. Amen.

## Selection 10

*Psalm XXXI*

IN thee, O Lord, do I put my trust; let me never be ashamed: deliver me in thy righteousness.

2 Bow down thine ear to me; deliver me speedily: be thou my strong rock, for an house of defence to save me.

3 For thou art my rock and my fortress; therefore for thy name's sake lead me, and guide me.

4 Pull me out of the net that they have laid privily for me: for thou art my strength.

5 Into thine hand I commit my spirit: thou has redeemed me, O Lord God of truth.

6 I have hated them that regard lying vanities: but I trust in the Lord.

7 I will be glad and rejoice in thy mercy: for thou hast considered my trouble; thou hast known my soul in adversities;

8 And hast not shut me up into the hand of the enemy: thou hast set my feet in a large room.

9 Have mercy upon me, O Lord, for I am in trouble: mine eye is consumed with grief, yea, my soul and my belly.

10 For my life is spent with grief, and my years with sighing: my strength faileth because of mine iniquity, and my bones are consumed.

11 I was a reproach among all mine enemies, but especially among my neighbours, and a fear to mine acquaintance: they that did see me without fled from me.

12 I am forgotten as a dead man out of mind: I am like a broken vessel.

13 For I have heard the slander of many: fear was on every side: while they took counsel together against me, they devised to take away my life.

14 But I trusted in thee, O Lord: I said, Thou art my God.

15 My times are in thy hand: deliver me from the hand of mine enemies, and from them that persecute me.

16 Make thy face to shine upon thy servant: save me for thy mercies' sake.

17 Let me not be ashamed, O Lord; for I have called upon thee: let the wicked be ashamed, and let them be silent in the grave.

18 Let the lying lips be put to silence; which speak grievous things proudly and contemptuously against the righteous.

19 Oh how great is thy goodness, which thou hast laid up for them that fear thee; which thou hast wrought for them that trust in thee before the sons of men!

20 Thou shalt hide them in the secret of thy presence from the pride of man: thou shalt keep them secretly in a pavilion from the strife of tongues.

21 Blessed be the Lord: for he hath shewed me his marvellous kindness in a strong city.

22 For I said in my haste, I am cut off from before thine eyes: nevertheless thou heardest the voice of my supplications when I cried unto thee.

23 O love the Lord, all ye his saints: for the Lord preserveth the faithful, and plentifully rewardeth the proud doer.

24 Be of good courage, and he shall strengthen your heart, all ye that hope in the Lord.

Glory be to the Father, and to the Son, and to the Holy Ghost.

As it was in the beginning, is now, and ever shall be, world without end. Amen.

## Selection 11

*Psalm XXXII*

BLESSED is he whose transgression is forgiven, whose sin is covered.

2 Blessed is the man unto whom the Lord imputeth not iniquity, and in whose spirit there is no guile.

3 When I kept silence, my bones waxed old through my roaring all the day long.

4 For day and night thy hand was heavy upon me: my moisture is turned into the drought of summer.

5 I acknowledged my sin unto thee, and mine iniquity have I not hid. I said, I will confess my transgressions unto the Lord; and thou forgavest the iniquity of my sin.

6 For this shall every one that is godly pray unto thee in a time when thou mayest be found: surely in the floods of great waters they shall not come nigh unto him.

7 Thou art my hiding place; thou shalt preserve me from trouble; thou shalt compass me about with songs of deliverance.

8 I will instruct thee and teach thee in the way which thou shalt go: I will guide thee with mine eye.

9 Be ye not as the horse, or as the mule, which have no understanding: whose mouth must be held in with bit and bridle, lest they come near unto thee.

10 Many sorrows shall be to the wicked: but he that trusteth in the Lord, mercy shall compass him about.

11 Be glad in the Lord, and rejoice, ye righteous: and shout for joy, all ye that are upright in heart.

*Psalm XXXIII*

12 Rejoice in the Lord, O ye righteous: for praise is comely for the upright.

13 Praise the Lord with harp: sing unto him with the psaltery and an instrument of ten strings.

14 Sing unto him a new song; play skilfully with a loud noise.

15 For the word of the Lord is right; and all his works are done in truth.

16 He loveth righteousness and judgment: the earth is full of the goodness of the Lord.

17 By the word of the Lord were the heavens made; and all the host of them by the breath of his mouth.

18 He gathereth the waters of the sea together as an heap: he layeth up the depth in storehouses.

19 Let all the earth fear the Lord: let all the inhabitants of the world stand in awe of him.

20 For he spake, and it was done; he commanded, and it stood fast.

21 The Lord bringeth the counsel of the heathen to nought: he maketh the devices of the people of none effect.

22 The counsel of the Lord standeth for ever, the thoughts of his heart to all generations.

Glory be to the Father, and to the Son, and to the Holy Ghost.

As it was in the beginning, is now, and ever shall be, world without end. Amen.

## Selection 12

*Psalm XXXIII: 12-22*

BLESSED is the nation whose God is the Lord; and the people whom he hath chosen for his own inheritance.

2 The Lord looketh from heaven; he beholdeth all the sons of men.

3 From the place of his habitation he looketh upon all the inhabitants of the earth.

4 He fashioneth their hearts alike; he considereth all their works.

5 There is no king saved by the multitude of an host : a mighty man is not delivered by much strength.

6 An horse is a vain thing for safety: neither shall he deliver any by his great strength.

7 Behold, the eye of the Lord is upon them that fear him, upon them that hope in his mercy ;

8 To deliver their soul from death, and to keep them alive in famine.

9 Our soul waiteth for the Lord : he is our help and our shield.

10 For our heart shall rejoice in him, because we have trusted in his holy name.

11 Let thy mercy, O Lord, be upon us, according as we hope in thee.

*Psalm XXXIV*

12 I will bless the Lord at all times : his praise shall continually be in my mouth.

13 My soul shall make her boast in the Lord : the humble shall hear thereof, and be glad.

14 O magnify the Lord with me, and let us exalt his name together.

15 I sought the Lord, and he heard me, and delivered me from all my fears.

16 They looked unto him, and were lightened : and their faces were not ashamed.

17 This poor man cried, and the Lord heard him, and saved him out of all his troubles.

18 The angel of the Lord encampeth round about them that fear him, and delivereth them.

19 O taste and see that the Lord is good : blessed is the man that trusteth in him.

20 O fear the Lord, ye his saints : for there is no want to them that fear him.

21 The young lions do lack, and suffer hunger : but they that seek the Lord shall not want any good thing.

22 Come, ye children, hearken unto me : I will teach you the fear of the Lord.

23 What man is he that desireth life, and loveth many days, that he may see good ?

24 Keep thy tongue from evil, and thy lips from speaking guile.

25 Depart from evil, and do good ; seek peace, and pursue it.

26 The eyes of the Lord are upon the righteous, and his ears are open unto their cry.

27 The face of the Lord is against them that do evil, to cut off the remembrance of them from the earth.

28 The righteous cry, and the Lord heareth, and delivereth them out of all their troubles.

29 The Lord is nigh unto them that are of a broken heart ; and saveth such as be of a contrite spirit.

30 Many are the afflictions of the righteous ; but the Lord delivereth him out of them all.

31 He keepeth all his bones : not one of them is broken.

32 Evil shall slay the wicked : and they that hate the righteous shall be desolate.

33 The Lord redeemeth the soul of his servants : and none of them that trust in him shall be desolate.

Glory be to the Father, and to the Son, and to the Holy Ghost.

As it was in the beginning, is now, and ever shall be, world without end. Amen.

## Selection 13

*Psalm XXXVI*

THE transgression of the wicked saith within my heart, that there is no fear of God before his eyes.

2 For he flattereth himself in his own

eyes, until his iniquity be found to be hateful.

3 The words of his mouth are iniquity and deceit: he hath left off to be wise, and to do good.

4 He deviseth mischief upon his bed; he setteth himself in a way that is not good; he abhorreth not evil.

5 Thy mercy, O Lord, is in the heavens; and thy faithfulness reacheth unto the clouds.

6 Thy righteousness is like the great mountains; thy judgments are a great deep: O Lord, thou preservest man and beast.

7 How excellent is thy lovingkindness, O God! therefore the children of men put their trust under the shadow of thy wings.

8 They shall be abundantly satisfied with the fatness of thy house; and thou shalt make them drink of the river of thy pleasures.

9 For with thee is the fountain of life: in thy light shall we see light.

10 O continue thy lovingkindness unto them that know thee; and thy righteousness to the upright in heart.

11 Let not the foot of pride come against me, and let not the hand of the wicked remove me.

12 There are the workers of iniquity fallen: they are cast down, and shall not be able to rise.

*Psalm XXXVII: 1-11*

13 Fret not thyself because of evil doers, neither be thou envious against the workers of iniquity.

14 For they shall soon be cut down like the grass, and wither as the green herb.

15 Trust in the Lord, and do good; so shalt thou dwell in the land, and verily thou shalt be fed.

16 Delight thyself also in the Lord; and he shall give thee the desires of thine heart.

17 Commit thy way unto the Lord; trust also in him; and he shall bring it to pass.

18 And he shall bring forth thy righteousness as the light, and thy judgment as the noon-day.

19 Rest in the Lord, and wait patiently for him: fret not thyself because of him who prospereth in his way, because of the man who bringeth wicked devices to pass.

20 Cease from anger, and forsake wrath: fret not thyself in any wise to do evil.

21 For evil doers shall be cut off: but those that wait upon the Lord, they shall inherit the earth.

22 For yet a little while, and the wicked shall not be: yea, thou shalt diligently consider his place, and it shall not be.

23 But the meek shall inherit the earth; and shall delight themselves in the abundance of peace.

Glory be to the Father, and to the Son, and to the Holy Ghost.

As it was in the beginning, is now, and ever shall be, world without end. Amen.

## Selection 14

*Psalm XXXVII: 12-40*

THE wicked plotteth against the just, and gnasheth upon him with his teeth.

2 The Lord shall laugh at him: for he seeth that his day is coming.

3 The wicked have drawn out the sword, and have bent their bow, to cast down the poor and needy, and to slay such as be of upright conversation.

4 Their sword shall enter into their own heart, and their bows shall be broken.

5 A little that a righteous man hath is better than the riches of many wicked.

6 For the arms of the wicked shall be broken: but the Lord upholdeth the righteous.

7 The Lord knoweth the days of the upright: and their inheritance shall be for ever.

8 They shall not be ashamed in the evil time: and in the days of famine they shall be satisfied.

9 But the wicked shall perish, and the enemies of the Lord shall be as the fat of lambs: they shall consume; into smoke shall they consume away.

10 The wicked borroweth, and payeth not again: but the righteous sheweth mercy, and giveth.

11 For such as be blessed of him shall inherit the earth; and they that be cursed of him shall be cut off.

12 The steps of a good man are ordered by the Lord: and he delighteth in his way.

13 Though he fall, he shall not be utterly cast down: for the Lord upholdeth him with his hand.

14 I have been young, and now am old; yet have I not seen the righteous forsaken, nor his seed begging bread.

15 He is ever merciful, and lendeth; and his seed is blessed.

16 Depart from evil, and do good; and dwell for evermore.

17 For the Lord loveth judgment, and forsaketh not his saints; they are preserved for ever: but the seed of the wicked shall be cut off.

18 The righteous shall inherit the land, and dwell therein for ever.

19 The mouth of the righteous speaketh wisdom, and his tongue talketh of judgment.

20 The law of his God is in his heart; none of his steps shall slide.

21 The wicked watcheth the righteous, and seeketh to slay him.

22 The Lord will not leave him in his hand, nor condemn him when he is judged.

23 Wait on the Lord, and keep his way, and he shall exalt thee to inherit the land: when the wicked are cut off, thou shalt see it.

24 I have seen the wicked in great power, and spreading himself like a green bay tree.

25 Yet he passed away, and, lo, he was not: yea, I sought him, but he could not be found.

26 Mark the perfect man, and behold the upright: for the end of that man is peace.

27 But the transgressors shall be destroyed together: the end of the wicked shall be cut off.

28 But the salvation of the righteous is of the Lord: he is their strength in the time of trouble.

29 And the Lord shall help them, and deliver them: he shall deliver them from the wicked, and save them, because they trust in him.

Glory be to the Father, and to the Son, and to the Holy Ghost.

As it was in the beginning, is now, and ever shall be, world without end. Amen.

## Selection 15

*Psalm XXXIX*

I SAID, I will take heed to my ways, that I sin not with my tongue: I will keep my mouth with a bridle, while the wicked is before me.

2 I was dumb with silence; I held my peace, even from good; and my sorrow was stirred.

3 My heart was hot within me; while

I was musing the fire burned: then spake I with my tongue.

4 Lord, make me to know mine end, and the measure of my days, what it is; that I may know how frail I am.

5 Behold, thou hast made my days as an handbreadth; and mine age is as nothing before thee: verily every man at his best state is altogether vanity.

6 Surely every man walketh in a vain shew: surely they are disquieted in vain: he heapeth up riches, and knoweth not who shall gather them.

7 And now, Lord, what wait I for? my hope is in thee.

8 Deliver me from all my transgressions: make me not the reproach of the foolish.

9 I was dumb, I opened not my mouth; because thou didst it.

10 Remove thy stroke away from me: I am consumed by the blow of thine hand.

11 When thou with rebukes dost correct man for iniquity, thou makest his beauty to consume away like a moth: surely every man is vanity.

12 Hear my prayer, O Lord, and give ear unto my cry; hold not thy peace at my tears: for I am a stranger with thee and a sojourner, as all my fathers were.

13 O spare me, that I may recover strength, before I go hence, and be no more.

*Psalm XL: 1-10*

14 I waited patiently for the Lord; and he inclined unto me, and heard my cry.

15 He brought me up also out of an horrible pit, out of the miry clay, and set my feet upon a rock, and established my goings.

16 And he hath put a new song in my mouth, even praise unto our God: many shall see it, and fear, and shall trust in the Lord.

17 Blessed is that man that maketh the Lord his trust, and respecteth not the proud, nor such as turn aside to lies.

18 Many, O Lord my God, are thy wonderful works which thou hast done, and thy thoughts which are to us-ward: they cannot be reckoned up in order unto thee: if I would declare and speak of them, they are more than can be numbered.

19 Sacrifice and offering thou didst not desire; mine ears hast thou opened: burnt-offering and sin-offering hast thou not required.

20 Then said I, Lo, I come: in the volume of the book it is written of me,

21 I delight to do thy will, O my God: yea, thy law is within my heart.

22 I have preached righteousness in the great congregation: lo, I have not refrained my lips, O Lord, thou knowest.

23 I have not hid thy righteousness within my heart; I have declared thy faithfulness and thy salvation: I have not concealed thy lovingkindness and thy truth from the great congregation.

Glory be to the Father, and to the Son, and to the Holy Ghost.

As it was in the beginning, is now, and ever shall be, world without end. Amen.

## Selection 16

*Psalm XL: 11-17*

WITHHOLD not thou thy tender mercies from me, O Lord: let thy lovingkindness and thy truth continually preserve me.

2 For innumerable evils have compassed me about: mine iniquities have taken hold upon me, so that I am not able to look up; they are more than the hairs of mine head: therefore my heart faileth me.

3 Be pleased, O Lord, to deliver me: O Lord, make haste to help me.

4 Let them be ashamed and confounded together that seek after my soul to destroy it; let them be driven backward and put to shame that wish me evil.

5 Let them be desolate for a reward of their shame that say unto me, Aha, aha.

6 Let all those that seek thee rejoice and be glad in thee: let such as love thy salvation say continually, The Lord be magnified.

7 But I am poor and needy; yet the Lord thinketh upon me: thou art my help and my deliverer; make no tarrying, O my God.

*Psalm XLII*

8 As the hart panteth after the water brooks, so panteth my soul after thee, O God.

9 My soul thirsteth for God, for the living God: when shall I come and appear before God?

10 My tears have been my meat day and night, while they continually say unto me, Where is thy God?

11 When I remember these things, I pour out my soul in me: for I had gone with the multitude, I went with them to the house of God, with the voice of joy and praise, with a multitude that kept holyday.

12 Why art thou cast down, O my soul? and why art thou disquieted in me? hope thou in God: for I shall yet praise him for the help of his countenance.

13 O my God, my soul is cast down within me: therefore will I remember thee from the land of Jordan, and of the Hermonites, from the hill Mizar.

14 Deep calleth unto deep at the noise of thy waterspouts: all thy waves and thy billows are gone over me.

15 Yet the Lord will command his lovingkindness in the daytime, and in the night his song shall be with me, and my prayer unto the God of my life.

16 I will say unto God my rock, Why hast thou forgotten me? why go I mourning because of the oppression of the enemy?

17 As with a sword in my bones, mine enemies reproach me; while they say daily unto me, Where is thy God?

18 Why art thou cast down, O my soul? and why art thou disquieted within me? hope thou in God: for I shall yet praise him, who is the health of my countenance, and my God.

*Psalm XLIII*

19 Judge me, O God, and plead my cause against an ungodly nation: O deliver me from the deceitful and unjust man.

20 For thou art the God of my strength: why dost thou cast me off? why go I mourning because of the oppression of the enemy?

21 O send out thy light and thy truth: let them lead me; let them bring me unto thy holy hill, and to thy tabernacles.

22 Then will I go unto the altar of God, unto God my exceeding joy: yea, upon the harp will I praise thee, O God my God.

23 Why art thou cast down, O my soul? and why art thou disquieted within me? hope in God: for I shall yet praise him, who is the health of my countenance, and my God.

Glory be to the Father, and to the Son, and to the Holy Ghost.

As it was in the beginning, is now, and ever shall be, world without end. Amen.

## Selection 17

*Psalm XLV*

MY heart is inditing a good matter: I speak of the things which I have made touching the King: my tongue is the pen of a ready writer.

2 Thou art fairer than the children of men: grace is poured into thy lips: therefore God hath blessed thee for ever.

3 Gird thy sword upon thy thigh, O most mighty, with thy glory and thy majesty.

4 And in thy majesty ride prosperously because of truth and meekness and righteousness; and thy right hand shall teach thee terrible things.

5 Thine arrows are sharp in the heart of the king's enemies; whereby the people fall under thee.

6 Thy throne, O God, is for ever and ever: the sceptre of thy kingdom is a right sceptre.

7 Thou lovest righteousness, and hatest wickedness: therefore God, thy God, hath anointed thee with the oil of gladness above thy fellows.

8 All thy garments smell of myrrh, and aloes, and cassia, out of the ivory palaces, whereby they have made thee glad.

9 Kings' daughters were among thy honourable women: upon thy right hand did stand the queen in gold of Ophir.

10 Hearken, O daughter, and consider, and incline thine ear; forget also thine own people, and thy father's house;

11 So shall the king greatly desire thy beauty: for he is thy Lord; and worship thou him.

12 And the daughter of Tyre shall be there with a gift; even the rich among the people shall entreat thy favour.

13 The King's daughter is all glorious within: her clothing is of wrought gold.

14 She shall be brought unto the King in raiment of needlework; the virgins her companions that follow her shall be brought unto thee.

15 With gladness and rejoicing shall they be brought: they shall enter into the king's palace.

16 Instead of thy fathers shall be thy children, whom thou mayest make princes in all the earth.

17 I will make thy name to be remembered in all generations: therefore shall the people praise thee for ever and ever.

*Psalm XLVI*

18 God is our refuge and strength, a very present help in trouble.

19 Therefore will not we fear, though the earth be removed, and though the mountains be carried into the midst of the sea;

20 Though the waters thereof roar and be troubled, though the mountains shake with the swelling thereof.

21 There is a river, the streams whereof shall make glad the city of God, the holy place of the tabernacles of the Most High.

22 God is in the midst of her; she shall not be moved: God shall help her, and that right early.

23 The heathen raged, the kingdoms were moved: he uttered his voice, the earth melted.

24 The Lord of hosts is with us; the God of Jacob is our refuge.

25 Come, behold the works of the Lord, what desolations he hath made in the earth.

26 He maketh wars to cease unto the end of the earth; he breaketh the bow, and cutteth the spear in sunder; he burneth the chariot in the fire.

27 Be still, and know that I am God: I will be exalted among the heathen, I will be exalted in the earth.

## SELECTIONS FROM THE PSALMS

28 The Lord of hosts is with us ; the God of Jacob is our refuge.

Glory be to the Father, and to the Son, and to the Holy Ghost.

As it was in the beginning, is now, and ever shall be, world without end. Amen.

## Selection 18

*Psalm XLVIII*

GREAT is the Lord, and greatly to be praised in the city of our God, in the mountain of his holiness.

2 Beautiful for situation, the joy of the whole earth, is mount Zion, on the sides of the north, the city of the great King.

3 God is known in her palaces for a refuge.

4 For lo, the kings were assembled, they passed by together.

5 They saw it, and so they marvelled ; they were troubled, and hasted away.

6 Fear took hold upon them there, and pain, as of a woman in travail.

7 Thou breakest the ships of Tarshish with an east wind.

8 As we have heard, so have we seen in the city of the Lord of hosts, in the city of our God : God will establish it for ever.

9 We have thought of thy lovingkindness, O God, in the midst of thy temple.

10 According to thy name, O God, so is thy praise unto the ends of the earth : thy right hand is full of righteousness.

11 Let mount Zion rejoice, let the daughters of Judah be glad, because of thy judgments.

12 Walk about Zion, and go round about her : tell the towers thereof.

13 Mark ye well her bulwarks, consider her palaces ; that ye may tell it to the generation following.

14 For this God is our God for ever and ever : he will be our guide even unto death.

*Psalm L*

15 The mighty God, even the Lord, hath spoken, and called the earth from the rising of the sun unto the going down thereof.

16 Out of Zion, the perfection of beauty, God hath shined.

17 Our God shall come, and shall not keep silence : a fire shall devour before him, and it shall be very tempestuous round about him.

18 He shall call to the heavens from above, and to the earth, that he may judge his people.

19 Gather my saints together unto me; those that have made a covenant with me by sacrifice.

20 And the heavens shall declare his righteousness : for God is judge himself.

21 Hear, O my people, and I will speak ; O Israel, and I will testify against thee : I am God, even thy God.

22 I will not reprove thee for thy sacrifices or thy burnt offerings, to have been continually before me.

23 I will take no bullock out of thy house, nor he goats out of thy folds.

24 For every beast of the forest is mine, and the cattle upon a thousand hills.

25 I know all the fowls of the mountains : and the wild beasts of the field are mine.

26 If I were hungry, I would not tell thee : for the world is mine, and the fulness thereof.

27 Will I eat the flesh of bulls, or drink the blood of goats ?

28 Offer unto God thanksgiving ; and pay thy vows unto the most High :

29 And call upon me in the day of trouble : I will deliver thee, and thou shalt glorify me.

30 But unto the wicked God saith, What hast thou to do to declare my statutes, or that thou shouldest take my covenant in thy mouth?

31 Seeing thou hatest instruction, and castest my words behind thee.

32 When thou sawest a thief, then thou consentedst with him, and hast been partaker with adulterers.

33 Thou givest thy mouth to evil, and thy tongue frameth deceit.

34 Thou sittest and speakest against thy brother; thou slanderest thine own mother's son.

35 These things hast thou done, and I kept silence; thou thoughtest that I was altogether such an one as thyself: but I will reprove thee, and set them in order before thine eyes.

36 Now consider this, ye that forget God, lest I tear you in pieces, and there be none to deliver.

37 Whoso offereth praise glorifieth me: and to him that ordereth his conversation aright will I shew the salvation of God.

Glory be to the Father, and to the Son, and to the Holy Ghost.

As it was in the beginning, is now, and ever shall be, world without end. Amen.

## Selection 19

### Psalm LI

HAVE mercy upon me, O God, according to thy lovingkindness: according unto the multitude of thy tender mercies blot out my transgressions.

2 Wash me thoroughly from mine iniquity, and cleanse me from my sin.

3 For I acknowledge my transgressions: and my sin is ever before me.

4 Against thee, thee only, have I sinned, and done this evil in thy sight: that thou mightest be justified when thou speakest, and be clear when thou judgest.

5 Behold, I was shapen in iniquity; and in sin did my mother conceive me.

6 Behold, thou desirest truth in the inward parts: and in the hidden part thou shalt make me to know wisdom.

7 Purge me with hyssop, and I shall be clean: wash me, and I shall be whiter than snow.

8 Make me to hear joy and gladness; that the bones which thou hast broken may rejoice.

9 Hide thy face from my sins, and blot out all mine iniquities.

10 Create in me a clean heart, O God; and renew a right spirit within me.

11 Cast me not away from thy presence; and take not thy Holy Spirit from me.

12 Restore unto me the joy of thy salvation; and uphold me with thy free Spirit.

13 Then will I teach transgressors thy ways; and sinners shall be converted unto thee.

14 Deliver me from blood-guiltiness, O God, thou God of my salvation: and my tongue shall sing aloud of thy righteousness.

15 O Lord, open thou my lips, and my mouth shall shew forth thy praise.

16 For thou desirest not sacrifice; else would I give it: thou delightest not in burnt offering.

17 The sacrifices of God are a broken spirit: a broken and a contrite heart, O God, thou wilt not despise.

18 Do good in thy good pleasure unto Zion: build thou the walls of Jerusalem.

19 Then shalt thou be pleased with the sacrifices of righteousness, with burnt offering and whole burnt offering: then shall they offer bullocks upon thine altar.

Glory be to the Father, and to the Son, and to the Holy Ghost.
As it was in the beginning, is now, and ever shall be, world without end. Amen.

## Selection 20

*Psalm LVII*

BE merciful unto me, O God, be merciful unto me: for my soul trusteth in thee: yea, in the shadow of thy wings will I make my refuge, until these calamities be overpast.

2 I will cry unto God Most High; unto God that performeth all things for me.

3 He shall send from heaven, and save me from the reproach of him that would swallow me up. God shall send forth his mercy and his truth.

4 My soul is among lions: and I lie even among them that are set on fire, even the sons of men, whose teeth are spears and arrows, and their tongue a sharp sword.

5 Be thou exalted, O God, above the heavens; let thy glory be above all the earth.

6 They have prepared a net for my steps; my soul is bowed down: they have digged a pit before me, into the midst whereof they are fallen themselves.

7 My heart is fixed, O God, my heart is fixed: I will sing and give praise.

8 Awake up, my glory; awake, psaltery and harp: I myself will awake early.

9 I will praise thee, O Lord, among the people: I will sing unto thee among the nations.

10 For thy mercy is great unto the heavens, and thy truth unto the clouds.

11 Be thou exalted, O God, above the heavens: let thy glory be above all the earth.

*Psalm LXII*

12 Truly my soul waiteth upon God: from him cometh my salvation.

13 He only is my rock and my salvation; he is my defence; I shall not be greatly moved.

14 How long will ye imagine mischief against a man? ye shall be slain all of you: as a bowing wall shall ye be, and as a tottering fence.

15 They only consult to cast him down from his excellency: they delight in lies: they bless with their mouth, but they curse inwardly.

16 My soul, wait thou only upon God; for my expectation is from him.

17 He only is my rock and my salvation: he is my defence; I shall not be moved.

18 In God is my salvation and my glory: the rock of my strength, and my refuge, is in God.

19 Trust in him at all times; ye people, pour out your heart before him: God is a refuge for us.

20 Surely men of low degree are vanity, and men of high degree are a lie: to be laid in the balance, they are altogether lighter than vanity.

21 Trust not in oppression, and become not vain in robbery: if riches increase, set not your heart upon them.

22 God hath spoken once; twice have I heard this; that power belongeth unto God.

23 Also unto thee, O Lord, belongeth mercy: for thou renderest to every man according to his work.

Glory be to the Father, and to the Son, and to the Holy Ghost.
As it was in the beginning, is now, and ever shall be, world without end. Amen.

## Selection 21

*Psalm LXIII*

O GOD, thou art my God ; early will I seek thee : my soul thirsteth for thee, my flesh longeth for thee in a dry and thirsty land, where no water is ;
2 To see thy power and thy glory, so as I have seen thee in the sanctuary.
3 Because thy lovingkindness is better than life, my lips shall praise thee.
4 Thus will I bless thee while I live : I will lift up my hands in thy name.
5 My soul shall be satisfied as with marrow and fatness ; and my mouth shall praise thee with joyful lips :
6 When I remember thee upon my bed, and meditate on thee in the night watches.
7 Because thou hast been my help, therefore in the shadow of thy wings will I rejoice.
8 My soul followeth hard after thee : thy right hand upholdeth me.
9 But those that seek my soul to destroy it, shall go into the lower parts of the earth.
10 They shall fall by the sword ; they shall be a portion for foxes.
11 But the king shall rejoice in God ; every one that sweareth by him shall glory : but the mouth of them that speak lies shall be stopped.

*Psalm LXV*

12 Praise waiteth for thee, O God, in Zion : and unto thee shall the vow be performed.
13 O thou that hearest prayer, unto thee shall all flesh come.
14 Iniquities prevail against me : as for our transgressions, thou shalt purge them away.
15 Blessed is the man whom thou choosest, and causest to approach unto thee, that he may dwell in thy courts : we shall be satisfied with the goodness of thy house, even of thy holy temple.
16 By terrible things in righteousness wilt thou answer us, O God of our salvation ; who art the confidence of all the ends of the earth, and of them that are afar off upon the sea :
17 Which by his strength setteth fast the mountains ; being girded with power :
18 Which stilleth the noise of the seas, the noise of their waves, and the tumult of the people.
19 They also that dwell in the uttermost parts are afraid at thy tokens : thou makest the out-goings of the morning and evening to rejoice.
20 Thou visitest the earth, and waterest it : thou greatly enrichest it with the river of God, which is full of water : thou preparest them corn, when thou hast so provided for it.
21 Thou waterest the ridges thereof abundantly : thou settlest the furrows thereof : thou makest it soft with showers : thou blessest the springing thereof.
22 Thou crownest the year with thy goodness ; and thy paths drop fatness.
23 They drop upon the pastures of the wilderness : and the little hills rejoice on every side.
24 The pastures are clothed with flocks ; the valleys also are covered over with corn ; they shout for joy, they also sing.

Glory be to the Father, and to the Son, and to the Holy Ghost.
As it was in the beginning, is now, and ever shall be, world without end. Amen.

## Selection 22

*Psalm LXVI*

MAKE a joyful noise unto God, all ye lands:
2 Sing forth the honour of his name : make his praise glorious.

3 Say unto God, How terrible art thou in thy works! through the greatness of thy power shall thine enemies submit themselves unto thee.

4 All the earth shall worship thee, and shall sing unto thee; they shall sing to thy name.

5 Come and see the works of God: he is terrible in his doing toward the children of men.

6 He turned the sea into dry land: they went through the flood on foot: there did we rejoice in him.

7 He ruleth by his power for ever; his eyes behold the nations: let not the rebellious exalt themselves.

8 O bless our God, ye people, and make the voice of his praise to be heard:

9 Which holdeth our soul in life, and suffereth not our feet to be moved.

10 For thou, O God, hast proved us: thou hast tried us, as silver is tried.

11 Thou broughtest us into the net; thou laidest affliction upon our loins.

12 Thou hast caused men to ride over our heads; we went through fire and through water: but thou broughtest us out into a wealthy place.

13 I will go into thy house with burnt offerings: I will pay thee my vows,

14 Which my lips have uttered, and my mouth hath spoken, when I was in trouble.

15 I will offer unto thee burnt sacrifices of fatlings, with the incense of rams; I will offer bullocks with goats.

16 Come and hear, all ye that fear God, and I will declare what he hath done for my soul.

17 I cried unto him with my mouth, and he was extolled with my tongue.

18 If I regard iniquity in my heart, the Lord will not hear me:

19 But verily God hath heard me; he hath attended to the voice of my prayer.

20 Blessed be God, which hath not turned away my prayer, nor his mercy from me.

*Psalm LXVII*

21 God be merciful unto us, and bless us; and cause his face to shine upon us; Selah.

22 That thy way may be known upon earth, thy saving health among all nations.

23 Let the people praise thee, O God; let all the people praise thee.

24 O let the nations be glad and sing for joy: for thou shalt judge the people righteously, and govern the nations upon earth.

25 Let the people praise thee, O God; let all the people praise thee.

26 Then shall the earth yield her increase; and God, even our own God, shall bless us.

27 God shall bless us; and all the ends of the earth shall fear him.

Glory be to the Father, and to the Son, and to the Holy Ghost.

As it was in the beginning, is now, and ever shall be, world without end. Amen.

## Selection 23

*Psalm LXVIII*

LET God arise, let his enemies be scattered: let them also that hate him flee before him.

2 As smoke is driven away, so drive them away: as wax melteth before the fire, so let the wicked perish at the presence of God.

3 But let the righteous be glad; let them rejoice before God: yea, let them exceedingly rejoice.

4 Sing unto God, sing praises to his name: extol him that rideth upon the heavens by his name Jah, and rejoice before him.

## SELECTIONS FROM THE PSALMS

5 A father of the fatherless, and a judge of the widows, is God in his holy habitation.

6 God setteth the solitary in families: he bringeth out those which are bound with chains: but the rebellious dwell in a dry land.

7 O God, when thou wentest forth before thy people, when thou didst march through the wilderness;

8 The earth shook, the heavens also dropped at the presence of God: even Sinai itself was moved at the presence of God, the God of Israel.

9 Thou, O God, didst send a plentiful rain, whereby thou didst confirm thine inheritance, when it was weary.

10 Thy congregation hath dwelt therein: thou, O God, hast prepared of thy goodness for the poor.

11 The Lord gave the word: great was the company of those that published it.

12 Kings of armies did flee apace: and she that tarried at home divided the spoil.

13 Though ye have lien among the pots, yet shall ye be as the wings of a dove covered with silver, and her feathers with yellow gold.

14 When the Almighty scattered kings in it, it was white as snow in Salmon.

15 The hill of God is as the hill of Bashan; an high hill as the hill of Bashan.

16 Why leap ye, ye high hills? this is the hill which God desireth to dwell in; yea, the Lord will dwell in it for ever.

17 The chariots of God are twenty thousand, even thousands of angels: the Lord is among them, as in Sinai, in the holy place.

18 Thou hast ascended on high, thou hast led captivity captive: thou hast received gifts for men; yea, for the rebellious also, that the Lord God might dwell among them.

19 Blessed be the Lord, who daily loadeth us with benefits, even the God of our salvation.

20 He that is our God is the God of salvation; and unto God the Lord belong the issues from death.

21 But God shall wound the head of his enemies, and the hairy scalp of such an one as goeth on still in his trespasses.

22 The Lord said, I will bring again from Bashan; I will bring my people again from the depths of the sea:

23 That thy foot may be dipped in the blood of thine enemies, and the tongue of thy dogs in the same.

24 They have seen thy goings, O God; even the goings of my God, my King, in the sanctuary.

25 The singers went before, the players on instruments followed after; among them were the damsels playing with timbrels.

26 Bless ye God in the congregations, even the Lord, from the fountain of Israel.

27 There is little Benjamin with their ruler, the princes of Judah and their council, the princes of Zebulun, and the princes of Naphtali.

28 Thy God hath commanded thy strength: strengthen, O God, that which thou hast wrought for us.

29 Because of thy temple at Jerusalem shall kings bring presents unto thee.

30 Rebuke the company of spearmen, the multitude of the bulls, with the calves of the people, till every one submit himself with pieces of silver: scatter thou the people that delight in war.

31 Princes shall come out of Egypt; Ethiopia shall soon stretch out her hands unto God.

32 Sing unto God, ye kingdoms of the earth; O sing praises unto the Lord;

33 To him that rideth upon the heav-

ens of heavens, which were of old; lo, he doth send out his voice, and that a mighty voice.

34 Ascribe ye strength unto God: his excellency is over Israel, and his strength is in the clouds.

35 O God, thou art terrible out of thy holy places: the God of Israel is he that giveth strength and power unto his people. Blessed be God.

Glory be to the Father, and to the Son, and to the Holy Ghost.

As it was in the beginning, is now, and ever shall be, world without end. Amen.

## Selection 24

### Psalm LXXI

IN thee, O Lord, do I put my trust; let me never be put to confusion.

2 Deliver me in thy righteousness, and cause me to escape: incline thine ear unto me, and save me.

3 Be thou my strong habitation, whereunto I may continually resort: thou hast given commandment to save me; for thou art my rock and my fortress.

4 Deliver me, O my God, out of the hand of the wicked, out of the hand of the unrighteous and cruel man.

5 For thou art my hope, O Lord God: thou art my trust from my youth.

6 By thee have I been holden up from the womb: thou art he that took me out of my mother's bowels: my praise shall be continually of thee.

7 I am as a wonder unto many; but thou art my strong refuge.

8 Let my mouth be filled with thy praise and with thy honour all the day.

9 Cast me not off in the time of old age; forsake me not when my strength faileth.

10 For mine enemies speak against me; and they that lay wait for my soul take counsel together,

11 Saying, God hath forsaken him: persecute and take him; for there is none to deliver him.

12 O God, be not far from me: O my God, make haste for my help.

13 Let them be confounded and consumed that are adversaries to my soul; let them be covered with reproach and dishonour that seek my hurt.

14 But I will hope continually, and will yet praise thee more and more.

15 My mouth shall shew forth thy righteousness and thy salvation all the day; for I know not the numbers thereof.

16 I will go in the strength of the Lord God: I will make mention of thy righteousness, even of thine only.

17 O God, thou hast taught me from my youth: and hitherto have I declared thy wondrous works.

18 Now also, when I am old and grayheaded, O God, forsake me not; until I have shewed thy strength unto this generation, and thy power to every one that is to come.

19 Thy righteousness also, O God, is very high, who hast done great things: O God, who is like unto thee?

20 Thou, which hast shewed me great and sore troubles, shalt quicken me again, and shalt bring me up again from the depths of the earth.

21 Thou shalt increase my greatness, and comfort me on every side.

22 I will also praise thee with the psaltery, even thy truth, O my God: unto thee will I sing with the harp, O thou Holy One of Israel.

23 My lips shall greatly rejoice when I sing unto thee; and my soul, which thou hast redeemed.

24 My tongue also shall talk of thy righteousness all the day long: for they

are confounded, for they are brought unto shame, that seek my hurt.

Glory be to the Father, and to the Son, and to the Holy Ghost.

As it was in the beginning, is now, and ever shall be, world without end. Amen.

## Selection 25

### Psalm LXXII

GIVE the king thy judgments, O God, and thy righteousness unto the king's son.

2 He shall judge thy people with righteousness, and thy poor with judgment.

3 The mountains shall bring peace to the people, and the little hills, by righteousness.

4 He shall judge the poor of the people, he shall save the children of the needy, and shall break in pieces the oppressor.

5 They shall fear thee as long as the sun and moon endure, throughout all generations.

6 He shall come down like rain upon the mown grass : as showers that water the earth.

7 In his days shall the righteous flourish ; and abundance of peace so long as the moon endureth.

8 He shall have dominion also from sea to sea, and from the river unto the ends of the earth.

9 They that dwell in the wilderness shall bow before him ; and his enemies shall lick the dust.

10 The kings of Tarshish and of the isles shall bring presents : the kings of Sheba and Seba shall offer gifts.

11 Yea, all kings shall fall down before him : all nations shall serve him.

12 For he shall deliver the needy when he crieth ; the poor also, and him that hath no helper.

13 He shall spare the poor and needy, and shall save the souls of the needy.

14 He shall redeem their soul from deceit and violence : and precious shall their blood be in his sight.

15 And he shall live, and to him shall be given of the gold of Sheba : prayer also shall be made for him continually ; and daily shall he be praised.

16 There shall be an handful of corn in the earth upon the top of the mountains ; the fruit thereof shall shake like Lebanon: and they of the city shall flourish like grass of the earth.

17 His name shall endure for ever : his name shall be continued as long as the sun : and men shall be blessed in him : all nations shall call him blessed.

18 Blessed be the Lord God, the God of Israel, who only doeth wondrous things.

19 And blessed be his glorious name for ever : and let the whole earth be filled with his glory. Amen, and Amen.

Glory be to the Father, and to the Son, and to the Holy Ghost.

As it was in the beginning, is now, and ever shall be, world without end. Amen.

## Selection 26

### Psalm LXXIII

TRULY God is good to Israel, even to such as are of a clean heart.

2 But as for me, my feet were almost gone ; my steps had well nigh slipped.

3 For I was envious at the foolish, when I saw the prosperity of the wicked.

4 For there are no bands in their death : but their strength is firm.

5 They are not in trouble as other men : neither are they plagued like other men.

6 Therefore pride compasseth them about as a chain ; violence covereth them as a garment.

7 Their eyes stand out with fatness: they have more than heart could wish.

8 They are corrupt, and speak wickedly concerning oppression : they speak loftily.

9 They set their mouth against the heavens, and their tongue walketh through the earth.

10 Therefore his people return hither: and waters of a full cup are wrung out to them.

11 And they say, How doth God know? and is there knowledge in the Most High ?

12 Behold, these are the ungodly, who prosper in the world ; they increase in riches.

13 Verily I have cleansed my heart in vain, and washed my hands in innocency.

14 For all the day long have I been plagued, and chastened every morning.

15 If I say, I will speak thus ; behold I should offend against the generation of thy children.

16 When I thought to know this, it was too painful for me ;

17 Until I went into the sanctuary of God ; then understood I their end.

18 Surely thou didst set them in slippery places ; thou castedst them down into destruction.

19 How are they brought into desolation, as in a moment! they are utterly consumed with terrors.

20 As a dream when one awaketh ; so O Lord, when thou awakest, thou shalt despise their image.

21 Thus my heart was grieved, and I was pricked in my reins.

22 So foolish was I, and ignorant : I was as a beast before thee.

23 Nevertheless I am continually with thee : thou hast holden me by my right hand.

24 Thou shalt guide me with thy counsel, and afterward receive me to glory.

25 Whom have I in heaven but thee ? and there is none upon earth that I desire beside thee.

26 My flesh and my heart faileth : but God is the strength of my heart, and my portion for ever.

27 For, lo, they that are far from thee shall perish : thou hast destroyed all them that go a whoring from thee.

28 But it is good for me to draw near to God : I have put my trust in the Lord God, that I may declare all thy works.

Glory be to the Father, and to the Son, and to the Holy Ghost.

As it was in the beginning, is now, and ever shall be, world without end. Amen.

## Selection 27

*Psalm LXXVII*

I CRIED unto God with my voice, even unto God with my voice ; and he gave ear unto me.

2 In the day of my trouble I sought the Lord : my sore ran in the night, and ceased not : my soul refused to be comforted.

3 I remembered God, and was troubled: I complained, and my spirit was overwhelmed.

4 Thou holdest mine eyes waking : I am so troubled that I cannot speak.

5 I have considered the days of old, the years of ancient times.

6 I call to remembrance my song in the night : I commune with mine own heart : and my spirit made diligent search.

7 Will the Lord cast off for ever ? and will he be favourable no more ?

8 Is his mercy clean gone for ever ? doth his promise fail for evermore ?

9 Hath God forgotten to be gracious? hath he in anger shut up his tender mercies?

10 And I said, This is my infirmity: but I will remember the years of the right hand of the most High.

11 I will remember the works of the Lord: surely I will remember thy wonders of old.

12 I will meditate also of all thy work, and talk of thy doings.

13 Thy way, O God, is in the sanctuary: who is so great a God as our God?

14 Thou art the God that doest wonders: thou hast declared thy strength among the people.

15 Thou hast with thine arm redeemed thy people, the sons of Jacob and Joseph.

16 The waters saw thee, O God, the waters saw thee; they were afraid: the depths also were troubled.

17 The clouds poured out water: the skies sent out a sound: thine arrows also went abroad.

18 The voice of thy thunder was in the heaven: the lightnings lightened the world: the earth trembled and shook.

19 Thy way is in the sea, and thy path in the great waters, and thy footsteps are not known.

20 Thou leddest thy people like a flock by the hand of Moses and Aaron.

Glory be to the Father, and to the Son, and to the Holy Ghost.

As it was in the beginning, is now, and ever shall be, world without end. Amen.

## Selection 28

*Psalm LXXX*

GIVE ear, O Shepherd of Israel, thou that leadest Joseph like a flock; thou that dwellest between the cherubims, shine forth.

2 Before Ephraim and Benjamin and Manasseh stir up thy strength, and come and save us.

3 Turn us again, O God, and cause thy face to shine; and we shall be saved.

4 O Lord God of hosts, how long wilt thou be angry against the prayer of thy people?

5 Thou feedest them with the bread of tears; and givest them tears to drink in great measure.

6 Thou makest us a strife unto our neighbours: and our enemies laugh among themselves.

7 Turn us again, O God of hosts, and cause thy face to shine; and we shall be saved.

8 Thou hast brought a vine out of Egypt: thou hast cast out the heathen and planted it.

9 Thou preparedst room before it, and didst cause it to take deep root, and it filled the land.

10 The hills were covered with the shadow of it, and the boughs thereof were like the goodly cedars.

11 She sent out her boughs unto the sea, and her branches unto the river.

12 Why hast thou then broken down her hedges, so that all they which pass by the way do pluck her?

13 The boar out of the wood doth waste it, and the wild beast of the field doth devour it.

14 Return, we beseech thee, O God of hosts: look down from heaven, and behold, and visit this vine;

15 And the vineyard which thy right hand hath planted, and the branch that thou madest strong for thyself.

16 It is burned with fire, it is cut down: they perish at the rebuke of thy countenance.

17 Let thy hand be upon the man of thy right hand, upon the son of man whom thou madest strong for thyself.

18 So will not we go back from thee: quicken us, and we will call upon thy name.

19 Turn us again, O Lord God of hosts, cause thy face to shine; and we shall be saved.

Glory be to the Father, and to the Son, and to the Holy Ghost.

As it was in the beginning, is now, and ever shall be, world without end. Amen.

## Selection 29

*Psalm LXXXIV*

HOW amiable are thy tabernacles, O Lord of hosts!

2 My soul longeth, yea, even fainteth for the courts of the Lord: my heart and my flesh crieth out for the living God.

3 Yea, the sparrow hath found an house, and the swallow a nest for herself, where she may lay her young, even thine altars, O Lord of hosts, my King, and my God.

4 Blessed are they that dwell in thy house: they will be still praising thee.

5 Blessed is the man whose strength is in thee; in whose heart are the ways of them.

6 Who passing through the valley of Baca make it a well; the rain also filleth the pools.

7 They go from strength to strength, every one of them in Zion appeareth before God.

8 O Lord God of hosts, hear my prayer: give ear, O God of Jacob.

9 Behold, O God our shield, and look upon the face of thine anointed.

10 For a day in thy courts is better than a thousand. I had rather be a doorkeeper in the house of my God, than to dwell in the tents of wickedness.

11 For the Lord God is a sun and shield: the Lord will give grace and glory: no good thing will he withhold from them that walk uprightly.

12 O Lord of hosts, blessed is the man that trusteth in thee.

*Psalm LXXXV*

13 Lord, thou hast been favourable unto thy land: thou hast brought back the captivity of Jacob.

14 Thou hast forgiven the iniquity of thy people, thou hast covered all their sin.

15 Thou hast taken away all thy wrath: thou hast turned thyself from the fierceness of thine anger.

16 Turn us, O God of our salvation, and cause thine anger toward us to cease.

17 Wilt thou be angry with us for ever? wilt thou draw out thine anger to all generations?

18 Wilt thou not revive us again: that thy people may rejoice in thee?

19 Shew us thy mercy, O Lord, and grant us thy salvation.

20 I will hear what God the Lord will speak: for he will speak peace unto his people, and to his saints: but let them not turn again to folly.

21 Surely his salvation is nigh them that fear him; that glory may dwell in our land.

22 Mercy and truth are met together; righteousness and peace have kissed each other.

23 Truth shall spring out of the earth; and righteousness shall look down from heaven.

24 Yea, the Lord shall give that which is good; and our land shall yield her increase.

25 Righteousness shall go before him; and shall set us in the way of his steps.

Glory be to the Father, and to the Son, and to the Holy Ghost.

As it was in the beginning, is now, and ever shall be, world without end. Amen.

## Selection 30

*Psalm LXXXVI*

BOW down thine ear, O Lord, hear me : for I am poor and needy.

2 Preserve my soul ; for I am holy : O thou my God, save thy servant that trusteth in thee.

3 Be merciful unto me, O Lord : for I cry unto thee daily.

4 Rejoice the soul of thy servant : for unto thee, O Lord, do I lift up my soul.

5 For thou, Lord, art good, and ready to forgive ; and plenteous in mercy unto all them that call upon thee.

6 Give ear, O Lord, unto my prayer ; and attend to the voice of my supplications.

7 In the day of my trouble I will call upon thee : for thou wilt answer me.

8 Among the gods there is none like unto thee, O Lord ; neither are there any works like unto thy works.

9 All nations whom thou hast made shall come and worship before thee, O Lord ; and shall glorify thy name.

10 For thou art great, and doest wondrous things : thou art God alone.

11 Teach me thy way, O Lord ; I will walk in thy truth : unite my heart to fear thy name.

12 I will praise thee, O Lord my God, with all my heart : and I will glorify thy name for evermore.

13 For great is thy mercy toward me : and thou hast delivered my soul from the lowest hell.

14 O God, the proud are risen against me, and the assemblies of violent men have sought after my soul ; and have not set thee before them.

15 But thou, O Lord, art a God full of compassion, and gracious, longsuffering, and plenteous in mercy and truth.

16 O turn unto me, and have mercy upon me ; give thy strength unto thy servant, and save the son of thine handmaid.

17 Shew me a token for good ; that they which hate me may see it, and be ashamed : because thou, Lord, has holpen me, and comforted me.

*Psalm LXXXVII*

18 His foundation is in the holy mountains.

19 The Lord loveth the gates of Zion more than all the dwellings of Jacob.

20 Glorious things are spoken of thee, O city of God.

21 I will make mention of Rahab and Babylon to them that know me : behold Philistia, and Tyre, with Ethiopia ; this man was born there.

22 And of Zion it shall be said, This and that man was born in her : and the highest himself shall establish her.

23 The Lord shall count, when he writeth up the people, that this man was born there.

24 As well the singers as the players on instruments shall be there : all my springs are in thee.

Glory be to the Father, and to the Son, and to the Holy Ghost.

As it was in the beginning, is now, and ever shall be, world without end. Amen.

## Selection 31

*Psalm LXXXIX*

I WILL sing of the mercies of the Lord for ever : with my mouth will I make known thy faithfulness to all generations.

2 For I have said, Mercy shall be built

up for ever: thy faithfulness shalt thou establish in the very heavens.

3 I have made a covenant with my chosen, I have sworn unto David my servant,

4 Thy seed will I establish for ever, and build up thy throne to all generations.

5 And the heavens shall praise thy wonders, O Lord: thy faithfulness also in the congregation of the saints.

6 For who in the heaven can be compared unto the Lord? who among the sons of the mighty can be likened unto the Lord?

7 God is greatly to be feared in the assembly of the saints, and to be had in reverence of all them that are about him.

8 O Lord God of hosts, who is a strong Lord like unto thee? or to thy faithfulness round about thee?

9 Thou rulest the raging of the sea: when the waves thereof arise, thou stillest them.

10 Thou hast broken Rahab in pieces, as one that is slain: thou hast scattered thine enemies with thy strong arm.

11 The heavens are thine, the earth also is thine: as for the world and the fulness thereof, thou hast founded them.

12 The north and the south thou hast created them: Tabor and Hermon shall rejoice in thy name.

13 Thou hast a mighty arm: strong is thy hand, and high is thy right hand.

14 Justice and judgment are the habitation of thy throne: mercy and truth shall go before thy face.

15 Blessed is the people that know the joyful sound: they shall walk, O Lord, in the light of thy countenance.

16 In thy name shall they rejoice all the day: and in thy righteousness shall they be exalted.

17 For thou art the glory of their strength: and in thy favour our horn shall be exalted.

18 For the Lord is our defence; and the Holy One of Israel is our king.

Glory be to the Father, and to the Son, and to the Holy Ghost.

As it was in the beginning, is now, and ever shall be, world without end. Amen.

## Selection 32

*Psalm XC*

LORD, thou hast been our dwellingplace in all generations.

2 Before the mountains were brought forth, or ever thou hadst formed the earth and the world, even from everlasting to everlasting, thou art God.

3 Thou turnest man to destruction; and sayest, Return, ye children of men.

4 For a thousand years in thy sight are but as yesterday when it is past, and as a watch in the night.

5 Thou carriest them away as with a flood; they are as a sleep; in the morning they are like grass which groweth up.

6 In the morning it flourisheth, and groweth up; in the evening it is cut down, and withereth.

7 For we are consumed by thine anger, and by thy wrath are we troubled.

8 Thou hast set our iniquities before thee, our secret sins in the light of thy countenance.

9 For all our days are passed away in thy wrath: we spend our years as a tale that is told.

10 The days of our years are threescore years and ten; and if by reason of strength they be fourscore years, yet is their strength labour and sorrow; for it is soon cut off, and we fly away.

11 Who knoweth the power of thine anger? even according to thy fear, so is thy wrath.

12 So teach us to number our days, that we may apply our hearts unto wisdom.
13 Return, O Lord, how long? and let it repent thee concerning thy servants.
14 O satisfy us early with thy mercy; that we may rejoice and be glad all our days.
15 Make us glad according to the days wherein thou hast afflicted us, and the years wherein we have seen evil.
16 Let thy work appear unto thy servants, and thy glory unto their children.
17 And let the beauty of the Lord our God be upon us: and establish thou the work of our hands upon us; yea, the work of our hands establish thou it.

Glory be to the Father, and to the Son, and to the Holy Ghost.

As it was in the beginning, is now, and ever shall be, world without end. Amen.

## Selection 33

*Psalm XCI*

HE that dwelleth in the secret place of the most High shall abide under the shadow of the Almighty.

2 I will say of the Lord, He is my refuge and my fortress: my God; in him will I trust.

3 Surely he shall deliver thee from the snare of the fowler, and from the noisome pestilence.

4 He shall cover thee with his feathers, and under his wings shalt thou trust: his truth shall be thy shield and buckler.

5 Thou shalt not be afraid for the terror by night; nor for the arrow that flieth by day.

6 Nor for the pestilence that walketh in darkness; nor for the destruction that wasteth at noonday.

7 A thousand shall fall at thy side, and ten thousand at thy right hand; but it shall not come nigh thee.

8 Only with thine eyes shalt thou behold and see the reward of the wicked.

9 Because thou hast made the Lord, which is my refuge, even the most High, thy habitation;

10 There shall no evil befall thee; neither shall any plague come nigh thy dwelling.

11 For he shall give his angels charge over thee, to keep thee in all thy ways.

12 They shall bear thee up in their hands, lest thou dash thy foot against a stone.

13 Thou shalt tread upon the lion and adder: the young lion and the dragon shalt thou trample under feet.

14 Because he hath set his love upon me, therefore will I deliver him: I will set him on high, because he hath known my name.

15 He shall call upon me, and I will answer him: I will be with him in trouble; I will deliver him, and honour him.

16 With long life will I satisfy him, and shew him my salvation.

Glory be to the Father, and to the Son, and to the Holy Ghost.

As it was in the beginning, is now, and ever shall be, world without end. Amen.

## Selection 34

*Psalm XCII*

IT is a good thing to give thanks unto the Lord, and to sing praises unto thy name, O Most High:

2 To shew forth thy loving-kindness in the morning, and thy faithfulness every night.

3 Upon an instrument of ten strings, and upon the psaltery; upon the harp with a solemn sound.

4 For thou, Lord, hast made me glad

through thy work: I will triumph in the works of thy hands.

5 O Lord, how great are thy works! and thy thoughts are very deep.

6 A brutish man knoweth not; neither doth a fool understand this.

7 When the wicked spring as the grass, and when all the workers of iniquity do flourish; it is that they shall be destroyed for ever.

8 But thou, Lord, art Most High for evermore.

9 For, lo, thine enemies, O Lord, for, lo, thine enemies shall perish; all the workers of iniquity shall be scattered.

10 But my horn shalt thou exalt like the horn of an unicorn: I shall be anointed with fresh oil.

11 Mine eye also shall see my desire on mine enemies, and mine ears shall hear my desire of the wicked that rise up against me.

12 The righteous shall flourish like the palm tree: he shall grow like a cedar in Lebanon.

13 Those that be planted in the house of the Lord shall flourish in the courts of our God.

14 They shall still bring forth fruit in old age; they shall be fat and flourishing.

15 To shew that the Lord is upright: he is my rock, and there is no unrighteousness in him.

*Psalm XCIII*

16 The Lord reigneth, he is clothed with majesty; the Lord is clothed with strength, wherewith he hath girded himself: the world also is stablished, that it cannot be moved.

17 Thy throne is established of old: thou art from everlasting.

18 The floods have lifted up, O Lord, the floods have lifted up their voice; the floods lift up their waves.

19 The Lord on high is mightier than the noise of many waters, yea, than the mighty waves of the sea.

20 Thy testimonies are very sure: holiness becometh thine house, O Lord, for ever.

Glory be to the Father, and to the Son, and to the Holy Ghost.

As it was in the beginning, is now, and ever shall be, world without end. Amen.

## Selection 35

*Psalm XCIV*

O LORD God, to whom vengeance belongeth; O God, to whom vengeance belongeth, shew thyself.

2 Lift up thyself, thou judge of the earth: render a reward to the proud.

3 Lord, how long shall the wicked, how long shall the wicked triumph?

4 How long shall they utter and speak hard things? And all the workers of iniquity boast themselves?

5 They break in pieces thy people, O Lord, and afflict thine heritage.

6 They slay the widow and the stranger, and murder the fatherless.

7 Yet they say, The Lord shall not see, neither shall the God of Jacob regard it.

8 Understand, ye brutish among the people: and ye fools, when will ye be wise?

9 He that planted the ear, shall he not hear? he that formed the eye, shall he not see?

10 He that chastiseth the heathen, shall not he correct? he that teacheth man knowledge, shall not he know?

11 The Lord knoweth the thoughts of man, that they are vanity.

12 Blessed is the man whom thou chastenest, O Lord, and teachest him out of thy law.

13 That thou mayest give him rest

from the days of adversity, until the pit be digged for the wicked.

14 For the Lord will not cast off his people, neither will he forsake his inheritance.

15 But judgment shall return unto righteousness : and all the upright in heart shall follow it.

16 Who will rise up for me against the evil-doers ? Or who will stand up for me against the workers of iniquity ?

17 Unless the Lord had been my help, my soul had almost dwelt in silence.

18 When I said, My foot slippeth; thy mercy, O Lord, held me up.

19 In the multitude of my thoughts within me thy comforts delight my soul.

20 Shall the throne of iniquity have fellowship with thee, which frameth mischief by a law ?

21 They gather themselves together against the soul of the righteous, and condemn the innocent blood.

22 But the Lord is my defence ; and my God is the rock of my refuge.

23 And he shall bring upon them their own iniquity, and shall cut them off in their own wickedness ; yea, the Lord our God shall cut them off.

Glory be to the Father, and to the Son, and to the Holy Ghost.

As it was in the beginning, is now, and ever shall be, world without end. Amen.

## Selection 36

### Psalm XCV

O COME, let us sing unto the Lord: let us make a joyful noise to the rock of our salvation.

2 Let us come before his presence with thanksgiving : and make a joyful noise unto him with psalms.

3 For the Lord is a great God : and a great King above all gods.

4 In his hand are the deep places of the earth : the strength of the hills is his also.

5 The sea is his and he made it : and his hands formed the dry land.

6 O come, let us worship and bow down : let us kneel before the Lord our maker.

7 For he is our God : and we are the people of his pasture, and the sheep of his hand.

8 To day if ye will hear his voice, harden not your heart as in the provocation, and as in the day of temptation in the wilderness.

9 When your fathers tempted me, proved me, and saw my work.

10 Forty years long was I grieved with this generation, and said, It is a people that do err in their hearts, and they have not known my ways :

11 Unto whom I sware in my wrath that they should not enter into my rest.

### Psalm XCVI

12 O sing unto the Lord a new song : sing unto the Lord, all the earth.

13 Sing unto the Lord, bless his name: shew forth his salvation from day to day.

14 Declare his glory among the heathen, his wonders among all people.

15 For the Lord is great, and greatly to be praised : he is to be feared above all gods.

16 For all the gods of the nations are idols : but the Lord made the heavens.

17 Honour and majesty are before him : strength and beauty are in his sanctuary.

18 Give unto the Lord, O ye kindreds of the people, give unto the Lord glory and strength.

19 Give unto the Lord the glory due unto his name : bring an offering, and come into his courts.

20 O worship the Lord in the beauty

of holiness: fear before him, all the earth.

21 Say among the heathen that the Lord reigneth: the world also shall be established that it shall not be moved: he shall judge the people righteously.

22 Let the heavens rejoice, and let the earth be glad; let the sea roar, and the fulness thereof.

23 Let the field be joyful, and all that is therein: then shall all the trees of the wood rejoice

24 Before the Lord: for he cometh, for he cometh to judge the earth: he shall judge the world with righteousness, and the people with his truth.

Glory be to the Father, and to the Son, and to the Holy Ghost.

As it was in the beginning, is now, and ever shall be, world without end. Amen.

## Selection 37

*Psalm XCVII*

THE Lord reigneth; let the earth rejoice; let the multitude of isles be glad thereof.

2 Clouds and darkness are round about him: righteousness and judgment are the habitation of his throne.

3 A fire goeth before him, and burneth up his enemies round about.

4 His lightnings enlightened the world; the earth saw, and trembled.

5 The hills melted like wax at the presence of the Lord, at the presence of the Lord of the whole earth.

6 The heavens declare his righteousness, and all the people see his glory.

7 Confounded be all they that serve graven images, that boast themselves of idols; worship him, all ye gods.

8 Zion heard, and was glad; and the daughters of Judah rejoiced because of thy judgments, O Lord.

9 For thou, Lord, art high above all the earth: thou art exalted far above all gods.

10 Ye that love the Lord, hate evil: he preserveth the souls of his saints; he delivereth them out of the hand of the wicked.

11 Light is sown for the righteous, and gladness for the upright in heart.

12 Rejoice in the Lord, ye righteous; and give thanks at the remembrance of his holiness.

*Psalm XCVIII*

13 O sing unto the Lord a new song: for he hath done marvellous things: his right hand, and his holy arm, hath gotten him the victory.

14 The Lord hath made known his salvation: his righteousness hath he openly shewed in the sight of the heathen.

15 He hath remembered his mercy and his truth toward the house of Israel: all the ends of the earth have seen the salvation of our God.

16 Make a joyful noise unto the Lord, all the earth: make a loud noise, and rejoice, and sing praise.

17 Sing unto the Lord with the harp; with the harp, and the voice of a psalm.

18 With trumpets and sound of cornet make a joyful noise before the Lord, the King.

19 Let the sea roar, and the fulness thereof; the world, and they that dwell therein.

20 Let the floods clap their hands: let the hills be joyful together

21 Before the Lord; for he cometh to judge the earth: with righteousness shall he judge the world, and the people with equity.

*Psalm XCIX*

22 The Lord reigneth; let the people

tremble : he sitteth between the cherubim : let the earth be moved.

23 The Lord is great in Zion ; and he is high above all the people.

24 Let them praise thy great and terrible name ; for it is holy.

25 The king's strength also loveth judgment ; thou dost establish equity, thou executest judgment and righteousness in Jacob.

26 Exalt ye the Lord our God, and worship at his footstool ; for he is holy.

27 Moses and Aaron among his priests, and Samuel among them that call upon his name, they called upon the Lord, and he answered them.

28 He spake unto them in the cloudy pillar : they kept his testimonies, and the ordinance that he gave them.

29 Thou answeredst them, O Lord our God : thou wast a God that forgavest them, though thou tookest vengeance of their inventions.

30 Exalt the Lord our God, and worship at his holy hill ; for the Lord our God is holy.

Glory be to the Father, and to the Son, and to the Holy Ghost.

As it was in the beginning, is now, and ever shall be, world without end. Amen.

## Selection 38

*Psalm C*

MAKE a joyful noise unto the Lord, all ye lands.

2 Serve the Lord with gladness : come before his presence with singing.

3 Know ye that the Lord he is God : it is he that hath made us, and not we ourselves ; we are his people, and the sheep of his pasture.

4 Enter into his gates with thanksgiving, and into his courts with praise : be thankful unto him, and bless his name.

5 For the Lord is good ; his mercy is everlasting ; and his truth endureth to all generations.

*Psalm CII: 1-28*

6 Hear my prayer, O Lord, and let my cry come unto thee.

7 Hide not thy face from me in the day when I am in trouble ; incline thine ear unto me : in the day when I call, answer me speedily.

8 For my days are consumed like smoke, and my bones are burned as an hearth.

9 My heart is smitten, and withered like grass ; so that I forget to eat my bread.

10 By reason of the voice of my groaning my bones cleave to my skin.

11 I am like a pelican of the wilderness : I am like an owl of the desert.

12 I watch, and am as a sparrow alone upon the house top.

13 Mine enemies reproach me all the day ; and they that are mad against me are sworn against me.

14 For I have eaten ashes like bread, and mingled my drink with weeping,

15 Because of thine indignation and thy wrath : for thou hast lifted me up, and cast me down.

16 My days are like a shadow that declineth ; and I am withered like grass.

17 But thou, O Lord, shalt endure for ever ; and thy remembrance unto all generations.

18 Thou shalt arise, and have mercy upon Zion : for the time to favour her, yea, the set time, is come.

19 For thy servants take pleasure in her stones, and favour the dust thereof.

20 So the heathen shall fear the name of the Lord, and all the kings of the earth thy glory.

21 When the Lord shall build up Zion, he shall appear in his glory.

22 He will regard the prayer of the destitute, and not despise their prayer.

23 This shall be written for the generation to come : and the people which shall be created shall praise the Lord.

24 For he hath looked down from the height of his sanctuary ; from heaven did the Lord behold the earth ;

25 To hear the groaning of the prisoner ; to loose those that are appointed to death ;

26 To declare the name of the Lord in Zion, and his praise in Jerusalem ;

27 When the people are gathered together, and the kingdoms, to serve the Lord.

28 He weakened my strength in the way ; he shortened my days.

29 I said, O my God, take me not away in the midst of my days : thy years are throughout all generations.

30 Of old hast thou laid the foundation of the earth : and the heavens are the work of thy hands.

31 They shall perish, but thou shalt endure : yea, all of them shall wax old like a garment ; as a vesture shalt thou change them, and they shall be changed :

32 But thou art the same, and thy years shall have no end.

33 The children of thy servants shall continue, and their seed shall be established before thee.

Glory be to the Father, and to the Son, and to the Holy Ghost.

As it was in the beginning, is now, and ever shall be, world without end. Amen.

## Selection 39

*Psalm CIII*

BLESS the Lord, O my soul : and all that is within me, bless his holy name.

2 Bless the Lord, O my soul, and forget not his benefits :

3 Who forgiveth all thine iniquities; who healeth all thy diseases ;

4 Who redeemeth thy life from destruction ; who crowneth thee with lovingkindness and tender mercies ;

5 Who satisfieth thy mouth with good things ; so that thy youth is renewed like the eagle's.

6 The Lord executeth righteousness and judgment for all that are oppressed.

7 He made known his ways unto Moses, his acts unto the children of Israel.

8 The Lord is merciful and gracious, slow to anger, and plenteous in mercy.

9 He will not always chide : neither will he keep his anger for ever.

10 He hath not dealt with us after our sins ; nor rewarded us according to our iniquities.

11 For as the heaven is high above the earth, so great is his mercy toward them that fear him.

12 As far as the east is from the west, so far hath he removed our transgressions from us.

13 Like as a father pitieth his children, so that Lord pitieth them that fear him.

14 For he knoweth our frame ; he remembereth that we are dust.

15 As for man, his days are as grass : as a flower of the field, so he flourisheth.

16 For the wind passeth over it, and it is gone ; and the place thereof shall know it no more.

17 But the mercy of the Lord is from everlasting to everlasting upon them that fear him, and his righteousness unto children's children ;

18 To such as keep his covenant, and to those that remember his commandments to do them.

19 The Lord hath prepared his throne

in the heavens; and his kingdom ruleth over all.

20 Bless the Lord, ye his angels, that excel in strength, that do his commandments, hearkening unto the voice of his word.

21 Bless ye the Lord, all ye his hosts; ye ministers of his, that do his pleasure.

22 Bless the Lord, all his works in all places of his dominion: bless the Lord, O my soul.

Glory be to the Father, and to the Son, and to the Holy Ghost.

As it was in the beginning, is now, and ever shall be, world without end. Amen.

## Selection 40

*Psalm CIV*

BLESS the Lord, O my soul. O Lord my God, thou art very great; thou art clothed with honour and majesty:

2 Who coverest thyself with light as with a garment: who stretchest out the heavens like a curtain:

3 Who layeth the beams of his chambers in the waters: who maketh the clouds his chariot: who walketh upon the wings of the wind:

4 Who maketh his angels spirits; his ministers a flaming fire:

5 Who laid the foundations of the earth, that it should not be removed for ever.

6 Thou coveredst it with the deep as with a garment: the waters stood above the mountains.

7 At thy rebuke they fled; at the voice of thy thunder they hasted away.

8 They go up by the mountains; they go down by the valleys unto the place which thou hast founded for them.

9 Thou hast set a bound that they may not pass over; that they turn not again to cover the earth.

10 He sendeth the springs into the valleys, which run among the hills.

11 They give drink to every beast of the field; the wild asses quench their thirst.

12 By them shall the fowls of the heaven have their habitation, which sing among the branches.

13 He watereth the hills from his chambers: the earth is satisfied with the fruit of thy works.

14 He causeth the grass to grow for the cattle, and herb for the service of man: that he may bring forth food out of the earth;

15 And wine that maketh glad the heart of man, and oil to make his face to shine, and bread which strengtheneth man's heart.

16 The trees of the Lord are full of sap; the cedars of Lebanon, which he hath planted;

17 Where the birds make their nests: as for the stork, the fir trees are her house.

18 The high hills are a refuge for the wild goats; and the rocks for the conies.

19 He appointed the moon for seasons: the sun knoweth his going down.

20 Thou makest darkness, and it is night: wherein all the beasts of the forest do creep forth.

21 The young lions roar after their prey, and seek their meat from God.

22 The sun ariseth, they gather themselves together, and lay them down in their dens.

23 Man goeth forth unto his work and to his labour until the evening.

24 O Lord, how manifold are thy works! in wisdom hast thou made them all: the earth is full of thy riches.

25 So is this great and wide sea, wherein are things creeping innumerable, both small and great beasts.

26 There go the ships: there is that

leviathan, whom thou hast made to play therein.

27 These all wait upon thee, that thou mayst give them their meat in due season.

28 That thou givest them, they gather: thou openest thine hand, they are filled with good.

29 Thou hidest thy face, they are troubled: thou takest away their breath, they die, and return to their dust.

30 Thou sendest forth thy spirit, they are created: and thou renewest the face of the earth.

31 The glory of the Lord shall endure for ever: the Lord shall rejoice in his works.

32 He looketh on the earth, and it trembleth: he toucheth the hills, and they smoke.

33 I will sing unto the Lord as long as I live: I will sing praise to my God while I have my being.

34 My meditation of him shall be sweet: I will be glad in the Lord.

35 Let the sinners be consumed out of the earth, and let the wicked be no more. Bless thou the Lord, O my soul. Praise ye the Lord.

Glory be to the Father, and to the Son, and to the Holy Ghost.

As it was in the beginning, is now, and ever shall be, world without end. Amen.

## Selection 41

*Psalm CVII: 1-22*

O GIVE thanks unto the Lord, for he is good: for his mercy endureth for ever.

2 Let the redeemed of the Lord say so, whom he hath redeemed from the hand of the enemy;

3 And gathered them out of the lands, from the east, and from the west, from the north, and from the south.

4 They wandered in the wilderness in a solitary way; they found no city to dwell in.

5 Hungry and thirsty, their soul fainted in them.

6 Then they cried unto the Lord in their trouble, and he delivered them out of their distresses.

7 And he led them forth by the right way, that they might go to a city of habitation.

8 Oh that men would praise the Lord for his goodness, and for his wonderful works to the children of men!

9 For he satisfieth the longing soul, and filleth the hungry soul with goodness.

10 Such as sit in darkness and in the shadow of death, being bound in affliction and iron;

11 Because they rebelled against the words of God, and contemned the counsel of the Most High:

12 Therefore he brought down their heart with labour; they fell down, and there was none to help.

13 Then they cried unto the Lord in their trouble, and he saved them out of their distresses.

14 He brought them out of darkness and the shadow of death, and brake their bands in sunder.

15 Oh that men would praise the Lord for his goodness, and for his wonderful works to the children of men!

16 For he hath broken the gates of brass, and cut the bars of iron in sunder.

17 Fools because of their transgression, and because of their iniquities, are afflicted.

18 Their soul abhorreth all manner of meat; and they draw near unto the gates of death.

19 Then they cry unto the Lord in

their trouble, and he saveth them out of their distresses.

20 He sent his word, and healed them, and delivered them from their destructions.

21 Oh that men would praise the Lord for his goodness, and for his wonderful works to the children of men!

22 And let them sacrifice the sacrifices of thanksgiving, and declare his works with rejoicing.

Glory be to the Father, and to the Son, and to the Holy Ghost.

As it was in the beginning, is now, and ever shall be, world without end. Amen.

## Selection 42

*Psalm CVII: 23-43*

THEY that go down to the sea in ships, that do business in great waters;

2 These see the works of the Lord, and his wonders in the deep.

3 For he commandeth, and raiseth the stormy wind, which lifteth up the waves thereof.

4 They mount up to the heaven, they go down again to the depths: their soul is melted because of trouble.

5 They reel to and fro, and stagger like a drunken man, and are at their wit's end.

6 Then they cry unto the Lord in their trouble, and he bringeth them out of their distresses.

7 He maketh the storm a calm, so that the waves thereof are still.

8 Then are they glad because they be quiet; so he bringeth them unto their desired haven.

9 Oh that men would praise the Lord for his goodness, and for his wonderful works to the children of men!

10 Let them exalt him also in the congregation of the people, and praise him in the assembly of the elders.

11 He turneth rivers into a wilderness, and the water-springs into dry ground;

12 A fruitful land into barrenness, for the wickedness of them that dwell therein.

13 He turneth the wilderness into a standing water, and dry ground into water-springs.

14 And there he maketh the hungry to dwell, that they may prepare a city for habitation;

15 And sow the fields, and plant vineyards, which may yield fruits of increase.

16 He blesseth them also, so that they are multiplied greatly; and suffereth not their cattle to decrease.

17 Again, they are minished and brought low through oppression, affliction, and sorrow.

18 He poureth contempt upon princes, and causeth them to wander in the wilderness, where there is no way.

19 Yet setteth he the poor on high from affliction, and maketh him families like a flock.

20 The righteous shall see it, and rejoice: and all iniquity shall stop her mouth.

21 Whoso is wise, and will observe these things, even they shall understand the lovingkindness of the Lord.

Glory be to the Father, and to the Son, and to the Holy Ghost.

As it was in the beginning, is now, and ever shall be, world without end. Amen.

## Selection 43

*Psalm CX*

THE Lord said unto my Lord, Sit thou at my right hand, until I make thine enemies thy footstool.

2 The Lord shall send the rod of thy

strength out of Zion: rule thou in the midst of thine enemies.

3 Thy people shall be willing in the day of thy power, in the beauties of holiness from the womb of the morning: thou hast the dew of thy youth.

4 The Lord hath sworn, and will not repent, Thou art a priest for ever after the order of Melchizedek.

5 The Lord at thy right hand shall strike through kings in the day of his wrath.

6 He shall judge among the heathen, he shall fill the places with the dead bodies; he shall wound the heads over many countries.

7 He shall drink of the brook in the way: therefore shall he lift up the head.

*Psalm CXI*

8 Praise ye the Lord. I will praise the Lord with my whole heart, in the assembly of the upright, and in the congregation.

9 The works of the Lord are great, sought out of all them that have pleasure therein.

10 His work is honourable and glorious: and his righteousness endureth for ever.

11 He hath made his wonderful works to be remembered: the Lord is gracious and full of compassion.

12 He hath given meat unto them that fear him: he will ever be mindful of his covenant.

13 He hath shewed his people the power of his works, that he may give them the heritage of the heathen.

14 The works of his hands are verity and judgment; all his commandments are sure.

15 They stand fast for ever and ever, and are done in truth and uprightness.

16 He sent redemption unto his people: he hath commanded his covenant for ever: holy and reverend is his name.

17 The fear of the Lord is the beginning of wisdom: a good understanding have all they that do his commandments: his praise endureth for ever.

*Psalm CXII*

18 Praise ye the Lord. Blessed is the man that feareth the Lord, that delighteth greatly in his commandments.

19 His seed shall be mighty upon earth: the generation of the upright shall be blessed.

20 Wealth and riches shall be in his house: and his righteousness endureth for ever.

21 Unto the upright there ariseth light in the darkness: he is gracious, and full of compassion, and righteous.

22 A good man sheweth favour, and lendeth: he will guide his affairs with discretion.

23 Surely he shall not be moved for ever: the righteous shall be in everlasting remembrance.

24 He shall not be afraid of evil tidings: his heart is fixed, trusting in the Lord.

25 His heart is established, he shall not be afraid, until he see his desire upon his enemies.

26 He hath dispersed, he hath given to the poor; his righteousness endureth for ever; his horn shall be exalted with honour.

27 The wicked shall see it, and be grieved; he shall gnash with his teeth, and melt away: the desire of the wicked shall perish.

Glory be to the Father, and to the Son, and to the Holy Ghost.

As it was in the beginning, is now, and ever shall be, world without end. Amen.

## SELECTIONS FROM THE PSALMS

### Selection 44

*Psalm CXIII*

PRAISE ye the Lord. Praise, O ye servants of the Lord, praise the name of the Lord.

2 Blessed be the name of the Lord from this time forth and for evermore.

3 From the rising of the sun unto the going down of the same the Lord's name is to be praised.

4 The Lord is high above all nations, and his glory above the heavens.

5 Who is like unto the Lord our God, who dwelleth on high.

6 Who humbleth himself to behold the things that are in heaven, and in the earth!

7 He raiseth up the poor out of the dust, and lifteth the needy out of the dunghill.

8 That he may set him with princes, even with the princes of his people.

9 He maketh the barren woman to keep house, and to be a joyful mother of children. Praise ye the Lord.

*Psalm CXV*

10 Not unto us, O Lord, not unto us, but unto thy name give glory, for thy mercy, and for thy truth's sake.

11 Wherefore should the heathen say, Where is now their God?

12 But our God is in the heavens; he hath done whatsoever he hath pleased.

13 Their idols are silver and gold, the work of men's hands.

14 They have mouths, but they speak not: eyes have they, but they see not.

15 They have ears, but they hear not: noses have they, but they smell not.

16 They have hands, but they handle not: feet have they, but they walk not: neither speak they through their throat.

17 They that make them are like unto them; so is every one that trusteth in them.

18 O Israel, trust thou in the Lord: he is their help and their shield.

19 O house of Aaron, trust in the Lord: he is their help and their shield.

20 Ye that fear the Lord, trust in the Lord: he is their help and their shield.

21 The Lord hath been mindful of us: he will bless us; he will bless the house of Israel; he will bless the house of Aaron.

22 He will bless them that fear the Lord, both small and great.

23 The Lord shall increase you more and more, you and your children.

24 Ye are blessed of the Lord which made heaven and earth.

25 The heaven, even the heavens, are the Lord's: but the earth hath he given to the children of men.

26 The dead praise not the Lord, neither any that go down into silence.

27 But we will bless the Lord from this time forth and for evermore. Praise the Lord.

Glory be to the Father, and to the Son, and to the Holy Ghost.

As it was in the beginning, is now, and ever shall be, world without end. Amen.

### Selection 45

*Psalm CXVI*

I LOVE the Lord, because he hath heard my voice and my supplications.

2 Because he hath inclined his ear unto me, therefore will I call upon him as long as I live.

3 The sorrows of death compassed me, and the pains of hell gat hold upon me: I found trouble and sorrow.

4 Then called I upon the name of the Lord; O Lord, I beseech thee, deliver my soul.

5 Gracious is the Lord, and righteous; yea, our God is merciful.
6 The Lord preserveth the simple: I was brought low, and he helped me.
7 Return unto thy rest, O my soul; for the Lord hath dealt bountifully with thee.
8 For thou hast delivered my soul from death, mine eyes from tears, and my feet from falling.
9 I will walk before the Lord in the land of the living.
10 I believed, therefore have I spoken: I was greatly afflicted.
11 I said in my haste, All men are liars.
12 What shall I render unto the Lord for all his benefits toward me?
13 I will take the cup of salvation, and call upon the name of the Lord.
14 I will pay my vows unto the Lord, now in the presence of all his people.
15 Precious in the sight of the Lord is the death of his saints.
16 O Lord, truly I am thy servant; I am thy servant, and the son of thy handmaid: thou hast loosed my bonds.
17 I will offer to thee the sacrifice of thanksgiving, and will call upon the name of the Lord.
18 I will pay my vows unto the Lord now in the presence of all his people.
19 In the courts of the Lord's house, in the midst of thee, O Jerusalem. Praise ye the Lord.

*Psalm CXVII*

20 O praise the Lord, all ye nations; praise him, all ye people.
21 For his merciful kindness is great toward us: and the truth of the Lord endureth for ever. Praise ye the Lord.

Glory be to the Father, and to the Son, and to the Holy Ghost.

As it was in the beginning, is now, and ever shall be, world without end. Amen.

## Selection 46

*Psalm CXVIII*

O GIVE thanks unto the Lord; for he is good: because his mercy endureth for ever.
2 Let Israel now say, that his mercy endureth for ever.
3 Let the house of Aaron now say, that his mercy endureth for ever.
4 Let them now that fear the Lord say, that his mercy endureth for ever.
5 I called upon the Lord in distress: the Lord answered me, and set me in a large place.
6 The Lord is on my side; I will not fear: what can man do unto me?
7 The Lord taketh my part with them that help me: therefore shall I see my desire upon them that hate me.
8 It is better to trust in the Lord than to put confidence in man.
9 It is better to trust in the Lord than to put confidence in princes.
10 All nations compassed me about: but in the name of the Lord will I destroy them.
11 They compassed me about; yea, they compassed me about: but in the name of the Lord I will destroy them.
12 They compassed me about like bees; they are quenched as the fire of thorns: for in the name of the Lord I will destroy them.
13 Thou hast thrust sore at me that I might fall: but the Lord helped me.
14 The Lord is my strength and song, and is become my salvation.
15 The voice of rejoicing and salvation is in the tabernacles of the righteous: the right hand of the Lord doeth valiantly.
16 The right hand of the Lord is exalted: the right hand of the Lord doeth valiantly.

17 I shall not die, but live, and declare the works of the Lord.

18 The Lord hath chastened me sore: but he hath not given me over unto death.

19 Open to me the gates of righteousness: I will go into them, and I will praise the Lord:

20 This gate of the Lord, into which the righteous shall enter.

21 I will praise thee: for thou hast heard me, and art become my salvation.

22 The stone which the builders refused is become the head stone of the corner.

23 This is the Lord's doing; it is marvellous in our eyes.

24 This is the day which the Lord hath made; we will rejoice and be glad in it.

25 Save now, I beseech thee, O Lord: O Lord, I beseech thee, send now prosperity.

26 Blessed be he that cometh in the name of the Lord: we have blessed you out of the house of the Lord.

27 God is the Lord, which hath shewed us light: bind the sacrifice with cords, even unto the horns of the altar.

28 Thou art my God, and I will praise thee: thou art my God, I will exalt thee.

29 O give thanks unto the Lord; for he is good: for his mercy endureth for ever.

Glory be to the Father, and to the Son, and to the Holy Ghost.

As it was in the beginning, is now, and ever shall be, world without end. Amen.

## Selection 47

*Psalm CXIX: 1-24*

BLESSED are the undefiled in the way, who walk in the law of the Lord.

2 Blessed are they that keep his testimonies, and that seek him with the whole heart.

3 They also do no iniquity: they walk in his ways.

4 Thou hast commanded us to keep thy precepts diligently.

5 O that my ways were directed to keep thy statutes!

6 Then shall I not be ashamed, when I have respect unto all thy commandments.

7 I will praise thee with uprightness of heart, when I shall have learned thy righteous judgments.

8 I will keep thy statutes: O forsake me not utterly.

9 Wherewithal shall a young man cleanse his way? by taking heed thereto according to thy word.

10 With my whole heart have I sought thee: O let me not wander from thy commandments.

11 Thy word have I hid in mine heart, that I might not sin against thee.

12 Blessed art thou, O Lord: teach me thy statutes.

13 With my lips have I declared all the judgments of thy mouth.

14 I have rejoiced in the way of thy testimonies, as much as in all riches.

15 I will meditate in thy precepts, and have respect unto thy ways.

16 I will delight myself in thy statutes: I will not forget thy word.

17 Deal bountifully with thy servant, that I may live, and keep thy word.

18 Open thou mine eyes, that I may behold wondrous things out of thy law.

19 I am a stranger in the earth: hide not thy commandments from me.

20 My soul breaketh for the longing that it hath unto thy judgments at all times.

21 Thou hast rebuked the proud that are cursed, which do err from thy commandments.

22 Remove from me reproach and contempt ; for I have kept thy testimonies.
23 Princes also did sit and speak against me : but thy servant did meditate in thy statutes.
24 Thy testimonies also are my delight and my counsellors.
Glory be to the Father, and to the Son, and to the Holy Ghost.
As it was in the beginning, is now, and ever shall be, world without end. Amen.

## Selection 48

*Psalm CXIX: 89-112*

FOR ever, O Lord, thy word is settled in heaven.
2 Thy faithfulness is unto all generations : thou hast established the earth, and it abideth.
3 They continue this day according to thine ordinances : for all are thy servants.
4 Unless thy law had been my delights, I should then have perished in mine affliction.
5 I will never forget thy precepts : for with them thou hast quickened me.
6 I am thine, save me ; for I have sought thy precepts.
7 The wicked have waited for me to destroy me : but I will consider thy testimonies.
8 I have seen an end of all perfection : but thy commandment is exceeding broad.
9 O how love I thy law! it is my meditation all the day.
10 Thou through thy commandments hast made me wiser than mine enemies : for they are ever with me.
11 I have more understanding than all my teachers : for thy testimonies are my meditation.

12 I understand more than the ancients, because I keep thy precepts.
13 I have refrained my feet from every evil way, that I might keep thy word.
14 I have not departed from thy judgments : for thou hast taught me.
15 How sweet are thy words unto my taste ! yea, sweeter than honey to my mouth.
16 Through thy precepts I get understanding : therefore I hate every false way.
17 Thy word is a lamp unto my feet, and a light unto my path.
18 I have sworn, and I will perform it, that I will keep thy righteous judgments.
19 I am afflicted very much : quicken me, O Lord, according unto thy word.
20 Accept, I beseech thee, the freewill-offerings of my mouth, O Lord, and teach me thy judgments.
21 My soul is continually in my hand : yet do I not forget thy law.
22 The wicked have laid a snare for me : yet I erred not from thy precepts.
23 Thy testimonies have I taken as an heritage for ever : for they are the rejoicing of my heart.
24 I have inclined mine heart to perform thy statutes always, even unto the end.
Glory be to the Father, and to the Son, and to the Holy Ghost.
As it was in the beginning, is now, and ever shall be, world without end. Amen.

## Selection 49

*Psalm CXXI*

I WILL lift up mine eyes unto the hills, from whence cometh my help.
2 My help cometh from the Lord, which made heaven and earth.
3 He will not suffer thy foot to be

moved: he that keepeth thee will not slumber.

4 Behold, he that keepeth Israel shall neither slumber nor sleep.

5 The Lord is thy keeper: the Lord is thy shade upon thy right hand.

6 The sun shall not smite thee by day, nor the moon by night.

7 The Lord shall preserve thee from all evil: he shall preserve thy soul.

8 The Lord shall preserve thy going out and thy coming in from this time forth, and even for evermore.

*Psalm CXXII*

9 I was glad when they said unto me, Let us go into the house of the Lord.

10 Our feet shall stand within thy gates, O Jerusalem.

11 Jerusalem is builded as a city that is compact together:

12 Whither the tribes go up, the tribes of the Lord, unto the testimony of Israel, to give thanks unto the name of the Lord.

13 For there are set thrones of judgment, the thrones of the house of David.

14 Pray for the peace of Jerusalem: they shall prosper that love thee.

15 Peace be within thy walls, and prosperity within thy palaces.

16 For my brethren and companions' sakes, I will now say, Peace be within thee.

17 Because of the house of the Lord our God I will seek thy good.

*Psalm CXXIV*

18 If it had not been the Lord who was on our side, now may Israel say;

19 If it had not been the Lord who was on our side, when men rose up against us;

20 Then they had swallowed us up quick, when their wrath was kindled against us:

21 Then the waters had overwhelmed us, the stream had gone over our soul:

22 Then the proud waters had gone over our soul.

23 Blessed be the Lord, who hath not given us as a prey to their teeth.

24 Our soul is escaped as a bird out of the snare of the fowlers: the snare is broken, and we are escaped.

25 Our help is in the name of the Lord, who made heaven and earth.

Glory be to the Father, and to the Son, and to the Holy Ghost.

As it was in the beginning, is now, and ever shall be, world without end. Amen.

## Selection 50

*Psalm CXXV*

THEY that trust in the Lord shall be as mount Zion, which cannot be removed, but abideth for ever.

2 As the mountains are round about Jerusalem, so the Lord is round about his people from henceforth even for ever.

3 For the rod of the wicked shall not rest upon the lot of the righteous; lest the righteous put forth their hands unto iniquity.

4 Do good, O Lord, unto those that be good, and to them that are upright in their hearts.

5 As for such as turn aside unto their crooked ways, the Lord shall lead them forth with the workers of iniquity: but peace shall be upon Israel.

*Psalm CXXVI*

6 When the Lord turned again the captivity of Zion, we were like them that dream.

7 Then was our mouth filled with laughter, and our tongue with singing: then said they among the heathen, The Lord hath done great things for them.

8 The Lord hath done great things for us; whereof we are glad.
9 Turn again our captivity, O Lord, as the streams in the south.
10 They that sow in tears shall reap in joy.
11 He that goeth forth and weepeth, bearing precious seed, shall doubtless come again with rejoicing, bringing his sheaves with him.

*Psalm CXXVII*

12 Except the Lord build the house, they labour in vain that build it : except the Lord keep the city, the watchman waketh but in vain.
13 It is vain for you to rise up early, to sit up late, to eat the bread of sorrows : for so he giveth his beloved sleep.
14 Lo, children are an heritage of the Lord : and the fruit of the womb is his reward.
15 As arrows are in the hand of a mighty man; so are children of the youth.
16 Happy is the man that hath his quiver full of them : they shall not be ashamed, but they shall speak with the enemies in the gate.

*Psalm CXXX*

17 Out of the depths have I cried unto thee, O Lord.
18 Lord, hear my voice : let thine ears be attentive to the voice of my supplications.
19 If thou, Lord, shouldst mark iniquities, O Lord, who shall stand?
20 But there is forgiveness with thee, that thou mayest be feared.
21 I wait for the Lord, my soul doth wait, and in his word do I hope.
22 My soul waiteth for the Lord more than they that watch for the morning : I say, more than they that watch for the morning.

23 Let Israel hope in the Lord : for with the Lord there is mercy, and with him is plenteous redemption.
24 And he shall redeem Israel from all his iniquities.
Glory be to the Father, and to the Son, and to the Holy Ghost.
As it was in the beginning, is now, and ever shall be, world without end. Amen.

## Selection 51

*Psalm CXXXII*

LORD, remember David, and all his afflictions :
2 How he sware unto the Lord, and vowed unto the mighty God of Jacob;
3 Surely I will not come into the tabernacle of my house, nor go up into my bed;
4 I will not give sleep to mine eyes, or slumber to mine eyelids,
5 Until I find out a place for the Lord, an habitation for the mighty God of Jacob.
6 Lo, we heard of it at Ephratah : we found it in the fields of the wood.
7 We will go into his tabernacles : we will worship at his footstool.
8 Arise, O Lord, into thy rest; thou, and the ark of thy strength.
9 Let thy priests be clothed with righteousness; and let thy saints shout for joy.
10 For thy servant David's sake turn not away the face of thine anointed.
11 The Lord hath sworn in truth unto David; he will not turn from it; Of the fruit of thy body will I set upon thy throne.
12 If thy children will keep my covenant and my testimony that I shall teach them, their children shall also sit upon thy throne for evermore.
13 For the Lord hath chosen Zion; he hath desired it for his habitation.

14 This is my rest for ever: here will I dwell; for I have desired it.

15 I will abundantly bless her provision: I will satisfy her poor with bread.

16 I will also clothe her priests with salvation: and her saints shall shout aloud for joy.

17 There will I make the horn of David to bud; I have ordained a lamp for mine anointed.

18 His enemies will I clothe with shame: but upon himself shall his crown flourish.

*Psalm CXXXIII*

19 Behold, how good and how pleasant it is for brethren to dwell together in unity!

20 It is like the precious ointment upon the head, that ran down upon the beard, even Aaron's beard: that went down to the skirts of his garments;

21 As the dew of Hermon, and as the dew that descended upon the mountains of Zion: for there the Lord commanded the blessing, even life for evermore.

*Psalm CXXXIV*

22 Behold, bless ye the Lord, all ye servants of the Lord, which by night stand in the house of the Lord.

23 Lift up your hands in the sanctuary and bless the Lord.

24 The Lord that made heaven and earth bless thee out of Zion.

Glory be to the Father, and to the Son, and to the Holy Ghost.

As it was in the beginning, is now, and ever shall be, world without end. Amen.

## Selection 52

*Psalm CXXXIX*

O LORD, thou hast searched me, and known me.

2 Thou knowest my downsitting and mine uprising, thou understandest my thought afar off.

3 Thou compassest my path and my lying down, and art acquainted with all my ways.

4 For there is not a word in my tongue, but lo, O Lord, thou knowest it altogether.

5 Thou hast beset me behind and before, and laid thine hand upon me.

6 Such knowledge is too wonderful for me; it is high, I cannot attain unto it.

7 Whither shall I go from thy Spirit? or whither shall I flee from thy presence?

8 If I ascend up into heaven, thou art there: if I make my bed in hell, behold, thou art there.

9 If I take the wings of the morning, and dwell in the uttermost parts of the sea;

10 Even there shall thy hand lead me, and thy right hand shall hold me.

11 If I say, Surely the darkness shall cover me; even the night shall be light about me.

12 Yea, the darkness hideth not from thee; but the night shineth as the day: the darkness and the light are both alike to thee.

13 For thou hast possessed my reins: thou hast covered me in my mother's womb.

14 I will praise thee; for I am fearfully and wonderfully made: marvellous are thy works; and that my soul knoweth right well.

15 My substance was not hid from thee, when I was made in secret, and curiously wrought in the lowest parts of the earth.

16 Thine eyes did see my substance, yet being unperfect; and in thy book all my members were written, which in con-

tinuance were fashioned, when as yet there was none of them.

17 How precious also are thy thoughts unto me, O God! how great is the sum of them!

18 If I should count them, they are more in number than the sand: when I awake, I am still with thee.

19 Surely thou wilt slay the wicked, O God: depart from me therefore, ye bloody men.

20 For they speak against thee wickedly, and thine enemies take thy name in vain.

21 Do not I hate them, O Lord, that hate thee? and am not I grieved with those that rise up against thee?

22 I hate them with perfect hatred: I count them mine enemies.

23 Search me, O God, and know my heart: try me, and know my thoughts:

24 And see if there be any wicked way in me, and lead me in the way everlasting.

Glory be to the Father, and to the Son, and to the Holy Ghost.

As it was in the beginning, is now, and ever shall be, world without end. Amen.

## Selection 53

*Psalm CXLII*

I CRIED unto the Lord with my voice: with my voice unto the Lord did I make my supplication.

2 I poured out my complaint before him; I shewed before him my trouble.

3 When my spirit was overwhelmed within me, then thou knewest my path. In the way wherein I walked have they privily laid a snare for me.

4 I looked on my right hand, and beheld, but there was no man that would know me: refuge failed me; no man cared for my soul.

5 I cried unto thee, O Lord: I said, Thou art my refuge and my portion in the land of the living.

6 Attend unto my cry; for I am brought very low: deliver me from my persecutors; for they are stronger than I.

7 Bring my soul out of prison, that I may praise thy name: the righteous shall compass me about; for thou shalt deal bountifully with me.

*Psalm CXLIV*

8 Blessed be the Lord my strength, which teacheth my hands to war, and my fingers to fight;

9 My goodness, and my fortress; my high tower, and my deliverer; my shield, and he in whom I trust; who subdueth my people under me.

10 Lord, what is man, that thou takest knowledge of him! or the son of man, that thou makest account of him!

11 Man is like to vanity: his days are as a shadow that passeth away.

12 Bow thy heavens, O Lord, and come down: touch the mountains, and they shall smoke.

13 Cast forth lightning, and scatter them: shoot out thine arrows, and destroy them.

14 Send thine hand from above; rid me, and deliver me out of great waters, from the hand of strange children;

15 Whose mouth speaketh vanity, and their right hand is a right hand of falsehood.

16 I will sing a new song unto thee, O God: upon a psaltery and an instrument of ten strings will I sing praises unto thee.

17 It is he that giveth salvation unto kings: who delivereth David his servant from the hurtful sword.

18 Rid me, and deliver me from the hand of strange children, whose mouth

speaketh vanity, and their right hand is a right hand of falsehood:

19 That our sons may be as plants grown up in their youth; that our daughters may be as corner stones, polished after the similitude of a palace:

20 That our garners may be full, affording all manner of store; that our sheep may bring forth thousands and ten thousands in our streets:

21 That our oxen may be strong to labour; that there be no breaking in, nor going out; that there be no complaining in our streets.

22 Happy is that people, that is in such a case: yea, happy is that people, whose God is the Lord.

Glory be to the Father, and to the Son, and to the Holy Ghost.

As it was in the beginning, is now, and ever shall be, world without end. Amen.

## Selection 54

*Psalm CXLV*

I WILL extol thee, my God, O king: and I will bless thy name for ever and ever.

2 Every day will I bless thee; and I will praise thy name for ever and ever.

3 Great is the Lord, and greatly to be praised; and his greatness is unsearchable.

4 One generation shall praise thy works to another, and shall declare thy mighty acts.

5 I will speak of the glorious honour of thy majesty, and of thy wondrous works.

6 And men shall speak of the might of thy terrible acts: and I will declare thy greatness.

7 They shall abundantly utter the memory of thy great goodness, and shall sing of thy righteousness.

8 The Lord is gracious, and full of compassion; slow to anger, and of great mercy.

9 The Lord is good to all: and his tender mercies are over all his works.

10 All thy works shall praise thee, O Lord; and thy saints shall bless thee.

11 They shall speak of the glory of thy kingdom, and talk of thy power;

12 To make known to the sons of men his mighty acts, and the glorious majesty of his kingdom.

13 Thy kingdom is an everlasting kingdom, and thy dominion endureth throughout all generations.

14 The Lord upholdeth all that fall, and raiseth up all those that be bowed down.

15 The eyes of all wait upon thee: and thou givest them their meat in due season.

16 Thou openest thine hand, and satisfiest the desire of every living thing.

17 The Lord is righteous in all his ways, and holy in all his works.

18 The Lord is nigh unto all them that call upon him, to all that call upon him in truth.

19 He will fulfil the desire of them that fear him: he also will hear their cry, and will save them.

20 The Lord preserveth all them that love him: but all the wicked will he destroy.

21 My mouth shall speak the praise of the Lord: and let all flesh bless his holy name for ever and ever.

Glory be to the Father, and to the Son, and to the Holy Ghost.

As it was in the beginning, is now, and ever shall be, world without end. Amen.

## Selection 55

### Psalm CXLVI

PRAISE ye the Lord. Praise the Lord, O my soul.

2 While I live will I praise the Lord: I will sing praises unto my God while I have any being.

3 Put not your trust in princes, nor in the son of man, in whom there is no help.

4 His breath goeth forth, he returneth to his earth; in that very day his thoughts perish.

5 Happy is he that hath the God of Jacob for his help, whose hope is in the Lord his God:

6 Which made heaven and earth, the sea, and all that therein is: which keepeth truth for ever:

7 Which executeth judgment for the oppressed: which giveth food to the hungry. The Lord looseth the prisoners:

8 The Lord openeth the eyes of the blind: the Lord raiseth them that are bowed down: the Lord loveth the righteous:

9 The Lord preserveth the strangers; he relieveth the fatherless and widow: but the way of the wicked he turneth upside down.

10 The Lord shall reign for ever, even thy God, O Zion, unto all generations. Praise ye the Lord.

### Psalm CXLVII

11 Praise ye the Lord: for it is good to sing praises unto our God; for it is pleasant; and praise is comely.

12 The Lord doth build up Jerusalem: he gathereth together the outcasts of Israel.

13 He healeth the broken in heart, and bindeth up their wounds.

14 He telleth the number of the stars; he calleth them all by their names.

15 Great is our Lord, and of great power: his understanding is infinite.

16 The Lord lifteth up the meek: he casteth the wicked down to the ground.

17 Sing unto the Lord with thanksgiving; sing praise upon the harp unto our God:

18 Who covereth the heaven with clouds, who prepareth rain for the earth, who maketh grass to grow upon the mountains.

19 He giveth to the beast his food, and to the young ravens which cry.

20 He delighteth not in the strength of the horse: he taketh not pleasure in the legs of a man.

21 The Lord taketh pleasure in them that fear him, in those that hope in his mercy.

22 Praise the Lord, O Jerusalem; praise thy God, O Zion.

23 For he hath strengthened the bars of thy gates; he hath blessed thy children within thee.

24 He maketh peace in thy borders, and filleth thee with the finest of the wheat.

25 He sendeth forth his commandment upon earth: his word runneth very swiftly.

26 He giveth snow like wool: he scattereth the hoarfrost like ashes.

27 He casteth forth his ice like morsels: who can stand before his cold?

28 He sendeth out his word, and melteth them: he causeth his wind to blow, and the waters flow.

29 He sheweth his word unto Jacob, his statutes and his judgments unto Israel.

30 He hath not dealt so with any nation: and as for his judgments, they have not known them. Praise ye the Lord.

Glory be to the Father, and to the Son, and to the Holy Ghost.

As it was in the beginning, is now, and ever shall be, world without end. Amen.

## Selection 56

*Psalm CXLVIII*

PRAISE ye the Lord. Praise ye the Lord from the heavens : praise him in the heights.

2 Praise ye him, all his angels : praise ye him, all his hosts.

3 Praise ye him, sun and moon : praise him, all ye stars of light.

4 Praise him, ye heavens of heavens, and ye waters that be above the heavens.

5 Let them praise the name of the Lord : for he commanded, and they were created.

6 He hath also stablished them for ever and ever : he hath made a decree which shall not pass.

7 Praise the Lord from the earth, ye dragons, and all deeps :

8 Fire, and hail ; snow, and vapours ; stormy wind fulfilling his word :

9 Mountains, and all hills ; fruitful trees, and all cedars :

10 Beasts, and all cattle ; creeping things, and flying fowl :

11 Kings of the earth, and all people ; princes, and all judges of the earth :

12 Both young men, and maidens ; old men, and children :

13 Let them praise the name of the Lord : for his name alone is excellent ; his glory is above the earth and heaven.

14 He also exalteth the horn of his people, the praise of all his saints ; even of the children of Israel ; a people near unto him. Praise ye the Lord.

*Psalm CXLIX*

15 Praise ye the Lord. Sing unto the Lord a new song, and his praise in the congregation of saints.

16 Let Israel rejoice in him that made him : let the children of Zion be joyful in their King.

17 Let them praise his name in the dance : let them sing praises unto him with the timbrel and harp.

18 For the Lord taketh pleasure in his people : he will beautify the meek with salvation.

19 Let the saints be joyful in glory : let them sing aloud upon their beds.

20 Let the high praises of God be in their mouth, and a two edged sword in their hand ;

21 To execute vengeance upon the heathen, and punishments upon the people ;

22 To bind their kings with chains, and their nobles with fetters of iron ;

23 To execute upon them the judgment written : this honour have all his saints. Praise ye the Lord.

*Psalm CL*

24 Praise ye the Lord. Praise God in his sanctuary : praise him in the firmament of his power.

25 Praise him for his mighty acts : praise him according to his excellent greatness.

26 Praise him with the sound of the trumpet : praise him with the psaltery and harp.

27 Praise him with the timbrel and dance : praise him with stringed instruments and organs.

28 Praise him upon the loud cymbals : praise him upon the high sounding cymbals.

29 Let every thing that hath breath praise the Lord. Praise ye the Lord.

Glory be to the Father, and to the Son, and to the Holy Ghost.

As it was in the beginning, is now, and ever shall be, world without end. Amen.

# THE COMMANDMENTS

## Selection 57

MINISTER. God spake all these words, saying: I am the Lord thy God. Thou shalt have no other gods before me.

PEOPLE. *Lord, have mercy upon us, and incline our hearts to keep this law.*

Thou shalt not make unto thee any graven image, or any likeness of anything that is in the heaven above, or that is in the earth beneath, or that is in the waters under the earth: thou shalt not bow down thyself to them nor serve them, for I the Lord thy God am a jealous God, visiting the iniquity of the fathers upon the children unto the third and fourth generation of them that hate me; and showing mercy unto thousands of them that love me and keep my commandments.

*Lord, have mercy upon us, and incline our hearts to keep this law.*

Thou shalt not take the name of the Lord thy God in vain; for the Lord will not hold him guiltless that taketh his name in vain.

*Lord, have mercy upon us, and incline our hearts to keep this law.*

Remember the sabbath day to keep it holy. Six days shalt thou labor and do all thy work: but the seventh day is the sabbath of the Lord thy God: in it thou shalt not do any work, thou, nor thy son, nor thy daughter, thy manservant, nor thy maidservant, nor thy cattle, nor thy stranger that is within thy gates; for in six days the Lord made heaven and earth, the sea, and all that in them is, and rested the seventh day; wherefore the Lord blessed the sabbath day and hallowed it.

*Lord, have mercy upon us, and incline our hearts to keep this law.*

Honor thy father and thy mother, that thy days may be long upon the land which the Lord thy God giveth thee.

*Lord, have mercy upon us, and incline our hearts to keep this law.*

Thou shalt not kill.

*Lord, have mercy upon us, and incline our hearts to keep this law.*

Thou shalt not commit adultery.

*Lord, have mercy upon us, and incline our hearts to keep this law.*

Thou shalt not steal.

*Lord, have mercy upon us, and incline our hearts to keep this law.*

Thou shalt not bear false witness against thy neighbor.

*Lord, have mercy upon us, and incline our hearts to keep this law.*

Thou shalt not covet thy neighbor's house, thou shalt not covet thy neighbor's wife, nor his manservant, nor his maidservant, nor his ox, nor his ass, nor anything that is thy neighbor's.

*Lord, have mercy upon us, and write all these thy laws in our hearts, we beseech thee.*

Hear also what our Lord Jesus Christ saith.

Thou shalt love the Lord thy God with all thy heart, and with all thy soul, and with all thy mind: This is the first and great commandment. And the second is like unto it: Thou shalt love thy neighbor as thyself. On these two commandments hang all the law and the prophets.

# THE LITANY

COMPILED FROM EVANGELICAL SERVICES IN USE SINCE THE REFORMATION.

## Selection 58

MINISTER. O God the Father of Heaven,
PEOPLE. *Have mercy upon us.*
O God the Son, Redeemer of the world,
*Have mercy upon us.*
O God the Holy Ghost, our Comforter and Guide,
*Have mercy upon us.*
O Lamb of God, that takest away the sin of the world,
*Have mercy upon us, and grant us thy peace.*
Remember not, Lord, our offences, nor the offences of our fathers; neither take thou vengeance of our sins; spare us, good Lord, spare thy people whom thou hast redeemed with thy most precious blood, and be not angry with us forever;
*Spare us, good Lord.*
From all evil and mischief; from sin, from the crafts and assaults of the devil, from thy wrath, and from everlasting death,
*Good Lord, deliver us.*
From all blindness of heart; from pride, vain glory, and hypocrisy; from envy, hatred, and malice, and all uncharitableness,
*Good Lord, deliver us.*
From all unhallowed and sinful affections, from all defilements of mind and body, from unbelief and contempt of thy word and commandments,

*Good Lord, deliver us.*
From dying suddenly and unprepared; from war, pestilence, and famine; from hardness of heart, despair of thy mercy, and grieving of thy Holy Spirit,
*Good Lord, deliver us.*
By the mystery of thy holy incarnation, by thy sacred birth and baptism, by thy fasting and temptation,
*Good Lord, deliver us.*
By thine agony and bloody sweat, by thy cross and passion, by thy precious death and burial, by thy glorious resurrection and ascension, and by the coming of the Holy Ghost the Comforter,
*Good Lord, deliver us.*
In all time of our affliction, in all time of our prosperity, in the hour of death, and in the day of judgment,
*Good Lord, deliver us.*
We sinners beseech thee to hear us, O Lord God, and that it may please thee to rule and govern thy holy church universal in the right way:
*We beseech thee to hear us, Good Lord.*
That it may please thee to keep in the true worshiping of thee, in righteousness and in holiness of life, thy servants the President of the United States, the Governor of this Commonwealth, [the chief magistrate of this city,] and all others in authority over us; endue them plenteously with thy grace and heavenly gifts, that they may rightly administer justice, wisely govern and faithfully protect thy

people whom thou hast committed to their care ;
*We beseech thee to hear us, good Lord.*

That it may please thee to preserve in purity of doctrine, in soundness of word, and in holiness of life, all pastors and ministers of thy church ; to send forth faithful laborers into thy harvest ; to encourage thy missionaries in our own land and among all nations ; and to grant the increase of thy word and the fruit of thy Spirit unto all that hear ;
*We beseech thee to hear us, good Lord.*

That it may please thee to comfort the sick and afflicted, especially those known to ourselves whom we name in our hearts before thee ; to succor all who are in danger ; to bless young children ; to show thy pity upon all prisoners and captives ; to defend and provide for fatherless children and widows, and all that are desolate and oppressed ; to keep in peace and safety the stranger in a strange land, and all who are far from home, that they may never want the comforting sense of thy presence ; and to have mercy upon all sorts and conditions of men ;
*We beseech thee to hear us, good Lord.*

That it may please thee to forgive our enemies, persecutors, and slanderers, and to turn their hearts ;
*We beseech thee to hear us, good Lord.*

That it may please thee to give and preserve to our use the kindly fruits of the earth, so as in due time we may enjoy them ;
*We beseech thee to hear us, good Lord.*

That it may please thee to give us true repentance, to forgive all our sins as we from our hearts forgive all who trespass against us, and to endue us with the grace of thy Holy Spirit to amend our lives according to thy holy word ;
*We beseech thee to hear us, good Lord.*

We poor sinners beseech thee to hear us, gracious Lord our God, and to keep us in everlasting communion with all thy faithful children who have entered into the joy of their Lord, especially with those who are dear to our souls, and with the whole church triumphant ; that we may all at last rest together in thy presence, from our labors.

*Glory be to him who is the resurrection and the life, in the church which waiteth for him and in that which surroundeth him for ever and ever. Amen.*

# THE APOSTLES' CREED.

I believe in God the Father Almighty, Maker of heaven and earth:

And in Jesus Christ his only Son our Lord; Who was conceived by the Holy Ghost, Born of the Virgin Mary; Suffered under Pontius Pilate, was crucified, dead, and buried; He descended into hell; The third day he rose again from the dead; He ascended into heaven, And sitteth on the right hand of God the Father Almighty; From thence he shall come to judge the quick and the dead.

I believe in the Holy Ghost; The holy Catholic Church; The Communion of Saints; The Forgiveness of sins; The Resurrection of the body; And the life everlasting. Amen.

# THE ORDER OF HYMNS, CHIEFLY AFTER THE APOSTLES' CREED.

THE CALL TO WORSHIP . . 1–24
GOD THE FATHER ALMIGHTY,
MAKER OF HEAVEN AND
EARTH . . . . . . 25–41
JESUS CHRIST
Advent and Birth . . . 42–60
Ministry and Example . . 61–83
Passion and Crucifixion . 84–96
Resurrection . . . . . 97–105
Ascension . . . . . . 106–112
Mediatorial Reign . . . 113–126
Second Coming and Judgment . . . . . . . 127–139
THE HOLY GHOST
The Holy Ghost . . . . 140–152
Inspiration . . . . . . 153–156
THE HOLY CATHOLIC CHURCH 157–169
Baptism and Confession of Faith . . . . . . . 170–180
The Lord's Supper . . . 181–187
Consecration and Service . 188–203
Charities and Missions . . 204–227
THE COMMUNION OF SAINTS 228–241

THE FORGIVENESS OF SINS
Invitation . . . . . . 242–265
Repentance . . . . . 266–280
Surrender and Acceptance 281–295
Redeeming Love . . . . 296–310
Conflict . . . . . . . 311–324
Trial and Trust . . . . 325–364
Prayer and Aspiration . . 365–377
THE RESURRECTION OF THE BODY
Burial of the Dead . . . 378–383
THE LIFE EVERLASTING . 384–405
TIMES AND SEASONS
The Lord's Day . . . . 406–427
Morning . . . . . . 428–432
Evening . . . . . . . 433–453
The New Year . . . . 454–458
Thanksgiving . . . . . 459–462
TRAVELLERS' HYMNS . . . 463–467
NATIONAL HYMNS . . . . 468–472
ANCIENT AND SCRIPTURAL HYMNS . . . . . . 473–489

# HYMNS

### 1 Christ Church  6.6.6.6.8.8.          CHARLES STEGGALL

1 Ye ho-ly an-gels bright, Who wait at God's right hand, Or

thro' the realms of light Fly at your Lord's command, As-sist our song, for

else the theme Too high doth seem for mor-tal tongue. A-MEN.

2 Ye blessèd souls at rest,
 Who ran this earthly race,
And now from sin released
 Behold the Saviour's face,
God's praises sound, as in His Light,
 With sweet delight, ye do abound.

3 Ye saints who toil below,
 Adore your heavenly King,
And onward as ye go
 Some joyful anthem sing.
Take what He gives and praise Him still,
 Through good or ill, who ever lives.

    4 My soul, bear thou thy part,
     Triumph in God above,
    And with a well-tuned heart,
     Sing thou the songs of love !
    Let all thy days till life shall end,
     Whate'er He send, be filled with praise.  Amen.
                                RICHARD BAXTER—adapted

## THE CALL TO WORSHIP

**2  Italian Hymn**  6.6.4.6.6.6.4.  FELICE GIARDINI

1 Come, Thou Al - might - y King, Help us Thy name to sing,

Help us to praise: Fa-ther! all glo - ri - ous, O'er all vic - to - ri - ous,

Come, and reign o - ver us, An - cient of Days! A - MEN.

2 Come, Thou incarnate Word,
Gird on Thy mighty sword;
  Our prayer attend;
Come, and Thy people bless,
And give Thy word success:
Spirit of holiness!
  On us descend.

3 Come, holy Comforter!
Thy sacred witness bear
  In this glad hour:
Thou, Who almighty art,
Now rule in every heart,
And ne'er from us depart,
  Spirit of power!

4 To the great One in Three,
The highest praises be,
  Hence evermore!
His sovereign majesty
May we in glory see,
And to eternity
  Love and adore.  Amen.

CHARLES WESLEY

## THE CALL TO WORSHIP

**3 Nicæa** 11s & 12s

J. B. DYKES

1 Ho-ly, Ho-ly, Ho - ly! Lord God Al- might-y! Ear - ly in the

morn - ing our song shall rise to Thee: Ho-ly, Ho-ly, Ho - ly,

mer-ci-ful and might-y, God in Three Persons, Blessèd Trini- ty!

2 Holy, Holy, Holy! all the saints adore Thee,
   Casting down their golden crowns around the glassy sea ;
  Cherubim and Seraphim falling down before Thee,
   Which wert, and art, and evermore shalt be.

3 Holy, Holy, Holy! though the darkness hide Thee,
   Though the eye of sinful man Thy glory may not see ;
  Only Thou art holy : there is none beside Thee
   Perfect in power, in love, and purity.

4 Holy, Holy, Holy! Lord God Almighty!
   All Thy works shall praise Thy Name, in earth, and sky, and sea :
  Holy, Holy, Holy! merciful and mighty,
   God in Three Persons, Blessèd Trinity! Amen.

REGINALD HEBER

## THE CALL TO WORSHIP

### 4 Grace Church L.M.
IGNACE PLEYEL

1 Come, O Cre - a - tor-Spir - it blest, And in our souls take up Thy rest;

A - MEN.

Come, with Thy grace and heavenly aid, To fill the hearts which Thou hast made.

2 Great Comforter, to Thee we cry;
O highest gift of God most high,
O Fount of life, O Fire of love,
And sweet anointing from above!

3 Kindle our senses from above,
And make our hearts o'erflow with love;
With patience firm, and virtue high,
The weakness of our flesh supply.

4 Far from us drive the foe we dread,
And grant us Thy true peace instead;
So shall we not, with Thee for guide,
Turn from the path of life aside. Amen.

LATIN HYMN 8th CENT. TR. CASWALL *ab. and alt.*

### 5 State Street S.M.
J. C. WOODMAN

1 Our heavenly Fa - ther calls, And Christ in-vites us near; With

## THE CALL TO WORSHIP

both our friendship shall be sweet, And our com-mun-ion dear.

2 God pities all my griefs;
He pardons every day;
Almighty to protect my soul,
And wise to guide my way.

3 How large His bounties are!
What various stores of good,
Diffused from my Redeemer's hand,
And purchased with His blood!

4 Jesus, my living Head,
I bless Thy faithful care;
Mine Advocate before the throne,
And my Forerunner there.

5 Here fix, my roving heart,
Here wait, my warmest love,
Till the communion be complete,
In nobler scenes above.   Amen.
PHILIP DODDRIDGE

## 6 Seymour 7s
From VON WEBER

1 Come, my soul, thy suit pre-pare, Je-sus loves to an-swer prayer;

He Him-self has bid thee pray, Therefore will not say thee nay.

2 Thou art coming to a King,
Large petitions with thee bring;
For His grace and power are such,
None can ever ask too much.

3 With my burden I begin,
Lord, remove this load of sin;
Let Thy blood, for sinners spilt,
Set my conscience free from guilt.

4 Lord, I come to Thee for rest,
Take possession of my breast;

There Thy blood-bought right main-
And without a rival reign.   [tain,

5 While I am a pilgrim here,
Let Thy love my spirit cheer;
As my Guide, my Guard, my Friend,
Lead me to my journey's end.

6 Show me what I have to do,
Every hour my strength renew;
Let me live a life of faith,
Let me die Thy people's death.   Amen.
JOHN NEWTON ab.

## THE CALL TO WORSHIP

**7  St. Leonard** C.M.D.                    HENRY HILES

1 Lord, when we bend be-fore Thy throne, And our con-fes-sions pour,
O may we feel the sins we own, And hate what we de-plore.
Our brok-en spir-its pity-ing see; And pen-i-tence im-part; Then let a kindling glance from Thee, Beam Hope upon the heart.

A-MEN.

2 When we disclose our wants in prayer,
   May we our wills resign;
And not a thought our bosoms share
   Which is not wholly Thine.
Let Faith each weak petition fill,
   And waft it to the skies;
And teach our hearts 't is goodness still,
   That grants it or denies.

3 When our responsive tongues essay
   Their grateful hymns to raise,
Grant that our souls may join the lay,
   And mount to Thee in praise.
Then on Thy glories, while we dwell,
   Thy mercies we'll renew,
Till Love divine transported tell
   Our God's our Father too.   Amen.
                        J. D. CARLYLE

## THE CALL TO WORSHIP

**8 Humility** L.M.  S. P. TUCKERMAN

1 Je-sus, where'er Thy peo-ple meet, There they behold Thy mer-cy-seat;

A-MEN.

Where'er they seek Thee, Thou art found, And ev'ry place is hallowed ground.

2 For Thou, within no walls confined,
Inhabitest the humble mind;
Such ever bring Thee where they come,
And going, take Thee to their home.

3 Dear Shepherd of Thy chosen few,
Thy former mercies here renew;
Here to our waiting hearts proclaim
The sweetness of Thy saving name.

4 Here may we prove the power of pray'r
To strengthen faith, and sweeten care,
To teach our faint desires to rise,
And bring all heaven before our eyes.

5 Lord, we are few, but Thou art near:
Nor short Thine arm, nor deaf Thine ear;
Oh, rend the heavens, come quickly down,
And make a thousand hearts Thine own.
Amen.
WILLIAM COWPER *ab.*

**9**

1 From every stormy wind that blows,
From every swelling tide of woes,
There is a calm, a sure retreat:
'T is found beneath the mercy-seat.

2 There is a place where Jesus sheds
The oil of gladness on our heads;
A place than all besides more sweet:
It is the blood-stained mercy-seat.

3 There is a spot where spirits blend,
Where friend holds fellowship with friend:
Though sundered far, by faith they meet,
Around one common mercy-seat.

4 Ah! whither could we flee for aid,
When tempted, desolate, dismayed;
Or how the hosts of hell defeat,
Had suffering saints no mercy-seat?

5 There, there on eagle wings we soar,
And time and sense seem all no more;
And heaven comes down our souls to greet,
And glory crowns the mercy-seat. Amen.
HUGH STOWELL

## THE CALL TO WORSHIP

### 10 Olmutz S.M.
Arr. by Lowell Mason

♩ = 104

1 Be - hold the throne of grace! The promise calls me near;

A - MEN.

There Je-sus shows a smiling face, And waits to an - swer prayer.

2 My soul! ask what thou wilt;
  Thou canst not be too bold;
Since His own blood for thee He spilt,
  What else can He withhold?

3 Thine image, Lord! bestow,
  Thy presence and Thy love;
I ask to serve Thee here below,
  And reign with Thee above.

4 Teach me to live by faith;
  Conform my will to Thine;
Let me victorious be in death,
  And then in glory shine. Amen.

JOHN NEWTON *ab.*

### 11 Beatitude C.M.
J. B. DYKES

♩ = 92

1. Talk with me, Lord: Thy - self re - veal, While here o'er earth I rove;

## THE CALL TO WORSHIP

Speak to my heart, and let it feel The kin-dling of Thy love.

2 With Thee conversing, I forget
  All time, and toil, and care ;
Labor is rest, and pain is sweet,
  If Thou, my God, art here.

3 Here then, my God, vouchsafe to stay,
  And make my heart rejoice ;
My bounding heart shall own Thy sway,
  And echo to Thy voice.

4 Thou callest me to seek Thy face ;
  'T is all I wish to seek ;
To attend the whispers of Thy grace,
  And hear Thee inly speak.

5 Let this my every hour employ,
  Till I Thy glory see,
Enter into my Master's joy,
  And find my heaven in Thee.  Amen.

CHARLES WESLEY *ab.*

## 12 St. Andrew S.M.

JOSEPH BARNBY

1 Sweet is Thy mer-cy, Lord; Be-fore Thy mer-cy-seat My soul, a-doring, pleads Thy word, And owns Thy mercy sweet.

2 My need, and Thy desires,
  Are all in Christ complete ;
Thou hast the justice truth requires,
  And I Thy mercy sweet.

3 Where'er Thy name is blest,
  Where'er Thy people meet,
There I delight in Thee to rest,
  And find Thy mercy sweet.

4 Light Thou my weary way,
  Lead Thou my wandering feet,
That while I stray on earth I may
  Still find Thy mercy sweet.

5 Thus shall the heavenly host
  Hear all my songs repeat
To Father, Son, and Holy Ghost,
  My joy, Thy mercy sweet.  Amen.

J. S. B. MONSELL

## THE CALL TO WORSHIP

**13 Hebron** 6.4.6.4.6.6.4.   A. B. SPRATT

1 Nearer, my God, to Thee; Nearer to Thee! Ev'n tho' it be a cross That raiseth me!

Still all my song shall be, Nearer, my God, to Thee, Nearer to Thee!

2 Though like a wanderer,
　The sun gone down,
Darkness be over me,
　My rest a stone;
Yet in my dreams I 'd be
Nearer, my God, to Thee,
　Nearer to Thee!

3 There let the way appear,
　Steps unto heaven;
All that Thou sendest me,
　In mercy given;
Angels to beckon me
Nearer, my God, to Thee,
　Nearer to Thee!

4 Then, with my waking thoughts,
　Bright with Thy praise,
Out of my stony griefs
　Bethel I 'll raise;
So by my woes to be
Nearer, my God, to Thee,
　Nearer to Thee!

5 Or if on joyful wing,
　Cleaving the sky,
Sun, moon, and stars forgot,
　Upward I fly,
Still all my song shall be,
Nearer, my God, to Thee,
　Nearer to Thee!　Amen.

SARAH F. ADAMS

**Bethany**　SECOND TUNE　LOWELL MASON

## THE CALL TO WORSHIP

**14 Olivet** 6.6.4.6.6.6.4.  LOWELL MASON

1 My faith looks up to Thee, Thou Lamb of Cal-va-ry,

Sav-iour di-vine! Now hear me while I pray; Take all my

A-MEN.

guilt a-way; Oh, let me, from this day, Be whol-ly Thine!

2 May Thy rich grace impart
Strength to my fainting heart,
My zeal inspire!
As Thou hast died for me,
Oh, may my love to Thee
Pure, warm, and changeless be —
A living fire!

3 While life's dark maze I tread,
And griefs around me spread,
Be Thou my guide;
Bid darkness turn to day,
Wipe sorrow's tears away,
Nor let me ever stray
From Thee aside.

4 When ends life's transient dream,
When death's cold, sullen stream
Shall o'er me roll,
Blest Saviour! then, in love,
Fear and distrust remove;
Oh, bear me safe above —
A ransomed soul! Amen.

RAY PALMER

## THE CALL TO WORSHIP

### 15 Marshall s.m.
G. J. Geer

1 Still, still with Thee, my God, I would de-sire to be:
By day, by night, at home, a-broad, I would be still with Thee.

A - MEN.

2 With Thee, when dawn comes in,
And calls me back to care,
Each day returning to begin
With Thee, my God, in prayer.

3 With Thee amid the crowd
That throngs the busy mart,
To hear Thy voice, 'mid clamor loud,
Speak softly to my heart.

4 With Thee, when day is done,
And evening calms the mind;
The setting, as the rising, sun
With Thee my heart would find.

5 With Thee, when darkness brings,
The signal of repose,
Calm in the shadow of Thy wings,
Mine eyelids I would close.

6 With Thee, in Thee, by faith
Abiding I would be;
By day, by night, in life, in death,
I would be still with Thee. Amen.

J. D. Burns *alt.*

### 16 Hermann c.m.
N. Hermann

1 Sweet is the memory of Thy grace, My God, my heavenly King;

## THE CALL TO WORSHIP

Let age to age Thy righteous-ness In sounds of glo-ry sing.

2 God reigns on high; but ne'er confines
His goodness to the skies;
Thro' the whole earth His bounty shines
And every want supplies.

3 With longing eyes Thy creatures wait
On Thee for daily food;
Thy liberal hand provides their meat,
And fills their mouth with good.

4 How kind are Thy compassions, Lord!
How slow Thine anger moves!
But soon He sends His pardoning word
To cheer the souls He loves.

5 Creatures, with all their endless race,
Thy power and praise proclaim;
But saints that taste Thy richer grace
Delight to bless Thy name. Amen.
ISAAC WATTS

### 17 Dominus regit me 8s & 7s
J. B. DYKES

1 The King of love my Shepherd is, Whose goodness fail-eth nev-er: I

noth-ing lack if I am His And He is mine for ev - er.

2 Where streams of living water flow
My ransomed soul He leadeth,
And, where the verdant pastures grow,
With food celestial feedeth.

3 Perverse and foolish, oft I strayed,
But yet in love He sought me,
And on His shoulder gently laid,
And home, rejoicing, brought me.

4 In death's dark vale I fear no ill
With Thee, dear Lord, beside me;
Thy rod and staff my comfort still,
Thy Cross before to guide me.

5 Thou spreadst a table in my sight,
Thy unction grace bestoweth,
And oh, the transport of delight
With which my cup o'erfloweth.

6 And so, through all the length of days,
Thy goodness faileth never;
Good Shepherd, may I sing Thy praise
Within Thy house forever! Amen.
H. W. BAKER

## THE CALL TO WORSHIP

**18 Resurrection** 8s & 7s 6l.    GERMAN

1 Come, ye faith-ful, raise the an-them, Cleave the skies with shouts of praise;
Sing to Him who found the ran-som, An-cient of e-ter-nal days;

A - MEN.

God E-ter-nal, Word In-carnate, Whom the Heaven of heavens obeys.

2 If His people walk in darkness,
   Through the thickest clouds of night,
He, according to His promise,
   Sends the pillar-beam of light;
Then they pass along His highway,
   Turning not to left or right.

3 When the thirsty pant for water,
   And no cooling streams are found,
He descends, like showers in Springtime
   Softening all the parchéd ground:
While the smitten Rock its torrents
   Pours in ample streams around.

4 Hungry souls that faint and languish
   By His bounteous hand are fed;
Yes, He gives them food immortal,
   Gives Himself, the living Bread,
Gives the chalice of His passion,
   Rich with blood on Calvary shed.

5 There for us and our redemption,
   See Him all His lifeblood pour!
There He wins our full salvation,
   Dies that we may die no more;
Then, arising, lives forever,
   Reigning where He was before.

6 Trust Him then, ye fearful pilgrims;
   Who shall pluck you from His hand?
Pledged He stands for your salvation,
   Who are fighting for His land.
Oh, that we amidst His true ones,
   Round His throne one day may stand. Amen.

JOB HUPTON *adapt. by* SMALE, *alt.*

## THE CALL TO WORSHIP

**19 Benedic Anima** 8n&7n6l.  JOHN GOSS

1 Praise, my soul, the King of heav-en, To His feet thy trib-ute bring.

Ransom'd, heal'd, restor'd, for-giv-en, Who, like me, His praise should sing?

A - MEN.

Al - le - lu - ia, Al - le - lu - ia, Praise the ev-er-last-ing King.

2 Praise Him for His grace and favor
  To our fathers in distress;
Praise Him still the same as ever,
  Slow to chide, and swift to bless;
    Alleluia, Alleluia!
  Glorious in His faithfulness.

3 Fatherlike, He tends and spares us,
  Well our feeble frame He knows;
In His hands He gently bears us,
  Rescues us from all our foes;
    Alleluia, Alleluia!
  Widely as His mercy flows.

4 Angels, help us to adore Him!
  Ye behold Him face to face!
Sun and moon bow down before Him,
  Dwellers all in time and space;
    Alleluia, Alleluia!
  Praise with us the God of grace.   Amen.

H. F. LYTE

## THE CALL TO WORSHIP

**20  Mirfield** C.M.          Arthur Cottman

1  O Jesus, King most wonderful! Thou Conqueror renowned! Thou

Sweetness most in-ef-fa-ble! In whom all joys are found!

2  When once Thou visitest the heart,
   Then truth begins to shine;
Then earthly vanities depart;
   Then kindles love divine.

3  O Jesus! Light of all below!
   Thou Fount of life and fire!
Surpassing all the joys we know,
   And all we can desire —

4  May every heart confess Thy name,
   And ever Thee adore;
And, seeking Thee, itself inflame
   To seek Thee more and more!

5  Thee may our tongues forever bless;
   Thee may we love alone;
And ever in our lives express
   The image of Thine own. Amen.

                     St. Bernard  Tr. Caswall

**21  Duke Street** L.M.          John Hatton

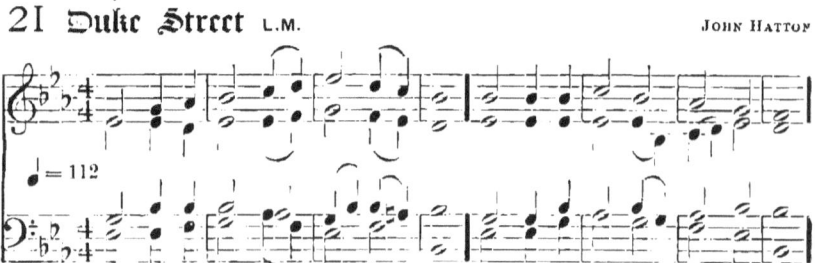

1  Come, let us sing the Song of songs, The saints in heaven began the strain,

## THE CALL TO WORSHIP

The homage which to Christ belongs: "Worthy the Lamb, for He was slain!"

2 Slain to redeem us by His blood,
  To cleanse from every sinful stain,
And make us kings and priests to God:
  "Worthy the Lamb, for He was slain!"

3 To Him who suffered on the tree,
  Our souls at His soul's price to gain,
Blessing, and praise, and glory be:
  "Worthy the Lamb, for He was slain!"

4 To Him enthroned by filial right,
  All power in heaven and earth pro-
Honor, and majesty, and might: [claim,
  "Worthy the Lamb, for He was slain!"

5 Come Holy Spirit from on high,
  Our faith, our hope, our love sustain,
Living to sing, and dying cry,
  "Worthy the Lamb, for He was slain!"
                                  Amen.
JAMES MONTGOMERY *ab.*

## 22 Aubrey C.M.
C. J. VINCENT JR.

1 A-rise, my soul! my joy-ful powers, And tri-umph in my God;

Awake, my voice! And loud proclaim His glorious grace abroad.

2 The arms of everlasting love
  Beneath my soul He placed,
And on the Rock of Ages set
  My slippery footsteps fast.

3 The city of my blest abode
  Is walled around with grace;

Salvation for a bulwark stands,
  To shield the sacred place.

4 Arise, my soul! awake, my voice!
  And tunes of pleasure sing;
Loud alleluias shall address
  My Saviour and my King.   Amen.
ISAAC WATTS *ak*

## THE CALL TO WORSHIP

**23 Innocents** 7s     Arr. by W. H. MONK

1 God e-ter-nal, Lord of all, Low-ly at Thy feet we fall,

All the earth doth worship Thee, We amidst the throng would be.

2 All the holy angels cry
"Hail, thrice holy God most high!"
Lord of all the heavenly powers,
Be the same loud anthem ours.

3 Glorified apostles raise
Night and day continual praise;
Hast Thou not a mission too
For Thy children here to do?

4 With Thy prophets' goodly line
We in mystic bond combine;
For Thou hast to babes revealed
Things that to the wise were sealed.

5 Martyrs, in a noble host,
Of Thy cross are heard to boast;
Since so bright the crown they wear,
Early we Thy cross would bear.

6 All Thy Church in heaven and earth,
Jesus! hail Thy spotless birth;
Seated on the judgment-throne,
Number us among Thine own! Amen.

J. E. MILLARD *ab*

## THE CALL TO WORSHIP

**24  Old Hundredth.** L.M.                                          GENEVA PSALTER

1 From all that dwell below the skies, Let the Cre-a-tor's praise a-rise; Let
2 E-ter-nal are Thy mercies, Lord! E-ter-nal truth attends Thy word: Thy

the Redeemer's name be sung, Thro' ev'ry land, by ev-'ry tongue.
praise shall sound from shore to shore, Till suns shall rise and set no more. Amen.

ISAAC WATTS

---

Praise God, from whom all blessings flow;
Praise Him, all creatures here below;
Praise Him above, ye heavenly host;
Praise Father, Son, and Holy Ghost. Amen.

---

*For other Hymns appropriate to Worship, see following Topics.*

GOD THE FATHER ALMIGHTY . . . . . . . 25–41
JESUS CHRIST; Mediatorial Reign . . . . . . . 113–126
THE HOLY GHOST . . . . . . . . 140–152
THE HOLY CATHOLIC CHURCH . . . . . . . 157–166
TIMES AND SEASONS; The Lord's Day . . . . . 406–427

## GOD THE FATHER ALMIGHTY

**25** 𝔏𝔭𝔬𝔫𝔰 10.10.11.11.  J. M. HAYDN

1 O wor-ship the King all glo-rious a - bove; O grate-ful - ly

sing His pow'r and His love; Our Shield and De - fend - er, the

A - MEN.

Ancient of days, Pa-vilioned in splendor, And girded with praise.

2 O tell of His might, O sing of His grace,
Whose robe is the light, whose canopy space;
His chariots of wrath the deep thunder-clouds form,
And dark is His path on the wings of the storm.

3 Thy bountiful care what tongue can recite?
It breathes in the air, it shines in the light;
It streams from the hills, it descends to the plain,
And sweetly distils in the dew and the rain.

4 Frail children of dust, and feeble as frail,
In Thee do we trust, nor find Thee to fail.
Thy mercies how tender! how firm to the end!
Our Maker, Defender, Redeemer, and Friend. Amen.

ROBERT GRANT *ab*

## MAKER OF HEAVEN AND EARTH

**26 Coronae** P87s&4.  W. H. Monk

1 God the Lord a King re-main-eth, Robed in His own glo-rious light!

God hath robed Him and He reigneth! He hath gird-ed Him with might!

Al - le - lu - ia! God is King in depth and height.  A - MEN.

2 In her everlasting station
   Earth is poised to swerve no more:
Thou hast laid Thy throne's foundation,
   From all time where thought can soar.
      Alleluia!
Lord, Thou art for evermore.

3 Lord, the water-floods have lifted,
   Ocean floods have lift their roar:
Now they pause where they have drifted,
   Now they burst upon the shore.
      Alleluia!
For the ocean's sounding store.

4 With all tones of waters blending,
   Glorious is the breaking deep!
Glorious, beauteous, without ending,
   God who reigns on heaven's high steep!
      Alleluia!
Songs of ocean never sleep.

5 Lord, the words Thy lips are telling,
   Are the perfect verity:
Of Thine high eternal dwelling
   Holiness shall inmate be!
      Alleluia!
Pure is all that lives with Thee!
          Amen.

JOHN KEBLE

## GOD THE FATHER ALMIGHTY

**27  Old Hundred Forty-eighth**  6.6.6.6.8.8.   WILLIAM CROFT

1 Oh, for a shout of joy, High as the theme we sing! To

this di-vine em-ploy Your hearts and voi-ces bring: Sound,

sound thro' all the earth abroad, The love, th' e-ter-nal love of God.

A - MEN.

2 Unnumbered myriads stand,
  Of seraphs bright and fair;
Or bow at His right hand,
  And pay their homage there:
But strive in vain, with loudest chord,
To sound the wondrous love of God.

3 Yet sinners saved by grace,
  In songs of lower key,
In every age and place,
  Have sung the mystery,—
Have told in strains of sweet accord,
The love, the sovereign love of God.

4 Though earth and hell assail,
  And doubts and fears arise,
The weakest shall prevail,
  And grasp the heavenly prize;
And through an endless age record
The love, th' unchanging love of God.

5 Oh, for a shout of joy,
  High as the theme we sing!
To this divine employ
  Your hearts and voices bring:
Sound, sound through all the earth abroad,
The love, th' eternal love, of God. Amen.

J. YOUNG

## MAKER OF HEAVEN AND EARTH

**28 Angel Voices** 8.5.8.5.8.7.        ARTHUR SULLIVAN

1 An-gel voic-es ev-er sing-ing Round Thy throne of light,

An-gel harps for-ev-er ring-ing Rest not day nor night: Thousands on-ly

live to bless Thee, And con-fess Thee, Lord of might!   A-MEN.

2 Thou, Who art beyond the farthest
  Mortal eye can scan,
Can it be that Thou regardest
  Songs of sinful man?
Can we know that Thou art near us,
  And wilt hear us? Yea! we can.

3 Yea, we know that Thou rejoicest
  O'er each work of Thine:
Thou didst ears, and hands, and voices,
  For Thy praise combine;
Craftsman's art and music's measure
  For Thy pleasure didst design.

4 Here, Great God, to-day we offer
  Of Thine own to Thee,
And for Thine acceptance proffer,
  All unworthily,
Hearts, and minds, and hands, and voices,
  In our choicest melody. Amen.

FRANCIS POTT

## GOD THE FATHER ALMIGHTY

### 29 Hummel C.M.
CHARLES ZEUNER

♩ = 69

1 I sing th' al-might-y power of God, That made the mountains rise,

A - MEN.

That spread the flowing seas a - broad, And built the loft-y skies.

2 I sing the wisdom that ordained
   The sun to rule the day;
The moon shines full at His command,
   And all the stars obey.

3 I sing the goodness of the Lord,
   That filled the earth with food;
He formed the creatures with His word,
   And then pronounced them good.

4 Lord, how Thy wonders are displayed,
   Where'er I turn mine eye;
If I survey the ground I tread,
   Or gaze upon the sky!

5 There's not a plant or flower below,
   But makes Thy glories known;
And clouds arise, and tempests blow,
   By order from Thy throne.

6 Creatures that borrow life from Thee
   Are subject to Thy care;
There's not a place where we can flee,
   But God is present there. Amen.

ISAAC WATTS

### 30 Dundee C.M.
SCOTCH PSALTER

♩ = 72

1 Great God! how in - fi - nite art Thou! What worthless worms are we!

## MAKER OF HEAVEN AND EARTH

Let the whole race of creatures bow, And pay their praise to Thee.

2 Thy throne eternal ages stood,
Ere seas or stars were made;
Thou art the ever-living God,
Were all the nations dead.

3 Eternity, with all its years,
Stands present in Thy view;
To Thee there's nothing old appears;
Great God! there's nothing new.

4 Our lives through various scenes are drawn,
And vexed with trifling cares;
While Thine eternal thought moves on
Thine undisturbed affairs.

5 Great God! how infinite art Thou!
What worthless worms are we!
Let the whole race of creatures bow,
And pay their praise to Thee. Amen.

ISAAC WATTS

## 31 Illo L.M.

LOWELL MASON

1 O blessèd God, to Thee I raise My voice in thankful hymns of praise;

And when my voice shall si-lent be, My silence shall be praise to Thee.

2 For voice and silence both impart
The filial homage of my heart;
And both alike are understood
By Thee, Thou Parent of all good—

3 Whose grace is all unsearchable,
Whose care for me no tongue can tell,
Who loves my loudest praise to hear,
And loves to bless my voiceless prayer.
Amen.

GREEK HYMN

## GOD THE FATHER ALMIGHTY

**32 Welfield** 8.8.6.8.8.6.     H. A. CROSBIE

1 Thy might-y work-ing, mighty God, Wakes all my pow'rs; I look a-broad,

And can no lon-ger rest; I, too, must sing when all things sing,

And from my heart the prais-es ring, The Highest lov-eth best. A-MEN.

2 If Thou, in Thy great love to us,
  Wilt scatter joy and beauty thus
    O'er this poor earth of ours;
What nobler glories shall be given
Hereafter in Thy shining heaven,
    Set round with golden towers!

3 What thrilling joy, when on our sight
  Christ's garden beams in cloudless light
    And rings with God's high praise;
Where all the thousand seraphim
In one accordant voice and hymn
    Their Alleluia raise!

4 Oh, were I there! oh, that I now
  Before Thy throne, my God, could bow,
    And bear my heavenly palm!
Then, like the angels, would I raise
My voice, and sing Thine endless praise
    In many a sweet-toned psalm. Amen.

PAUL GERHARDT *ab.*

## MAKER OF HEAVEN AND EARTH

**33 Darwall** 6.6.6.6.8.8.  JOHN DARWALL

1 O ho-ly, ho-ly Lord, Cre-a-tion's sov'reign King! Thy

maj-es-ty a-dored Let all cre-a-tion sing: Who wast, and

A - MEN.

art, and art to be; Nor time shall see Thy sway de - part.

2 Great are Thy works of praise,
  O God of boundless might!
All just and true Thy ways,
  Thou King of saints, in light!
Let all above, and all below,
Conspire to show Thy power and love.

3 Who shall not fear Thee, Lord!
  And magnify Thy name?
Thy judgments, sent abroad,
  Thy holiness proclaim:
Nations shall throng from every shore,
And all adore in one loud song.

    4 While thus the powers on high
      Their swelling chorus raise,
    Let earth and man reply
      And echo back the praise:
    Thy glory own, first, last, and best,
    God ever blest, and God alone! Amen.

HENRY WARE, Jr. *ab.*

## GOD THE FATHER ALMIGHTY

**34 Church Triumphant** L.M.        J. W. ELLIOTT

1 The Lord is King! Lift up thy voice, O earth, and all ye heav'ns rejoice!

From world to world the joy shall ring, "The Lord omnipotent is King!"

2 The Lord is King! Who then shall dare
Resist His will, distrust His care?
Or murmur at His wise decrees,
Or doubt His royal promises?

3 The Lord is King! Child of the dust,
The Judge of all the earth is just;
Holy and true are all His ways,
Let every creature speak His praise.

4 Oh, when His wisdom can mistake,
His might decay, His love forsake,
Then may His children cease to sing,
"The Lord omnipotent is King!"

5 Alike pervaded by His eye,
All parts of His dominion lie;
This world of ours and worlds unseen,
And thin the boundary between.

6 One Lord, one empire, all secures;
He reigns! and life and death are yours;
Through earth and heaven one song shall ring,
"The Lord omnipotent is King!" Amen.

                         JOSIAH CONDER *ab.*

**35 Windsor** C.M.        GEORGE KIRBYE

1 My God, how won-der-ful Thou art! Thy maj-es-ty how bright!

## MAKER OF HEAVEN AND EARTH

How glorious is Thy mer-cy-seat, In depths of burn-ing light!

2 How dread are Thine eternal years,
O everlasting Lord!
By prostrate spirits day and night,
Incessantly adored!

3 O how I fear Thee, living God!
With deepest, tenderest fears;
And worship Thee with trembling hope
And penitential tears!

4 Yet I may love Thee, too, O Lord,
Almighty as Thou art,
For Thou hast stooped to ask of me
The love of my poor heart.

5 How wonderful, how beautiful
The sight of Thee must be!
Thine endless wisdom, boundless power,
And awful purity! Amen.

F. W. FABER ab.

## 36 Tallis' Ordinal C.M.

THOMAS TALLIS

1 O Lord, how good, how great art Thou, In heaven and earth the same: There

an-gels at Thy footstool bow, Here babes Thy grace proclaim.

2 When glorious in the nightly sky
Thy moon and stars I see,
Oh, what is man, I wondering cry,
To be so loved by Thee.

3 To him Thou hourly deign'st to give
New mercies from on high;
Didst quit Thy throne with him to live,
For him in pain to die.

4 Close to Thine own bright seraphim
His favored path is trod;
And all beside are serving him,
That he may serve his God.

5 O Lord, how good, how great art Thou,
In heaven and earth the same:
There angels at Thy footstool bow,
Here babes Thy grace proclaim. Amen.

H. F. LYTE

## GOD THE FATHER ALMIGHTY

**37 St. Ann's** C.M.  WILLIAM CROFT

1 Our God, our help in ages past, Our hope for years to come, Our shelter from the stormy blast, And our eternal home!

2 Under the shadow of Thy throne
Thy saints have dwelt secure;
Sufficient is Thine arm alone,
And our defence is sure.

3 Before the hills in order stood,
Or earth received her frame,
From everlasting Thou art God,
To endless years the same.

4 Thy word commands our flesh to dust,
"Return, ye sons of men;"
All nations rose from earth at first,
And turn to earth again.

5 Time, like an ever-rolling stream,
Bears all its sons away;
They fly, forgotten, as a dream
Dies at the opening day.

6 Our God, our help in ages past,
Our hope for years to come,
Be Thou our guard while troubles last,
And our eternal home!  Amen.

ISAAC WATTS *ab.*

**38**

1 God moves in a mysterious way
His wonders to perform;
He plants His footsteps in the sea,
And rides upon the storm.

2 Deep in unfathomable mines
Of never-failing skill,
He treasures up His bright designs,
And works His sovereign will.

3 Ye fearful saints, fresh courage take;
The clouds ye so much dread
Are big with mercy, and shall break
In blessings on your head.

4 Judge not the Lord by feeble sense,
But trust Him for His grace;
Behind a frowning providence
He hides a smiling face.

5 His purposes will ripen fast,
Unfolding every hour;
The bud may have a bitter taste,
But sweet will be the flower.

6 Blind unbelief is sure to err,
And scan His work in vain:
God is His own Interpreter,
And He will make it plain.  Amen.

WILLIAM COWPER

## MAKER OF HEAVEN AND EARTH

**39 Grostete** L.M.  H. W. GREATOREX

1 Lord of all be-ing, thron'd a-far, Thy glo-ry flames from sun and star; Cen-tre and soul of ev-'ry sphere, Yet to each loving heart how near.

2 Sun of our life, Thy quickening ray
Sheds on our path the glow of day;
Star of our hope, Thy softened light
Cheers the long watches of the night.

3 Our midnight is Thy smile withdrawn;
Our noontide is Thy gracious dawn;
Our rainbow arch Thy mercy's sign;
All, save the clouds of sin, are Thine.

4 Lord of all life, below, above,
Whose light is truth, whose warmth is love,
Before Thy ever-blazing throne
We ask no lustre of our own.

5 Grant us Thy truth to make us free,
And kindling hearts that burn for Thee,
Till all Thy living altars claim
One holy light, one heavenly flame.
Amen.
O. W. HOLMES

**Louvan** L.M.   SECOND TUNE   V. C. TAYLOR

## GOD THE FATHER ALMIGHTY

### 40 Magdalena 7s&6s D.
John Stainer

1 O God, the Rock of A-ges, Who evermore hast been, What time the tempest

ra-ges, Our dwelling-place serene: Before Thy first creations, O Lord, the same as

now, To end-less gen-er-a-tions The Ev - er - last - ing Thou!  A - MEN.

2 Our years are like the shadows
  On sunny hills that lie,
Or grasses in the meadows
  That blossom but to die:
A sleep, a dream, a story
  By strangers quickly told,
An unremaining glory
  Of things that soon are old.

3 O Thou, who canst not slumber,
  Whose light grows never pale,
Teach us aright to number
  Our years before they fail.
On us Thy mercy lighten,
  On us Thy goodness rest,
And let Thy Spirit brighten
  The hearts Thyself hast blest.

4 Lord, crown our faith's endeavor
  With beauty and with grace,
Till, clothed in light forever,
  We see Thee face to face:
A joy no language measures;
  A fountain brimming o'er;
An endless flow of pleasures;
  An ocean without shore  Amen.

E. H. Bickersteth

## MAKER OF HEAVEN AND EARTH

**41 Regent Square** 8s&7s6l.    HENRY SMART

1 Guide me, O Thou great Je-ho-vah, Pilgrim thro' this bar-ren land:

I am weak, but Thou art might-y; Hold me with Thy powerful hand;

A - MEN.

Bread of heav-en, Bread of heaven, Feed me till I want no more.

    2 Open Thou the crystal fountain
      Whence the healing streams do flow;
    Let the fiery, cloudy pillar
      Lead me all my journey through;
        Strong Deliverer,
    Be Thou still my Strength and Shield.

    3 When I tread the verge of Jordan,
      Bid my anxious fears subside;
    Bear me through the swelling current,
      Land me safe on Canaan's side;
        Songs of praises
    I will ever give to Thee. Amen.
                WILLIAM WILLIAMS *alt.*

*See also hymns under* THE FORGIVENESS OF SINS: Trial and Trust. 325–364.

## JESUS CHRIST

### 42 Langdale 8s & 7s
RICHARD REDHEAD

1 Hark! a thrilling voice is sounding; "Christ is nigh!" it seems to say; "Cast away the dreams of dark-ness, O ye chil-dren, of the day."

2 Startled at the solemn warning,
   Let the earth-bound soul arise;
Christ, her Sun, all sloth dispelling,
   Shines upon the morning skies.

3 Lo! the Lamb so long expected
   Comes with pardon down from heaven;
Let us haste, with tears of sorrow,
   One and all to be forgiven.

4 So, when next He comes in glory,
   Wrapping all the earth in fear,
May He then as our Defender
   On the clouds of heaven appear.

5 Honor, glory, virtue, merit,
   To the Father and the Son,
With the co-eternal Spirit,
   While eternal ages run. Amen.

LATIN HYMN 5th Cent. Tr. CASWALL

### 43 Laus Deo 6s & 5s 12l.
JOSEPH BARNBY

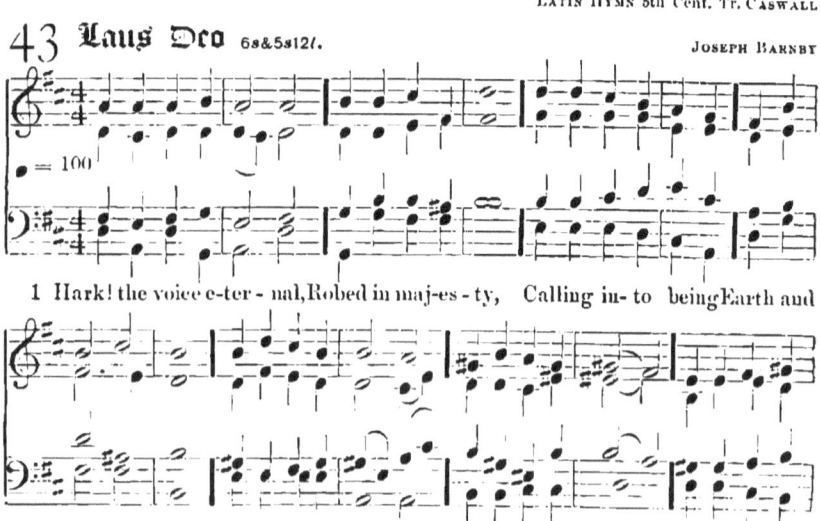

1 Hark! the voice e-ter-nal, Robed in maj-es-ty, Calling in-to being Earth and sea and sky; Hark! in countless numbers All the angel-throng Hail cre-a-tion's

## ADVENT AND BIRTH

morning With one burst of song. High in re-gal glo - ry, 'Mid eternal light,

A - MEN.

Reign, O King im-mor - tal, Ho - ly, in - fi - nite.

2 Bright the world and glorious,
  Calm both earth and sea,
Noble in its grandeur
  Stood man's purity;
Came the great transgression,
  Came the saddening fall,
Death and desolation
  Breathing over all.
    Still in regal glory,
    'Mid eternal light,
    Reigned the King immortal,
    Holy, infinite.

3 Long the nations waited,
  Through the troubled night,
Looking, longing, yearning
  For the promised light.
Prophets saw the morning
  Breaking far away,
Minstrels sang the splendor
  Of that opening day.
    Whilst in regal glory,
    'Mid eternal light,
    Reigned the King immortal,
    Holy, infinite.

4 Brightly dawned the Advent
  Of the new-born King,
Joyously the watchers
  Heard the angels sing.
Sadly closed the evening
  Of His hallowed life,

As the noontide darkness
  Veiled the last dread strife.
Lo! again in glory,
  'Mid eternal light,
Reigns the King immortal,
  Holy, infinite.

5 Lo! again He cometh,
  Robed in clouds of light,
As the Judge eternal,
  Armed with power and might.
Nations to His footstool
  Gathered then shall be;
Earth shall yield her treasures,
  And her dead, the sea.
    Till the trumpet soundeth,
    'Mid eternal light
    Reign, Thou King immortal,
    Holy, infinite.

6 Jesus! Lord and Master,
  Prophet, Priest and King,
To Thy feet triumphant
  Hallowed praise we bring.
Thine the pain and weeping,
  Thine the victory;
Power, and praise, and honor,
  Be, O Lord, to Thee.
    High in regal glory,
    'Mid eternal light,
    Reign, O King immortal,
    Holy, infinite. Amen.

J. JULIAN.

*JESUS CHRIST*

### 44 St. Saviour C.M.
F. G. BAKER

1 Hark, the glad sound, the Saviour comes, The Saviour promised long! Let

A - MEN.

ev - ery heart pre-pare a throne, And ev - ery voice a song.

2 He comes the prisoners to release
In Satan's bondage held;
The gates of brass before Him burst,
The iron fetters yield.

3 He comes from thickest films of vice
To clear the mental ray,
And on the eyes oppressed with night
To pour celestial day.

4 He comes the broken heart to bind,
The bleeding soul to cure:
And with the treasures of His grace
To enrich the humble poor.

5 Our glad Hosannas, Prince of Peace,
Thy welcome shall proclaim;
And heaven's eternal arches ring
With Thy belovéd Name. Amen.

PHILIP DODDRIDGE *ab.*

### 45 Nativity C.M.
HENRY LAHEE

1 Joy to the world! the Lord is come; Let earth re - ceive her King;

## ADVENT AND BIRTH

Let ev-'ry heart pre-pare Him room, And heav'n and nature sing.

2 Joy to the earth! the Saviour reigns;
  Let men their songs employ;
While fields and floods, rocks, hills, and
  Repeat the sounding joy.  [plains

3 No more let sins and sorrows grow,
  Nor thorns infest the ground;
He comes to make His blessings flow
  Far as the curse is found.

4 He rules the world with truth and grace,
  And makes the nations prove
The glories of His righteousness,
  And wonders of His love.  Amen.

ISAAC WATTS

**Antioch** C.M.  SECOND TUNE  From HANDEL, arr. by LOWELL MASON

♩ = 76

## JESUS CHRIST

**46 Arthur's Seat** 6.6.6.6.8.8.  *Arr. from* JOHN GOSS

1 Hark, hark, the notes of joy Roll o'er the heaven-ly plains, And

seraphs find em - ploy For their sublim-est strains; Some new delight in

heav'n is known; Loud ring the harps a - round the throne. A - MEN.

2 Hark, hark, the sounds draw nigh,
　The joyful hosts descend;
Jesus forsakes the sky,
　To earth His footsteps bend;
He comes to bless our fallen race,
He comes with messages of grace.

3 Bear, bear the tidings round,
　Let every mortal know
What love in God is found,
　What pity He can show;
Ye winds that blow, ye waves that roll,
Bear the glad news from pole to pole.

4 Strike, strike the harps again,
　To great Immanuel's name;
Arise, ye sons of men,
　And all His grace proclaim:
Angels and men, wake every string,
'Tis God the Saviour's praise we sing. Amen.

ANDREW REED

*ADVENT AND BIRTH*

## 47 St. George's Chapel 7sD.

G. J. ELVEY

1 He has come! the Christ of God, Left for us His glad a-bode;
Stooping from His throne of bliss, To this dark-some wil-der-ness:
He has come! the Prince of Peace; Come to bid our sor-rows cease,
Come to scat-ter with His light All the shadows of our night.

2 He the Mighty King has come!
Making this poor earth His home;
Come to bear our sin's sad load;
Son of David, Son of God.
He has come, whose name of grace
Speaks deliverance to our race,
Left for us His glad abode;
Son of Mary, Son of God

3 Unto us a Child is born!
Ne'er has earth beheld a morn
Among all the morns of time,
Half so glorious in its prime.
Unto us a Son is given!
He has come from God's own heaven,
Bringing with Him from above
Holy peace and holy love. Amen.

HORATIUS BONAR

## JESUS CHRIST

### 48 Mendelssohn 7s 10l.
From MENDELSSOHN

1 Hark! the herald angels sing Glory to the new-born King; Peace on earth, and mercy mild, God and sinners reconciled! Joyful, all ye nations, rise, Join the triumph of the skies; With th'angelic host proclaim Christ is born in Bethlehem! Hark! the herald angels sing Glory to the new-born King.

2 Christ, by highest heaven adored;
Christ, the Everlasting Lord.
Late in time behold Him come,
Offspring of the Virgin's womb:
Veiled in flesh the Godhead see;
Hail the Incarnate Deity,
Pleased as man with men to dwell,
Jesus, our Emmanuel.
  Hark! the herald angels sing
  Glory to the new-born King.

3 Hail, the heavenly Prince of Peace!
Hail, the Sun of righteousness!
Light and life to all He brings,
Risen with healing in His wings.
Mild He lays His glory by,
Born that man no more may die,
Born to raise the sons of earth,
Born to give them second birth.
  Hark! the herald angels sing
  Glory to the new-born King. Amen.

CHARLES WESLEY

## ADVENT AND BIRTH

### 49 Carol C.M.D.     R. S. WILLIS

1. It came up-on the midnight clear, That glo-rious song of old, From an-gels bend-ing near the earth, To touch their harps of gold: "Peace on the earth, good-will to men From heaven's all-gra-cious King." The world in sol - emn stillness lay To hear the an - gels sing.

A - MEN.

2 Still through the cloven skies they come
   With peaceful wings unfurled;
And still their heavenly music floats
   O'er all the weary world:
Above its sad and lowly plains
   They bend on hovering wing,
And ever o'er its Babel sounds
   The blessèd angels sing.

3 Yet with the woes of sin and strife
   The world has suffered long;
Beneath the angel-strain have rolled
   Two thousand years of wrong;
And man, at war with man, hears not
   The love-song which they bring:
Oh, hush the noise, ye men of strife,
   And hear the angels sing.

4 And ye, beneath life's crushing load,
   Whose forms are bending low,
Who toil along the climbing way
   With painful steps and slow,—
Look now; for glad and golden hours
   Come swiftly on the wing;
Oh, rest beside the weary road,
   And hear the angels sing.

5 For lo, the days are hastening on
   By prophet bards foretold,
When with the ever-circling years
   Comes round the age of gold:
When Peace shall over all the earth
   Its ancient splendors fling,
And the whole world give back the song
   Which now the angels sing.    Amen.
                                                E. H. Sears.

## JESUS CHRIST

### 50 Gould C.M.
J. E. GOULD

1 Calm, on the list'ning ear of night, Come heaven's melodious strains,

A - MEN.

Where wild Ju-dea stretches far Her sil - ver - man - tled plains.

2 Celestial choirs, from courts above,
Shed sacred glories there;
And angels, with their sparkling lyres,
Make music on the air.

3 The answering hills of Palestine
Send back their glad reply;
And greet from all their holy heights,
The dayspring from on high.

4 O'er the blue depths of Galilee
There comes a holier calm;
And Sharon waves, in solemn praise,
Her silent groves of palm.

5 "Glory to God!" the sounding skies
Loud with their anthems ring;
"Peace to the earth—good-will to men,
From heaven's eternal King." Amen.

E. H. SEARS ab.

### 51 Nativity New 8.6.6.8.6.6.
F. C. MAKER

1 All my heart this night rejoices, As I hear, far and near, Sweetest angel voices:

"Christ is born," their choirs are singing
Till the air everywhere, Now with joy is ringing.

2 Hark! a voice from yonder manger,
  Soft and sweet, doth entreat,
" Flee from woe and danger;
  Brethren, come: from all that grieves you
  You are freed; all you need
I will surely give you."

3 Come, then, let us hasten yonder;
  Here let all, great and small,
Kneel in awe and wonder;
  Love Him who with love is yearning;
  Hail the star that from far
Bright with hope is burning. Amen.
          PAUL GERHARDT Tr. WINKWORTH *ab*.

## 52 Wareham L.M.
WILLIAM KNAPP

1 All praise to Thee, e-ter-nal Lord, Who wore the garb of flesh and blood:

And chose a manger for Thy throne, While worlds on worlds were Thine alone.

2 Once did the skies before Thee bow;
A virgin's arms contain Thee now:
While angels who in Thee rejoice
Now listen for Thine infant voice.

3 A little child Thou art our guest,
That weary ones in Thee may rest;
Forlorn and lowly is Thy birth,
That we may rise to heaven from earth.

4 Thou comest in the darksome night
To make us children of the light,
To make us, in the realms divine,
Like Thine own angels round Thee shine.

5 All this for us Thy love hath done;
By this to Thee our love is won:
For this we tune our cheerful lays,
And shout our thanks in ceaseless praise.
                Amen.
    MARTIN LUTHER

## JESUS CHRIST

**53  Manger** Irregular — CARL REINECKE

♩ = 92

*1 Thou didst leave Thy throne and Thy kingly crown
When Thou camest to earth for me;

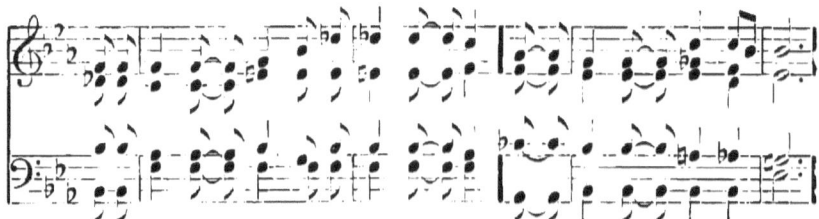

But in Bethlehem's home was there found no room For Thy ho-ly na-tiv-i-ty.

A-MEN.

O come to my heart, Lord Jesus; O come, There is room in my heart for Thee.

2 Heaven's arches rang when the angels sang,
Proclaiming Thy royal degree;
But in lowly birth Thou didst come to earth,
And in great humility:
O come, etc.

3 The foxes found rest, and the birds their nest
In the shade of the forest tree;
But Thy couch was the sod, O Thou Son of God,
In the deserts of Galilee.
O come, etc.

4 Thou camest, O Lord, with the living word
That should set Thy people free;
But with mocking scorn, and with crown of thorn,
They bore Thee to Calvary.
O come, etc.

5 When heaven's arches shall ring and her choir shall sing
At Thy coming to victory,
Let Thy voice call me home, saying,
"Yet there is room,
There is room at My side for thee:"
O come, etc.    Amen.

\* *The ties are to be noticed only in singing the syllables correspondingly marked.*   EMILY E. S. ELLIOTT

## 54 Irby 8.7.8.7.7.7.
H. J. GAUNTLETT

1 Once in roy-al Da-vid's cit-y Stood a low-ly cat-tle-shed,
Where a moth-er laid her Ba-by In a man-ger for His bed;
Ma-ry was that mother mild, Je-sus Christ her lit-tle Child.

A-MEN.

2 He came down to earth from heaven,
  Who is God and Lord of all,
And His shelter was a stable,
  And His cradle was a stall:
With the poor, and mean, and lowly,
Lived on earth our Saviour Holy.

3 And, thro' all His wondrous Childhood,
  He would honor, and obey,
Love, and watch the lowly maiden
  In whose gentle arms He lay;
Christian children all must be
Mild, obedient, good as He.

4 For He is our childhood's Pattern,
  Day by day like us He grew,
He was little, weak and helpless,
  Tears and smiles like us He knew:
And He feeleth for our sadness,
And He shareth in our gladness.

5 And our eyes at last shall see Him,
  Through His own redeeming love,
For that Child so dear and gentle
  Is our Lord in Heaven above:
And He leads His children on
To the place where He is gone.

6 Not in that poor lowly stable,
  With the oxen standing by,
We shall see Him; but in Heaven,
  Set at God's Right Hand on high;
When like stars His children crowned
All in white shall wait around. Amen.

MRS. C. F. ALEXANDER.

*ADVENT AND BIRTH*

### 56 St. Matthew C.M.D.
WILLIAM CROFT

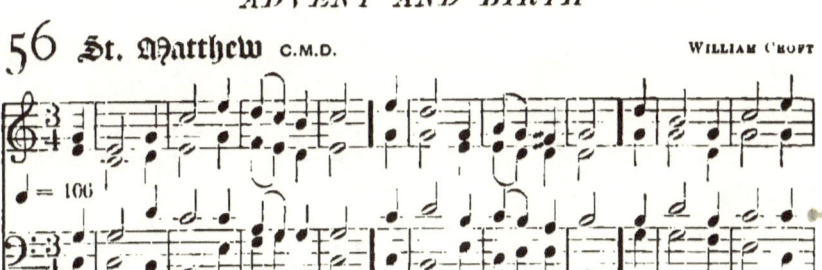

1 O lit-tle town of Bethlehem! How still we see thee lie; Above thy deep and

dreamless sleep The si-lent stars go by; Yet in thy dark streets shineth The

everlasting Light; The hopes and fears of all the years Are met in thee to-night.

2 For Christ is born of Mary,
  And gathered all above,
While mortals sleep, the angels keep
  Their watch of wondering love.
O morning stars, together
  Proclaim the holy birth!
And praises sing to God the King,
  And peace to men on earth.

3 How silently, how silently,
  The wondrous gift is given!
So God imparts to human hearts
  The blessings of His heaven.
No ear may hear His coming,
  But in this world of sin,
Where meek souls will receive Him still,
  The dear Christ enters in.

4 O holy Child of Bethlehem!
  Descend to us, we pray;
Cast out our sin, and enter in,
  Be born in us to-day.
We hear the Christmas angels
  The great glad tidings tell;
O come to us, abide with us,
  Our Lord Emmanuel! Amen.

PHILLIPS BROOKS

## JESUS CHRIST

**57 Alma Lux** 6s&5sD. with Chorus     FRANCES R. HAVERGAL.

1 From the eastern mountains Pressing on they come,
   Wise men in their wisdom To His humble home;

Stirr'd by deep devotion, Hasting from afar, Ever journeying onward,
   Guided by a star.

A · MEN.

Light of Life that shineth Ere the worlds began,
   Draw Thou near, and lighten Every heart of man.

2 There their Lord and Saviour
   Meek and lowly lay,
Wondrous light that led them
   Onward on their way,
Ever now to lighten
   Nations from afar,
As they journey homeward
   By that guiding star.
      Light of Life, etc.

3 Thou who in a manger
   Once hast lowly lain,
Who dost now in glory
   O'er all kingdoms reign,
Gather in the heathen,
   Who in lands afar
Ne'er have seen the brightness
   Of Thy guiding star.
      Light of Life, etc.

## ADVENT AND BIRTH

4 Onward through the darkness
  Of the lonely night,
Shining still before them,
  With Thy kindly light,
Guide them, Jew and Gentile,
  Homeward from afar,
Young and old together,
  By Thy guiding star.
    Light of Life, etc.

5 Until every nation,
  Whether bond or free,
'Neath Thy starlit banner,
  Jesus, follows Thee
O'er the distant mountains
  To that heavenly home,
Where nor sin nor sorrow
  Evermore shall come.
    Light of Life, etc.   Amen.

GODFREY THRING

## 58 Dir 7s 6l.

CONRAD KOCHER

♩= 96

1 As with gladness men of old, Did the guiding star behold; As with joy they hailed its [light,

A - MEN.

Leading onward, beaming bright;
          So, most gracious Lord, may we Evermore be led to Thee.

2 As with joyful steps they sped
  To that lowly manger-bed,
There to bend the knee before
Him whom heaven and earth adore,
  So may we with willing feet,
  Ever seek the mercy-seat.

3 As they offered gifts most rare,
  At that manger rude and bare,
  So may we with holy joy,
  Pure and free from sin's alloy,
All our costliest treasures bring,
Christ, to Thee our heavenly King.

4 Holy Jesus! every day
  Keep us in the narrow way;
And, when earthly things are past,
Bring our ransomed souls at last
  Where they need no star to guide,
  Where no clouds Thy glory hide.

5 In the heavenly country bright,
  Need they no created light;
Thou its Light, its Joy, its Crown,
Thou its Sun which goes not down;
  There forever may we sing
  Alleluias to our King.   Amen.

W. C. DIX

## JESUS CHRIST

### 59 Oblations  11s & 10s
WILLIAM SPARK

1 Bright-est and best of the sons of the morn-ing, Dawn on our

dark-ness and lend us Thine aid! Star of the East, the ho-ri-zon a-

A · MEN.

dorn-ing, Guide where our in-fant Re-deem-er is laid.

2 Cold on His cradle the dewdrops are shining,
　Low lies His head with the beasts of the stall;
Angels adore Him, in slumber reclining,
　Maker and Monarch and Saviour of all.

3 Say, shall we yield Him in costly devotion
　Odors of Edom and offerings divine;
Gems of the mountain and pearls of the ocean,
　Myrrh from the forest or gold from the mine?

4 Vainly we offer each ample oblation,
　Vainly with gifts would His favor secure;
Richer by far is the heart's adoration,
　Dearer to God are the prayers of the poor.

5 Brightest and best of the sons of the morning,
　Dawn on our darkness and lend us Thine aid:
Star of the East, the horizon adorning,
　Guide where our infant Redeemer is laid.   Amen.

REGINALD HEBER

## ADVENT AND BIRTH

**60 Regent Square** 8s & 7s 6l.     HENRY SMART

1 Angels, from the realms of glory, Wing your flight o'er all the earth;

Ye who sang creation's story, Now proclaim Messiah's birth!

Come and worship, Come and worship, Worship Christ, the new-born King.

2 Shepherds, in the field abiding,
  Watching o'er your flocks by night;
God with man is now residing,
  Yonder shines the infant-light:
    Come and worship,
Worship Christ, the new-born King.

3 Sages, leave your contemplations;
  Brighter visions beam afar:
Seek the great Desire of nations,
  Ye have seen His natal star:
    Come and worship,
Worship Christ, the new-born King.

4 Saints, before the altar bending,
  Watching long in hope and fear,
Suddenly the Lord, descending,
  In His temple shall appear:
    Come and worship,
Worship Christ, the new-born King.   Amen.

JAMES MONTGOMERY

*JESUS CHRIST*

## 61 Winchester New L.M.
BARTHOLOMÄUS CRASSELIUS

1 On Jordan's bank the Baptist's cry
Announces that the Lord is nigh;
Awake, and hearken, for He brings
Glad tidings of the King of kings.

2 Then cleansed be every breast from sin;
Make straight the way for God within;
Prepare we in our hearts a home,
Where such a mighty Guest may come.

3 For Thou art our salvation, Lord,
Our Refuge, and our great Reward;
Without Thy grace we waste away,
Like flowers that wither and decay.

4 To heal the sick stretch out Thine hand,
And bid the fallen sinner stand;
Shine forth, and let Thy light restore
Earth's own true loveliness once more.

5 All praise, Eternal Son, to Thee
Whose advent doth Thy people free,
Whom with the Father we adore
And Holy Ghost for evermore. Amen.

PARIS BREVIARY  Tr. CHANDLER

## 62 Grace Church L.M.
IGNACE PLEYEL

1 And didst Thou, Lord, our sorrows take? And didst Thou, Lord, our burdens bear?

## MINISTRY AND EXAMPLE

Didst Thou for love of us forsake Those glorious heights, that heavenly air?

2 Oh, could our weakness move Thy might?
Our mis'ry make us sought of Thee?
Our gloom allure Thy glory bright?
Our sins win down Thy purity?

3 We who so tenderly were sought,
Shall we not joyful seekers be,
And to Thy feet divinely brought,
Help weaker souls, dear Lord, to Thee?

4 Celestial Seeker, send us forth!
Almighty Lover, teach us love!
When shall we yearn to help our earth,
As yearned the Holy One above? Amen.

T. H. GILL

## 63 Armagh c.m.
JAMES TURLE

1 What grace, O Lord, and beau-ty shone A-round Thy steps be-low;

What patient love was seen in all Thy life and death of woe!

2 For, ever on Thy burden'd heart
A weight of sorrow hung;
Yet no ungentle, murmuring word
Escaped Thy silent tongue.

3 Thy foes might hate, despise, revile,
Thy friends unfaithful prove,
Unwearied in forgiveness still,
Thy heart could only love.

4 Oh, give us hearts to love like Thee,
Like Thee, O Lord, to grieve
Far more for others' sins, than all
The wrongs that we receive.

5 One with Thyself, may every eye,
In us, Thy brethren, see
The gentleness and grace that spring
From union, Lord, with Thee. Amen.

EDWARD DENNY

*JESUS CHRIST*

## 64 Hasliell L.M.
F. K. GLEZEN

1 How sweet-ly flowed the gospel sound From lips of gen-tle-ness and grace,

A-MEN.

When listening thousands gathered round, And joy and gladness filled the place!

2 From heaven He came, of heaven He spoke,
To heaven He led His followers' way;
Dark clouds of gloomy night He broke,
Unvailing an immortal day.

3 "Come, wanderers, to my Father's home;
Come, all ye weary ones, and rest;"
Yes, sacred Teacher, we will come,
Obey Thee, love Thee, and be blest.
Amen.
JOHN BOWRING *ab.*

## 65

1 How beauteous were the marks divine,
That in Thy meekness used to shine;
That lit Thy lonely pathway, trod
In wondrous love, O Son of God!

2 Oh, who like Thee, so calm, so bright,
So pure, so made to live in light?
Oh, who like Thee did ever go
So patient through a world of woe?

3 Oh, who like Thee so humbly bore
The scorn, the scoffs of men, before?
So meek, forgiving, godlike, high,
So glorious in humility?

4 E'en death, which sets the prisoner free,
Was pain, and scoff, and scorn to Thee;
Yet love thro' all Thy torture glowed,
And mercy with Thy life-blood flowed.

5 Oh, in Thy light be mine to go,
Illuming all my way of woe!
And give me ever on the road
To trace Thy footsteps, Son of God! Amen.
A. C. COXE

*MINISTRY AND EXAMPLE*

**66 Beatitude** C.M.  J. B. DYKES

1 O Son of Man, Thyself hast proved Our trials and our tears; Life's thankless toil, and scant re-pose; Death's ag-o-nies and fears.

2 In all things like Thy brethren Thou
  Wast made, yet free from sin;
  But how unlike to us, O Lord!—
  Replies the voice within.

3 O Son of God, in glory raised,
  Thou sittest on Thy throne:
  Thence, by Thy pleadings and Thy grace,
  Still succoring Thine own.

4 Brother and Saviour, Friend and Judge,
  To Thee, O Christ, be given
  To bind upon Thy crown, the names
  Elect in earth and heaven. Amen.
                                    JOSEPH ANSTICE

**67**

1 Oh, mean may seem this house of clay,
  Yet 'twas the Lord's abode;
  Our feet may mourn this thorny way,
  Yet here Immanuel trod.

2 This fleshly robe the Lord did wear;
  This watch the Lord did keep;
  These burdens sore the Lord did bear;
  These tears the Lord did weep.

3 O vale of tears no longer sad,
  Wherein the Lord did dwell!
  O happy robe of flesh that clad
  Our own Immanuel!

4 But not this fleshly robe alone
  Shall link us, Lord, to Thee;
  Not only in the tear and groan
  Shall the dear kindred be.

5 We shall be reckoned for Thine own,
  Because Thy heaven we share,
  Because we sing around Thy throne,
  And Thy bright raiment wear.

6 O mighty grace, our life to live,
  To make our earth divine!
  O mighty grace, Thy heaven to give
  And lift our life to Thine! Amen.
                                    T. H. GILL

*JESUS CHRIST*

### 68 Filius Dei C.M.D.
A. R. GAUL

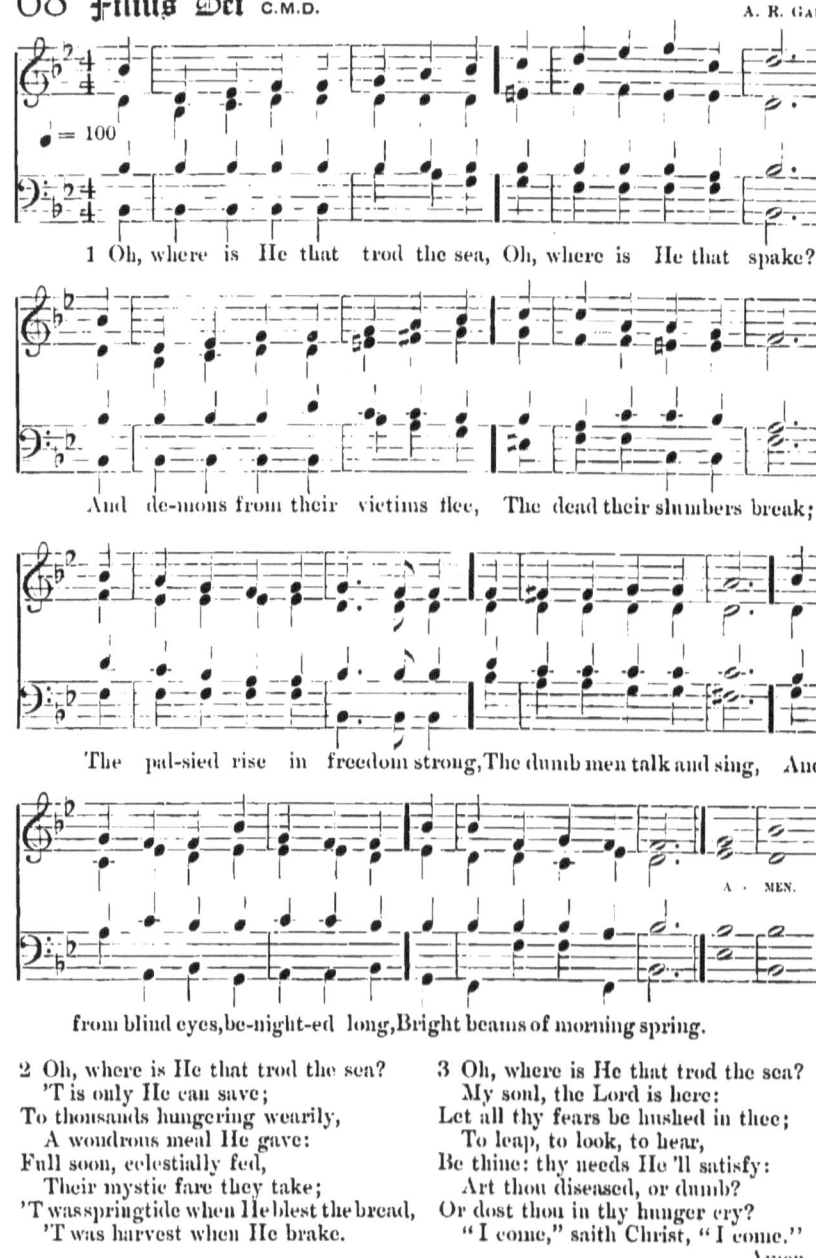

♩ = 100

1 Oh, where is He that trod the sea, Oh, where is He that spake?
And de-mons from their victims flee, The dead their slumbers break;
The pal-sied rise in freedom strong, The dumb men talk and sing, And
from blind eyes, be-night-ed long, Bright beams of morning spring.
A - MEN.

2 Oh, where is He that trod the sea?
   'Tis only He can save;
To thousands hungering wearily,
   A wondrous meal He gave:
Full soon, celestially fed,
   Their mystic fare they take;
'Twas springtide when He blest the bread,
   'Twas harvest when He brake.

3 Oh, where is He that trod the sea?
   My soul, the Lord is here:
Let all thy fears be hushed in thee;
   To leap, to look, to hear,
Be thine: thy needs He'll satisfy:
   Art thou diseased, or dumb?
Or dost thou in thy hunger cry?
   "I come," saith Christ, "I come."
              Amen.
T. T. LYNCH *ab*

## MINISTRY AND EXAMPLE

**69 Euroclydon** 6s & 4s D.  E. K. Glezen

1 Fierce was the wild bil-low, Dark was the night, Oars labored heav-i-ly,

Foam glimmered white, Trembled the mar-i-ners, Per-il was nigh;
Then said the God of God, "Peace! it is I!"  A-MEN.

2 Ridge of the mountain-wave,
   Lower thy crest!
Wail of Euroclydon,
   Be thou at rest!
Sorrow can never be,
   Darkness must fly,
Where saith the Light of Light,
   "Peace! It is I!"

3 Jesus, Deliverer,
   Come Thou to me:
Soothe Thou my voyaging
   Over life's sea;
Thou, when the storm of death
   Roars, sweeping by,
Whisper, Thou Truth of Truth,
   "Peace! It is I!" Amen.

ANATOLIUS Tr. NEALE

## JESUS CHRIST

**70** Deliverance C.M.D.   JOSEPH BARNBY

1 Thine arm, O Lord, in days of old Was strong to heal and save;

It triumphed o'er dis-ease and death, O'er dark-ness and the grave:

To Thee they went, the blind, the dumb, The palsied and the lame, The

lep-er with his taint-ed life, The sick with fevered frame.

2 And lo, Thy touch brought life and health,
Gave speech, and strength, and sight;
And youth renewed and frenzy calmed
Owned Thee, the Lord of Light:
And now, O Lord, be near to bless,
Almighty as of yore,
In crowded street, by restless couch,
As by Gennesareth's shore.

3 Be Thou our great Deliverer still,
Thou Lord of Life and Death;
Restore and quicken, soothe and bless
With Thine almighty breath.
To hands that work and eyes that see,
Give wisdom's heavenly lore,
That whole and sick, and weak and strong,
May praise Thee evermore. Amen.

E. H. PLUMPTRE *ab.*

## MINISTRY AND EXAMPLE

**71 Rosslyn** Irregular — C. R. CUFF

1 I think, when I read that sweet story of old, When Jesus was here among men, How He

called little children as lambs to His fold, I should like to have been with them then;

2 I wish that His hands had been placed on my head,
  That His arm had been thrown around me,
And that I might have seen His kind look when He said,
  "Let the little ones come unto Me."

3 Yet still to His footstool in prayer I may go,
  And ask for a share in His love;
And if I now earnestly seek Him below,
  I shall see Him and hear Him above:

4 In that beautiful place He has gone to prepare
  For all that are washed and forgiven,
And many dear children are gathering there,
  "For of such is the kingdom of heaven."

5 But thousands and thousands who wander and fall,
  Never heard of that heavenly home;
I should like them to know there is room for them all,
  And that Jesus has bid them to come.

6 I long for the joy of that glorious time,
  The sweetest, and brightest, and best,
When the dear little children of every clime
  Shall crowd to His arms and be blest.   Amen.

Mrs. JEMIMA LUKE

## JESUS CHRIST

**72 Faith** C.M.      J. B. DYKES

1 Im-mor-tal Love, for ev-er full, For ev-er flow-ing free, For ev-er shared, for ev-er whole, A nev-er-eb-bing sea!

2 Blow, winds of God, awake and blow
The mists of earth away!
Shine out, O Light Divine, and show
How wide and far we stray!

3 We may not climb the heavenly steeps
To bring the Lord Christ down:
In vain we search the lowest deeps,
For Him no depths can drown.

4 But warm, sweet, tender, even yet
A present help is He;
And faith has still its Olivet,
And love its Galilee.

5 The healing of His seamless dress
Is by our beds of pain;
We touch Him in life's throng and press,
And we are whole again.

6 Thro' Him the first fond prayers are said
Our lips of childhood frame,
The last low whispers of our dead
Are burdened with His name.

7 O Lord and Master of us all!
Whate'er our name or sign,
We own Thy sway, we hear Thy call,
We test our lives by Thine. Amen.

J. G. WHITTIER

**Serenity** C.M.     SECOND TUNE     Arr. from W. V. WALLACE

## MINISTRY AND EXAMPLE

**73 Galilee** 8s & 7s    ALBERT LOWE

1 Je-sus calls us; o'er the tu-mult Of our life's wild rest-less sea

Day by day His sweet voice soundeth, Saying, "Christian, follow Me;"

2 As of old, Saint Andrew heard it
　By the Galilean lake,
Turned from home, and toil, and kindred,
　Leaving all for His dear sake.

3 Jesus calls us from the worship
　Of the vain world's golden store,
From each idol that would keep us,
　Saying, "Christian, love Me more."

4 In our joys and in our sorrows,
　Days of toil and hours of ease,
Still He calls, in cares and pleasures,
　That we love Him more than these.

5 Jesus calls us; by Thy mercies,
　Saviour, make us hear Thy call,
Give our hearts to Thine obedience,
　Serve and love Thee best of all.
　　　　　　　　Amen.

Mrs. C. F. ALEXANDER

**Dorrnance** 8s & 7s    SECOND TUNE    I. B. WOODBURY

## JESUS CHRIST

### 74 Marshall S.M.
G. J. Geer

♩ = 104

1 Thou say'st, 'Take up thy cross, O man, and fol-low Me';
The night is black, the feet are slack, Yet we would fol-low Thee.

2 But, O dear Lord, we cry,
That we Thy face could see!
Thy blessèd face one moment's space—
Then might we follow Thee!

3 Dim tracts of time divide
Those golden days from me;
Thy voice comes strange o'er years of change;
How can we follow Thee?

4 Comes faint and far Thy voice
From vales of Galilee;
Thy vision fades in ancient shades;
How should we follow Thee?

5 O heavy cross — of faith
In what we cannot see!
As once of yore Thyself restore
And help to follow Thee!

6 If not as once Thou cam'st
In true humanity,
Come yet as guest within the breast
That burns to follow Thee.

7 Within our heart of hearts
In nearest nearness be:
Set up Thy throne within Thine own:—
Go, Lord: we follow Thee. Amen.

F. T. Palgrave *ab.*

### 75 Hamburg L.M.
Arr. by Lowell Mason

♩ = 100

1 My dear Redeemer, and my Lord, I read my du-ty in Thy word;

## MINISTRY AND EXAMPLE

But in Thy life the law ap-pears, Drawn out in living charac - ters.

2 Such was Thy truth, and such Thy zeal,
Such deference to Thy Father's will,
Such love, and meekness so divine,
I would transcribe and make them mine.

3 Cold mountains and the midnight air
Witnessed the fervor of Thy prayer;
The desert Thy temptation knew,
Thy conflict and Thy victory too.

4 Be Thou my pattern; make me bear
More of Thy gracious image here;
Then God, the Judge, shall own my name
Among the followers of the Lamb. Amen.

ISAAC WATTS

## 76 Angelus L.M.

J. G. W. SCHEFFLER

1 O Master, let me walk with Thee In lowly paths of service free;

Tell me Thy secret; help me bear The strain of toil, the fret of care.

2 Help me the slow of heart to move
By some clear winning word of love;
Teach me the wayward feet to stay,
And guide them in the homeward way.

3 Teach me Thy patience; still with Thee
In closer, dearer company;
In work that keeps faith sweet and strong,
In trust that triumphs over wrong,

4 In hope that sends a shining ray
Far down the future's broadening way;
In peace that only Thou canst give,
With Thee, O Master, let me live! Amen.

WASHINGTON GLADDEN

## JESUS CHRIST

### 77 Trust. 8s & 7s
From MENDELSSOHN

1 Lord, I know Thy grace is nigh me, Though Thyself I can-not see;
Je-sus, Master, pass not by me; Son of Da-vid, pit-y me.

A - MEN.

2 While I sit in weary blindness,
Longing for the blessèd light,
Many taste Thy loving-kindness;
"Lord, I would receive my sight."

3 I would see Thee and adore Thee,
And Thy word the power can give;
Hear the sightless soul implore Thee:
Let me see Thy face and live.

4 Ah, what touch is this that thrills me?
What this burst of strange delight?
Lo, the rapturous vision fills me!
This is Jesus! this is sight!

5 Room, ye saints that throng behind Him!
Let me follow in the way;
I will teach the blind to find Him
Who can turn their night to day. Amen.

H. D. GANSE

### 78 St. Mark. C.M.
H. J. GAUNTLETT

1 The Saviour!—what a no-ble flame Was kindled in His breast, When,

## MINISTRY AND EXAMPLE

hast-ing to Je-ru-sa-lem, He march'd before the rest!

2 With all His sufferings full in view,
And woes to us unknown,
Forth to the task His spirit flew:
'Twas love that urged Him on.

3 Lord, we return Thee what we can;
Our hearts shall sound abroad
Salvation to the dying Man,
And to the rising God!

4 And while Thy bleeding glories here
Engage our wondering eyes,
We learn our lighter cross to bear,
And hasten to the skies. Amen.

WILLIAM COWPER

### 79 St. Drostane L.M.
J. B. DYKES

♩ = 104

1 Ride on! ride on in maj-es-ty! In low-ly pomp ride on to die: O

Christ, Thy triumphs now begin O'er captive death and conquered sin.

2 Ride on! ride on in majesty!
The wingèd squadrons of the sky
Look down with sad and wondering eyes
To see the approaching sacrifice.

3 Ride on! ride on in majesty!
The last and fiercest strife is nigh:
The Father on His sapphire throne
Expects His own anointed Son.

4 Ride on! ride on in majesty!
In lowly pomp ride on to die;
Bow thy meek head to mortal pain;
Then take, O God, Thy power, and reign. Amen.

H. H. MILMAN ab.

## 80 St. Anselm 7s & 6s D.
JOSEPH BARNBY

1 O how shall I re-ceive Thee, How meet Thee on Thy way; Blest hope of ev-'ry na-tion, My soul's de-light and stay? O Je-sus, Je-sus, give me Now by Thine own pure light, To know whate'er is pleas-ing And wel-come in Thy sight.

2 Thy Zion palms is strewing,
 With branches fresh and fair;
My soul, in praise awaking,
 Her anthem shall prepare.
Perpetual thanks and praises
 Forth from my heart shall spring;
And to Thy Name the service
 Of all my powers I bring.

3 Ye who with guilty terror
 Are trembling, fear no more:
With love and grace the Saviour
 Shall you to hope restore.
He comes, who contrite sinners
 Will with the children place,
The children of His Father,
 The heirs of life and grace. Amen.

PAUL GERHARDT Tr. RUSSELL ab

## MINISTRY AND EXAMPLE

### 81 Hosanna  L.M. with Chorus
J. B. DYKES

1 Ho-san-na to the liv-ing Lord! Ho-san-na to th' In-car-nate Word,

To Christ, Cre-a-tor, Saviour, King, Let earth, let heav'n, Ho-san-na sing!

Ho-san-na! Lord! Ho-san-na in the high - est! A MEN.

2 Hosanna, Lord! Thine angels cry;
Hosanna, Lord! Thy saints reply;
Above, beneath us, and around,
The dead and living swell the sound;
   Hosanna! Lord! Hosanna in the highest!

3 O Saviour! with protecting care,
Return to this Thy house of prayer!
Assembled in Thy sacred name,
Where we Thy parting promise claim!
   Hosanna! Lord! Hosanna in the highest!

4 But, chiefest, in our cleansèd breast,
Eternal! bid Thy Spirit rest,
And make our secret soul to be
A temple pure, and worthy Thee!
   Hosanna! Lord! Hosanna in the highest!

5 So, in the last and dreadful day,
When earth and heaven shall melt away,
Thy flock, redeem'd from sinful stain,
Shall swell the sound of praise again:
   Hosanna! Lord! Hosanna in the highest!
                Amen.

REGINALD HEBER.

## JESUS CHRIST

**82 Tours** 7s & 6s D.  
BERTHOLD TOURS

♩ = 126

1 When, His sal-va-tion bring-ing, To Zi-on Je-sus came,
The child-ren all stood sing-ing, Ho-san-na to His name;
Nor did their zeal of-fend Him, But, as He rode a-long, He
let them still at-tend Him, Well pleased to hear their song. A-MEN.

2 And since the Lord retaineth
His love for children still,
Though now as King He reigneth
On Zion's heavenly hill,
We'll flock around His banner,
Who sits upon the throne,
And raise a loud hosanna,
To David's royal Son.

3 For should we fail proclaiming
Our great Redeemer's praise,
The stones, our silence shaming,
Would their hosanna raise.
But should we only render
The tribute of our words?
No; while our hearts are tender,
They, too, should be the Lord's. Amen.

JOHN KING

## MINISTRY AND EXAMPLE

**83 St. Theodulph** 7s & 6s D. — MELCHIOR TESCHNER

1 All glory, laud, and honor
To Thee, Redeemer, King!
To whom the lips of children
Made sweet hosannas ring.
Thou art the King of Israel,
Thou David's royal Son,
Who in the Lord's name comest,
The King and blessèd One.

2 The company of angels
 Are praising Thee on high,
And mortal men, and all things
 Created make reply.
The people of the Hebrews
 With palms before Thee went,
Our praise and prayer and anthems
 Before Thee we present.

3 To Thee before Thy passion
 They sang their hymns of praise;
To Thee now high exalted
 Our melody we raise.
Thou didst accept their praises;
 Accept the prayers we bring,
Who in all good delightest,
 Thou good and gracious King. Amen.

ST. THEODULPH Tr. NEALE ab. alt.

## JESUS CHRIST

### 84 Babylon's Streams L.M.
SCOTCH PSALTER

1 'Tis midnight,—and on Olive's brow, The star is dimm'd that lately shone;
'Tis midnight,—in the garden now The suffering Saviour prays alone.

2 'Tis midnight,—and, from all removed,
Immanuel wrestles, lone with fears;
E'en the disciple that He loved
Heeds not his Master's grief and tears.

3 'Tis midnight,—and for others' guilt
The Man of sorrows weeps in blood;
Yet He, who hath in anguish knelt,
Is not forsaken by His God.

4 'Tis midnight,— and, from ether-plains,
Is borne the song that angels know;
Unheard by mortals are the strains
That sweetly soothe the Saviour's woe. Amen.

W. B. TAPPAN

### Olive's Brow L.M. SECOND TUNE
W. B. BRADBURY

## PASSION AND CRUCIFIXION

### 85 St. Cross L.M.
J. B. DYKES

1 Oh, come and mourn with me a-while; Oh, come ye to the Sav-iour's side;

Oh, come, to-geth-er let us mourn; Je-sus, our Love, is cru-ci-fied.

A-MEN.

2 Have we no tears to shed for Him,
While soldiers scoff and Jews deride?
Ah! look how patiently He hangs;
Jesus, our Love, is crucified.

3 Seven times He spake, seven words of love;
And all three hours His silence cried

For mercy on the souls of men;
Jesus, our Love, is crucified.

4 O Love of God; O Son of Man!
In this dread act your strength is tried;
And victory remains with love;
For He, our Love, is crucified. Amen.

F. W. FABER *ab.*

### 86 Federal Street L.M.
H. K. OLIVER

1 O the sweet wonders of that cross Where my Redeem-er loved and died:
2 I would for-ev-er speak His name In sounds to mor-tal ears unknown;

A-MEN.

Her noblest life my spir-it draws From His dear wounds and bleeding side.
With angels join to praise the Lamb, And worship at His Father's throne. Amen.

ISAAC WATTS *ab.*

## JESUS CHRIST

**87 St. Denys** 8s&7s6l.  W. H. MONK

1 Now, my soul, thy voice up-rais-ing, Tell in sweet and mourn-ful strain,

How the Cru-ci-fied, en-dur-ing Grief and wounds and dy - ing pain,

A - MEN.

Freely of His love was offered, Sin-less, was for sin-ners slain.

2 See! His hands and feet are fastened:
So He makes His people free!
Not a wound whence blood is flowing
But a fount of grace shall be:
Yea, the very nails which nail Him
Nail us, also, to the tree!

3 Thro' His heart the spear is piercing,
Though His foes have seen Him die;
Blood and water thence are streaming
In a tide of mystery;
Water from our guilt to cleanse us,
Blood to win us crowns on high.

4 Jesus, may those precious fountains
Life to thirsting souls afford:
Let them be our present healing,
And at length our great reward:
So a ransomed world shall ever
Praise Thee, its redeeming Lord.   Amen.

SANTOLIUS MAGLORIANUS

## PASSION AND CRUCIFIXION

**88  Passion Chorale** 7s&6sD.   H. L. HASLER

1 O sacred Head, now wounded, With grief and shame weighed down, Now scornfully sur-

rounded With thorns, Thine only crown; O sacred Head, what glo-ry, What

bliss, till now was Thine! Yet, though despised and gory, I joy to call Thee mine.

2 What Thou, my Lord, hast suffered,
  Was all for sinner's gain:
Mine, mine was the transgression,
  But Thine the deadly pain:
Lo, here I fall, my Saviour!
  'T is I deserve Thy place;
Look on me with Thy favor,
  Vouchsafe to me Thy grace.

3 The joy can ne'er be spoken,
  Above all joys beside,
When in Thy body broken
  I thus with safety hide:
My Lord of life, desiring
  Thy glory now to see,
Beside Thy cross expiring,
  I'd breathe my soul to Thee.

4 What language shall I borrow
  To thank Thee, dearest Friend?
For this, Thy dying sorrow,
  Thy pity without end?
Oh, make me Thine forever;
  And should I fainting be,
Lord, let me never, never,
  Outlive my love to Thee!

5 Be near when I am dying,
  Oh, show Thy cross to me!
And for my succor flying,
  Come, Lord, to set me free!
These eyes, new faith receiving,
  From Jesus shall not move:
For he who dies believing,
  Dies safely through Thy love. Amen.

ST. BERNARD  Tr. ALEXANDER

## JESUS CHRIST

**89 Frederika** C.M.D.  E. K. GLEZEN

1 There is a green hill far a-way Without a cit-y wall,
Where the dear Lord was cru-ci-fied, Who died to save us all.

2 We may not know, we can-not tell, What pains He had to bear,
But we be-lieve it was for us He hung and suffered there.

A - MEN.

3 He died that we might be forgiven,
He died to make us good,
That we might go at last to heaven,
Saved by His precious blood.

4 There was no other good enough
To pay the price of sin,
He only could unlock the gate
Of heaven, and let us in.

\* 5 Oh, dearly, dearly has He loved,
And we must love Him too,
And trust in His redeeming blood,
And try His works to do. Amen.

Mrs. C. F. ALEXANDER

## PASSION AND CRUCIFIXION

**90 Sychar** 8s&7s — J. B. Dykes

1 In the cross of Christ I glo-ry, Towering o'er the wrecks of time;
All the light of sacred sto-ry Gathers round its head sublime.

2 When the woes of life o'ertake me,
Hopes deceive and fears annoy,
Never shall the cross forsake me:
Lo! it glows with peace and joy.

3 When the sun of bliss is beaming
Light and love upon my way,
From the cross the radiance streaming,
Adds new lustre to the day.

4 Bane and blessing, pain and pleasure,
By the cross are sanctified;
Peace is there, that knows no measure,
Joys that through all time abide.

5 In the cross of Christ I glory,
Towering o'er the wrecks of time;
All the light of sacred story
Gathers round its head sublime. Amen.

JOHN BOWRING

**Rathbun** 8s&7s — SECOND TUNE — I. CONKEY

## JESUS CHRIST

### 91 Hendon 7s 5l.
C. H. A. Malan

1 Ask ye what great thing I know That delights and stirs me so? What the high reward I win? Whose the name I glory in? Jesus Christ, the Crucified.

2 What is faith's foundation strong?
What awakes my lips to song?
He who bore my sinful load,
Purchased for me peace with God,
Jesus Christ, the Crucified.

3 Who defeats my fiercest foes?
Who consoles my saddest woes?
Who revives my fainting heart,
Healing all its hidden smart?
Jesus Christ, the Crucified.

4 Who is Life in life to me?
Who the Death of death will be?
Who will place me on His right
With the countless hosts of light?
Jesus Christ, the Crucified.

5 This is that great thing I know;
This delights and stirs me so:
Faith in Him who died to save,
Him who triumphed o'er the grave,
Jesus Christ, the Crucified. Amen.

B. H. Kennedy

### 92 Rockingham (Eng.) L.M.
Edward Miller

1 When I survey the wondrous cross On which the Prince of Glo-ry died,

## PASSION AND CRUCIFIXION

My richest gain I count but loss, And pour contempt on all my pride.

2 Forbid it, Lord, that I should boast,
　Save in the death of Christ, my God:
All the vain things that charm me most,
　I sacrifice them to His blood.

3 See, from His head, His hands, His feet,
　Sorrow and love flow mingled down!

Did e'er such love and sorrow meet?
　Or thorns compose so rich a crown?

4 Were the whole realm of nature mine,
　That were a tribute far too small;
Love so amazing, so divine,
　Demands my soul, my life, my all.
　　　　　　　　　　　　Amen.

　　　　　　　　　　ISAAC WATTS ab.

## 93 Sicilian Mariner's Hymn 8s&7s

♩=126

1 Sweet the mo-ments, rich in bless-ing, Which be-fore the cross I spend,

Life, and health, and peace possessing, From the sinner's dying Friend.

2 Truly blessèd is this station,
　Low before His cross to lie,
While I see divine compassion,
　Beaming in His gracious eye.

3 Here it is I find my heaven
　While upon the Lamb I gaze:
Love I much? I've much forgiven;
　I'm a miracle of grace.

4 For Thy sorrows we adore Thee,
　For the pains that wrought our peace;

Gracious Saviour! we implore Thee
　In our souls Thy love increase.

5 Love and grief our hearts dividing,
　With our tears His feet we bathe;
Constant still, in faith abiding,
　Life deriving from His death.

6 Here in tender, grateful sorrow
　With my Saviour will I stay;
Here new hope and strength will borrow;
　Here will love my fears away. Amen.

　　　　　　JAMES ALLEN alt. W. SHIRLEY

## JESUS CHRIST

### 94. St. Agnes C.M.
*J. B. Dykes*

1 There is a foun-tain fill'd with blood, Drawn from Im-man-uel's veins;

And sinners, plunged beneath that flood, Lose all their guilty stains.

2 The dying thief rejoiced to see
That fountain in his day;
And there have I, as vile as he,
Washed all my sins away.

3 Dear, dying Lamb! Thy precious blood
Shall never lose its power,
Till all the ransomed church of God
Be saved, to sin no more.

4 E'er since, by faith, I saw the stream
Thy flowing wounds supply,
Redeeming love has been my theme,
And shall be till I die.

5 Then, in a nobler, sweeter song,
I'll sing Thy power to save,
When this poor, lisping, stammering tongue
Lies silent in the grave. Amen.

WILLIAM COWPER *ab.*

### Cowper C.M. — SECOND TUNE
*Lowell Mason*

## PASSION AND CRUCIFIXION

### 95 Ravenscroft 8₇7₇&4      RICHARD REDHEAD

1 Hark! the voice of love and mer-cy Sounds a-loud from Cal-va-ry;

See! it rends the rocks a-sun-der, Shakes the earth and veils the sky:

"It is fin-ished!" Hear the dy-ing Sav-iour cry. A-MEN.

2 "It is finished!"— Oh, what pleasure
Do these precious words afford!
Heavenly blessings, without measure,
  Flow to us from Christ, the Lord:
    "It is finished!"
Saints, the dying words record.

3 Tune your harps anew, ye seraphs;
Join to sing the pleasing theme:
All on earth, and all in heaven,
  Join to praise Immanuel's name:
    Alleluia!
Glory to the bleeding Lamb! Amen.

JONATHAN EVANS

---

See also Hymns under —

THE HOLY CATHOLIC CHURCH
    The Lord's Supper . . . . . . . 181 – 187
THE FORGIVENESS OF SINS
    Repentance . . . . . . . . 266 – 280
    Redeeming Love . . . . . . 296 – 310

## JESUS CHRIST

### 96. Rock of Ages. 7s6l.
RICHARD REDHEAD

1 Rest-ing from His work to-day, In the tomb the Sav-iour lay;

Still He slept, from head to feet Shrouded in the wind-ing-sheet,

Ly-ing in the rock a-lone, Hid-den by the seal-èd stone.

A-MEN.

2 Late at even there was seen
Watching long the Magdalene;
Early, ere the break of day,
Sorrowful she took her way
To the holy garden glade,
Where her buried Lord was laid.

3 So with Thee, till life shall end,
I would solemn vigil spend:
Let me hew Thee, Lord, a shrine
In this rocky heart of mine,
Where in pure embalmèd cell
None but Thou may ever dwell.

4 Myrrh and spices will I bring,
True affection's offering;
Close the door from sight and sound
Of the busy world around;
And in patient watch remain
Till my Lord appear again. Amen.

T. W. WHYTEHEAD.

## RESURRECTION

**97 Magdalen College** 8.8.6.8.8.6.    WILLIAM HAYNES

1 Come see the place where Jesus lay, And hear angelic watchers say,

"He lives, who once was slain: Why seek the living 'midst the dead?

Remember how the Saviour said, That He would rise again."

2 O joyful sound! O glorious hour,
When by His own almighty power
  He rose and left the grave!
Now let our songs His triumph tell,
Who burst the bands of death and hell,
  And ever lives to save.

3 The First-begotten of the dead,
For us He rose, our glorious Head,
  Immortal life to bring;       [die,
What though the saints like Him shall
They share their Leader's victory,
  And triumph with their King.

4 No more they tremble at the grave,
For Jesus will their spirits save,
  And raise their slumbering dust:
O risen Lord, in Thee we live,
To Thee our ransomed souls we give,
  To Thee our bodies trust.   Amen.

THOMAS KELLY *ab.* and *alt.*

## JESUS CHRIST

**98 Easter Hymn** 7s with Alleluia  
W. H. MONK

1 Christ, the Lord, is risen to-day, Al-le-lu - ia! Sons of men and

an-gels say, Al - le - lu - ia! Raise your joys and triumphs high!

Al-le-lu - ia! Sing, ye heavens, and earth reply! Alle - lu - ia!

2 Love's redeeming work is done,
                                  Alleluia!
Fought the fight, the battle won;
                                  Alleluia!
Lo! our Sun's eclipse is o'er;
                                  Alleluia!
Lo! He sets in blood no more.
                                  Alleluia!

3 Vain the stone, the watch, the seal,
                                  Alleluia!
Christ hath burst the gates of hell;
                                  Alleluia!
Death in vain forbids Him rise;
                                  Alleluia!
Christ hath opened Paradise.
                                  Alleluia!

4 Lives again our glorious King;
                                  Alleluia!
"Where, O Death, is now thy sting?"
                                  Alleluia!
Once He died our souls to save;
                                  Alleluia!
"Where's thy victory, boasting grave?"
                                  Alleluia!

5 Soar we now where Christ has led,
                                  Alleluia!
Following our exalted Head;
                                  Alleluia!
Made like Him, like Him we rise;
                                  Alleluia!
Ours the cross, the grave, the skies!
                            Alleluia! Amen.

CHARLES WESLEY *alt.*

## RESURRECTION

**Nuremberg** 7s · SECOND TUNE without Alleluia · J. R. AHLE

**99 Holy Cross** C.M. · JOHN STAINER

1 I say to all men far and near, That He is risen a-gain; That
He is with us now and here, And ev-er shall re-main.

2 And what I say, let each this morn
  Go tell it to his friend,
That soon in every place shall dawn
  His kingdom without end.

3 Now first to souls who thus awake
  Seems earth a fatherland:
A new and endless life they take
  With rapture from His hand.

4 The fears of death and of the grave
  Are whelmed beneath the sea,
And every heart, now light and brave,
  May face the things to be.

5 The way of darkness that He trod
  To heaven at last shall come,
And he who hearkens to His word,
  Shall reach His Father's home. Amen.

FRIEDRICH VON HARDENBERG  Tr. WINKWORTH

*JESUS CHRIST*

## 100 Lancashire 7s & 6s
HENRY SMART

♩ = 108

1 The day of re-sur-rec-tion, Earth, tell it out a-broad:
The Pass-o-ver of glad-ness, The Pass-o-ver of God.
From death to life e-ter-nal, From this world to the sky,
Our Christ hath brought us o-ver, With hymns of vic-to-ry.

A-MEN.

2 Our hearts be pure from evil,
  That we may see aright
The Lord in rays eternal
  Of resurrection-light;
And, listening to His accents,
  May hear, so calm and plain,
His own "All hail!" and, hearing,
  May raise the victor-strain.

3 Now let the heavens be joyful,
  Let earth her song begin;
Let the round world keep triumph,
  And all that is therein;
Invisible and visible,
  Their notes let all things blend,
For Christ the Lord hath risen,
  Our Joy that hath no end. Amen.

ST. JOHN OF DAMASCUS Tr. NEALE

## RESURRECTION

**101 Lur Coi** 8s & 7s D.   ARTHUR SULLIVAN

1 Al - le - lu - ia! Al - le - lu - ia! Hearts to heaven and voic-es raise;

Sing to God a hymn of glad-ness, Sing to God a hymn of praise;

He, who on the Cross a Vic-tim For the world's sal - va - tion bled,

A - MEN.

Je-sus Christ, the King of glo-ry, Now is ris-en from the dead.

2 Christ is risen, Christ the first-fruits
  Of the holy harvest field,
Which with all its full abundance
  At His second coming yield;
Then the golden ears of harvest
  Will their heads before Him wave,
Ripened by His glorious sunshine
  From the furrows of the grave.

3 Christ is risen, we are risen;
  Shed upon us heavenly grace,
Rain, and dew, and gleams of glory
  From the brightness of Thy face;
That we, with our hearts in heaven,
  Here on earth may fruitful be,
And by Angel-hands be gathered,
  And be ever, Lord, with Thee. Amen.
      CHRISTOPHER WORDSWORTH  *ab.*

*JESUS CHRIST*

## 102 St. Fulbert C.M.
H. J. GAUNTLETT

1 Ye choirs of New Je-ru-sa-lem, Your sweetest notes employ, The Paschal victory to hymn In strains of holy joy. Alle-lu-ia! . .

2 For Judah's Lion bursts His chains,
   Crushing the serpent's head;
And cries aloud thro' death's domains
   To wake the imprisoned dead.
           Alleluia!

3 Devouring depths of hell their prey
   At His command restore;
His ransomed hosts pursue their way
   Where Jesus goes before. Alleluia!

4 Triumphant in His glory now
   To Him all power is given;
To Him in one communion bow
   All saints in earth and heaven.
           Alleluia!

5 While we, His soldiers, praise our King,
   His mercy we implore,
Within His palace bright to bring
   And keep us evermore. Alleluia!

6 All glory to the Father be,
   All glory to the Son,
All glory, Holy Ghost, to Thee,
   While endless ages run. Alleluia! Amen.

FULBERT, of Chartres Tr. CAMPBELL

## Hummel C.M.  SECOND TUNE (without Alleluia)
CHARLES ZEUNER

*RESURRECTION*

A - MEN.

103 **St. Albinus** 7.8.7.8. with Alleluia      H. J. GAUNTLETT

♩ = 100

1 Je-sus lives! no longer now, Can thy ter-rors,Death,ap - pal us; Je-sus

A - MEN.

lives! by this we know Thou, O Grave,canst not enthral us. Allelu - ia!

    2 Jesus lives: henceforth is death
       But the gate of Life immortal;
       This shall calm our trembling breath,
       When we pass its gloomy portal. Alleluia!

    3 Jesus lives: for us He died:
       Then, alone to Jesus living,
       Pure in heart may we abide,
       Glory to our Saviour giving. Alleluia!

    4 Jesus lives: our hearts know well
       Nought from us His love shall sever;
       Life, nor death, nor powers of hell
       Tear us from His keeping ever. Alleluia!

    5 Jesus lives: to Him the throne
       Over all the world is given:
       May we go where He is gone,
       Rest and reign with Him in heaven. Alleluia!
                                      Amen.
                                   C. F. GELLERT Tr. COX

## JESUS CHRIST

### 104 Palestrina 8.8.8.4.

From PALESTRINA

1 The strife is o'er, the bat-tle done; The vic-to-ry of life is won;

The song of tri-umph has be-gun. Al-le-lu-ia!

2 The powers of death have done their worst,
But Christ their legions hath dispersed;
Let shouts of holy joy outburst.
           Alleluia!

3 The three sad days have quickly sped,
He rises glorious from the dead;
All glory to our risen Head!
           Alleluia!

4 Lord, by the stripes which wounded Thee,
From death's dread sting Thy servants free,
That we may live and sing to Thee.
           Alleluia!   Amen.

LATIN HYMN 12th Cent   Tr. POTT

## RESURRECTION

**105** Eversley 6s & 5s D.  J. W. ELLIOTT

1 Welcome, happy morn-ing! Age to age shall say: Hell to-day is

vanquished, Heaven is won to-day! Lo the dead is liv-ing, God for ev-er-

more! Him, their true Cre-a-tor All His works a-dore. A-MEN.

2 Earth with joy confesses,
   Clothing her for spring,
All good gifts returned, with
   Her returning King:
Bloom in every meadow,
   Leaves on every bough,
Speak His sorrows ended,
   Hail His triumph now.

3 Maker and Redeemer,
   Life and health of all,
Thou, from heaven beholding
   Human nature's fall,
Of the Father's Godhead
   True and only Son,
Manhood to deliver,
   Manhood didst put on.

4 Thou, of life the author,
   Death didst undergo,
Tread the path of darkness,
   Saving strength to show;
Come then, true and faithful,
   Now fulfil Thy word,
'Tis Thine own third morning,
   Rise, my buried Lord!

5 Loose the souls long-prisoned,
   Bound with Satan's chain;
All that now is fallen
   Raise to life again;
Show Thy face in brightness,
   Bid the nations see,
Bring again our daylight;
   Day returns with Thee. Amen.

VENANTIUS FORTUNATUS Tr. ELLERTON *ab*.

## JESUS CHRIST

### 106 Koenig L.M.D.
JOSEPH BARNBY

1 Our Lord is ris-en from the dead, Our Je-sus is gone up on high; The

powers of hell are captive led, Dragg'd to the portals of the sky. There His triumphal

chariot waits, And an-gels chant the sol-emn lay: "Lift up your heads, ye

A · MEN.

heavenly gates! Ye ev-er-last-ing doors! give way!"

2 Loose all your bars of massy light,
   And wide unfold the ethereal scene:
He claims those mansions as His right;
   Receive the King of glory in.
Who is the King of glory — who?
   The Lord who all our foes o'ercame;
The world, sin, death, and hell o'erthrew;
   And Jesus is the conqueror's name.

3 Lo! His triumphal chariot waits,
   And angels chant the solemn lay:
"Lift up your heads, ye heavenly gates!
   Ye everlasting doors! give way!"
Who is the King of glory — who?
   The Lord of glorious power possessed;
The King of saints and angels too,
   God over all, forever blessed    Amen.

CHARLES WESLEY

## ASCENSION

**107** Ascension  7s with Alleluia  W. H. MONK

1 Hail the day that sees Him rise, Al - le - lu - ia! Ravished from our wish-ful eyes; Al - le - lu - ia! Christ, a-while to mor-tals given, Al - le - lu - ia! Reascends His na-tive heav'n. Alle-lu - ia! A - MEN.

2 There for Him high triumph waits;
  Alleluia!
Lift your heads, eternal gates:
  Alleluia!
Wide unfold the radiant scene;
  Alleluia!
Take the King of glory in!
  Alleluia!

3 Circled round with angel powers,
  Alleluia!
Their triumphant Lord and ours,
  Alleluia!
Conqueror over death and sin;
  Alleluia!
Take the King of glory in!
  Alleluia!

4 Him though highest heaven receives,
  Alleluia!
Still He loves the earth He leaves:
  Alleluia!
Though returning to His throne,
  Alleluia!
Still He calls mankind His own.
  Alleluia!

5 See, He lifts His hands above;
  Alleluia!
See, He shows the prints of love:
  Alleluia!
Hark, His gracious lips bestow
  Alleluia!
Blessings on His Church below.
  Alleluia! Amen.

CHARLES WESLEY

## JESUS CHRIST

**108 St. Saviour** C.M. — F. G. Baker

1 Triumphant, Christ ascends on high,
The glorious work complete,
Sin, death, and hell, low vanquished lie,
Beneath His awful feet.

2 There, with eternal glory crowned,
The Lord, the Conqueror, reigns;
His praise the heavenly choirs resound
In their immortal strains.

3 Amid the splendors of His throne,
Unchanging love appears;
The names He purchased for His own,
Still on His heart He bears.

4 Still with prevailing power He pleads
Their cause for whom He died;
His Spirit's sacred influence sheds,
Their Comforter and Guide.

5 Oh, the rich depths of love divine!
Of bliss a boundless store!
Dear Saviour, let me call Thee mine;
I can not wish for more.

6 On Thee alone my hope relies;
Beneath Thy cross I fall,—
My Lord, my life, my sacrifice,
My Saviour, and my all! Amen.

ANNE STEELE

**109**

1 The head that once was crowned with thorns
Is crowned with glory now;
A royal diadem adorns
The mighty victor's brow.

2 The highest place that heaven affords
Is His, is His by right,
The King of kings, and Lord of lords,
And heaven's eternal light.

3 The joy of all who dwell above,
The joy of all below,
To whom He manifests His love,
And grants His name to know.

4 To them the cross, with all its shame,
With all its grace is given:
Their name an everlasting name,
Their joy the joy of heaven.

5 The cross He bore is life and health,
Though shame and death to Him;
His people's hope, His people's wealth,
Their everlasting theme. Amen.

THOMAS KELLY

## ASCENSION

**110 Abridge** C.M.                              Isaac Smith

1 Th' e-ter-nal gates lift up their heads, The doors are o-pened wide;

The King of glo-ry is gone up Un-to His Father's side.

2 Thou art gone in before us, Lord,
   Thou hast prepared a place,
That we may be where now Thou art,
   And look upon Thy face.

3 And ever on Thine earthly path
   A gleam of glory lies;
A light still breaks behind the cloud
   That veils Thee from our eyes.

4 Lift up our thoughts, lift up our songs,
   And let Thy grace be given:
That while we linger yet below,
   Our hearts may be in heaven;

5 That where Thou art at God's right hand,
   Our hope, our love may be:
Dwell in us now, that we may dwell
   For evermore in Thee.   Amen.

                      Mrs. C. F. Alexander

## JESUS CHRIST

### III Moultrie 8s & 7s D.

GERARD COBB

1 Christ, a-bove all glo-ry seat-ed! King e-ter-nal, strong to save!

Dy-ing, Thou hast death de-feat-ed, Buried, Thou hast spoiled the grave.

Thou art gone, where now is giv-en, What no mor-tal might could gain:

A-MEN.

On th' e-ter-nal throne of heaven, In Thy Father's pow'r to reign.

2 There Thy kingdoms all adore Thee,
   Heaven above and earth below,
While the depths of hell before Thee,
   Trembling and defeated, bow.
We, O Lord! with hearts adoring,
   Follow Thee above the sky:
Hear our prayers Thy grace imploring,
   Lift our souls to Thee on high.

3 So when Thou again in glory
   On the clouds of heaven shalt shine,
We, Thy flock, may stand before Thee,
   Owned for evermore as Thine.
Hail! all hail! In Thee confiding,
   Jesus, Thee shall all adore,
In Thy Father's might abiding
   With one Spirit evermore! Amen.

LATIN 7th Cent.

## ASCENSION

**112  Corona** 8,7,3&4           W. H. MONK

1 Look, ye saints; the sight is glorious; See the "Man of sorrows" now;

From the fight returned victorious, Ev-'ry knee to Him shall bow;

Crown Him! Crown Him! Crowns become the Victor's brow.

2 Crown the Saviour, angels, crown Him;
  Rich the trophies Jesus brings;
  In the seat of power enthrone Him,
  While the vault of heaven rings;
    Crown Him! Crown Him!
  Crown the Saviour King of kings.

3 Sinners in derision crowned Him,
  Mocking thus the Saviour's claim;
  Saints and angels crowd around Him,
  Own His title, praise His name:
    Crown Him! Crown Him!
  Spread abroad the Victor's fame!

4 Hark! those bursts of acclamation!
  Hark! those loud, triumphant chords!
 Jesus takes the highest station;
   O what joy the sight affords!
     Crown Him! Crown Him!
   King of kings, and Lord of lords. Amen.

THOMAS KELLY

## JESUS CHRIST

### 113 Miles Lane C.M.
WILLIAM SHRUBSOLE

♩ = 84

1 All hail the pow'r of Je-sus' name! Let an-gels pros-trate fall; Bring forth the roy-al di-a-dem, And crown Him, crown Him, crown Him, crown Him Lord of all. A-MEN.

2 Crown Him, ye martyrs of our God,
Who from His altar call;
Extol the stem of Jesse's rod,
And crown Him Lord of all.

3 Ye chosen seed of Israel's race,
Ye ransomed from the fall,
Hail Him who saves you by His grace,
And crown Him Lord of all.

4 Sinners, whose love can ne'er forget
The wormwood and the gall;

Go spread your trophies at His feet,
And crown Him Lord of all.

5 Let every kindred, every tribe,
On this terrestrial ball,
To Him all majesty ascribe,
And crown Him Lord of all.

6 O that with yonder sacred throng
We at His feet may fall;
We'll join the everlasting song,
And crown Him Lord of all. Amen.

EDWARD PERRONETT

### Coronation C.M.     SECOND TUNE
OLIVER HOLDEN

♩ = 84

## MEDIATORIAL REIGN

A-MEN.

### 114 Italian Hymn  6.6.4.6.6.6.4.   FELICE GIARDINI

♩ = 92

1 Come, all ye saints of God, Wide through the earth a-broad
Spread Jesus' fame: Tell what His love hath done: Trust in His name a-lone;

Shout to His lof-ty throne, "Worthy the Lamb!"  A-MEN.

2 Hence, gloomy doubts and fears!
  Dry up your mournful tears;
  Swell the glad theme:
  To Christ, our gracious King,
  Strike each melodious string;
  Join heart and voice to sing,
  "Worthy the Lamb!"

3 Hark! how the choirs above,
  Filled with the Saviour's love,
  Dwell on His name!
  There, too, may we be found,
  With light and glory crowned,
  While all the heavens resound,
  "Worthy the Lamb!"  Amen.

JAMES BODEN

## JESUS CHRIST

**115 Church Triumphant** L.M.  J. W. ELLIOTT

1 Hail to the Prince of life and peace, Who holds the keys of death and hell!

A - MEN.

The spacious world unseen is His, And sov'reign pow'r becomes Him well.

2 In shame and torment once He died;
But now He lives for evermore:
Bow down, ye saints, around His seat,
And, all ye angel-bands, adore.

3 So live for ever, glorious Lord,
To crush Thy foes and guard Thy friends;
While all Thy chosen tribes rejoice
That Thy dominion never ends.

4 Worthy Thy hand to hold the keys,
Guided by wisdom and by love;
Worthy to rule o'er mortal life,
O'er worlds below, and worlds above.

5 For ever reign, victorious King!
Wide thro' the earth Thy name be known;
And call my longing soul to sing
Sublimer anthems near Thy throne.
Amen.

PHILIP DODDRIDGE *ab.*

**116 St. Thomas** S.M.  AARON WILLIAMS

1 A-wake, and sing the song Of Mo- ses and the Lamb!

## MEDIATORIAL REIGN

Wake ev-'ry heart and ev-'ry tongue, To praise the Saviour's name!

2 Sing of His dying love;
Sing of His rising power:
Sing how He intercedes above
For those whose sins He bore.

3 Sing on your heavenly way,
Ye ransomed sinners, sing!
Sing on, rejoicing every day
In Christ, th' exalted King.

4 Soon shall we hear Him say,
"Ye blessèd children, come!"
Soon shall He call us hence away
To our eternal home.

5 Soon shall our raptured tongue
His endless praise proclaim,
And sweeter voices tune the song
Of Moses and the Lamb. Amen.

WILLIAM HAMMOND ab.

## 117 Tunbridge L.M.
RICHARD REDHEAD

1 Go, wor-ship at Im-man-uel's feet; See in His face what wonders meet;

Earth is too nar-row to express His worth, His glory, or His grace.

2 Nor earth, nor seas, nor sun, nor stars,
Nor heaven, His full resemblance bears:
His beauties we can never trace,
Till we behold Him face to face.

3 Oh, let me climb those higher skies,
Where storms and darkness never rise:
There He displays His power abroad,
And shines, and reigns, th' incarnate God.
Amen.

ISAAC WATTS ab.

## JESUS CHRIST

**118 Harwell** 8.7.8.7.7.7.8.6.     Lowell Mason

1 Hark! ten thousand harps and voices Sound the note of praise above: Jesus reigns, and heaven re-

joices; Jesus reigns, the God of love; See, He sits on yonder throne; Jesus rules the world a-lone. Al-le-lu-ia! Al-le-lu-ia! Al-le-lu-ia! A-men.

2 King of glory, reign forever!
  Thine an everlasting crown;
Nothing from Thy love shall sever
  Those whom Thou hast made Thine own:
Happy objects of Thy grace,
Destined to behold Thy face.
    Alleluia! Amen.

3 Saviour, hasten Thine appearing;
  Bring, oh, bring the glorious day,
When, the awful summons hearing,
  Heaven and earth shall pass away!
Then, with golden harps we'll sing,
"Glory, glory to our King!"
    Alleluia! Amen. Amen.

THOMAS KELLY *ab.*

**119 Dedham** C.M.     William Gardner

1 Come, let us join our cheerful songs With an-gels round the throne;

## MEDIATORIAL REIGN

Ten thousand thousand are their tongues, But all their joys are one.

2 "Worthy the Lamb that died," they cry,
"To be exalted thus!"
"Worthy the Lamb!" our lips reply,
"For He was slain for us!"

3 Jesus is worthy to receive
Honor and power divine;
And blessings, more than we can give,
Be, Lord, forever Thine!

4 Let all that dwell above the sky,
And air, and earth, and seas,
Conspire to lift Thy glories high,
And speak Thine endless praise.

5 The whole creation join in one
To bless the sacred name
Of Him who sits upon the throne,
And to adore the Lamb! Amen.

ISAAC WATTS

## 120 Wilmot 8s & 7s.

Arr. from VON WEBER

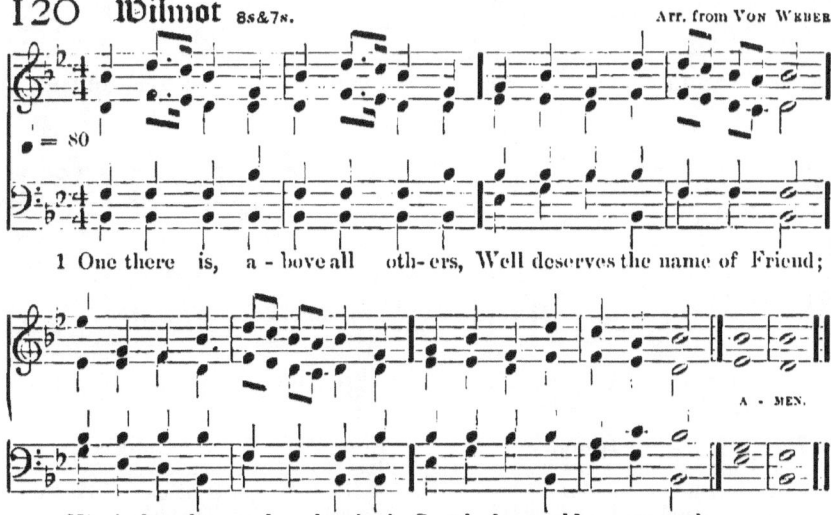

1 One there is, above all others, Well deserves the name of Friend;
His is love beyond a brother's, Costly, free, and knows no end.

2 Which of all our friends, to save us,
Could or would have shed his blood?
But our Jesus died to have us
Reconciled in Him to God.

3 When He lived on earth abased,
Friend of sinners was His name;
Now above all glory raised,
He rejoices in the same.

4 Oh! for grace our hearts to soften,
Teach us, Lord, at length, to love;
We, alas! forget too often
What a friend we have above. Amen.

JOHN NEWTON ab. and alt.

## JESUS CHRIST

**121 Darwall** 6.6.6.6.8.8.    JOHN DARWALL

1 Come, ev-'ry pi-ous heart That loves the Sav-iour's name, Your

no-blest pow'r ex-ert To cel-e-brate His fame: Tell all a-

bove, and all be-low, The debt of love to Him you owe.

A - MEN.

2 He left His starry crown,
  And laid His robes aside;
On wings of love came down,
  And wept, and bled, and died:
What He endured, oh, who can tell,
To save our souls from death and hell.

3 From the dark grave He rose,
  The mansion of the dead;
And thence His mighty foes
  In glorious triumph led;
Up through the sky the conqueror rode,
And reigns on high, the Saviour, God.

4 From thence He'll quickly come,
  His chariot will not stay,
And bear our spirits home
  To realms of endless day:
There shall we see His lovely face,
And ever be in His embrace.

5 Jesus, we ne'er can pay
  The debt we owe Thy love;
Yet tell us how we may
  Our gratitude approve:
Our hearts, our all, to Thee we give;
The gift, though small, do Thou receive.
                                Amen.
SAMUEL STENNETT

## MEDIATORIAL REIGN

### 122 Adoration 6.6.6.6.8.8.
W. H. HAVERGAL

1 Re-joice, the Lord is King, Your Lord and King a-dore, Mor-

tals, give thanks and sing, And tri-umph ever-more: Lift up your heart, lift

up your voice, Re-joice, a-gain I say, re-joice.

2 Jesus the Saviour reigns,
  The God of truth and love;
When He had purged our stains
  He took His seat above:
Lift up your heart, lift up your voice,
Rejoice, again I say, rejoice.

3 His kingdom cannot fail,
  He rules o'er earth and heaven;
The keys of death and hell
  Are to our Jesus given:
Lift up your heart, lift up your voice,
Rejoice, again I say, rejoice.

4 He sits at God's right hand
  Till all His foes submit,
And bow to His command,
  And fall beneath His feet:
Lift up your heart, lift up your voice,
Rejoice, again I say, rejoice.

5 He all His foes shall quell,
  Shall all our sins destroy,
And every bosom swell
  With pure seraphic joy:
Lift up your heart, lift up your voice,
Rejoice, again I say, rejoice

6 Rejoice in glorious hope;
  Jesus, the Judge, shall come,
And take His servants up
  To their eternal home:
We soon shall hear the archangel's voice,
The trump of God shall sound, Rejoice. Amen.

CHARLES WESLEY

## JESUS CHRIST

**123 Koenig** L.M.D.  
Small notes for the organ.  
JOSEPH BARNBY

1 O God of God! O Light of Light! Thou Prince of Peace, Thou King of Kings; To Thee, where angels know no night, The song of praise for-ev-er rings:—To Him who sits up-on the throne, The Lamb once slain for sin-ful men, Be honor, might; all by Him won; Glory and praise! Amen, Amen.

2 Nations afar, in ignorance deep;  
  Isles of the sea, where darkness lay;  
These hear His voice, they wake from sleep,  
  And throng with joy the upward way.  
They cry with us, "Send forth Thy light,  
  O Lamb, once slain for sinful men;  
Burst Satan's bonds, O God of Might,  
  Set all men free!" Amen, Amen.

3 Sing to the Lord a glorious song,  
  Sing to His name, His love forth tell;  
Sing on, heaven's hosts, His praise prolong;  
  Sing, ye who now on earth do dwell:—  
Worthy the Lamb for sinners slain,  
  From angels, praise; and thanks from men.  
Worthy the Lamb, enthroned to reign,  
  Glory and power! Amen, Amen, Amen.

J. JULIAN, ab.

## MEDIATORIAL REIGN

**124 Lur Coi** 8s & 7s D.                           ARTHUR SULLIVAN

1 Hail, Thou once despiséd Jesus! Hail, Thou Galilean King! Thou didst suffer

to release us, Thou didst free salvation bring. Hail, Thou agonizing Saviour,

Bearer of our sin and shame! By Thy merits we find favor; Life is given thro' Thy name.

2 Paschal Lamb, by God appointed,
   All our sins on Thee were laid;
By Almighty love anointed
   Thou hast full atonement made:
All Thy people are forgiven
   Through the virtue of Thy blood;
Opened is the gate of Heaven;
   Peace is made for man with God.

3 Jesus, hail; Enthroned in glory,
   There for ever to abide.
All the heavenly hosts adore Thee,
   Seated at Thy Father's side!
There for sinners Thou art pleading;
   There Thou dost our place prepare;
Ever for us interceding
   Till in glory we appear.

4 Worship, honor, power, and blessing,
   Thou art worthy to receive;
Loudest praises, without ceasing,
   Meet it is for us to give!
Help, ye bright angelic spirits,
   Bring your sweetest, noblest lays,
Help to sing our Saviour's merits,
   Help to chant Immanuel's praise! Amen.

JOHN BAKEWELL *alt.*

## JESUS CHRIST

**125** Diademata  S.M.D.  G. J. Elvey

1 Crown Him with many crowns, The Lamb upon His throne: Hark! how the heav'nly

anthem drowns All mu-sic but its own! A-wake, my soul, and sing  Of

A - MEN.

Him who died for thee; And hail Him as thy matchless King Thro' all eternity.

2 Crown Him the Lord of love!
  Behold His hands and side,—
Rich wounds, yet visible above,
  In beauty glorified:
No angel in the sky
  Can fully bear that sight,
But downward bends his burning eye
  At mysteries so bright.

3 Crown Him the Lord of peace!
  Whose power a sceptre sways
In heaven and earth, that wars may cease,
  And all be prayer and praise.
His reign shall know no end;
  And round His piercéd feet
Fair flowers of Paradise extend
  Their fragrance ever sweet.

4 Crown Him the Lord of years!
  The Potentate of time,
Creator of the rolling spheres
  Ineffably sublime!
All hail, Redeemer, hail!
  For Thou hast died for me:
Thy praise shall never, never fail
  Throughout eternity. Amen.

MATTHEW BRIDGES *ab.*

## MEDIATORIAL REIGN

**126 Alleluia** 8s & 7s with Alleluia — ALBERT LOWE

1 Lord of ev-'ry land and na-tion, "Ancient of e-ter-nal days,"
Sounded thro' the wide cre-a-tion, Be Thy just and law-ful praise.
Al-le-lu-ia! Al-le-lu-ia! Al-le-lu-ia! A-men.

2 For the grandeur of Thy nature,
  Grand beyond a seraph's thought,
For created works of power,
  Works with skill and kindness wrought.
    Alleluia! Amen.

3 But Thy rich, Thy free redemption,
  Dark through brightness all along;
Thought is poor, and poor expression;
  Who can sing that awful song?
    Alleluia! Amen.

4 "Brightness of the Father's glory,"
  Shall Thy praise unuttered lie?
Shun, my tongue, the guilty silence;
  Sing the Lord who came to die.
    Alleluia! Amen.

5 From the highest throne in glory,
  To the Cross of deepest woe,
All to ransom guilty captives—
  Flow my praise, forever flow.
    Alleluia! Amen.

6 Go, return, immortal Saviour;
  Leave Thy footstool, take Thy throne;
Thence return, and reign forever;
  Be the kingdom all Thine own.
    Alleluia! Amen. Amen.

ROBERT ROBINSON

## JESUS CHRIST

**127　St. Cephas** 6s&5sD.　　　　　　　H. A. CROSBIE

1 At the name of Je - sus Ev-'ry knee shall bow, Ev-'ry tongue con-

fess Him King of glo-ry now. 'Tis the Father's pleasure We should call Him

Lord, Who from the be-gin - ning Was the mighty Word.

A - MEN.

2 At His voice creation
　Sprang at once to sight,
All the angel faces,
　All the hosts of light,
Thrones and dominations,
　Stars upon their way,
All the heavenly orders
　In their great array.

3 Humbled for a season,
　To receive a name
From the lips of sinners
　Unto whom He came,
Faithfully He bore it
　Spotless to the last,
Brought it back victorious,
　When from death He passed.

4 In your hearts enthrone Him;
　There let Him subdue
All that is not holy,
　All that is not true:
Crown Him as your Captain
　In temptation's hour:
Let His will enfold you
　In its light and power.

5 Brothers, this Lord Jesus
　Shall return again,
With His Father's glory,
　With His angel train;
For all wreaths of empire
　Meet upon His brow,
And our hearts confess Him
　King of glory now. Amen.

CAROLINE M. NOEL.

## SECOND COMING AND JUDGMENT

### 128 Benedic Anima 8s & 7s 6l.
JOHN GOSS

1 Je - sus came, the heavens a-dor-ing, Came with peace from realms on high;

Je - sus came for man's re-demption, Low-ly came on earth to die;

Al - le - lu - ia! Al - le - lu - ia! Came in deep hu-mil - i - ty.

2 Jesus comes again in mercy,
   When our hearts are bowed with care;
Jesus comes again in answer
   To an earnest heartfelt prayer;
     Alleluia! Alleluia!
Comes to save us from despair.

3 Jesus comes to hearts rejoicing,
   Bringing news of sins forgiven;
Jesus comes in sounds of gladness,
   Leading souls redeemed to heaven;
     Alleluia! Alleluia!
Now the gate of death is riven.

4 Jesus comes in joy and sorrow,
   Shares alike our hopes and fears;
Jesus comes whate'er befalls us,
   Glads our hearts, and dries our tears;
     Alleluia! Alleluia!
Cheering ev'n our failing years.

5 Jesus comes on clouds triumphant,
   When the heavens shall pass away;
Jesus comes again in glory;
   Let us then our homage pay,
     Alleluia! ever singing
Till the dawn of endless day. Amen.
                   GODFREY THRING

## JESUS CHRIST

**129 Wilmot** 8s & 7s  
Arr. from VON WEBER

♩ = 80

1 Come, Thou long ex-pect-ed Je - sus, Born to set Thy peo-ple free;
From our fears and sins re-lease us, Let us find our rest in Thee.

A · MEN.

2 Israel's strength and consolation,
   Hope of all the saints Thou art;
  Dear desire of every nation,
   Joy of every longing heart.

3 Born, Thy people to deliver;
   Born a child, and yet a King;
  Born to reign in us forever,
   Now Thy gracious kingdom bring.

4 By Thine own eternal Spirit,
   Rule in all our hearts alone;
  By Thine all-sufficient merit,
   Raise us to Thy glorious throne. Amen.

CHARLES WESLEY

**130 Eagley** C.M.  
J. WALCH

♩ = 100

1 Light of the lone - ly pil-grim's heart, Star of the com - ing day,

## SECOND COMING AND JUDGMENT

Arise, and, with Thy morning beams, Chase all our griefs away.

2 Come, blessèd Lord, bid every shore
And answering island sing
The praises of Thy royal name,
And own Thee as their King.

3 Bid the whole earth responsive now
To the bright world above,
Break forth in rapturous strains of joy
In memory of Thy love.

4 Lord, Lord, Thy fair creation groans,
The air, the earth, the sea,
In unison with all our hearts,
And calls aloud for Thee.

5 Come, then, with all Thy quickening powers,
With one awakening smile,
And bid the serpent's trail no more
Thy beauteous realms defile.

6 Thine was the cross, with all its fruits
Of grace and peace divine:
Be Thine the crown of glory now,
The palm of victory Thine.   Amen.

EDWARD DENNY

## 131 Sienna s.m.
W. H. DEANE

1 Come, Lord, and tar - ry not; Bring the long-looked-for day;
Oh! why these years of waiting here, These ages of de - lay?

2 Come, for Thy saints still wait;
Daily ascends their sigh:
The Spirit and the Bride say, "Come!"
Dost Thou not hear the cry?

3 Come, for creation groans,
Impatient of Thy stay,
Worn out with these long years of ill,
These ages of delay.

4 Come, and make all things new;
Build up this ruined earth:
Restore our faded Paradise,
Creation's second birth.

5 Come and begin Thy reign
Of everlasting peace;
Come, take the kingdom to Thyself,
Great King of righteousness.   Amen.

HORATIUS BONAR *ab.*

## JESUS CHRIST

### 132 Supplication. 8s & 7s D.
W. H. MONK

1 Light of those whose dreary dwelling Borders on the shades of death!

Come, and by Thy-self re-veal-ing, Dis-si-pate the clouds be-neath:

Thou of heav'n and earth Cre-a-tor, In our deep-est darkness rise,—

A - MEN.

Scattering all the night of na-ture, Pour-ing day up-on our eyes.

2 Still we wait for Thine appearing;
   Life and joy Thy beams impart,
Chasing all our fears, and cheering
   Every poor benighted heart:
Come and manifest Thy favor
   To the ransomed helpless race;
Come, Thou universal Saviour!
   Come, and bring the Gospel grace.

3 Save us, in Thy great compassion,
   O Thou mild, pacific Prince!
Give the knowledge of Salvation,
   Give the pardon of our sins;
By Thine all-restoring merit,
   Every burdened soul release;
Every weary, wandering spirit,
   Guide into Thy perfect peace. Amen.

CHARLES WESLEY

## SECOND COMING AND JUDGMENT

**133 Islington** 6.6.6.6.8.7.8.7.  G. M. GARRETT

1 Christ, that ever reigneth, Christ, that here remaineth, Christ, within us dwelling,

Christ, in praise excelling; Him we proclaim, His glorious name; To our Creator

ren - der Homage all due; lowly and true Homage to Him we tender. A-MEN.

2 Heaven's high host rejoices,
Lifting up all voices,
  Jubilant with gladness;—
  Yet the earth with sadness
Dreading her fate God doth await,
Who judgment strict revealeth;
Merciful Power, save in that hour
Those whom Thy passion healeth!

3 Raise us, cleansed, to regions
Where the angel legions
  Round Thee aye are soaring;
  With the saints adoring;
Grant us Thy peace, bid dangers cease,
And Thou, Thy mercy sending,
Christ, give us rest, where, with the blest,
Thy reign is never ending. Amen.

E. A. DAYMAN.

## JESUS CHRIST

### 134 Veni Immanuel L.M.6l.  CHARLES GOUNOD

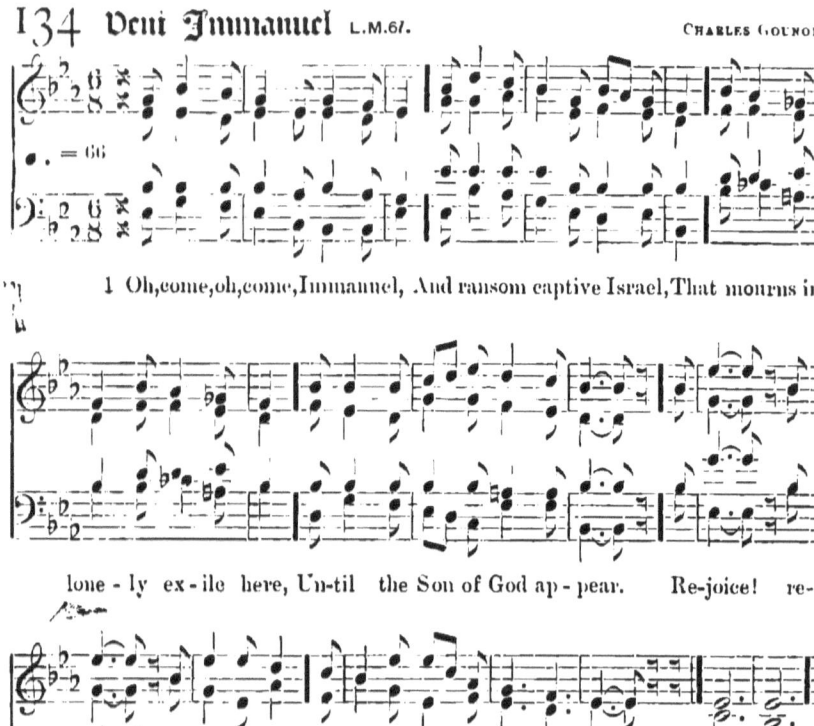

♩. = 66

1 Oh, come, oh, come, Immanuel, And ransom captive Israel, That mourns in lone-ly ex-ile here, Un-til the Son of God ap-pear. Re-joice! re-joice! Im-man-u-el Shall come to thee, O Is-ra-el!

A-MEN.

2 Draw nigh, draw nigh, O Morning Star,
And bring us comfort from afar:
And banish far from us the gloom
Of sinful night and endless doom.
Rejoice! rejoice! Immanuel
Shall come to thee, O Israel!

3 Draw nigh, draw nigh, O David's Key,
The heavenly gate unfolds to Thee;
Make safe the way that leads on high,
And close the path to misery.
Rejoice! rejoice! Immanuel
Shall come to thee, O Israel!

4 Draw nigh, draw nigh, O Lord of Might,
Who once, from Sinai's flaming height,
Didst give the trembling tribes Thy law
In cloud, and majesty, and awe.
Rejoice! rejoice! Immanuel
Shall come to thee, O Israel!  Amen.

Tr. J. M. NEALE.

## SECOND COMING AND JUDGMENT

**135  Greenland** 7s & 6s D.  *Lausanne Psalter*

1 Rejoice, rejoice, believers! And let your lights appear; The shades of eve are

thickening, And dark-er night is near; The Bridegroom is advan-cing; Each

hour He draws more nigh; Up! watch and pray, nor slumber; At midnight comes the cry.

2 See that your lamps are burning,
   Replenish them with oil;
Look now for your salvation,
   The end of sin and toil.
The watchers on the mountain
   Proclaim the Bridegroom near,
Go meet Him as He cometh,
   With alleluias clear.

3 Our hope and expectation,
   O Jesus, now appear;
Arise, Thou Sun so longed for,
   O'er this benighted sphere.
With hearts and hands uplifted,
   We plead, O Lord, to see
The day of earth's redemption,
   And ever be with Thee.   Amen.

LAURENTIUS LAURENTI Tr. BORTHWICK *ab. and sl. alt.*

## JESUS CHRIST

**136 Ravenscroft** 8s7s&4      RICHARD REDHEAD

1 Lo, He comes, with clouds descending, Once for fa-vor'd sin-ners slain:

Thousand thousand saints at-tend-ing Swell the tri-umph of His train:

Al - le - lu - ia! God ap-pears on earth to reign.

2 Every eye shall now behold Him,
   Robed in dreadful majesty:
Those who set at nought and sold Him,
   Pierced, and nailed Him to the tree,
     Deeply wailing,
Shall the true Messiah see.

3 Every island, sea, and mountain,
   Heaven and earth, shall flee away:
All who hate Him must, confounded,
   Hear the trump proclaim the day;
     Come to judgment,
Come to judgment, come away.

4 Now redemption, long expected,
   See in solemn pomp appear;
All His saints, by man rejected,
   Now shall meet Him in the air,
     Alleluia!
See the day of God appear.

5 Yea, Amen; let all adore Thee,
   High on Thine eternal throne:
Saviour, take the power and glory;
   Claim the kingdom for Thine own.
     O come quickly,
Alleluia! Come, Lord, come. Amen.

From JOHN CENNICK and CHARLES WESLEY

## SECOND COMING AND JUDGMENT

**137** Melita L.M.6l.  J. B. Dykes

1 Come, quickly come, dread Judge of all;
For awful though Thine advent be,
All shadows from the truth will fall,
And falsehood die in sight of Thee:
O quickly come: for doubt and fear
Like clouds dissolve when Thou art near.

2 Come, quickly come, great King of all;
Reign all around us, and within;
Let sin no more our souls enthral,
Let pain and sorrow die with sin:
O quickly come: for Thou alone
Canst make Thy scattered people one.

3 Come, quickly come, true Life of all,
For death is mighty all around;
On every home his shadows fall,
On every heart his mark is found:
O quickly come: for grief and pain
Can never cloud Thy glorious reign.

4 Come, quickly come, true Light of all;
For gloomy night broods o'er our way;
And weakly souls begin to fall
With weary watching for the day:
O quickly come: for round Thy throne
No eye is blind, no night is known.
Amen.

LAURENCE TUTTIETT

## JESUS CHRIST

### 138 St. Sebastian 7s6l.

S. S. WESLEY

1 When this pass-ing world is done, When has sunk yon glar-ing sun;

When I stand with Christ in glory, Look-ing o'er life's finished story:

Then, Lord, shall I ful - ly know—Not till then—how much I owe.

2 When I stand before the throne,
Dressed in beauty not my own;
When I see Thee as Thou art,
Love Thee with unsinning heart:
Then, Lord, shall I fully know—
Not till then — how much I owe.

3 When the praise of heaven I hear,
Loud as thunders to the ear,
Loud as many waters' noise,
Sweet as harp's melodious voice:
Then, Lord, shall I fully know—
Not till then — how much I owe. Amen.

R. M. McCheyne

## SECOND COMING AND JUDGMENT

**139 Germany** L.M.           From BEETHOVEN

1 Jesus, Thy blood and righteousness, My beauty are, my glorious dress; 'Midst flaming worlds, in these arrayed, With joy shall I lift up my head.

2 When from the dust of death I rise
To claim my mansion in the skies,
E'en then this shall be all my plea —
Jesus hath lived, hath died for me.

3 Bold shall I stand in Thy great day,
For who aught to my charge shall lay?
Fully absolved through these I am,
From sin and fear, from guilt and shame.

4 Thou God of power, Thou God of love,
Let the whole world Thy mercy prove;
Now let Thy word o'er all prevail;
Now take the spoils of death and hell.

5 O let the dead now hear Thy voice;
Now bid Thy banished ones rejoice;
Their beauty this, their glorious dress,
Jesus, Thy blood and righteousness.
                          Amen.
ZINZENDORF N. L.   Tr. WESLEY

*See also Hymns under —*

THE LIFE EVERLASTING  . . . . . . . . . . 384–405

## THE HOLY GHOST

### 140 St. Cuthbert 8.6.8.4.
J. B. DYKES

1 Our blest Re-deem-er, ere He breathed His tender last fare-well,

A Guide, a Com-fort-er, bequeathed With us to dwell. A-MEN.

2 He came sweet influence to impart,
  A gracious, willing guest,
While He can find one humble heart
  Wherein to rest.

3 And His that gentle voice we hear,
  Soft as the breath of even,
That checks each thought, that calms
    each fear,
  And speaks of heaven.

4 And every virtue we possess,
  And every conquest won,
And every thought of holiness,
  Are His alone.

5 Spirit of purity and grace,
  Our weakness, pitying see;
Oh, make our hearts Thy dwelling-
    place,
  And worthier Thee! Amen.

HARRIET AUBER ab.

### 141 Winchester Old C.M.
ESTES' PSALTER

1 When God of old came down from heav'n, In power and wrath He came;

## THE HOLY GHOST

Before His feet the clouds were riven, Half darkness and half flame.

2 But when He came the second time,
He came in power and love;
Softer than gale at morning prime,
Hovered His holy Dove.

3 The fires, that rushed on Sinai down
In sudden torrents dread,
Now gently light, a glorious crown,
On every sainted head.

4 And, as on Israel's awe-struck ear
The voice exceeding loud,
The trump that angels quake to hear,
Thrilled from the deep dark cloud;

5 So, when the Spirit of our God
Came down His flock to find,
A voice from heaven was heard abroad,
A rushing mighty wind.

6 It fills the Church of God, it fills
The sinful world around;
Only in stubborn hearts and wills
No place for it is found.

7 Come, Lord, come Wisdom, Love, and
Open our ears to hear;      [Power,
Let us not miss the accepted hour;
Save, Lord, by love or fear.  Amen.

JOHN KEBLE *ab.*

## 142

1 Our God! our God! Thou shinest here,
    Thine own this latter day:
  To us Thy radiant steps appear:
    We watch Thy glorious way.

2 Thou tookest once our flesh; Thy face
    Once on our darkness shone;
  Yet through each age new births of grace
    Still make Thy glory known.

3 Not only olden ages felt
    The presence of the Lord;
  Not only with the fathers dwelt
    Thy Spirit and Thy word.

4 Doth not the Spirit still descend
    And bring the heavenly fire?
  Doth not He still Thy Church extend,
    And waiting souls inspire?

5 Come, Holy Ghost! in us arise;
    Be this Thy mighty hour!
  And make Thy willing people wise
    To know Thy day of power.  Amen.

T. H. GILL

## THE HOLY GHOST

**143** St. Agnes C.M.     J. B. DYKES

1 Come, Ho- ly Spir - it, heaven - ly Dove, With all Thy quickening powers,

Kindle a flame of sa - cred love, In these cold hearts of ours!

2 Look, how we grovel here below,
   Fond of these trifling toys!
Our souls can neither fly nor go
   To reach eternal joys.

3 In vain we tune our formal songs;
   In vain we strive to rise:
Hosannas languish on our tongues,
   And our devotion dies.

4 Dear Lord, and shall we ever live
   At this poor dying rate,
Our love so faint, so cold to Thee,
   And Thine to us so great?

5 Come, Holy Spirit, heavenly Dove,
   With all Thy quickening powers,
Come, shed abroad a Saviour's love,
   And that shall kindle ours. Amen.
                          ISAAC WATTS

**144** Armagh C.M.     JAMES TURLE

1 Why should the chil - dren of a King Go mourn-ing all their days?

## THE HOLY GHOST

Great Comfort-er! de-scend and bring Some tokens of Thy grace.

2 Dost Thou not dwell in all the saints,
And seal the heirs of heaven?
When wilt Thou banish my complaints,
And show my sins forgiven?

3 Assure my conscience of her part
In the Redeemer's blood;
And bear Thy witness with my heart,
That I am born of God.

4 Thou art the earnest of His love,
The pledge of joys to come;
And Thy soft wings, celestial Dove,
Will safe convey me home. Amen.

ISAAC WATTS

145 **Thatcher** S.M.　　　　　　　　　　From HANDEL

♩ = 100

1 Come, Ho - ly Spir - it, come! Let thy bright beams a - rise;

Dis-pel the sor - row from our minds, The darkness from our eyes.

2 Revive our drooping faith,
Our doubts and fears remove,
And kindle in our breasts the flame
Of never-dying love.

3 Convince us of our sin,
Then lead to Jesus' blood,
And to our wondering view reveal
The secret love of God.

4 'Tis Thine to cleanse the heart,
To sanctify the soul,
To pour fresh life in every part,
And new-create the whole.

5 Dwell therefore in our hearts,
Our minds from bondage free;
Then we shall know, and praise, and love
The Father, Son, and Thee. Amen.

JOSEPH HART ab.

## THE HOLY GHOST

**146 Olivet** 6.6.4.6.6.6.4.  LOWELL MASON

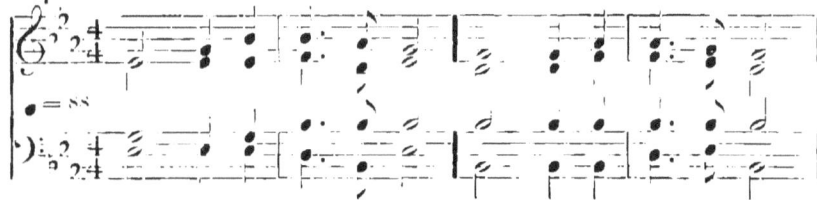

1 Come, Ho-ly Ghost,—in love Shed on us from a-bove
Thine own bright ray! Di-vine-ly good Thou art: Thy sa-cred gifts impart
To glad-den each sad heart: Oh, come to - day!

2 Come, tend'rest Friend, and best,
Our most delightful guest,
　With soothing power;
Rest, which the weary know,
Shade, 'mid the noontide glow,
Peace, when deep griefs o'erflow,—
　Cheer us this hour!

3 Come, Light serene, and still
Our inmost bosoms fill;
　Dwell in each breast:

We know no dawn but Thine;
Send forth Thy beams divine,
On our dark souls to shine,
　And make us blest!

4 Come, all the faithful bless:
Let all, who Christ confess,
　His praise employ:
Give virtue's rich reward;
Victorious death accord,
And, with our glorious Lord,
　Eternal joy!  Amen.

ROBERT II. OF FRANCE  Tr. PALMER

**147 St. Ambrose** 7.7.7.5.  GREGORIAN arr. GAUNTLETT

1 Gracious Spir-it, Ho - ly Ghost, Taught by Thee, we cov - et most,

## THE HOLY GHOST

Of Thy gifts at Pen-te-cost, Ho-ly, heaven-ly Love.

2 Love is kind, and suffers long;
Love is meek, and thinks no wrong;
Love than death itself more strong:
  Give us heavenly Love.

3 Prophecy will fade away,
Melting in the light of day;
Love will ever with us stay:
  Give us heavenly Love.

4 Faith will vanish into sight;
Hope be emptied in delight:

Love in heaven will shine more bright.
  Give us heavenly Love.

5 Faith and Hope and Love we see
Joining hand in hand agree:
But the greatest of the three,
And the best, is Love.

6 From the overshadowing
Of Thy gold and silver wing
Shed on us, who to Thee sing,
  Holy, heavenly Love.  Amen.
        CHRISTOPHER WORDSWORTH *alt.*

148 **Rodbourne** 7.7.7.5.                R. HAKING

♩ = 88

1 Ho-ly Ghost, the In-fi-nite, Shine up-on our nature's night
With Thy blessèd in-ward light, Com-fort-er Di-vine.

2 We are sinful, cleanse us, Lord;
We are faint, Thy strength afford;
Lost, until by Thee restored.
  Comforter Divine!

3 Like the dew, Thy peace distil;
Guide, subdue our wayward will,
Things of Christ unfolding still,
  Comforter Divine!

4 In us, for us, intercede,
And with voiceless groaning plead

Our unutterable need,
  Comforter Divine!

5 In us "Abba, Father," cry,
Earnest of our bliss on high,
Seal of immortality,
  Comforter Divine!

6 Search for us the depths of God;
Bear us up the starry road,
To the height of Thine abode,
  Comforter Divine!  Amen.
        GEORGE RAWSON *alt.*

## THE HOLY GHOST

### 149 Hebron L.M.
Lowell Mason

1 Sure the blest Comfort-er is nigh; 'Tis He sustains my fainting heart:

A — MEN.

Else would my hope for-ev-er die, And every cheering ray depart.

2 When some kind promise glads my soul,
Do I not find His healing voice
The tempest of my fears control,
And bid my drooping powers rejoice?

3 Whene'er, to call the Saviour mine,
With ardent wish my heart aspires,—
Can it be less than power divine,
That animates these strong desires?

4 And, when my cheerful hope can say,—
I love my God and taste His grace,—
Lord! is it not Thy blissful ray,
That brings this dawn of sacred peace?

5 Let Thy kind Spirit in my heart
For ever dwell, O God of love!
And light and heavenly peace impart,—
Sweet earnest of the joys above.
Amen.

Anne Steele *ab.*

### 150 Downton C.M.
S. S. Wesley

1 O Spir-it of the liv - ing God, Brooding with dove - like wings

## THE HOLY GHOST

O - ver the helpless and the weak A-mong cre - a - ted things!

2 Where should our feebleness find
Our helplessness a stay, [strength,
Didst Thou not bring us strength and
And comfort, day by day? [help,

3 Great are Thy consolations, Lord,
And mighty is Thy power,
In sickness and in solitude,
In sorrow's darkest hour.

4 Oh, if the souls that now despise
And grieve Thee, heavenly Dove,
Would seek Thee, and would welcome Thee,
How would they prize Thy love! Amen.

JANE E. BROWNE

## 151 Hermon C.M.
LOWELL MASON

1 Thy home is with the humble, Lord! The simplest are the best;

Thy lodging is in childlike hearts; Thou makest there Thy rest.

2 Dear Comforter! eternal Love!
If Thou wilt stay with me,
Of lowly thoughts and simple ways
I'll build a house for Thee.

3 Who made this beating heart of mine
But Thou, my heavenly Guest?
Let no one have it, then, but Thee,
And let it be Thy rest. Amen.

F. W. FABER ab.

## THE HOLY GHOST

**152  Dalehurst** C.M.  ARTHUR COTTMAN

1 The glo-ry of the spring how sweet! The new-born life how glad! What joy the hap-py earth to greet In new, bright raiment clad!

2 Divine Renewer! Thee I bless;
  I greet Thy going forth:
I love Thee in the loveliness
  Of Thy renewed earth.

3 But oh, these wonders of Thy grace,
  These nobler works of Thine,
These marvels sweeter far to trace,
  These new-births more divine!

4 These sinful souls Thou hallowest,
  These hearts Thou makest new,
These mourning souls by Thee made blest,
  These faithless hearts made true:

5 This new-born glow of faith so strong,
  This bloom of love so fair;
This new-born ecstasy of song
  And fragrancy of prayer!

6 Creator Spirit, work in me
  These wonders sweet of Thine!
Divine Renewer, graciously
  Renew this heart of mine!

7 Still let new life and strength upspring,
  Still let new joy be given!
And grant the glad new song to ring
  Through the new earth and heaven.   Amen.

T. H. GILL.

## INSPIRATION

**153 Aurelia** 7s & 6s D.                               S. S. WESLEY

1 O Word of God incarnate, O Wisdom from on high, O Truth unchanged, un-

changing, O Light of our dark sky! We praise Thee for the radiance That,

from the hallowed page, A lantern to our footsteps, Shines on from age to age.

2 The Church from Thee, her Master,
   Received the gift divine;
And still that light she lifteth
   O'er all the earth to shine.
It is the golden casket
   Where gems of truth are stored;
It is the heaven-drawn picture
   Of Thee, the living Word.

3 It floateth like a banner
   Before God's host unfurled;
It shineth like a beacon
   Above the darkling world;
It is the chart and compass
   That o'er life's surging sea,
'Mid mists, and rocks, and quicksands,
   Still guide, O Christ, to Thee.

4 O make Thy Church, dear Saviour,
   A lamp of purest gold,
To bear before the nations
   Thy true light, as of old.
O teach Thy wandering pilgrims
   By this their path to trace,
Till, clouds and darkness ended,
   They see Thee face to face.  Amen.
                      W. W. How

## THE HOLY GHOST

### 154. St. Stephen C.M.
WILLIAM JONES

1 The Spir-it breathes up-on the word, And brings the truth to sight:
Pre-cepts and promis-es af-ford A sanc-ti-fy-ing light.

2 A glory gilds the sacred page,
  Majestic, like the sun;
It gives a light to every age,
  It gives, but borrows none.

3 The hand that gave it still supplies
  The gracious light and heat;
His truths upon the nations rise,
  They rise, but never set.

4 Let everlasting thanks be Thine,
  For such a bright display
As makes a world of darkness shine
  With beams of heavenly day.

5 My soul rejoices to pursue
  The steps of Him I love,
Till glory breaks upon my view
  In brighter worlds above. Amen.

WILLIAM COWPER

### 155. Evan C.M.
W. H. HAVERGAL

1 How pre-cious is the Book Divine: By in-spi-ra-tion given:

## INSPIRATION

Bright as a lamp its doctrines shine, To guide our souls to heaven.

2 Its light, descending from above,
Our gloomy world to cheer;
Displays a Saviour's boundless love,
And brings His glories near.

3 It shows to man his wandering ways,
And where his feet have trod;
And brings to view the matchless grace
Of a forgiving God.

4 It sweetly cheers our drooping hearts,
In this dark vale of tears;
Life, light, and joy it still imparts,
And quells our rising fears.

5 This lamp, thro' all the tedious night
Of life, shall guide our way,
Till we behold the clearer light
Of an eternal day. Amen.

JOHN FAWCETT *ab*.

## 156 Armagh C.M.

JAMES TURLE

♩ = 92

1 Lamp of our feet, where-by we trace Our path when wont to stray;
Stream, from the fount of heavenly grace, Brook, by the traveller's way.

2 Bread of our souls, whereon we feed;
True manna from on high;
Our guide and chart, wherein we read
Of realms beyond the sky.

3 Pillar of fire, through watches dark,
And radiant cloud by day;
When waves would whelm our tossing bark,
Our anchor and our stay.

4 Word of the everlasting God,
Will of His glorious Son,
Without thee, how could earth be trod,
Or heaven itself be won?

5 Lord, grant us all aright to learn
The wisdom it imparts;
And to its heavenly teaching turn,
With simple, childlike hearts. Amen.

BERNARD BARTON

157 Aurelia 7s & 6s D.  S. S. WESLEY

1 The Church's one foundation  Is Jesus Christ, her Lord; She is His new cre-

a-tion  By water and the Word: From heav'n He came and sought her, To

be His holy bride; With His own blood He bought her, And for her life He died.

2 Elect from every nation,
 Yet one o'er all the earth,
Her charter of salvation
 One Lord, one faith, one birth;
One Holy Name she blesses,
 Partakes one holy food,
And to one hope she presses,
 With every grace endued.

3 'Mid toil and tribulation,
 And tumult of her war,
She waits the consummation
 Of peace for evermore;
Till with the vision glorious
 Her longing eyes are blest,
And the great Church victorious
 Shall be the Church at rest.

4 Yet she on earth hath union
 With God, the Three in One,
And mystic sweet communion
 With those whose rest is won:
Oh, happy ones and holy!
 Lord, give us grace that we
Like them, the meek and lowly,
 On high may dwell with Thee. Amen.

S. J. STONE ab.

## 158 Austria 8s & 7s D.
F. J. HAYDN

1 Glorious things of thee are spoken, Zion, city of our God!

He whose word cannot be broken, Formed thee for His own abode:

On the Rock of Ages founded— What can shake thy sure repose?

With salvation's walls surrounded, Thou may'st smile at all thy foes.

2 See, the streams of living waters
   Springing from eternal love,
Well supply thy sons and daughters,
   And all fear of want remove;
Who can faint, while such a river
   Ever flows their thirst t' assuage?
Grace, which like the Lord, the giver,
   Never fails from age to age.

3 Round each habitation hovering,
   See the cloud and fire appear!
For a glory and a covering,
   Showing that the Lord is near:
He who gives them daily manna,
   He who listens when they cry—
Let Him hear the loud hosanna,
   Rising to His throne on high. Amen.

JOHN NEWTON *ab.*

## THE HOLY CATHOLIC CHURCH

### 159 State Street S.M.
J. C. WOODMAN

1 I love Thy king-dom, Lord! The house of Thine a-bode, The

Church, our blest Re-deemer saved With His own precious blood.

2 I love Thy Church, O God!
Her walls before Thee stand,
Dear as the apple of Thine eye,
And graven on Thy hand.

3 For her my tears shall fall,
For her my prayers ascend;
To her my cares and toils be given,
Till toils and cares shall end.

4 Beyond my highest joy
I prize her heavenly ways—
Her sweet communion, solemn vows,
Her hymns of love and praise.

5 Jesus, Thou friend divine,
Our Saviour and our King,
Thy hand from every snare and foe,
Shall great deliverance bring.

6 Sure as Thy truth shall last,
To Zion shall be given
The brightest glories earth can yield,
And brighter bliss of heaven. Amen.

TIMOTHY DWIGHT

### 160 Mirfield C.M.
ARTHUR COTTMAN

1 Cit-y of God, how broad and far, Outspread Thy walls sub-lime! The

## THE HOLY CATHOLIC CHURCH

true Thy charter'd freemen are, Of ev-'ry age and clime.

2 One holy Church, one army strong,
One steadfast high intent,
One working band, one harvest song,
One King Omnipotent!

3 How purely hath Thy speech come down
From man's primeval youth!
How grandly hath Thine empire grown,
Of Freedom, Love, and Truth!

4 How gleam Thy watch-fires thro' the
With never-fainting ray! [night
How rise Thy towers, serene and bright,
To meet the dawning day!

5 In vain the surge's angry shock,
In vain the drifting sands;
Unharmed, upon the Eternal Rock,
The Eternal City stands. Amen.

SAMUEL JOHNSON

161  St. Stephen C.M.     WILLIAM JONES

♩ = 84

1 One ho-ly Church of God appears Through every age and race, Un-

wast-ed by the lapse of years, Unchanged by changing place.

2 From oldest time, on farthest shores,
Beneath the pine or palm,
One Unseen Presence she adores,
With silence, or with psalm.

3 The truth is her prophetic gift,
The soul her sacred page;
And feet on mercy's errand swift,
Do make her pilgrimage.

4 O living Church, thine errand speed,
Fulfil thy task sublime;
With bread of life earth's hunger feed;
Redeem the evil time! Amen.

SAMUEL LONGFELLOW ab.

## THE HOLY CATHOLIC CHURCH

**162 Renovation** S.M. — From HUMMEL

1 Far down the ages now, Her journey well-nigh done,
The pilgrim church pursues her way, In haste to reach the crown.

2 The story of the past
Comes up before her view:
How well it seems to suit her still,
Old, and yet ever new.

3 'Tis the same story still
Of sin and weariness,
Of grace and love still flowing down
To pardon and to bless.

4 No wider is the gate,
No broader is the way,
No smoother is the ancient path,
That leads to light and day.

5 No slacker grows the fight,
No feebler is the foe,
Nor less the need of armor tried,
Of shield and spear and bow.

6 Thus onward still we press
Through evil and through good,
Through pain and poverty and want,
Through peril and through blood.

7 Still faithful to our God,
And to our Captain true,
We follow where He leads the way,
The kingdom in our view. Amen.

HORATIUS BONAR *ab.*

**163 St. Ann's** C.M. — WILLIAM CROFT

1 Oh, where are kings and empires now, Of old that went and came?

## THE HOLY CATHOLIC CHURCH

But, Lord, Thy Church is praying yet, A thousand years the same.

2 We mark her goodly battlements,
And her foundations strong;
We hear within the solemn voice
Of her unending song.

3 For not like kingdoms of the world
Thy holy Church, O God! ['ning her,
Though earthquake shocks are threat-
And tempests are abroad;

4 Unshaken as eternal hills,
Immovable she stands,
A mountain that shall fill the earth,
A house not made by hands. Amen.

A. C. COXE

### 164 Mozart L.M.
Arr. from MOZART

♩ = 100

1 Triumphant Zi-on, lift thy head, From dust and darkness and the dead;

Though humbled long, awake at length, And gird thee with thy Saviour's strength.

2 Put all thy beauteous garments on
And let thy various charms be known:
The world thy glories shall confess,
Decked in the robes of righteousness.

3 No more shall foes unclean invade,
And fill thy hallowed walls with dread;
No more shall hell's insulting host
Their victory and thy sorrows boast.

4 God, from on high, thy groans will hear;
His hand thy ruins shall repair;
Reared and adorned by love divine,
Thy towers and battlements shall shine.

5 Grace shall dispose my heart and voice,
To share and echo back her joys;
Nor will her watchful monarch cease,
To guard her in eternal peace. Amen.

PHILIP DODDRIDGE

## THE HOLY CATHOLIC CHURCH

**165 Dulce Carmen** 8s & 7s 6l.  J. M. HAYDN

1 Al - le - lu - ia! song of glad-ness, Song of ev - er - last - ing joy;

Al - le - lu - ia! song the sweetest That can an - gel hosts em-ploy;

A - MEN.

Hymning in God's ho-ly presence, Their high praise e-ter-nal-ly.

2 Alleluia! Church victorious,
   Thou may'st lift this joyful strain:
Alleluia! songs of triumph
   Well befit the ransomed train;
We our songs must raise with sadness,
   While in exile we remain.

3 Alleluia! strains of gladness
   Suit not souls with anguish torn;
Alleluia! notes of sadness
   Best befit our state forlorn;
For, in this dark world of sorrow,
   We with tears our sins must mourn.

4 But one earnest supplication,
   Holy God, we raise to Thee;
Bring us to Thy blissful presence,
   Make us all Thy joys to see;
Then we'll sing our alleluia,
   Sing to all eternity.  Amen.

LATIN HYMN 11th Century  Tr. NEALE

## THE HOLY CATHOLIC CHURCH

**166 Cloisters** 11.11.11.5.  JOSEPH BARNBY

1 Lord of our life, and God of our sal-va-tion, Star of our

night, and Hope of ev-ery na-tion, Hear and re-ceive Thy

Church's sup-pli-ca-tion, Lord God Al-might-y.  A-MEN.

2 Lord, Thou canst help when earthly armor faileth,
Lord, Thou canst save when deadly sin assaileth,
Lord, o'er Thy rock nor death nor hell prevaileth:
    Grant us Thy peace, Lord:

3 Peace in our hearts, our evil thoughts assuaging,
Peace in Thy Church, where brothers are engaging,
Peace, when the world its busy war is waging;
    Calm Thy foes raging.

4 Grant us Thy help till backward they are driven,
Grant them Thy truth, that they may be forgiven,
Grant peace on earth, and after we have striven,
    Peace in Thy heaven. Amen.

LATIN HYMN 8th Cent. Tr. PUSEY

## THE HOLY CATHOLIC CHURCH

### 167 London C.M.
WILLIAM CROFT

♩ = 76

1 A-rise, O King of grace, a-rise, And en-ter to Thy rest;

Lo! Thy Church waits with longing eyes Thus to be owned and blessed. A-MEN.

2 Enter with all Thy glorious train,
Thy Spirit and Thy Word;
All that the ark did once contain
Could no such grace afford.

3 Here, mighty God, accept our vows,
Here let Thy praise be spread:
Bless the provisions of Thy house,
And fill Thy poor with bread.

4 Here let the Son of David reign,
Let God's Anointed shine;
Justice and truth His court maintain
With love and power divine.

5 Here let Him hold a lasting throne;
And as His kingdom grows,
Fresh honors shall adorn His crown,
And shame confound His foes. Amen.

ISAAC WATTS

### 168 Leighton S.M.
H. W. GREATOREX

♩ = 88

1 How beauteous are their feet Who stand on Zi-on's hill, Who bring sal-

## THE HOLY CATHOLIC CHURCH

va - tion on their tongues, And words of peace re - veal!

2 How charming is their voice
How sweet the tidings are!
"Zion, behold thy Saviour King;
He reigns and triumphs here."

3 How happy are our ears,
That hear this joyful sound,
Which kings and prophets waited for,
And sought, but never found!

4 How blessèd are our eyes,
That see this heavenly light!
Prophets and kings desired it long,
But died without the sight.

5 The watchmen join their voice,
And tuneful notes employ;
Jerusalem breaks forth in songs,
And deserts learn the joy.

6 The Lord makes bare His arm
Through all the earth abroad;
Let every nation now behold
Their Saviour and their God. Amen.

ISAAC WATTS

### 169 Duke Street L.M.  JOHN HATTON

♩ = 112

1 We bid thee welcome, in the name Of Je-sus, our ex - alt - ed Head,
Come as a servant; so He came And we receive thee in His stead.

2 Come as a shepherd; guard and keep
This fold from hell, and earth, and sin;
Nourish the lambs, and feed the sheep,
The wounded heal, the lost bring in.

3 Come as a teacher, sent from God,
Charged His whole counsel to declare;
Lift o'er our ranks the prophet's rod,
While we uphold thy hands with prayer.

4 Come as a messenger of peace,
Filled with the Spirit, fired with love;
Live to behold our large increase,
And die to meet us all above. Amen.

JAMES MONTGOMERY ab.

## THE HOLY CATHOLIC CHURCH

### 170 Siloam C.M. (Eng.)     St. Albans Tune Book

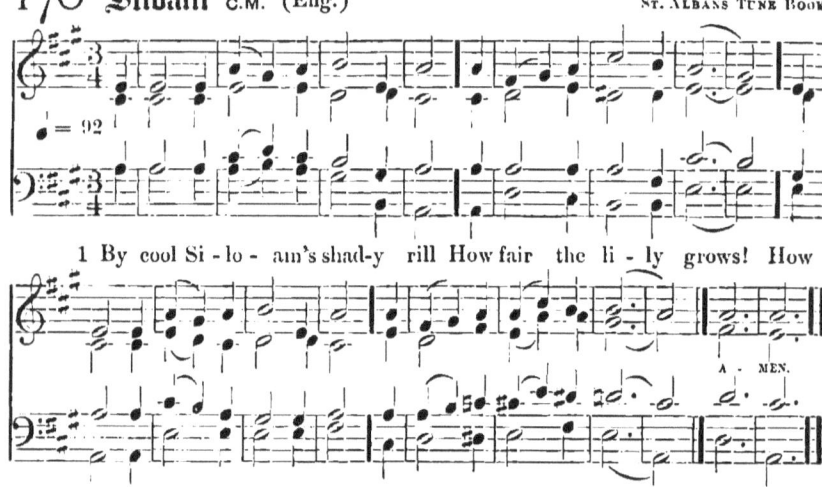

1 By cool Siloam's shady rill How fair the lily grows! How sweet the breath, beneath the hill, Of Sharon's dewy rose!

2 Lo! such the child whose early feet
The paths of peace have trod;
Whose secret heart, with influence sweet,
Is upward drawn to God.

3 By cool Siloam's shady rill
The lily must decay;
The rose that blooms beneath the hill
Must shortly fade away.

4 And soon, too soon, the wintry hour
Of man's maturer age

May shake the soul with sorrow's power
And stormy passion's rage.

5 O Thou, whose infant feet were found
Within Thy Father's shrine,
Whose years, with changeless virtue
Were all alike divine!   [crowned,

6 Dependent on Thy bounteous breath,
We seek Thy grace alone
In childhood, manhood, age and death,
To keep us still Thine own.   Amen.

REGINALD HEBER

### 171

1 See, Israel's gentle Shepherd stands,
With all-engaging charms;
Hark! how He calls the tender lambs,
And folds them in His arms.

2 "Permit them to approach," He cries,
"Nor scorn their humble name;

It was to bless such souls as these
The Lord of angels came."

3 We bring them, Lord, with fervent
And yield them up to Thee: [prayer,
Joyful that we ourselves are Thine,
Thine let our offspring be.   Amen.

PHILIP DODDRIDGE ab.

### Siloam C.M.     SECOND TUNE     I. B. WOODBURY

## BAPTISM AND CONFESSION OF FAITH

**172 Guter Hirt** 8s&7s

JOSEPH BARNBY

♩ = 88

1 Saviour! who Thy flock art feeding With the shepherd's kindest care, All the

fee-ble gen-tly leading, While the lambs Thy bo-som share;—

2 Now, these little ones receiving,
   Fold them in Thy gracious arm;
   There, we know, Thy word believing,
   Only there, secure from harm.

3 Never, from Thy pasture roving,
   Let them be the lion's prey;
   Let Thy tenderness, so loving,
   Keep them all life's dangerous way.

4 Then, within Thy fold eternal,
   Let them find a resting-place;
   Feed in pastures ever vernal,
   Drink the rivers of Thy grace. Amen.

W. A. MUHLENBURG

## THE HOLY CATHOLIC CHURCH

**173 Kirby Bedon** 6.6.4.6.6.6.4.    E. Bennett

1 Shepherd of tender youth, Guiding in love and truth Thro' devious ways;

Christ our triumphant King, We come Thy name to sing; Hither our children bring, Tributes of praise.

2 Thou art our holy Lord,
O all-subduing Word,
  Healer of strife:
Thou didst Thyself abase,
That from sin's deep disgrace
Thou mightest save our race,
  And give us life.

3 Thou art the great High Priest;
Thou hast prepared the feast
  Of heavenly love;
While in our mortal pain
None calls on Thee in vain;
Help Thou dost not disdain,
  Help from above.

4 Ever be near our side,
Our Shepherd and our Guide,
  Our staff and song:
Jesus, Thou Christ of God,
By Thine enduring word
Lead us where Thou hast trod,
  Make our faith strong.

5 So now, and till we die,
Sound we Thy praises high,
  And joyful sing:
Let all Thy holy throng
Who to Thy Church belong,
Unite and swell the song
  To Christ our King.   Amen.

CLEMENT OF ALEXANDRIA   Tr. DEXTER

## BAPTISM AND CONFESSION OF FAITH

### 174 Peterborough L.M.D.
CH. PS. AND HY. BOOK

1 Arm these Thy soldiers, mighty Lord, With shield of faith and Spirit's sword;
Forth to the battle may they go, And boldly fight against the foe,
With banner of the cross unfurled, And by it overcome the world;
And so at last receive from Thee The palm and crown of victory.

2 Come, ever-blessèd Spirit, come,
And make Thy servant's hearts Thy home;
May each a living temple be,
Hallowed forever, Lord, to Thee;
Enrich that temple's holy shrine
With sevenfold gifts of grace divine;
With wisdom, light, and knowledge bless,
Strength, counsel, fear, and godliness.

3 O Trinity in Unity
One only God, and Persons Three;
In whom, through whom, by whom we live,
To Thee we praise and glory give;
Oh, grant us so to use Thy grace,
That we may see Thy glorious face,
And ever with the heavenly host
Praise Father, Son, and Holy Ghost.
Amen.

CHRISTOPHER WORDSWORTH *ab.*

## THE HOLY CATHOLIC CHURCH

**175 Rockingham** (Eng.) L.M.        EDWARD MILLER

1 Oh, sweetly breathe the lyres above, When angels touch the quivering string, And wake, to chant Immanuel's love, Such strains as angel-lips can sing!

2 And sweet, on earth, the choral swell,
From mortal tongues, of gladsome lays;
When pardoned souls their raptures tell,
And, grateful, hymn Immanuel's praise.

3 Jesus, Thy name our souls adore;
We own the bond that makes us Thine;
And carnal joys, that charmed before,
For Thy dear sake we now resign.

4 Our hearts, by dying love subdued,
Accept Thine offered grace to-day:
Beneath the cross, with blood bedewed,
We bow and give ourselves away.

5 In Thee we trust—on Thee rely;
Though we are feeble, Thou art strong;
Oh, keep us till our spirits fly
To join the bright, immortal throng!
      Amen.

RAY PALMER

**176 St. Mabyn** 8s & 7s       A. H. BROWN

1 Something ev-ery heart is lov-ing; If not Je-sus, none can rest;

## BAPTISM AND CONFESSION OF FAITH

Lord, my heart to Thee is giv-en, Take it, for it loves Thee best.

2 Thus I cast the world behind me;
   Jesus most beloved shall be;
Beauteous more than all things beauteous,
   He alone is joy to me.

3 Bright with all eternal radiance
   Is the glory of Thy face;
Thou art loving, sweet, and tender,
   Full of pity, full of grace.

4 Keep my heart still faithful to Thee,
   That my earthly life may be
But a shadow to that glory
   Of my hidden life in Thee. Amen.
                    GERHARD TERSTEEGEN

### 177 Lancaster C.M.
SAMUEL HOWARD

♩ = 92

1 I'm not ashamed to own my Lord, Nor to defend His cause,
Maintain the honor of His word, The glory of His cross.

2 Jesus, my God! I know His name,
   His Name is all my trust,
Nor will He put my soul to shame,
   Nor let my hope be lost.

3 Firm as His throne His promise stands,
   And He can well secure
What I've committed to His hands,
   Till the decisive hour.

4 Then will He own my worthless name
   Before His Father's face,
And in the New Jerusalem
   Appoint my soul a place. Amen.
                    ISAAC WATTS

## THE HOLY CATHOLIC CHURCH

### 178 St. Andrew S.M.
JOSEPH BARNBY

1 Like No-ah's wea-ry dove, That soared the earth around, But not a rest-ing place a-bove The cheerless wa-ters found;

A-MEN.

2 O cease, my wandering soul,
   On restless wing to roam;
All the wide world, to either pole,
   Has not for thee a home.

3 Behold the ark of God,
   Behold the open door;
Hasten to gain that dear abode,
   And rove, my soul, no more.

4 There, safe thou shalt abide,
   There, sweet shall be thy rest,
And every longing satisfied,
   With full salvation blest. Amen.

W. A. MUHLENBERG *ab.*

### 179 Service 7s
From MENDELSSOHN

1 Peo-ple of the liv-ing God, I have sought the world around,

## BAPTISM AND CONFESSION OF FAITH

Paths of sin and sor-row trod, Peace and comfort nowhere found.

2 Now to you my spirit turns —
Turns, a fugitive unblest;
Brethren, where your altar burns,
Oh, receive me into rest!

3 Lonely I no longer roam,
Like the cloud, the wind, the wave:
Where you dwell shall be my home,
Where you die shall be my grave;—

4 Mine the God whom you adore,
Your Redeemer shall be mine;
Earth can fill my soul no more,
Every idol I resign. Amen.

JAMES MONTGOMERY *ab.*

## 180 Dismission L.M.

H. W. BAKER

♩ = 100

1 Je - sus and shall it ev - er be A mortal man ashamed of Thee?

Ashamed of Thee whom angels praise, Whose glories shine through endless days?

2 Ashamed of Jesus! sooner far
Let evening blush to own a star:
He sheds the beams of light divine
O'er this benighted soul of mine.

3 Ashamed of Jesus, that dear Friend
On whom my hopes of heaven depend!
No, when I blush, be this my shame,
That I no more revere His name.

4 Ashamed of Jesus! yes, I may,
When I've no guilt to wash away,
No tear to wipe, no good to crave,
No fear to quell, no soul to save.

5 Till then, nor is my boasting vain,
Till then I boast a Saviour slain;
And O, may this my glory be,
That Christ is not ashamed of me.
Amen.

JOSEPH GRIGG *alt.* by BENJAMIN FRANCIS

## THE HOLY CATHOLIC CHURCH

**181 Ratisbon** 7s6l.   SACHSEN CHORALBUCH

♩ = 76

1 Man-y cen-tu-ries have fled Since our Sav-iour broke the bread.

And this sa-cred feast or-dained, Ev-er by His Church re-tained:

A - MEN.

Those His bod-y who discern, Thus shall meet till His re-turn.

2 Through the Church's long eclipse,
When, from priest or pastor's lips,
Truth divine was never heard,—
'Mid the famine of the word,
Still these symbols witness gave
To His love who died to save.

3 Come, the blessèd emblems share,
Which the Saviour's death declare;
Come, on truth immortal feed;
For His flesh is meat indeed:
Saviour, witness with the sign,
That our ransomed souls are Thine. Amen.

JOSIAH CONDER *ab.*

## THE LORD'S SUPPER

**182 St. Edith** 7s & 6s D.     E. HUSBAND

1 O bread to pil-grims giv-en, O food that an-gels eat;

O man-na sent from heav-en, For heaven-born na-tures meet!

Give us, for Thee long pin-ing, To eat till rich-ly filled;

Till, earth's delights re-sign-ing, Our ev-'ry wish is stilled. A-MEN.

2 O water, life bestowing,
  Forth from the Saviour's heart,
A fountain purely flowing,
  A fount of love Thou art!
Oh, let us, freely tasting,
  Our burning thirst assuage!
Thy sweetness never wasting,
  Avails from age to age.

3 Jesus, this Feast receiving,
  We Thee, unseen, adore;
Thy faithful word believing,
  We taste, and doubt no more.
Give us, Thou true and loving,
  On earth to live in Thee:
Then, death the veil removing,
  Thy glorious face to see. Amen.

TH. AQUINAS Tr. PALMER

## THE HOLY CATHOLIC CHURCH

### 183 In Memoriam 8.8.8.4.
F. C. Maker

1 By Christ redeemed, in Christ restored, We keep the mem-o-ry a-dored,

And show the death of our dear Lord Un-til He come.

2 His body broken in our stead
Is here, in this memorial bread;
And so our feeble love is fed,
    Until He come.

3 His fearful drops of agony,
His life-blood shed for us we see;
The wine shall tell the mystery,
    Until He come.

4 And thus that dark betrayal night,
With the last advent we unite—
The shame, the glory, by this rite,
    Until He come.

5 Until the trump of God be heard,
Until the ancient graves be stirred,
And with the great commanding word,
    The Lord shall come.

6 O blessèd hope! with this elate
Let not our hearts be desolate,
But strong in faith, in patience wait
    Until He come. Amen.
                GEORGE RAWSON

### 184 Merton C.M.
J. P. Jewson alt.

1 Ac-cord-ing to Thy gra-cious word, In meek hu-mil-i-ty,

## THE LORD'S SUPPER

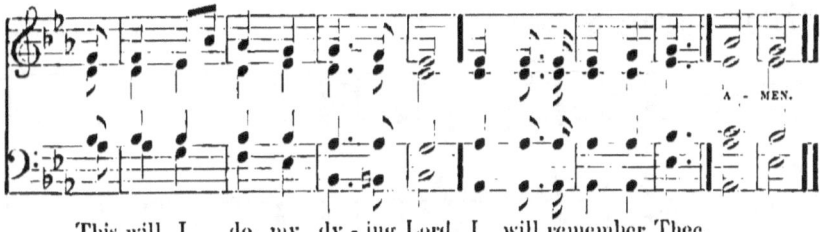

This will I do, my dy-ing Lord, I will remember Thee.

2 Thy body, broken for my sake,
My bread from heaven shall be;
Thy sacramental cup I take,
And thus remember Thee.

3 Gethsemane can I forget?
Or there Thy conflict see,
Thine agony and bloody sweat,
And not remember Thee?

4 When to the cross I turn mine eyes
And rest on Calvary,
O Lamb of God, my sacrifice,
I must remember Thee;

5 Remember Thee, and all Thy pains,
And all Thy love to me;
Yes, while a breath, a pulse remains,
Will I remember Thee.

6 And when these failing lips grow dumb,
And mind and memory flee,
When Thou shalt in Thy kingdom come,
Jesus, remember me. Amen.
JAMES MONTGOMERY

### 185 Eucharistic Hymn 9.8.9.8.      J. S. B. HODGES

1 Bread of the world, in mer-cy bro-ken, Wine of the soul, in mer-cy shed,

By whom the words of life were spoken, And in whose death our sins are dead.

2 Look on the heart by sorrow broken,
Look on the tears by sinners shed;
And be Thy feast to us the token
That by Thy grace our souls are fed. Amen.
REGINALD HEBER

## THE HOLY CATHOLIC CHURCH

**186 Guildford** 7s6l.      WILLIAM HAYNES

1 "Till He come:" oh, let the words Lin-ger on the trembling chords;

Let the lit-tle while be-tween In their gold-en light be seen;

A . MEN.

Let us think how heaven and home Lie beyond that —"Till He come."

2 When the weary ones we love
Enter on their rest above,
Seems the earth so poor and vast,
All our life-joy overcast?
Hush, be every murmur dumb;
It is only —"Till He come."

3 Clouds and conflicts round us press;
Would we have our sorrow less?
All the sharpness of the cross,
All that tells the world is loss,
Death and darkness, and the tomb,
Only whisper —"Till He come."

4 See, the feast of love is spread,
Drink the wine, and break the bread;
Sweet memorials,— till the Lord
Call us round His heavenly board;
Some from earth, from glory some,
Severed only —"Till He come." Amen.

E. H. BICKERSTETH

## THE LORD'S SUPPER

**187** Dismission L.M.      H. W. Baker

1 Je - sus, Thou joy of lov-ing hearts! Thou Fount of life, Thou Light of men!

From the best bliss that earth imparts, We turn unfilled to Thee again.

2 Thy truth unchanged hath ever stood;
  Thou savest those that on Thee call;
  To them that seek Thee, Thou art good,
  To them that find Thee, All in all.

3 We taste Thee, O Thou living Bread,
  And long to feast upon Thee still:
  We drink of Thee, the Fountain Head,
  And thirst, our souls from Thee to fill.

4 Our restless spirits yearn for Thee,
  Where'er our changeful lot is cast;
  Glad, when Thy gracious smile we see,
  Blest, when our faith can hold Thee fast.

5 O Jesus, ever with us stay;
  Make all our moments calm and bright;
  Chase the dark night of sin away;
  Shed o'er the world Thy holy light.
                     Amen.

                  ST. BERNARD   Tr. PALMER

---

*See also Hymns under —*

**JESUS CHRIST**
    Passion and Crucifixion     .    .    . 84 – 96
    Mediatorial Reign   .    .    .    113 – 126

**THE FORGIVENESS OF SINS**
    Repentance .           .    .    266 – 280.
    Redeeming Love .    .    .    .    296 – 310

## THE HOLY CATHOLIC CHURCH

**188 St. Michael** S.M.     Date's Psalter

1 Ye servants of the Lord, Each in his of-fice wait, Observant of His heavenly word, And watchful at His gate. A-MEN.

2 Let all your lamps be bright,
   And trim the golden flame:
Gird up your loins, as in His sight,
   For awful is His Name.

3 Watch: 't is your Lord's command,
   And while we speak, He 's near;
Mark the first signal of His hand,
   And ready all appear.

4 O happy servant he,
   In such a posture found!
He shall his Lord with rapture see,
   And be with honor crowned. Amen.

                                  PHILIP DODDRIDGE

**189 Olmutz** S.M.     Arr. by Lowell Mason

1 A charge to keep I have, A God to glo-ri-fy;

## CONSECRATION AND SERVICE

A nev-er dy-ing soul to save, And fit it for the sky.

2 To serve the present age,
My calling to fulfil;
Oh, may it all my powers engage
To do my Master's will.

3 Arm me with jealous care,
As in Thy sight to live;
And oh, Thy servant, Lord, prepare
A strict account to give.

4 Help me to watch and pray,
And on Thyself rely,
Assured, if I my trust betray,
I shall forever die. Amen.
CHARLES WESLEY

### 190 State Street S.M.
J. C. WOODMAN

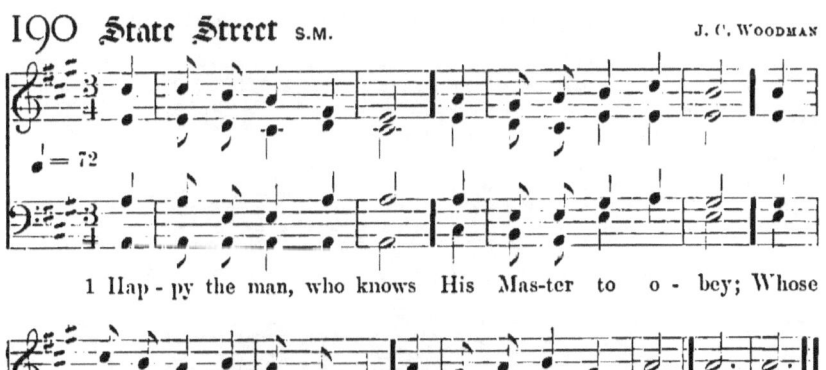

♩ = 72

1 Hap-py the man, who knows His Mas-ter to o-bey; Whose

life of care and la-bor flows, Where God points out the way.

2 He riseth to his task,
Soon as the word is given,
Nor waits, nor doth a question ask,
When orders come from heaven.

3 Nothing he calls his own;
Nothing he hath to say;
His feet are shod for God alone,
And God alone obey.

4 Give us, O God, this mind,
Which waits for Thy command,
And doth its highest pleasure find
In Thy great work to stand. Amen.
T. C. UPHAM

## THE HOLY CATHOLIC CHURCH

**191 St. Gertrude** 6s&5sD.  ARTHUR SULLIVAN

2 Like a mighty army
  Moves the church of God;
  Brothers, we are treading
  Where the saints have trod:
We are not divided,
  All one body we,
One in hope and doctrine,
  One in charity.
    Onward, etc.

3 Crowns and thrones may perish,
  Kingdoms rise and wane;
But the church of Jesus
  Constant will remain.
Gates of hell can never
  'Gainst that church prevail;
We have Christ's own promise
  And that cannot fail.
    Onward, etc. Amen.
S. BARING-GOULD

*CONSECRATION AND SERVICE*

## 192 Amerton S.M.
WILLIAM HAYNES

1 Soldiers of Christ, a-rise!.. And put your ar-mor on,...
Strong in the strength which God supplies Thro' His eternal Son,—

2 Strong in the Lord of hosts,
  And in His mighty power:
Who in the strength of Jesus trusts
Is more than conqueror.

3 Stand, then, in His great might,
  With all His strength endued;
But take, to arm you for the fight,
The panoply of God.

4 That having all things done,
  And all your conflicts past,
Ye may o'ercome, through Christ alone,
And stand entire at last. Amen.
CHARLES WESLEY ab.

## Silver Street S.M. SECOND TUNE
ISAAC SMITH

## THE HOLY CATHOLIC CHURCH

**193  Alma Lur** 11s            Frances R. Havergal.

1 On our way rejoic-ing as we homeward move, Hearken to our praises,
O Thou God of love! Is there grief or sad-ness? Thine it can-not be!
Is our sky beclouded? clouds are not from Thee! On our way re-joic-ing
as we homeward move, Hearken to our praises, O Thou God of love!

A - MEN.

2 If with honest-hearted love for God and man,
Day by day Thou find us doing what we can,
Thou who giv'st the seed-time wilt give large increase,
Crown the head with blessings, fill the heart with peace.
    On our way rejoicing, etc.

3 On our way rejoicing gladly let us go;
Conquered hath our Leader, vanquished is our foe!
Christ without, our safety, Christ within, our joy;
Who, if we be faithful, can our hope destroy?
    On our way rejoicing, etc.    Amen.

J. S. B. Monsell *alt.*

## CONSECRATION AND SERVICE

**194** Jesus Magister Bone  7s & 6s D.    J. B. DYKES

1 O Je-sus, I have prom-ised To serve Thee to the end; Be Thou for ev - er

near me, My Mas-ter and my Friend! I shall not fear the bat - tle If
Thou art by my side, Nor wander from the pathway If Thou wilt be my Guide.

2 O let me hear Thee speaking
  In accents clear and still,
Above the storms of passion,
  The murmurs of self-will.
O speak to reassure me,
  To hasten or control;
O speak to make me listen,
  Thou Guardian of my soul.

3 O Jesus, Thou hast promised,
  To all who follow Thee,
That where Thou art in glory,
  There shall Thy servant be;
And, Jesus, I have promised
  To serve Thee to the end;
O give me grace to follow
  My Master and my Friend! Amen.

J. E. BODE ab.

## THE HOLY CATHOLIC CHURCH

195 **Ellacombe** 7s & 6s D.   OLD GERMAN MELODY

1 Go for-ward, Christian sol - dier, Be-neath His ban-ner true:
The Lord Him-self, thy Lead - er, Shall all thy foes sub-due.
His love fore-tells thy tri - als, He knows thine hour-ly need;
He can, with bread of heav - en, Thy fainting spir-it feed.

A - MEN.

2 Go forward, Christian soldier,
  Fear not the secret foe;
Far more are o'er thee watching
  Than human eyes can know.
Trust only Christ, thy Captain,
  Cease not to watch and pray;
Heed not the treach'rous voices,
  That lure thy soul astray.

3 Go forward, Christian soldier,
  Fear not the gathering night;
The Lord has been thy shelter,
  The Lord will be thy light;
When morn His face revealeth,
  Thy dangers all are past;
O pray that faith and virtue
  May keep thee to the last. Amen.

LAURENCE TUTTIETT

## 196 CONSECRATION AND SERVICE

1 Lead on, O King Eternal!
  The day of march has come:
Henceforth in fields of conquest
  Thy tents shall be our home.
Through days of preparation
  Thy grace has made us strong,
And now, O King Eternal,
  We lift our battle song.

2 Lead on, O King Eternal!
  Till Sin's fierce war shall cease,
And Holiness shall whisper
  The sweet amen of Peace;

For not with swords loud clashing,
  Nor roll of stirring drums,
But deeds of love and mercy
  The heavenly kingdom comes.

3 Lead on, O King Eternal!
  We follow not with fears,
For gladness breaks like morning
  Where e'er Thy face appears;
Thy cross is lifted o'er us—
  We journey in its light;
The crown awaits the conquest—
  Lead on, O God of might! Amen.

ERNEST W. SHURTLEFF

## 197 Pearsall 7s&6sD.    ST. GALL. CATH. GESANGBUCH

1 O happy band of pilgrims, If onward ye will tread With Jesus as your Fel-low, To Je-sus as your head! O hap-py, if ye la-bor As Jesus did for men! O happy, if ye hunger As Jesus hunger'd then!

A-MEN.

2 The Faith by which ye see Him,
  The Hope, in which ye yearn,
The Love that through all troubles
  To Him alone will turn,—
What are they but forerunners
  . To lead you to His sight?
What are they, save the effluence
  Of Uncreated Light?

3 The Cross that Jesus carried
  He carried as your due:
The crown that Jesus weareth
  He weareth it for you;
O happy band of pilgrims
  Look upward to the skies;—
Where such a light affliction
  Shall win you such a prize! Amen.

ST. JOSEPH OF THE STUDIUM, Tr. NEALE *ab.*

## THE HOLY CATHOLIC CHURCH

**198 Italian Hymn** 6.6.4.6.6.6.4.    FELICE GIARDINI

1 Christ for the world we sing; The world to Christ we bring,

With lov-ing zeal: The poor, and them that mourn, The faint and

o-ver-borne, Sin-sick and sor-row-worn, Whom Christ doth heal. A-MEN.

2 Christ for the world we sing;
The world to Christ we bring
 With fervent prayer;
The wayward and the lost,
By restless passion tossed,
Redeemed, at countless cost,
 From dark despair.

3 Christ for the world we sing;
The world to Christ we bring,
 With one accord;
With us the work to share,
With us reproach to dare,
With us the cross to bear,
 For Christ our Lord.

4 Christ for the world we sing;
The world to Christ we bring,
 With joyful song;
The new-born souls, whose days,
Reclaimed from error's ways,
Inspired with hope and praise,
 To Christ belong. Amen.

SAMUEL WOLCOTT

## CONSECRATION AND SERVICE

**199** Greenland 7s & 6s D.    LAUSANNE PSALTER

1 Stand up!—stand up for Je - sus! Ye soldiers of the cross; Lift high His royal

banner, It must not suffer loss; From victory unto vic-tory His army He shall

lead, Till every foe is vanquished And Christ is Lord in-deed.   A - MEN.

2 Stand up!—stand up for Jesus!
　The trumpet call obey;
Forth to the mighty conflict,
　In this His glorious day;
"Ye that are men, now serve Him,"
　Against unnumbered foes;
Your courage rise with danger,
　And strength to strength oppose.

3 Stand up!—stand up for Jesus!
　Stand in His strength alone:
The arm of flesh will fail you;
　Ye dare not trust your own:
Put on the gospel armor,
　And watching unto prayer,
Where duty calls or danger,
　Be never wanting there.

4 Stand up!—stand up for Jesus!
　The strife will not be long;
This day the noise of battle,
　The next the victor's song:
To him that overcometh,
　A crown of life shall be;
He with the King of Glory
　Shall reign eternally!  Amen.
　　　　　GEORGE DUFFIELD

## THE HOLY CATHOLIC CHURCH

**200 Albans.** 6s & 5s 12l.   J. M. HAYDN

1 Forward be our watchword, Hearts and voices joined; Seek the things before us,

Not a look be-hind. Burns the fier-y pil-lar At our army's head;

Who shall dream of shrinking, By our captain led. Forward, out of er - ror,

A - MEN.

Leave behind the night; Forward thro' the darkness, Forward in-to light.

2 Forward, flock of Jesus,
　Salt of all the earth;
Till each yearning purpose
　Spring to glorious birth;
Sick, they ask for healing,
　Blind, they grope for day;

Pour upon the nations
　Wisdom's loving ray.
Forward, out of error,
　Leave behind the night;
Forward through the darkness,
　Forward into Light!

## CONSECRATION AND SERVICE

3 Glories upon glories
  Hath our God prepared,
  By the souls that love Him
  One day to be shared;
  Eye hath not beheld them,
  Ear hath never heard;
  Nor of these hath uttered
    Thought or speech a word:
      Forward, marching eastward
        Where the heaven is bright,
      Till the veil be lifted,
        Till our faith be sight!

4 Far o'er yon horizon
  Rise the city towers,
  Where our God abideth,
  That fair home is ours:
  Flash the streets with jasper,
  Shine the gates with gold:
  Flows the gladdening river
    Shedding joys untold:
      Thither, onward thither,
        In the Spirit's might:
      Pilgrims to your country,
        Forward into Light!  Amen.
                    HENRY ALFORD *ab.*

### 201  7s
J. B. CALKIN

1 Soldiers who to Christ belong, Trust ye in His word, be strong;

For His promises are sure, His rewards for aye endure.

2 His no crowns that pass away;
  His no palm that sees decay;
  His the joy that shall not fade:
  His the light that knows no shade:

3 His the home for spirits blest,
  Where He gives them peaceful rest,
  Far above the starry skies,
  In the bliss of Paradise.

4 Here on earth ye can but clasp
  Things that perish in the grasp;
  Lift your hearts then to the skies:
  God Himself shall be your prize.

5 Praise we now with saints at rest
  FATHER, SON, and SPIRIT Blest;
  For His promises are sure,
  His rewards shall aye endure.  Amen.
        PARIS BREVIARY adap. from ISAAC WILLIAMS

## THE HOLY CATHOLIC CHURCH

**202 St. Theresa** 6s&5sD. with Chorus    ARTHUR SULLIVAN

1 Brightly gleams our banner, Pointing to the sky, Waving on Christ's

soldiers To their home on high! Marching through the desert, Gladly thus we pray,

Still with hearts united, Singing on our way,— Brightly gleams our banner,

Pointing to the sky, Waving on Christ's soldiers To their home on high!

2 Jesus, Lord and Master,
  At Thy sacred feet,
Here, with hearts rejoicing,
  See Thy children meet.
Often have we left Thee,
  Often gone astray;
Keep us mighty Saviour,
  In the narrow way.
    Brightly gleams, etc.

3 Pattern of our childhood,
  Once Thyself a child,
Make our childhood holy,
  Pure, and meek, and mild.
In the hour of danger
  Whither can we flee,
Save to Thee, dear Saviour,
  Only unto Thee?
    Brightly gleams, etc.

## CONSECRATION AND SERVICE

4 All our days direct us,
In the way we go;
Crown us still victorious
Over every foe:
Bid Thine angels shield us
When the storm-clouds lower;
Pardon Thou and save us
In the last dread hour.
Brightly gleams; etc.

5 Then with Saints and Angels
May we join above,
Offering prayers and praises
At Thy Throne of love.
When the march is over,
Then come rest and peace,
Jesus in His beauty!
Songs that never cease!
Brightly gleams, etc. Amen.

T. J. POTTER AND OTHERS

203 Children's Service 7.6.8.8.6.  E. K. GLEZEN

♩ = 88

1 Oh, what can lit - tle hands do, To please the King of heaven?
The lit - tle hands some work may try To help the poor in
mis - er - y: Such grace to mine be given. A-MEN.

2 Oh, what can little lips do,
To please the King of heaven?
The little lips can praise and pray,
And gentle words of kindness say:
Such grace to mine be given.

3 Oh, what can little eyes do,
To please the King of heaven?
The little eyes can upward look,
And learn to read God's holy Book:
Such grace to mine be given.

4 Oh, what can little hearts do,
To please the King of heaven?
Our hearts, if God His Spirit send,
Can love and trust their Saviour-Friend:
Such grace to mine be given.

5 When hearts, and hands, and lips unite
To please the King of heaven,
And serve the Saviour with delight,
They are most precious in His sight:
Such grace to mine be given. Amen.

FABIN

## THE HOLY CATHOLIC CHURCH

### 204 Schumann S.M.

From SCHUMANN

♩ = 88

1 We give Thee but Thine own, Whate'er the gift may be: All that we have is Thine a-lone, A trust, O Lord, from Thee.

A - MEN.

2 May we Thy bounties thus
As stewards true receive,
And gladly, as Thou blessest us,
To Thee our first-fruits give.

3 Oh, hearts are bruised and dead;
And homes are bare and cold;
And lambs for whom the Shepherd bled
Are straying from the fold!

4 To comfort and to bless,
To find a balm for woe,
To tend the lone and fatherless,
Is angels' work below.

5 The captive to release,
To God the lost to bring,
To teach the way of life and peace,—
It is a Christ-like thing.

6 And we believe Thy word,
Though dim our faith may be,—
Whate'er for Thine we do, O Lord,
We do it unto Thee. Amen.

W. W. How

### 205 Dedham C.M.

WILLIAM GARDNER

♩ = 72

1 Fa-ther of mer-cies! send Thy grace, All powerful, from a-bove,

## CHARITIES AND MISSIONS

To form in our o-be-dient souls The im-age of Thy love.

2 Oh, may our sympathizing breasts
   The generous pleasure know,
Kindly to share in others' joy,
   And weep for others' woe.

3 When the most helpless sons of grief,
   In low distress are laid,
Soft be our hearts their pains to feel,
   And swift our hands to aid.

4 So Jesus looked on dying man,
   When throned above the skies;
And mid th' embraces of His God
   He felt compassion rise.

5 On wings of love the Saviour flew,
   To raise us from the ground,
And made the richest of His blood,
   A balm for every wound. Amen.

PHILIP DODDRIDGE

### 206 Holy Trinity  C.M.

JOSEPH BARNBY

1 Lord, lead the way the Saviour went, By lane and cell ob-scure, And

let love's treasures still be spent, Like His, up-on the poor.

2 Like Him, thro' scenes of deep distress,
   Who bore the world's sad weight,
We, in their crowded loneliness,
   Would seek the desolate.

3 For Thou hast placed us side by side
   In this wide world of ill;
And that Thy followers may be tried,
   The poor are with us still.

4 Mean are all offerings we can make;
   Yet Thou hast taught us, Lord,
If given for the Saviour's sake,
   They lose not their reward. Amen.

WILLIAM CROSSWELL

## 207 Thatcher S.M.
From HANDEL

1 Sow in the morn thy seed, At eve hold not thy hand;
To doubt and fear give thou no heed, Broadcast it o'er the land.

2 Beside all waters sow,
   The highway furrows stock,
Drop it where thorns and thistles grow,
   Scatter it on the rock.

3 The good, the fruitful ground
   Expect not here nor there;
O'er hill and dale by plots 't is found;
   Go forth, then, everywhere.

4 Thou know'st not which may thrive
   The late or early sown;
Grace keeps the precious germs alive
   When and wherever strown.

5 And duly shall appear,
   In verdure, beauty, strength;
The tender blade, the stalk, the ear,
   And the full corn at length.

6 Thou canst not toil in vain;
   Cold, heat, the moist and dry,
Shall foster and mature the grain
   For garners in the sky.

7 Then, when the glorious end,
   The day of God, shall come,
The angel-reapers shall descend,
   And heaven sing, "Harvest home!"
                     Amen.
JAMES MONTGOMERY *ab*.

## 208 St. Alban S.M.
R. R. CHOPE

1 Teach me, my God and King, In all things Thee to see; And

## CHARITIES AND MISSIONS

what I do in an-y thing, To do it as for Thee!

2 To scorn the senses' sway,
 While still to Thee I tend;
 In all I do, be Thou the way,
 In all, be Thou the end.

3 All may of Thee partake;
 Nothing so small can be,
 But draws, when acted for Thy sake,
 Greatness and worth from Thee.

4 If done beneath Thy laws,
 Ev'n servile labors shine;
 Hallowed is toil, if this the cause;
 The meanest work, divine. Amen.

GEORGE HERBERT and JOHN WESLEY

**209 Service** 7s        From MENDELSSOHN

♩ = 76

1 Saviour, who Thy life didst give, That our souls might ransomed be,

Rest we not, till all the world Hears that love, and turns to Thee.

2 Help us, that we falter not,
 Though the fields are white and wide,
 And the reapers, sorely pressed,
 Call for aid on every side.

3 Guide us, that with swifter feet
 We may speed us on our way,
 Leading darkened nations forth
 Into Thine eternal day.

4 Sweet the service — blest the toil —
 Thine alone the glory be;
 Oh, baptize our souls anew;
 Consecrate us all to Thee. Amen.

AMELIA DE F. LOCKWOOD

## 210 Nativity C.M.
Henry Lahee

1 Workman of God, O lose not heart,
But learn what God is like;
And in the darkest battle-field
Thou shalt know where to strike.

2 Thrice blest is he to whom is given
The instinct that can tell
That God is on the field, when He
Is most invisible.

3 Blest too is he who can divine,
Where real right doth lie,
And dares to take the side that seems
Wrong to man's blindfold eye.

4 God's glory is a wondrous thing,
Most strange in all its ways,
And, of all things on earth, least like
What men agree to praise.

5 Then learn to scorn the praise of men,
And learn to lose with God;
For Jesus won the world through shame,
And beckons thee His road.

6 For right is right, since God is God;
And right the day must win;
To doubt would be disloyalty,
To falter would be sin. Amen.

F. W. Faber ab.

## 211 Mendon L.M.
Arr. Lowell Mason

1 Go, labor on; spend and be spent, Thy joy to do the Father's will;

## CHARITIES AND MISSIONS

It is the way the Master went, Should not the servant tread it still?

2 Go, labor on while it is day;
   The world's dark night is hastening on;
   Speed, speed thy work, cast sloth away,
   It is not thus that souls are won.

3 Toil on, faint not, keep watch and pray,
   Be wise the erring soul to win:
   Go forth into the world's highway,
   Compel the wanderer to come in.

4 Toil on, and in thy toil rejoice;
   For toil comes rest, for exile, home;
   Soon shalt thou hear the Bridegroom's voice,
   The midnight peal, "Behold, I come." Amen.

                             HORATIUS BONAR *ab.*

### 212 St. Mark C.M.  H. J. GAUNTLETT

1 Oh, still in accents sweet and strong Sounds forth the ancient word, "More

reap-ers for white harvest fields, More laborers for the Lord!"

2 We hear the call; in dreams no more
   In selfish ease we lie,
   But girded for our Father's work,
   Go forth beneath His sky.

3 Where prophets' word, and martyrs'
   And prayers of saints were sown, [blood,
   We, to their labors entering in,
   Would reap where they have strown.

4 O Thou whose call our hearts has stirred!
   To do Thy will we come;
   Thrust in our sickles at Thy word,
   And bear our harvest home. Amen.

                           SAMUEL LONGFELLOW

## 213 Greenland 7s & 6s D.

LAUSANNE PSALTER

1 Light of the world, we hail Thee Flushing the eastern skies; Never shall darkness

veil Thee Again from human eyes; Too long, alas, withholden, Now spread from shore to

shore, Thy light, so glad and gold-en, Shall set on earth no more. A-MEN.

2 Light of the world, Thy beauty
   Steals into every heart,
And glorifies with duty
   Life's poorest, humblest part;
Thou robest in Thy splendor
   The simple ways of men,
And helpest them to render
   Light back to Thee again.

3 Light of the world, before Thee
   Our spirits prostrate fall;
We worship, we adore Thee,
   Thou Light, the life of all;
With Thee is no forgetting
   Of all Thine hand hath made;
Thy rising hath no setting,
   Thy sunshine hath no shade.

4 Light of the world, illumine
   This darkened land of Thine,
Till everything that's human
   Be filled with what's divine;
Till every tongue and nation,
   From sin's dominion free,
Rise in the new creation
   Which springs from Love and Thee. Amen.

J. S. B. MONSELL.

## CHARITIES AND MISSIONS

### 214 Missionary Chant L.M.
CHARLES ZEUNER

1 Ye Christian heralds! go, pro-claim Sal-va-tion thro' Immanuel's name;

To distant climes the tidings bear, And plant the Rose of Sharon there.

  2 He'll shield you with a wall of fire,
   With holy zeal your hearts inspire,
   Bid raging winds their fury cease,
   And hush the tempest into peace.

  3 And when our labors all are o'er,
   Then may we meet to part no more,—
   Meet with the ransomed throng, to fall,
   And crown the Saviour Lord of all! Amen.
            B. H. DRAPER

### 215

  1 Sovereign of worlds, display Thy power;
   Be this Thy Zion's favored hour;
   O bid the morning star arise;
   O point the heathen to the skies.

  2 Set up Thy throne where Satan reigns,
   In western wilds and eastern plains;
   Far let the gospel's sound be known;
   Make Thou the universe Thine own.

  3 Speak, and the world shall hear Thy voice;
   Speak, and the desert shall rejoice:
   Dispel the gloom of heathen night;
   Bid every nation hail the light. Amen.
            B. H. DRAPER

## THE HOLY CATHOLIC CHURCH

**216 Mornington** S.M.    LORD MORNINGTON

1 O Lord our God, a - rise, The cause of truth main - tain,

And wide o'er all the peopled world Ex-tend her bless-èd reign.

2 Thou Prince of life, arise,
  Nor let Thy glory cease;
Far spread the conquests of Thy grace,
  And bless the earth with peace.

3 Thou Holy Ghost, arise,
  Expand Thy quickening wing,
And o'er a dark and ruined world
  Let light and order spring.

4 All on the earth, arise,
    To God the Saviour sing;
  From shore to shore, from earth to heaven,
    Let echoing anthems ring. Amen.
          RALPH WARDLAW

**217 Waltham** L.M.    J. B. CALKIN

1 Up - lift the banner! Let it float Skyward and seaward, high and wide: The

## CHARITIES AND MISSIONS

sun shall light its shining folds, The Cross on which the Saviour died.

2 Uplift the banner! Angels bend
  Wondering in silence o'er the sign,
And vainly seek to comprehend
  The wonder of the love Divine.

3 Uplift the banner! Heathen lands
  Far off shall see the glorious sight,
And nations, gathering at the call,
  Their spirits kindle in its light.

4 Uplift the banner! Let it float
  Sky-ward and sea-ward, high and wide;
Our glory, only in the Cross,
  Our only hope, the Crucified.

5 Uplift the banner! Wide and high,
  Sea-ward and sky-ward let it shine:
Nor skill, nor might, nor merit ours;
  We conquer only in the sign. Amen.

G. W. DOANE

### 218 Thatcher S.M.     From HANDEL

2 Over our spirits first
  Extend thy healing reign;
Then raise and quench the sacred thirst
  That never pains again.

3 Come, kingdom of our God,
  And make the broad earth thine;
Stretch o'er her lands and isles the rod
  That flowers with grace divine.

4 Soon may all tribes be blest
  With fruit from life's glad tree;
And in its shade, like brothers, rest,
  Sons of one family.

5 Come, kingdom of our God,
  And raise the glorious throne
In worlds by the undying trod,
  When God shall bless His own. Amen.

JOHN JOHNS

## THE HOLY CATHOLIC CHURCH

**219** Zion 8s7s&4    Thomas Hastings

1. O'er the gloomy hills of darkness, Cheered by no celestial ray, Sun of righteousness! arising, Bring the bright, the glorious day! Send the gospel

To the earth's remotest bound; Send the gospel To the earth's remotest bound.

2 Kingdoms wide that sit in darkness,—
Grant them, Lord, the glorious light!
And, from eastern coast to western,
May the morning chase the night;
And redemption,
Freely purchased, win the day.

3 Fly abroad, thou mighty gospel!
Win and conquer, never cease;
May thy lasting, wide dominion
Multiply and still increase;
Sway Thy sceptre,
Saviour! all the world around. Amen.

WILLIAM WILLIAMS *ab.*

**220** Resurrection 8s7s&4    GERMAN

1. On the mountain's top appearing, Lo! the sacred herald stands,
Welcome news to Zion bearing — Zion, long in hostile lands:

## CHARITIES AND MISSIONS

Mourning captive! Mourning captive! God Himself shall loose thy bands.

2 Has thy night been long and mournful?
Have thy friends unfaithful prov'd?
Have thy foes been proud and scornful,
By thy sighs and tears unmov'd?
    Cease thy mourning;
Zion still is well-beloved.

3 God, thy God, will now restore thee;
He Himself appears thy Friend;
All thy foes shall flee before thee;
Here their boasts and triumphs end:
    Great deliverance
Zion's King vouchsafes to send.

4 Peace and joy shall now attend thee;
All thy warfare now is past;
God, thy Saviour, will defend thee;
Victory is thine at last:
    All thy conflicts
End in everlasting rest. Amen.
THOMAS KELLY

### 221 Nuremberg 7s
J. R. AHLE

1 Wake the song of ju-bi-lee, Let it ech-o o'er the sea!

Now is come the promised hour; Jesus reigns with glorious power.

2 All ye nations, join and sing,
Praise your Saviour, praise your King;
Let it sound from shore to shore —
"Jesus reigns forevermore!"

3 Hark! the desert lands rejoice;
And the islands join their voice;
Joy! the whole creation sings,—
"Jesus is the King of kings!" Amen.
LEONARD BACON

## 222 Webb 7s&6s D.

G. J. WEBB

1 The morning light is breaking; The darkness disappears;

The sons of earth are waking To penitential tears;

Each breeze that sweeps the ocean Brings tidings from afar,
Of nations in commotion, Prepared for Zion's war.

2 See heathen nations bending
  Before the God we love,
And thousand hearts ascending
  In gratitude above;
While sinners now confessing,
  The gospel call obey,
And seek the Saviour's blessing,—
  A nation in a day.

3 Blest river of salvation!
  Pursue thy onward way;
Flow thou to every nation,
  Nor in thy richness stay:
Stay not till all the lowly
  Triumphant reach their home;
Stay not till all the holy
  Proclaim —"The Lord is come!"
        Amen.

S. F. SMITH *ab*.

## CHARITIES AND MISSIONS

**223 Yarmouth** 7s & 6s D.  LOWELL MASON

1 Hail to the Lord's anointed, Great David's greater Son!
Hail in the time appointed, His reign on earth begun!

He comes to break oppression, To set the captive free,
To take away transgression,

To take away transgression, To take away transgression, And rule in equity.

2 He comes with succor speedy
To those who suffer wrong:
To help the poor and needy,
And help the weak be strong;
To give them songs for sighing,
Their darkness turn to light;
||: Whose souls condemned and dying,:||
Were precious in His sight.

3 He shall come down like showers
Upon the fruitful earth,
And love and joy, like flowers,
Spring in His path to birth;
Before Him on the mountains,
Shall peace, the herald, go:
||: And righteousness in fountains,:||
From hill to valley flow.

4 Kings shall fall down before Him,
And gold and incense bring,
All nations shall adore Him,
His praise all people sing;
O'er every foe victorious,
He on His throne shall rest,
||: From age to age more glorious,:||
All-blessing and all-blest.

5 For Him shall prayer unceasing
And daily vows ascend;
His kingdom still increasing,—
A kingdom without end;
The tide of time shall never
His covenant remove;
||: His name shall stand forever,—:||
That name to us is—Love! Amen.

JAMES MONTGOMERY *ab.*

## THE HOLY CATHOLIC CHURCH

**224  Missionary Hymn** 7s & 6s D.  LOWELL MASON

1 From Greenland's icy mountains, From India's coral strand, Where Afric's sunny

fountains Roll down their golden sand,—From many an ancient riv-er, From

A - MEN.

many a palmy plain, They call us to deliver Their land from error's chain.

2 What though the spicy breezes
  Blow soft o'er Ceylon's isle,
Though every prospect pleases,
  And only man is vile;
In vain with lavish kindness
  The gifts of God are strown;
The heathen in his blindness,
  Bows down to wood and stone!

3 Shall we, whose souls are lighted
  With wisdom from on high,—
Shall we, to men benighted,
  The lamp of life deny?
Salvation, oh, salvation!
  The joyful sound proclaim,
Till earth's remotest nation
  Has learned Messiah's name.

4 Waft, waft, ye winds, His story,
  And you, ye waters, roll,
Till, like a sea of glory,
  It spreads from pole to pole;
Till o'er our ransomed nature
  The Lamb for sinners slain,
Redeemer, King, Creator,
  In bliss returns to reign.  Amen.

REGINALD HEBER

## CHARITIES AND MISSIONS

**225  Missionary Chant** L.M.  CHARLES ZEUNER

1 Jesus shall reign where'er the sun Does his successive journeys run;
His kingdom stretch from shore to shore, Till moons shall wax and wane no more.

2 For Him shall endless prayer be made,
And praises throng to crown His head:
His name, like sweet perfume, shall rise,
With every morning sacrifice.

3 People and realms of every tongue,
Dwell on His love with sweetest song;
And infant voices shall proclaim
Their early blessings on His name.

4 Blessings abound where'er He reigns;
The prisoner leaps to loose his chains:
The weary find eternal rest,
And all the sons of want are blest.

5 Let every creature rise and bring
Peculiar honors to our King:
Angels descend with songs again,
And earth repeat the loud amen. Amen.
ISAAC WATTS ab.

**226**

1 Kingdoms and thrones to God belong;
Crown Him, ye nations, in your song;
His wondrous name and power rehearse;
His honors shall enrich your verse.

2 Proclaim Him King, pronounce Him blest;
He's your defence, your joy, your rest:
When terrors rise, and nations faint,
God is the strength of every saint. Amen.
ISAAC WATTS ab.

**227**

1 Soon may the last glad song arise
Through all the millions of the skies—
That song of triumph which records
That all the earth is now the Lord's!

2 Let thrones and powers and kingdoms be
Obedient, mighty God, to Thee!
And, over land and stream and main,
Wave Thou the sceptre of Thy reign!

3 Oh, let that glorious anthem swell,
Let host to host the triumph tell,
That not one rebel heart remains,
But over all the Saviour reigns! Amen.
Mrs. VOKE

*See also Hymns under --*

JESUS CHRIST
   Ministry and Example . . . . 61 – 83
   Mediatorial Reign . . . . 113 – 126
THE HOLY CATHOLIC CHURCH . . . . 157 – 169

## THE COMMUNION OF SAINTS

**228 All Saints** C.M.D.  H. S. CUTLER

*1 The Son of God goes forth to war, A kingly crown to gain; His blood-red banner

streams afar, Who follows in His train? Who best can drink his cup of woe, Tri-

umphant over pain; Who patient bears his cross below, He follows in His train.

A - MEN.

2 The martyr first, whose eagle eye
 Could pierce beyond the grave,
Who saw his Master in the sky,
 And called on Him to save;
Like Him, with pardon on his tongue,
 In midst of mortal pain,
He prayed for them that did the wrong:
 Who follows in His train?

3 A glorious band, the chosen few,
 On whom the Spirit came;
Twelve valiant saints, their hope they knew,
 And mocked the cross and flame:
They met the tyrant's brandished steel,
 The lion's gory mane;
They bowed their necks, the death to feel:
 Who follows in their train?

4 A noble army, men and boys,
 The matron and the maid,
Around the Saviour's throne rejoice,
 In robes of light arrayed;
They climbed the steep ascent of heaven
 Through peril, toil, and pain;
O God! to us may grace be given
 To follow in their train! Amen.

\* *May be sung to St. Ann's.*   REGINALD HEBER.

## THE COMMUNION OF SAINTS

### 229 Unser Herrscher 7s&6sD.
GERMAN

1 Let our Choir new anthems raise: Wake the morn with gladness:

God Himself to joy and praise Turns the martyrs' sadness:

Bright the day that won their crown, Opened heaven's bright portal,

A-MEN.

As they laid the mortal down To put on th' immortal.

2 Never flinched they from the flame,
From the torture never;
Vain the foeman's sharpest aim,
Satan's best endeavor:
For by faith they saw the land
Decked in all its glory,
Where triumphant now they stand
With the victor's story.

3 Up and follow, Christian men!
Press through toil and sorrow;
Spurn the night of fear, and then,
Oh, the glorious morrow!
Who will venture on the strife?
Blest who first begin it;
Who will grasp the Land of Life?
Warriors, up and win it. Amen.

St. Joseph of the Studium Tr. Neale *ab*

## THE COMMUNION OF SAINTS

### 230 Pleyel's Hymn 7s
*Arr. from PLEYEL*

1 Chil-dren of the heavenly King, As ye jour-ney, sweet-ly sing;

A-MEN.

Sing your Saviour's worthy praise, Glorious in His works and ways.

2 Ye are travelling home to God
In the way the fathers trod;
They are happy now, and ye
Soon their happiness shall see.

3 Shout, ye little flock, and blest!
You on Jesus' throne shall rest;
There your seat is now prepared;
There your kingdom and reward.

4 Fear not, brethren; joyful stand
On the borders of your land;
Jesus Christ, your Father's Son,
Bids you undismayed go on.

5 Lord, obediently we go,
Gladly leaving all below:
Only Thou our Leader be,
And we still will follow Thee. Amen.

JOHN CENNICK *ab.*

### 231 Boylston S.M.
*LOWELL MASON*

1 Blest be the tie that binds Our hearts in Christ-ian love:

## THE COMMUNION OF SAINTS

The fel-low-ship of kindred minds Is like to that a - bove.

2 Before our Father's throne
We pour our ardent prayers;
Our fears, our hopes, our aims are one,
Our comforts and our cares.

3 We share our mutual woes,
Our mutual burdens bear;
And often for each other flows
The sympathizing tear.

4 When we at death must part,
It gives us inward pain;

But we shall still be joined in heart,
And hope to meet again.

5 This glorious hope revives
Our courage by the way;
While each in expectation lives,
And longs to see the day.

6 From sorrow, toil, and pain,
And sin, we shall be free,
And perfect love and friendship reign
Through all eternity. Amen.
JOHN FAWCETT

### 232 Evan C.M. W. H. HAVERGAL

♩ = 88

1 How sweet, how heavenly is the sight, When those who love the Lord,

In one an-oth-er's peace delight, And so ful - fill His word.

2 When each can feel his brother's sigh,
And with him bear a part!
When sorrow flows from eye to eye,
And joy from heart to heart!

3 When, free from envy, scorn, and pride,
Our wishes all above,
Each can his brother's failings hide,
And show a brother's love!

4 When love, in one delightful stream,
Through every bosom flows,
When union sweet, and dear esteem,
In every action glows.

5 Love is the golden chain that binds
The happy souls above;
And he's an heir of heaven who finds
His bosom glow with love. Amen.
JOSEPH SWAIN

## THE COMMUNION OF SAINTS

**233** Sarum 10s3l, with Alleluia          JOSEPH BARNBY

1 For all the saints, who from their labors rest, Who Thee by

faith before the world confess'd, Thy name, O Jesus,

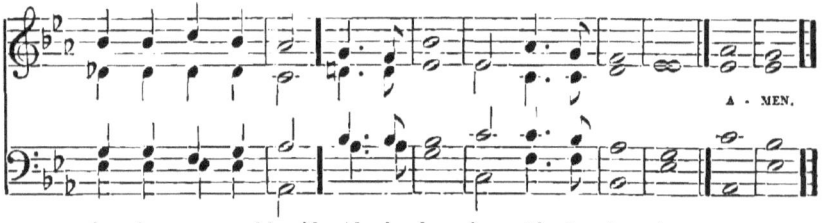

be for-ev-er bless'd, Al-le-lu-ia, Al-le-lu-ia.

A - MEN.

2 Thou wast their Rock, their Fortress and their Might;
Thou, Lord, their Captain in the well-fought fight;
Thou, in the darkness drear, their one true Light.
                        Alleluia.

3 O may Thy soldiers, faithful, true, and bold,
Fight as the saints who nobly fought of old,
And win with them the victor's crown of gold.
                        Alleluia.

4 O blest Communion, fellowship divine!
We feebly struggle, they in glory shine;
Yet all are one in Thee, for all are Thine.
                        Alleluia.

5 And when the strife is fierce, the warfare long,
Steals on the ear the distant triumph-song,
And hearts are brave again, and arms are strong.
                        Alleluia.

6 The golden evening brightens in the west;
Soon, soon to faithful warriors comes Thy rest;
Sweet is the calm of Paradise the blest.
                        Alleluia.

## THE COMMUNION OF SAINTS

7 But lo, there breaks a yet more glorious day;
The saints triumphant rise in bright array;
The King of Glory passes on His way.
                    Alleluia.

8 From earth's wide bounds, from ocean's farthest coast,
Through gates of pearl streams in the countless host,
Singing to Father, Son, and Holy Ghost.
              Alleluia.   Amen.
                              W. W. How

### 234  St. Theodulph  7s&6sD.     MELCHIOR TESCHNER

1 From all Thy saints in war-fare, For all Thy saints at rest, To Thee, O bless-èd

Je - sus, All prais-es be ad-dress'd. Thou, Lord, didst win the battle, That

they might conqu'rors be; Their crowns of living glory Are lit with rays from Thee.

2 Apostles, prophets, martyrs,
    And all the sacred throng,
Who wear the spotless raiment,
    Who raise the ceaseless song;
For these, passed on before us,
    Saviour. we Thee adore,
And, walking in their footsteps,
    Would serve Thee evermore.

3 Then praise we God, the Father,
    And praise we God, the Son,
And God the Holy Spirit,
    Eternal Three in One;
Till all the ransom'd number
    Fall down before the throne,
And honor, power, and glory
    Ascribe to God alone.   Amen.
                         EARL NELSON ab.

## THE COMMUNION OF SAINTS

### 235 Holy Trinity C.M.
JOSEPH BARNBY

1 Hap-py the souls to Je-sus joined, And sav'd by grace a-lone; Walk-

ing in all His ways, they find Their heav'n on earth be-gun. A-MEN.

2 The church triumphant in Thy love,
Their mighty joys we know:
They sing the Lamb in hymns above,
And we in hymns below.

3 Thee, in Thy glorious realm, they praise,
And bow before Thy throne;
We in the kingdom of Thy grace;—
The kingdoms are but one.

4 The holy to the holiest leads;
From thence our spirits rise;
And he that in Thy statutes treads
Shall meet Thee in the skies. Amen.

CHARLES WESLEY

### 236 Lancaster C.M.
SAMUEL HOWARD

1 Give me the wings of faith, to rise With-in the veil, and see

## THE COMMUNION OF SAINTS

The saints a-bove, how great their joys, How bright their glories be.

2 Once they were mourning here below,
  And wet their couch with tears;
  They wrestled hard, as we do now,
  With sins, and doubts, and fears.

3 I ask them, whence their victory
      came;
  They, with united breath,
  Ascribe their conquest to the Lamb,
  Their triumph to His death.

4 They marked the footsteps that He
      trod;
  His zeal inspired their breast;
  And following their incarnate God,
  Possess the promised rest.

5 Our glorious Leader claims our praise,
  For His own pattern given,
  While the long cloud of witnesses
  Show the same path to heaven.  Amen.
                        ISAAC WATTS

### 237  St. Michael  s.m.
DAYE'S PSALTER

1 For all Thy saints, O Lord, Who strove in Thee to live,
Who followed Thee, obeyed, adored, Our grateful hymn receive.

2 For all Thy saints, O Lord,
    Accept our thankful cry,
  Who counted Thee their great reward,
    And strove in Thee to die.

3 They all in life and death,
    With Thee, their Lord, in view,
  Learned from Thy Holy Spirit's breath,
    To suffer and to do.

4 For this Thy name we bless,
    And humbly pray that we
  May follow them in holiness,
    And live and die in Thee.  Amen.
                    RICHARD MANT  ab.

## THE COMMUNION OF SAINTS

**238 Nativity** C.M.     HENRY LAHEE

1 Sing we the song of those who stand A-round th' e-ter-nal throne, Of

ev-ery kin-dred, clime, and land, A mul-ti-tude un-known.

2 Life's poor distinctions vanish here;
   To-day, the young, the old,
Our Saviour and His flock appear
   One Shepherd and one fold.

3 Toil, trial, suffering, still await
   On earth the pilgrim-throng;
Yet learn we, in our low estate,
   The Church-triumphant's song.

4 "Worthy the Lamb for sinners slain,"
   Cry the redeemed above,
"Blessing and honor to obtain,
   And everlasting love."

5 "Worthy the Lamb," on earth we sing,
   "Who died our souls to save;
Henceforth, O Death, where is thy sting?
   Thy victory, O Grave?"

6 Then, alleluia, power, and praise
   To God in Christ be given;
May all who now this anthem raise,
   Renew the strain in heaven. Amen.

JAMES MONTGOMERY

## THE COMMUNION OF SAINTS

**239 Warwick** C.M.     SAMUEL STANLEY

1 Come, let us join our friends a-bove That have ob-tained the prize, And

on the ea-gle wings of love To joys ce-les-tial rise. A-MEN.

2 Let all the saints terrestrial sing
   With those to glory gone;
For all the servants of our King
   In earth and heaven are one.

3 One family, we dwell in Him,
   One Church above, beneath,
Though now divided by the stream,
   The narrow stream of death.

4 One army of the living God,
   To His command we bow;
Part of His host have crossed the flood,
   And part are crossing now.

5 E'en now to their eternal home
   Some happy spirits fly;
And we are to the margin come,
   And soon expect to die.

6 Dear Saviour, be our constant Guide;
   Then, when the word is given,
Bid Jordan's narrow stream divide,
   And land us safe in heaven. Amen.

CHARLES WESLEY *ab. and alt*

## THE COMMUNION OF SAINTS

**240  Promise** 8s & 7s D.      HENRY SMART

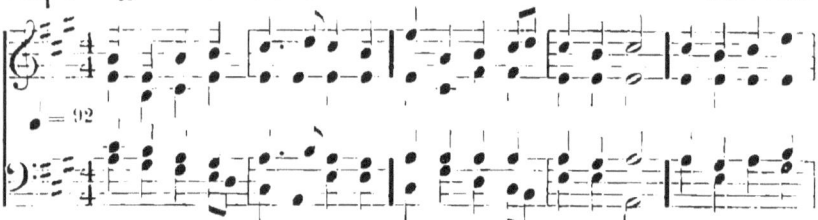

1 Thro' the night of doubt and sorrow, Onward goes the pilgrim band, Singing songs of

expectation, Marching to the Promis'd Land, Clear before us thro' the darkness Gleams and

burns the guiding Light; Brother clasps the hand of brother,
Stepping fearless thro' the night.

2 One the light of God's own presence,
  O'er His ransomed people shed,
Chasing far the gloom and terror,
  Brightening all the path we tread;—
One the object of our journey,
  One the faith which never tires,
One the earnest looking forward,
  One the hope our God inspires.

3 One the strain the lips of thousands
  Lift as from the heart of one;
One the conflict, one the peril,
  One the march in God begun;—
One the gladness of rejoicing
  On the far eternal shore,
Where the One almighty Father
  Reigns in love for evermore.

4 Onward therefore, pilgrim brothers,
  Onward with the Cross our aid!
Bear its shame and fight its battle,
  Till we rest beneath its shade!
Soon shall come the great awaking,
  Soon the rending of the tomb;
Then, a scattering of all shadows,
  And the end of toil and gloom.   Amen.

BERNHARDT S. INGEMANN   Tr. S. BARING-GOULD

## THE COMMUNION OF SAINTS

**241 Risenholme** 8.8.8.4.      H. J. GAUNTLETT

1 Fa-ther of all, from land and sea The nations sing, "Thine, Lord, are we,

Count-less in num-ber, but in Thee May we be one."

2 O Son of God, whose love so free
For men did make Thee man to be,
United to our God in Thee,
   May we be one.

3 Thou, Lord, didst once for all atone;
Thee may both Jew and Gentile own
Of their two walls the Corner Stone,
   Making them one.

4 Join high and low, join young and old,
In love that never waxes cold;
Under one Shepherd, in one fold,
   Make us all one.

5 So, when the world shall pass away,
May we awake with joy and say,
"Now in the bliss of endless day
   We all are one." Amen.
          CHRISTOPHER WORDSWORTH *ab.*

*See also Hymns under —*

THE HOLY CATHOLIC CHURCH . . . . . 157 – 169
THE LIFE EVERLASTING . . . . . 384 – 405

## THE FORGIVENESS OF SINS

### 242 Aubrey C.M.
C. J. VINCENT JR.

1 Sal-va-tion! oh, the joyful sound, 'Tis pleasure to our ears,
A sov'reign balm for ev-ery wound, A cor-dial for our fears.

2 Salvation! let the echo fly
The spacious earth around,
While all the armies of the sky
Conspire to raise the sound. Amen.

ISAAC WATTS *ah.*

### 243 Ratisbon 7s6l.
SACHSEN CHORALBUCH

1 From the Cross, up-lift-ed high, Where the Sav-iour deigns to die,
What me-lo-dious sounds I hear, Bursting on my ravished ear! —

## INVITATION

"Love's redeeming work is done—Come and welcome, sin-ner, come!"

2 "Spread for thee, the festal board
See with richest dainties stored;
To thy Father's bosom pressed;
Yet again a child confessed,
Never from His house to roam;
Come and welcome, sinner, come!"

3 "Soon the days of life shall end—
Lo, I come—your Saviour, Friend!
Safe your spirit to convey
To the realms of endless day,
Up to my eternal home—
Come and welcome, sinner, come!"
Amen.

THOMAS HAWEIS *ab.*

## 244 Mornington S.M.

LORD MORNINGTON

♩ = 72

1 Grace! 'tis a charm-ing sound, Har-mo-nious to the ear;
Heaven with the ech-o shall resound, And all the earth shall hear.

2 Grace first contrived the way
To save rebellious man;
And all the steps that grace display,
Which drew the wondrous plan.

3 Grace taught my wandering feet
To tread the heavenly road;
And new supplies each hour I meet
While pressing on to God.

4 Grace all the work shall crown,
Through everlasting days;
It lays in heaven the topmost stone,
And well deserves the praise. Amen.

PHILIP DODDRIDGE

## THE FORGIVENESS OF SINS

### 245. St. Edith. 7s & 6s D.
E. HUSBAND

1 O Jesus, Thou art standing
Outside the fast-closed door;
In lowly patience waiting
To pass the threshold o'er:
Shame on us, Christian brothers,
His name and sign who bear;
O shame, thrice shame upon us,
To keep Him standing there!

2 O Jesus, Thou art knocking:
And lo! that hand is scarred,
And thorns Thy brow encircle,
And tears Thy face have marred.
O love that passeth knowledge,
So patiently to wait!
O sin that hath no equal,
So fast to bar the gate!

3 O Jesus, Thou art pleading
In accents meek and low,
"I died for you, my children,
And will ye treat me so?"
O Lord, with shame and sorrow
We open now the door;
Dear Saviour, enter, enter,
And leave us nevermore! Amen.

W. W. How

## 246

1 The King of glory standeth
  Beside that heart of sin,
His mighty voice commandeth
  The raging waves within;
The floods of deepest anguish
  Roll backward at His will,
As o'er the storm ariseth
  His mandate, "Peace, be still."

2 At times, with sudden glory,
  He speaks, and all is done!
Without one stroke of battle
  The victory is won:
While we with joy beholding,
  Can scarce believe it true,
That e'en our kingly Jesus
  Can form such hearts anew.

3 But sometimes in the stillness,
  He gently draweth near,
And whispers words of welcome
  Into the sinner's ear;
With anxious heart He waiteth
  The answer of His cry,
That oft repeated question,
  "O wherefore wilt thou die?"

4 O Christ, His love is mighty!
  Long-suffering is His grace!
And glorious is the splendor
  That beameth from His face!
Our hearts up-leap in gladness,
  When we behold that love,
As we go singing onward
  To dwell with Him above.  Amen.
Mrs. C. L. S. BANCROFT.

## 247  Stephanos  8.5.8.3.                    H. W. BAKER.

1 Art thou wea-ry, art thou lan-guid, Art thou sore dis-tress'd?

"Come to Me," saith One, "and, com-ing, Be at rest."
A - MEN.

2 Hath He marks to lead me to Him,
    If He be my guide?
  "In His feet and hands are wound-prints,
    And His side."

3 Is there diadem, as Monarch,
    That His brow adorns?
  "Yea, a crown, in very surety,
    But of thorns."

4 If I find Him, if I follow,
    What His guerdon here?
  "Many a sorrow, many a labor,
    Many a tear."

5 If I still hold closely to Him,
    What hath He at last?
  "Sorrow vanquished, labor ended,
    Jordan passed."

6 If I ask Him to receive me,
    Will He say me nay?
  "Not till earth, and not till heaven
    Pass away."

7 Finding, following, keeping, struggling,
    Is He sure to bless?
  "Saints, apostles, prophets, martyrs,
    Answer, 'Yes.'"  Amen.
J. M. NEALE.

## 248 Heber C.M.

GEO. KINGSLEY

1 Ye wretch-ed, hun-gry, starv-ing poor, Be-hold a roy-al feast;

A-MEN.

Where mercy spreads her bounteous store, For every humble guest.

2 See, Jesus stands with open arms;
He calls, He bids you come:
Guilt holds you back, and fear alarms;
But see, there yet is room.

3 Room in the Saviour's bleeding heart:
There love and pity meet;
Nor will He bid the soul depart
That trembles at His feet.

4 In Him the Father, reconciled,
Invites your souls to come;
The rebel shall be called a child,
And kindly welcomed home.

5 There, with united heart and voice,
Before the eternal throne,
Ten thousand thousand souls rejoice
In ecstacies unknown.

6 And yet ten thousand thousand more
Are welcome still to come:
Ye longing souls, the grace adore;
Approach, there yet is room. Amen.

ANNE STEELE ab.

## 249 Beatitude C.M.

J. B. DYKES

1 Think well how Je-sus trusts Himself Un-to our child-ish love!

## INVITATION

As though by His free ways with us Our ear-nest-ness to prove.

2 His sacred name a common word
 On earth He loves to hear;
 There is no majesty in Him
 Which love may not come near.
3 The light of love is round His feet,
 His paths are never dim;

And He comes nigh to us when we
 Dare not come nigh to Him.
4 Let us be simple with Him, then,
 Not backward, stiff, nor cold,
 As though our Bethlehem could be
 What Sinai was of old. Amen.

F. W. FABER *ab.*

## 250 Service 7s

From MENDELSSOHN

1 Come, said Je-sus' sa-cred voice, Come, and make my paths your choice;
 I will guide you to your home; Weary pil-grim, hith-er come.

2 Thou who, homeless and forlorn,
 Long hast borne the proud world's scorn;
 Long hast roamed the barren waste,
 Weary wanderer, hither haste.

3 Hither come, for here is found
 Balm that flows for every wound!
 Peace, that ever shall endure,
 Rest, eternal, sacred, sure. Amen.

ANNA L. BARBAULD *ab.*

## Horton 7s   SECOND TUNE.   N. VON WARTENSEE Arr.

## THE FORGIVENESS OF SINS

**251 Bethany** (English) 8s&7sD.     HENRY SMART

1 Was there ever kindest shepherd Half so gentle, half so sweet
As the Saviour who would

have us Come and gather round His feet? There's a wideness in God's mercy Like the

wideness of the sea; There's a kindness in His justice Which is more than liberty.

2 There is no place where earth's sor-
   rows
Are more felt than up in heaven;
There is no place where earth's failings
Have such kindly judgment given.
There is welcome for the sinner,
   And more graces for the good;
There is mercy with the Saviour;
   There is healing in His blood.

3 There is grace enough for thou-
   sands
Of new worlds as great as this;
There is room for fresh creations
In that upper home of bliss;
For the love of God is broader
   Than the measure of man's mind;
And the heart of the Eternal
   Is most wonderfully kind.

4 But we make His love too narrow
   By false limits of our own;
And we magnify His strictness
   With a zeal He will not own.
There is plentiful redemption
   In the blood that has been shed;
There is joy for all the members,
   In the sorrows of the Head. Amen.

F. W. FABER *ab.*

## INVITATION

### 252 The Saviour's Call  6s & 4s
LOWELL MASON

1 To-day the Saviour calls: Ye wanderers, come: O ye benighted souls, Why longer roam?

2 To-day the Saviour calls;
Oh, hear Him now;
Within these sacred walls
To Jesus bow.

3 To-day the Saviour calls;
For refuge fly;
The storm of justice falls,
And death is nigh.

4 The Spirit calls to-day;
Yield to His power;
O, grieve Him not away:
'Tis mercy's hour.   Amen.

THOMAS HASTINGS

### 253 Peregrinus  8.6.8.6.4.
A. R. GAUL

1 Return, O wanderer, to thy home, Thy Father calls for thee; No longer now an
2 Return, O wanderer, to thy home, 'Tis Jesus calls for thee; The Spirit and the

ex-ile roam  In guilt and mis-er-y:  Re-turn, re - turn.
Bride say, "Come," Oh, now for ref-uge flee  Re-turn, re - turn.   Amen.

THOMAS HASTINGS  al.

254 Blumenthal 7s D.   JACQUES BLUMENTHAL

1 Sin-ners, turn; why will ye die? God, your Ma-ker, asks you why;

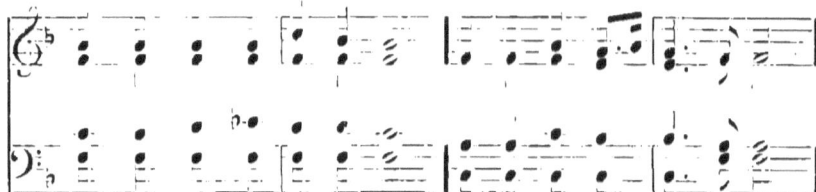

God, who did your be-ing give, Made you with Him-self to live:

He the fa-tal cause demands, Asks the work of His own hands,

A-MEN.

Why, ye thankless creatures, why Will ye cross His love, and die?

2 Sinners, turn; why will ye die?
God, your Saviour, asks you why;
He, who did your souls retrieve,
Died Himself that ye might live.
Will ye let Him die in vain,
Crucify your Lord again?
Why, ye ransomed sinners, why
Will ye slight His grace and die?

3 Sinners, turn; why will ye die?
God, the Spirit, asks you why;
God, who daily with you strove,
Wooed you to embrace His love.
Will ye not His grace receive?
Will ye still refuse to live?
Why, ye long-sought sinners, why
Will ye grieve your God, and die?
  Amen.

CHARLES WESLEY ab.

**255** Lyte  S.M.  J. P. WILKES

1 Did Christ o'er sin-ners weep, And shall our cheeks be dry? Let floods of pen-i-ten-tial grief Burst forth from ev-ery eye.

A-MEN.

2 The Son of God in tears,
    Angels with wonder see!
Be thou astonished, O my soul,
    He shed those tears for thee.

3 He wept that we might weep;
    Each sin demands a tear;
In heaven alone no sin is found,
    And there's no weeping there. Amen.

BENJAMIN BEDDOME

**256**

1 And canst thou, sinner, slight
    The call of love Divine?
Shall God with tenderness invite,
    And gain no thought of thine?

2 Wilt thou not cease to grieve
    The Spirit from thy breast,
Till He thy wretched soul shall leave
    With all thy sins oppressed?

3 To-day, a pardoning God
    Will hear the suppliant pray;
To-day, a Saviour's cleansing blood
    Will wash thy guilt away. Amen.

Mrs. A. B. HYDE

## THE FORGIVENESS OF SINS

**257  St. Bees**  7s                              J. B. DYKES

1 Hark, my soul! it is the Lord, 'Tis thy Sav-iour, hear His word:

Je-sus speaks, and speaks to thee; "Say, poor sinner, lov'st thou me?"

2 "Mine is an unchanging love,
Higher than the heights above,
Deeper than the depths beneath,
Free and faithful, strong as death."

3 "Thou shalt see my glory soon,
When the work of grace is done;
Partner of my throne shalt be:
Say, poor sinner, lov'st thou me?"

4 Lord, it is my chief complaint,
That my love is weak and faint;
Yet I love Thee and adore!
Oh, for grace to love Thee more!  Amen.

WILLIAM COWPER *ab.*

**258**

1 Sinner, rouse thee from thy sleep,
Wake, and o'er thy folly weep;
Raise thy spirit dark and dead,
Jesus waits His light to shed.

2 Leave thy folly, cease from crime,
From this hour redeem thy time;
Life secure without delay,
Evil is the mortal day.

3 Be not blind and foolish still;
Call'd of Jesus, learn His will:
Jesus calls from death and night,
Jesus waits to shed His light.  Amen.

H. U. ONDERDONK

**259  Olney**  S.M.                              LOWELL MASON

1 The Spir-it, in our hearts, Is whispering, "Sin-ner, come;" The

## INVITATION

Bride, the Church of Christ, proclaims To all His chil-dren, "Come!"

2 Let him that heareth say
 To all about him, "Come!"
Let him that thirsts for righteousness,
 To Christ, the fountain, come!

3 Yes, whosoever will,
 Oh, let him freely come,
And freely drink the stream of life;
 'T is Jesus bids him come.

4 Lo! Jesus, who invites,
 Declares, "I quickly come:"
Lord, even so! we wait Thine hour;
 Jesus, my Saviour, come! Amen.

H. C. ONDERDONK

## 260 Summons S.M.

J. B. CALKIN

1 Now is th'ac-cept-ed time, Now is the day of grace; Now

sinners! come, without de-lay, And seek the Saviour's face.

2 Now is the accepted time,
 The Saviour calls to-day;
To-morrow it may be too late;—
 Then why should you delay?

3 Now is the accepted time,
 The gospel bids you come;
And every promise in His word
 Declares there yet is room.

4 Lord, draw reluctant souls,
 And feast them with Thy love;
Then will the angels spread their wings
 And bear the news above. Amen.

JOHN DOBELL ob.

## THE FORGIVENESS OF SINS

### 261 Jesus Magister Bone 7s & 6s D.
J. B. DYKES

1 To-day Thy mercy calls me To wash away my sin, How-ev-er great my trespass, What-ev-er I have been; However long from mercy, My heart has turned away,

Thy precious blood can cleanse me, And make me white to-day.

2 To-day Thy gate is open,
And all who enter in
Shall find a Father's welcome,
And pardon for their sin;
The past shall be forgotten,
A present joy be given,
A future grace be promised,
A glorious crown in heaven.

3 O all embracing mercy,
O ever open door,
What should I do without Thee,
When heart and eyes run o'er?
When all things seem against me,
To drive me to despair,
I know one gate is open,
One ear will hear my prayer. Amen.

OSWALD ALLEN *ab.*

### 262 Federal Street L.M.
H. K. OLIVER

1 Be-hold a Stran-ger at the door! He gently knocks, has knocked before;

## INVITATION

Has waited long,is wait-ing still: You treat no other friend so ill.

2 Oh, lovely attitude! He stands,
With melting heart and open hands:
Oh, matchless kindness!—and He shows
This matchless kindness to His foes!

3 Rise, touched with gratitude divine;
Turn out His enemy and thine;
Turn out the soul-enslaving sin,
And let the heavenly Stranger in.

4 Sovereign of souls! Thou Prince of peace,
O may Thy gentle reign increase!
Throw wide the door, each willing mind,
And be His empire all mankind! Amen.

JOSEPH GRIGG *ab. and alt.*

## 263

1 God calling yet! shall I not hear?
Earth's pleasures shall I still hold dear?
Shall life's swift passing years all fly,
And still my soul in slumber lie?

2 God calling yet! and shall He knock,
And I my heart the closer lock?
He still is waiting to receive,
And shall I dare His Spirit grieve?

3 God calling yet! and shall I give
No heed, but still in bondage live?
I wait, but He does not forsake;
He calls me still; my heart, awake!

4 God calling yet! I cannot stay;
My heart I yield without delay:
Vain world, farewell, from thee I part;
The voice of God hath reached my heart.
Amen.

GERHARD TERSTEEGEN Tr. BORTHWICK *ab. and alt.*

## Bera L.M.   SECOND TUNE   J. E. GOULD

## THE FORGIVENESS OF SINS

### 264 Invitation 6s&3
F. C. Maker

1 Come to the Saviour now! He gently calleth thee;
In true repentance bow, Before Him bend the knee.
He waiteth to bestow Salvation, peace, and love, True joy on earth below, A home in heaven above. Come, come, come!

A-MEN.

2 Come to the Saviour now!
  Ye who have wandered far,
Renew your solemn vow,
  For His by right you are.
Come, like poor wandering sheep
  Returning to His fold;
His arm will safely keep,
  His love will ne'er grow cold.
Come, come, come!

3 Come to the Saviour, all!
  Whate'er your burdens be;
Hear now His loving call—
  "Cast all your care on me."
Come, and for every grief,
  In Jesus you will find
A sure and safe relief,
  A loving Friend and kind.
Come, come, come! Amen.

J. M. Wigner

## 265 Langran 10s

JAMES LANGRAN

1 Weary of earth, and laden with my sin, I look at heaven, and long to enter in; But there no evil thing may find a home: And yet I hear a voice that bids me "Come!"

2 So vile I am, how dare I hope to stand
In the pure glory of that holy land?
Before the whiteness of that throne appear?
Yet there are hands stretched out to draw me near.

3 It is the voice of Jesus that I hear,
His are the hands stretched out to draw me near,
And His the blood that can for all atone,
And set me faultless there before the throne.

4 'Twas He who found me on the deathly wild,
And made me heir of heaven, the Father's child,
And day by day, whereby my soul may live,
Gives me His grace of pardon, and will give.

5 Yea, Thou wilt answer for me, righteous Lord:
Thine all the merits, mine the great reward;
Thine the sharp thorns, and mine the golden crown;
Mine the life won, and Thine the life laid down. Amen.

S. J. STONE *ab.*

*See also Hymns under —*

THE HOLY GHOST                140–152

## THE FORGIVENESS OF SINS

### 266 Lachrymae 7s 3l
ARTHUR SULLIVAN

1 Lord, in this Thy mer-cy's day, Ere it pass for aye a-way, On our knees we fall and pray.

2 Holy Jesus, grant us tears,
Fill us with heart-searching fears,
Ere that day of doom appears.

3 Lord, on us Thy Spirit pour,
Kneeling lowly at the door,
Ere it close for evermore.

4 By Thy night of agony,
By Thy supplicating cry,
By Thy willingness to die;

5 By Thy tears of bitter woe
For Jerusalem below,
Let us not Thy love forego.

6 Judge and Saviour of our race,
Grant us, when we see Thy face,
With Thy ransomed ones a place.  Amen.

ISAAC WILLIAMS

### 267 Penitence L.M.
ST. ALBANS TUNE BOOK

1 Just as I am, with-out one plea, But that Thy blood was shed for me,

## REPENTANCE

And that Thou bid'st me come to Thee, O Lamb of God, I come! I come!

2 Just as I am, and waiting not
To rid my soul of one dark blot, [spot,
To Thee, whose blood can cleanse each
O Lamb of God, I come! I come!

3 Just as I am, though tossed about,
With many a conflict, many a doubt,
Fighting within, and fears without,
O Lamb of God, I come! I come!

4 Just as I am — poor, wretched, blind;
Sight, riches, healing of the mind,
Yea, all I need, in Thee I find,
O Lamb of God, I come! I come!

5 Just as I am, Thou wilt receive,
Wilt welcome, pardon, cleanse, relieve;
Because Thy promise I believe,
O Lamb of God, I come! I come!

6 Just as I am, Thy love unknown
Has broken every barrier down;
Now, to be Thine, yea, Thine alone,
O Lamb of God, I come! I come! Amen.

CHARLOTTE ELLIOTT

### Hamburg L.M.   SECOND TUNE   Arr. by LOWELL MASON

## 268 St. Agnes C.M.

J. B. DYKES

1 When, wounded sore, the strick-en soul Lies bleeding and un-bound,

One on-ly hand, a pierc-ed hand, Can heal the sin-ner's wound.

2 When sorrows swell the laden breast,
And tears of anguish flow,
One only heart, a broken heart,
Can feel the sinner's woe.

3 When penitence has wept in vain
Over some foul, dark spot,
One only stream, a stream of blood,
Can wash away the blot.

4 'T is Jesus' blood that washes white,
His hand that brings relief,
His heart that's touched with all our joys,
And feeleth for our grief.

5 Lift up Thy bleeding hand, O Lord!
Unseal that cleansing tide;
We have no shelter from our sin
But in Thy wounded side. Amen.

Mrs. C. F. Alexander

## 269 Rock of Ages 7s6l.

RICHARD REDHEAD

1 Rock of A-ges! cleft for me; Let me hide my-self in Thee!

## REPENTANCE

Let the wa-ter and the blood, From Thy riv-en side that flowed,

Be of sin the doub-le cure,—Cleanse me from its guilt and power.

2 Could my zeal no respite know,
Could my tears forever flow,
All for sin could not atone:
Thou must save, and Thou alone!
Nothing in my hand I bring,
Simply to Thy cross I cling.

3 While I draw this fleeting breath,
When my eyelids close in death,
When I soar to worlds unknown,
See Thee on Thy judgment throne,—
Rock of Ages! cleft for me,
Let me hide myself in Thee! Amen.
A. M. Toplady ob.

*The original from which stanza 2 is compiled.*

Not the labors of my hands
Can fulfil Thy law's demands:
Could my zeal no respite know,
Could my tears forever flow,
All for sin could not atone:
Thou must save, and Thou alone!

Nothing in my hand I bring,
Simply to Thy cross I cling;
Naked, come to Thee for dress;
Helpless, look to Thee for grace;
Foul, I to the fountain fly:
Wash me, Saviour, or I die.

**Toplady** 7s6l.     SECOND TUNE     THOMAS HASTINGS

## THE FORGIVENESS OF SINS

### 270 Service 7s
From MENDELSSOHN

1 Ho-ly Fa-ther, hear my cry; Ho-ly Sav-iour, bend Thine ear;

Ho-ly Spir-it, come Thou nigh: Father, Sav-iour, Spir-it, hear!

2 Father, save me from my sin;
Saviour, I Thy mercy crave;
Gracious Spirit, make me clean:
Father, Son, and Spirit, save!

3 Father, let me taste Thy love;
Saviour, fill my soul with peace;
Spirit, come my heart to move:
Father, Son, and Spirit, bless!

4 Father, Son, and Spirit—Thou
One Jehovah, shed abroad
All Thy grace within me now;
Be my Father and my God!   Amen.

HORATIUS BONAR

### 271 Eisenach L.M.
J. H. SCHEIN

1 Father of heaven, whose love profound   A ransom for our souls hath found,

## REPENTANCE

Before Thy throne we sinners bend;To us Thy pardoning love extend.

2 Almighty Son, incarnate Word,
Our Prophet, Priest, Redeemer, Lord,
Before Thy throne we sinners bend:
To us Thy saving grace extend.

3 Eternal Spirit, by whose breath
The soul is raised from sin and death,
Before Thy throne we sinners bend:
To us Thy quickening power extend.

4 Jehovah,—Father, Spirit, Son,—
Mysterious Godhead, Three in one,
Before Thy throne we sinners bend:
Grace, pardon, life, to us extend. Amen.

EDWARD COOPER

272 **Rodbourne** 7.7.7.5. R. HAKING

1 Lord of mer-cy and of might! Of mankind the Life and Light!
Mak-er,Teach-er In-fi-nite! Je-sus,hear and save.

2 Strong Creator! Saviour mild!
Humbled to a mortal Child,
Captive, beaten, bound, reviled,
Jesus, hear and save.

3 Throned above celestial things,
Borne aloft on angels' wings,
Lord of lords, and King of kings,
Jesus, hear and save.

4 Soon to come to earth again,
Judge of angels and of men,
Hear us now, and hear us then,
Jesus, hear and save. Amen.

REGINALD HEBER

## THE FORGIVENESS OF SINS

### 273 Flavian C.M.
BARBER'S PSALM TUNES

1 Approach, my soul, the mer-cy-seat, Where Je-sus an-swers prayer: There humbly fall be-fore His feet, For none can per-ish there.

A-MEN.

2 Bowed down beneath a load of sin,
By Satan sorely pressed,
By war without, and fears within,
I come to Thee for rest.

3 Be Thou my shield and hiding-place,
That, sheltered near Thy side,
I may my fierce accuser face,
And tell him, Thou hast died.

4 O wondrous love, to bleed and die,
To bear the cross and shame,
That guilty sinners, such as I,
Might plead Thy gracious Name. Amen.

JOHN NEWTON ab.

### 274 Audi Nos 6s & 5s
WILLIAM JONES

A-MEN.

1 Jesus, meek and gentle, Son of God, Most High;
Pitying, loving Saviour, Hear Thy children's cry.

2 Pardon our offences,
Loose our captive chains,
Break down every idol
Which our soul detains.

4 Lead us on our journey,
Be Thyself the Way
Through terrestrial darkness
To celestial day.

3 Give us holy freedom,
Fill our hearts with love,
Draw us, holy Jesus,
To the realms above.

5 Jesus, meek and gentle,
Son of God Most High;
Pitying, loving Saviour,
Hear Thy children's cry. Amen.

G. R. PRYNNE

## REPENTANCE

**275  Magdalena** 7s & 6s

JOHN STAINER

1 I need Thee, precious Jesus, For I am full of sin; My soul is dark and

guilt-y, My heart is dead with-in.  I need the cleansing fountain Where

I can always flee, The blood of Christ most precious, The sinner's perfect plea. A-MEN.

2 I need Thee, precious Jesus,
   For I am very poor;
A stranger and a pilgrim,
   I have no earthly store.
I need the love of Jesus,
   To cheer me on my way,
To guide my doubting footsteps,
   To be my strength and stay.

3 I need Thee, precious Jesus,
   I need a friend like Thee,
A friend to soothe and pity,
   A friend to care for me.
I need the heart of Jesus
   To feel each anxious care,
To tell my every trouble,
   And all my sorrows share.

4 I need Thee, precious Jesus,
   And hope to see Thee soon,
Encircled with the rainbow,
   And seated on Thy throne:
There, with Thy blood-bought children,
   My joy shall ever be
To sing Thy praises, Jesus,
   To gaze, my Lord, on Thee.  Amen.

FREDERIC WHITFIELD

## THE FORGIVENESS OF SINS

### 276 Penitence L.M.
ST. ALBANS TUNE BOOK

1 Oh, that my load of sin were gone! Oh, that I could at last submit

At Jesus' feet to lay it down, To lay my soul at Jesus' feet.

2 Rest for my soul I long to find;
Saviour of all, if mine Thou art,
Give me Thy meek and lowly mind,
And stamp Thine image on my heart.

3 Break off the yoke of inbred sin,
And fully set my spirit free;
I cannot rest till pure within,
Till I am wholly lost in Thee.

4 Fain would I learn of Thee, my God;
The light and easy burden prove,
The Cross, all stained with hallow'd blood,
The labor of Thy dying love.

5 I would, but Thou must give the power,
My heart from every sin release;
Bring near, bring near the joyful hour,
And fill me with Thy perfect peace.
Amen.
CHARLES WESLEY ab.

### 277 Rest (Eng.) 7s
RICHARD REDHEAD

1 Depth of mer-cy!—can there be Mer-cy still re-served for me?

## REPENTANCE

Can my God His wrath forbear? Me, the chief of sin-ners spare?

2 I have long withstood His grace;
Long provoked Him to His face:
Would not hearken to His calls;
Grieved Him by a thousand falls.

3 There for me the Saviour stands;
Shows His wounds and spreads His hands;
God is love! I know, I feel:
Jesus weeps, and loves me still. Amen.

CHARLES WESLEY ab.

## 278 St. Mary C.M.

TYE'S PSALTER

1 O Lord, turn not Thy face a-way From them that low-ly lie,
La-ment-ing sore their sin-ful life With tears and bit-ter cry.

2 Thy mercy-gates are open wide
To them that mourn their sin;
Oh! shut them not against us, Lord,
But let us enter in.

3 We need not to confess our fault,
For surely Thou canst tell:
What we have done, and what we are,
Thou knowest very well.

4 Wherefore to beg and to entreat
With tears we come to Thee,
As children that have done amiss
Fall at their father's knee.

5 And need we, then, O Lord, repeat
The blessing which we crave,
When Thou dost know, before we speak,
The thing that we would have?

6 Mercy, good Lord, mercy we ask,
This is the total sum,
For mercy, Lord, is all our suit;
Lord, let Thy mercy come. Amen.

JOHN MARCHANT alt.

## THE FORGIVENESS OF SINS

**279** Chalvey S.M.D.  L. G. HAYNE

1 I was a wandering sheep, I did not love the fold, I did not love my

Shepherd's voice, I would not be controlled. I was a wayward child, I

did not love my home, I did not love my Father's voice, I loved afar to roam.

2 The Shepherd sought His sheep,
　The Father sought His child;
They followed me o'er vale and hill,
　O'er deserts waste and wild.
They found me nigh to death,
　Famished, and faint, and lone;
They bound me with the bands of love;
　They saved the wandering one.

3 Jesus my Shepherd is,
　'Twas He that loved my soul,
'Twas He that washed me in His blood,
　'Twas He that made me whole.
'Twas He that sought the lost,
　That found the wandering sheep,
'Twas He that brought me to the fold,
　'Tis He that still doth keep.

4 I was a wandering sheep,
　I would not be controlled;
But now I love my Shepherd's voice,
　I love, I love the fold!
I was a wayward child;
　I once preferred to roam;
But now I love my Father's voice,—
　I love, I love His home! Amen.

HORATIUS BONAR ab.

## REPENTANCE

**280 St. Christopher** 7.6.8.6.8.6.8.6.   F. C. Maker

1 Beneath the Cross of Jesus I fain would take my stand, The shadow of a mighty Rock Within a weary land; A home within the wilderness, A rest upon the way, From the burning of the noon-tide heat, And the burden of the day.

2 Upon the Cross of Jesus,
Mine eye at times can see
The very dying form of One
Who suffered there for me.
And from my smitten heart with tears,
These wonders I confess,—
The wonder of His glorious love,
And my own worthlessness.

3 I take, O Cross, thy shadow,
For my abiding-place:
I ask no other sunshine than
The sunshine of His face;
Content to let the world go by,
To know no gain nor loss,
My sinful self my only shame,
My glory all the Cross.  Amen.

ELIZ. C. CLEPHANE

## THE FORGIVENESS OF SINS

### 281 Supplication. 8s & 7s D.
W. H. Monk

1 Take my heart, O Fa-ther, take it; Make and keep it all Thine own—

Let Thy Spir-it melt and break it — This proud heart of sin and stone.

Fa-ther, make me pure and low-ly, Fond of peace and far from strife;

Turning from the paths unho-ly Of this vain and sin-ful life.

2 Ever let Thy grace surround me;
   Strengthen me with power divine,
Till Thy cords of love have bound me:
   Make me to be wholly Thine.
May the blood of Jesus heal me,
   And my sins be all forgiven;
Holy Spirit, take and seal me,
   Guide me in the path to heaven. Amen.

## 282 Magdalena 7s & 6s

JOHN STAINER

1 I lay my sins on Jesus, The spotless Lamb of God; He bears them all and

frees us From the ac-curs-ed load: I bring my guilt to Je-sus, To

A - MEN.

wash my crimson stains White in His blood most precious, Till not a stain remains.

2 I lay my wants on Jesus;
  All fullness dwells in Him;
He heals all my diseases,
  He doth my soul redeem:
I lay my griefs on Jesus,
  My burdens and my cares;
He from them all releases,
  He all my sorrow shares.

3 I rest my soul on Jesus,
  This weary soul of mine;
His right hand me embraces,
  I on His breast recline:
I love the name of Jesus,
  Immanuel, Christ, the Lord,
Like fragrance on the breezes,
  His name abroad is poured.

4 I long to be like Jesus,
  Meek, loving, lowly, mild;
I long to be like Jesus,
  The Father's holy child:
I long to be with Jesus
  Amid the heavenly throng,
To sing with saints His praises,
  To learn the angels' song. Amen.

HORATIUS BONAR

## THE FORGIVENESS OF SINS

### 283 Bethany (English) 8s & 7s D.   Henry Smart

1 Jesus, I my cross have taken, All to leave and follow Thee;
Destitute, despised, for-

saken, Thou, from hence, my all shalt be. Perish ev-ery fond ambition, All I've

sought, or hoped, or known, Yet how rich is my condition,
God and heaven are still my own.

2 Take, my soul, thy full salvation,
    Rise o'er sin, and fear, and care;
Joy to find in every station
    Something still to do or bear;
Think what Spirit dwells within thee;
    Think what Father's smiles are thine;
Think that Jesus died to win thee;
    Child of heaven, canst thou repine?

3 Haste thee on from grace to glory,
    Armed by faith and winged by prayer!
Heaven's eternal day's before thee,
    God's own hand shall guide thee there:
Soon shall close thy earthly mission,
    Swift shall pass thy pilgrim days,
Hope shall change to glad fruition,
    Faith to sight, and prayer to praise. Amen.

H. F. Lyte *ab.*

## SURRENDER AND ACCEPTANCE

**Ellesdie** 8s&7sD.  SECOND TUNE  Arr. from Mozart

### 284 Tallis' Ordinal C.M.
Thomas Tallis

♩ = 80

1 O Gift of gifts! O Grace of faith! My God, how can it be
That Thou, who hast discerning love, Shouldst give that gift to me!

A - MEN.

2 Ah, Grace! into unlikeliest hearts
It is Thy boast to come;
The glory of Thy light to find
In darkest spots a home.

3 How many hearts Thou migh'st have had
More innocent than mine!
How many souls more worthy far
Of that sweet touch of Thine!

4 Thy choice, O God of goodness! then
I lovingly adore;
Oh, give me grace to keep Thy grace,
And grace to long for more! Amen.

F. W. Faber ab.

## THE FORGIVENESS OF SINS

### 285 Vox Dilecti  C.M.D.  *Small notes for Organ.*  J. B. DYKES

1 I heard the voice of Je-sus say, "Come un-to Me and rest;

Lay down, thou wea-ry one, lay down Thy head up-on My breast!"

I came to Je-sus as I was, Wea-ry and worn and sad,

I found in Him a rest-ing place, And He has made me glad.  A MEN.

2 I heard the voice of Jesus say,
 "Behold, I freely give
The living water; thirsty one,
 Stoop down and drink, and live!"
I came to Jesus, and I drank
 Of that life-giving stream;
My thirst was quenched, my soul revived,
 And now I live in Him.

3 I heard the voice of Jesus say,
 "I am this dark world's Light:
Look unto Me, thy morn shall rise,
 And all thy day be bright!"
I looked to Jesus, and I found
 In Him my star, my sun;
And in that light of life I'll walk,
 Till travelling days are done.  Amen

HORATIUS BONAR

## SURRENDER AND ACCEPTANCE

**286** Emmaus C.M.

1 All that I was, my sin, my guilt, My death, was all my own;
All that I am I owe to Thee, My gracious God a-lone.

2 The evil of my former state
Was mine, and only mine;
The good in which I now rejoice
Is Thine, and only Thine.

3 The darkness of my former state,
The bondage, all was mine,
The light of life in which I walk,
The liberty, is Thine.

4 Thy grace first made me feel my sin,
It taught me to believe;
Then in believing, peace I found,
And now I live, I live.

5 All that I am, even here on earth,
All that I hope to be,
When Jesus comes, and glory dawns,
I owe it, Lord to Thee.    Amen.

HORATIUS BONAR

**287**

1 Lord, I believe; Thy power I own,
Thy word I would obey;
I wander comfortless and lone,
When from Thy truth I stray.

2 Lord, I believe; but gloomy fears
Sometimes bedim my sight;
I look to Thee with prayers and tears,
And cry for strength and light.

3 Lord, I believe; but oft I know,
My faith is cold and weak;
My weakness strengthen, and bestow
The confidence I seek!

4 Yes! I believe; and only Thou
Canst give my soul relief;
Lord! to Thy truth my spirit bow;
"Help Thou mine unbelief!"   Amen.

J. R. WREFORD

## THE FORGIVENESS OF SINS

### 288 Lisbon S.M.
DANIEL READ

1 Dear Sav-iour, I am thine, By ev-er-last-ing bands; My name, my heart, I would resign; My soul is in Thy hands.

A-MEN.

2 To Thee I still would cleave
With ever growing zeal;
Let millions tempt me Christ to leave,
They never shall prevail.

3 His Spirit shall unite
My soul to Him, my Head:
Shall form me to His image bright,
And teach His paths to tread.

4 Death may my soul divide
From this abode of clay;
But love shall keep me near His side,
Through all the gloomy way.

5 Since Christ and we are one,
What should remain to fear?
If He in heaven has fixed His throne,
He'll fix His members there. Amen.

PHILIP DODDRIDGE alt.

### 289 St. Austell 7s
A. H. BROWN

1 Prince of Peace, con-trol my will; Bid this strug-gling heart be still;

## SURRENDER AND ACCEPTANCE

Bid my fears and doubtings cease; Hush my spir-it in - to peace.

2 Thou hast bought me with Thy blood,
Opened wide the gate to God;
Peace I ask,—but peace must be,
Lord, in being one with Thee.

3 May Thy will, not mine, be done;
May Thy will and mine be one;
Chase these doubtings from my heart;
Now Thy perfect peace impart.

4 Saviour, at Thy feet I fall;
Thou, my life, my God, my all!
Let Thy happy servant be
One forevermore with Thee!  Amen.

MARY S. B. DANA  *ab.*

## 290  Tunbridge L.M.

RICHARD REDHEAD

1 Lift up your heads, ye might-y gates! Be-hold the King of glo-ry waits;

The King of kings is drawing near; The Saviour of the world is here.

2 O blest the land, the city blest
Where Christ the Ruler is confessed;
O happy hearts and happy homes,
To whom this King of triumph comes.

3 Fling wide the portals of your heart,
Make it a temple set apart
From earthly use for heaven's employ,
Adorned with prayer and love and joy.

4 Redeemer, come! I open wide
My heart to Thee: here, Lord, abide!
Let me Thy inner presence feel,
Thy grace and love in me reveal.

5 So shall your Sovereign enter in;
And new and nobler life begin:
Thy Holy Spirit guide us on,
Until the glorious crown be won.  Amen.

GEORGE WEISSEL  Tr. WINKWORTH *ab. and alt.*

## THE FORGIVENESS OF SINS

**291 Tristitia** L.M.6l.  JOSEPH BARNBY

1 Jesus, my Lord, my God, my all! Hear me, blest Saviour! when I call;
Hear me, and from Thy dwelling-place Pour down the rich-es of Thy grace:
Je-sus, my Lord! I Thee a-dore, O make me love Thee more and more.

A - MEN.

2 Jesus! what didst Thou find in me,
That Thou hast dealt so lovingly?
How great the joy that Thou hast brought,
So far exceeding hope or thought!
  Jesus, my Lord! I Thee adore,
  O make me love Thee more and more.

3 Jesus! of Thee shall be my song;
To Thee my heart and soul belong;
All that I have or am is Thine,
And Thou, blest Saviour! Thou art mine.
  Jesus, my Lord! I Thee adore,
  O make me love Thee more and more.
      Amen.
HENRY COLLINS *ab.*

**292 Manoah** C.M.  Arr. from ROSSINI

1 If Thou im-part Thy-self to me, No oth-er good I need:

## SURRENDER AND ACCEPTANCE

If Thou, the Son, shalt make me free, I shall be free in-deed.

2 I can not rest till in Thy blood
   I full redemption have;
But Thou, through whom I come to God,
   Canst to the utmost save.

3 From sin,— the guilt, the power, the [pain,
   Thou wilt redeem my soul:
Lord, I believe — and not in vain;
   My faith shall make me whole.

4 I, too, with Thee, shall walk in white;
   With all Thy saints shall prove
The length, and breadth, and depth, and height
   Of everlasting Love. Amen.

## 293 Thatcher s.m.
*From* HÄNDEL

♩ = 100

1 Dear Lord and Mas-ter mine, Thy hap-py ser-vant see:
My Conqueror, with what joy di-vine Thy captive clings to Thee.

2 I love Thy yoke to wear,
   To feel Thy gracious bands,
Sweetly restrainéd by Thy care,
   And happy in Thy hands.

3 No bar would I remove;
   No bond would I unbind;
Within the limits of Thy love
   Full liberty I find.

4 I would not walk alone,
   But still with Thee, my God;
At every step my blindness own,
   And ask of Thee the road.

5 The weakness I enjoy
   That casts me on Thy breast;
The conflicts that Thy strength employ
   Make me divinely blest.

6 Dear Lord and Master mine,
   Still keep Thy servant true;
My Guardian and my Guide divine,
   Bring, bring Thy pilgrim through.

7 My Conqueror and my King,
   Still keep me in Thy train;
And with Thee Thy glad captive bring,
   When Thou return'st to reign. Amen.

T. H. GILL

## THE FORGIVENESS OF SINS

### 294  Weston 8s&7sD.
J. E. Roe

1 Love divine, all love excelling,—Joy of heaven, to earth come down! Fix in us Thy

humble dwelling, All Thy faithful mercies crown; Jesus! Thou art all compassion,

Pure, unbounded love Thou art; Visit us with Thy salvation,
　　Enter every trembling heart.

2 Breathe, oh, breathe Thy loving Spirit
　Into every troubled breast!
Let us all in Thee inherit,
　Let us find Thy promised rest;
Take away the love of sinning,
　Alpha and Omega be,—
End of faith, as its beginning,
　Set our hearts at liberty.

3 Come, almighty to deliver,
　Let us all Thy grace receive;
Speedily return, and never,
　Never more Thy temples leave!
Thee we would be always blessing;
　Serve Thee as Thy hosts above;
Pray, and praise Thee without ceasing;
　Glory in Thy perfect love.

4 Finish, then, Thy new creation,
　Pure, unspotted may we be:
Let us see our whole salvation
　Perfectly secured by Thee!
Changed from glory into glory,
　Till in heaven we take our place;
Till we cast our crowns before Thee,
　Lost in wonder, love, and praise.   Amen.

CHARLES WESLEY *sl. alt.*

## SURRENDER AND ACCEPTANCE

### 295 Rosefield 7s6l.
C. H. A. Malan

1 Bless-ed are the sons of God, They are bought with Jesus' blood;

They are ransomed from the grave; Life e - ter - nal they shall have:

With them numbered may we be, Here, and in e - ter - ni - ty. A - men.

2 They are justified by grace,
They enjoy the Saviour's peace;
All their sins are washed away;
They shall stand in God's great day:
With them numbered may we be,
Here, and in eternity.

3 They are lights upon the earth,
Children of a heavenly birth,—
One with God, with Jesus one:
Glory is in them begun:
With them numbered may we be,
Here, and in eternity. Amen.

Joseph Humphrey

---

See also *Hymns under* —

Jesus Christ
    Ministry and Example . . . . . . . . 61 - 83
    Passion and Crucifixion . . . . . . . . 84 - 96
The Holy Ghost . . . . . . . . . 140 - 152
The Holy Catholic Church
    Consecration and Service . . . . , . 188 - 203

## THE FORGIVENESS OF SINS

**296 Nuremberg** 7s  
J. R. AHLE

1 Now be-gin the heavenly theme, Sing a-loud in Je-sus' name:

Ye who Je-sus' kindness prove, Triumph in re-deeming love.

2 Ye who see the Father's grace  
Beaming in the Saviour's face,  
As to Canaan on ye move,  
Praise and bless redeeming love.

3 Mourning souls, dry up your tears;  
Banish all your guilty fears;  
See your guilt and curse remove,  
Cancelled by redeeming love.

4 Welcome, all by sin opprest,  
Welcome to His sacred rest;  
Nothing brought Him from above,  
Nothing but redeeming love.

5 Hither, then, your music bring,  
Strike aloud each joyful string;  
Mortals, join the host above,  
Join to praise redeeming love. Amen.

JOHN LANGFORD

**297 Dedham** C.M.  
WILLIAM GARDNER

1 Oh, for a thousand tongues to sing My dear Re-deem-er's praise! The

## REDEEMING LOVE

glo - ries of my God and King; The tri-umphs of His grace!

2 My gracious Master and my God!
   Assist me to proclaim,
   To spread, through all the earth abroad,
   The honors of Thy name.

3 Jesus—the name that calms my fears,
   That bids my sorrows cease;

'T is music to my ravished ears:
'T is life, and health, and peace.

4 He breaks the power of reigning sin,
   He sets the prisoner free:
   His blood can make the foulest clean;
   His blood availed for me. Amen.

CHARLES WESLEY ab.

## 298 Bishopsgate L.M.

1 A-wake, my soul, to joy-ful lays, And sing thy great Redeemer's praise; He just-ly claims a song from me: His lov-ing-kind-ness is so free!

2 He saw me ruined in the fall,
   Yet loved me, notwithstanding all;
   He saved me from my lost estate:
   His loving-kindness is so great!

3 Through mighty hosts of cruel foes,
   Where earth and hell my way oppose,
   He safely leads my soul along:
   His loving-kindness is so strong!

4 Often I feel my sinful heart
   Prone from my Jesus to depart;

And though I have Him oft forgot,
His loving-kindness changes not.

5 So when I pass death's gloomy vale,
   And life and mortal powers shall fail,
   O may my last expiring breath
   His loving-kindness sing in death.

6 Then shall I mount and soar away
   To the bright world of endless day;
   There shall I sing, with sweet surprise,
   His loving-kindness in the skies. Amen.

SAMUEL MEDLEY ab.

## THE FORGIVENESS OF SINS

### 299 St. Leonard C.M.D.
HENRY HILES

1 Ma-jes-tic sweet-ness sits enthroned Up-on the Saviour's brow;

His head with ra-diant glo-ries crown'd, His lips with grace o'erflow:

No mor-tal can with Him compare, A-mong the sons of men; Fair-

er is He than all the fair That fill the heav-enly train. A-MEN.

2 He saw me plunged in deep distress,
  He flew to my relief;
For me He bore the shameful Cross,
  And carried all my grief:
To Him I owe my life and breath,
  And all the joys I have;
He makes me triumph over death,
  He saves me from the grave.

3 To heaven, the place of His abode,
  He brings my weary feet;
Shows me the glories of my God,
  And makes my joy complete:
Since from His bounty I receive
  Such proofs of love divine,
Had I a thousand hearts to give,
  Lord! they should all be Thine! Amen.

SAMUEL STENNETT

## REDEEMING LOVE

**300 Lauda Zion** 8.8.8.5.  Arr. from MENDELSSOHN

1 Sing of Je - sus, sing for ev - er  Of the love that changes nev - er;

Who or what from Him can sev - er Those He makes His own?  A - MEN.

2 With His blood the Lord has bought them;
When they knew Him not, He sought them,
And from all their wanderings brought them,
    His the praise alone.

3 Through the desert Jesus leads them,
With the bread of heaven He feeds them,
And through all the way He speeds them,
    To their home above.

4 There they see the Lord who bought them,
Him who came from heaven, and sought them,
Him who by His Spirit taught them,
    Him they serve and love.

5 Let His people sing with gladness,
Other mirth than this is madness,
Mirth it is that ends in sadness,
    Be it far away.

6 'T is the saints have solid treasure,
They can sing with holy pleasure,
And their joy will know no measure,
    In the final day.  Amen.

THOMAS KELLY

## THE FORGIVENESS OF SINS

### 301 Blessed Saviour 6s&5sD.

1 Saviour, blessèd Saviour,
  Listen whilst we sing,
Hearts and voices raising
  Praises to our King.
All we have we offer,
  Body, soul, and spirit,
All we yield to Thee.

2 Nearer, ever nearer,
  Christ, we draw to Thee,
Deep in adoration
  Bending low the knee:
Thou for our redemption
  Cam'st on earth to die;
Thou, that we might follow,
  Hast gone up on high.

3 Great and ever greater
  Are Thy mercies here,
True and everlasting
  Are the glories there,
Where no pain, nor sorrow,
  Toil, nor care, is known,
Where the angel-legions
  Circle round Thy throne.

4 Clearer still and clearer
  Dawns the light from heaven,
In our sadness bringing
  News of sin forgiven.
Life has lost its shadows,
  Pure the light within;
Thou hast shed Thy radiance
  On a world of sin.

5 Brighter still and brighter
  Glows the western sun,
Shedding all its gladness
  O'er our work that's done.
Time will soon be over,
  Toil and sorrow past,
May we, Blessèd Saviour,
  Find a rest at last. Amen.

GODFREY THRING *ab*

## REDEEMING LOVE

**302 Christ Church** 6.6.6.6.8.8.  CHARLES STEGGALL

1 Je-sus, trans-port-ing sound! The joy of earth and heaven! No

oth-er help is found, None oth-er name is given, By which we can sal-

va-tion have: But Je-sus came the world to save. A-MEN.

2 Jesus, harmonious Name!
　It charms the hosts above:
They evermore proclaim,
　And wonder at His love:
'T is all their happiness to gaze,
O Jesus Christ, on Thy blest Face.

3 His Name the sinner hears,
　And is from sin set free;
'T is music in his ears,
　'T is life and victory:
Glad songs of praise his lips employ;
His heart is filled with holy joy.

4 Jesus, for all mankind
　The Lamb of God once slain;
Who hast Thy life resigned
　For every soul of man:
O Sovereign Son, to Thee we cry;
Let Thy blood cleanse us; else we die. Amen.

CHARLES WESLEY ab.

## THE FORGIVENESS OF SINS

### 303 Ariel 8.8.6.8.8.6.  Lowell Mason

1 Oh, could I speak the matchless worth, Oh, could I sound the glories forth

Which in my Saviour shine! I'd soar, and touch the heavenly strings, And vie with Gabriel

while he sings, In notes almost divine, In notes al - most di - vine. A - MEN.

2 I'd sing the precious blood He spilt,
My ransom from the dreadful guilt
  Of sin and wrath divine:
I'd sing His glorious righteousness,
In which all perfect, heavenly dress,
  My soul shall ever shine.

3 I'd sing the characters He bears,
And all the forms of love He wears,
  Exalted on His throne:
In loftiest songs of sweetest praise,
I would to everlasting days
  Make all His glories known.

4 Well, the delightful day will come
When my dear Lord will bring me home,
  And I shall see His face;
Then with my Saviour, Brother, Friend,
A blest eternity I'll spend,
  Triumphant in His grace. Amen.

SAMUEL MEDLEY *ab.*

## REDEEMING LOVE

**304** **Ouseley** 6.6.4.6.6.6.4.  F. A. G. OUSELEY

1 Jesus, Thy name I love,
All other names above,
Jesus, my Lord!
O Thou art all to me:
Nothing to please I see,
Nothing apart from Thee,
Jesus, my Lord!

2 When unto Thee I flee,
Thou wilt my refuge be,
Jesus, my Lord!
What need I now to fear?
What earthly grief or care,
Since Thou art ever near,
Jesus, my Lord!

3 Soon Thou wilt come again;
I shall be happy then,
Jesus, my Lord!
Then Thine own face I'll see,
Then I shall like Thee be,
Then evermore with Thee,
Jesus, my Lord! Amen.

JAMES GEORGE DECK *ab.*

## THE FORGIVENESS OF SINS

### 305 Eagley C.M.
J. WALCH

1 Je-sus! I love Thy charm-ing name, 'Tis mu-sic to mine ear;

A-MEN.

Fain would I sound it out so loud That earth and heaven should hear.

2 Yes! Thou art precious to my soul,
   My transport and my trust;
   Jewels to Thee are gaudy toys,
   And gold is sordid dust.

3 All my capacious powers can wish,
   In Thee doth richly meet;
   Not to mine eyes is light so dear,
   Nor friendship half so sweet.

4 Thy grace still dwells upon my heart,
   And sheds its fragrance there;
   The noblest balm of all its wounds,
   The cordial of its care. Amen.

PHILIP DODDRIDGE ab.

### 306

1 Jesus, these eyes have never seen
   That radiant form of Thine!
   The vail of sense hangs dark between
   Thy blessèd face and mine!

2 I see Thee not, I hear Thee not,
   Yet art Thou oft with me;
   And earth hath ne'er so dear a spot,
   As where I meet with Thee.

3 Like some bright dream that comes
   When slumbers o'er me roll,[unsought,
   Thine image ever fills my thought,
   And charms my ravished soul.

4 Yet though I have not seen, and still
   Must rest in faith alone;
   I love Thee, dearest Lord!— and will,
   Unseen, but not unknown.

5 When death these mortal eyes shall seal,
   And still this throbbing heart,
   The rending vail shall Thee reveal,
   All glorious as Thou art! Amen.

RAY PALMER

## REDEEMING LOVE

**307** Heber C.M.           Geo. Kingsley

1 Jesus! the ver-y thought of Thee With sweetness fills the breast;
But sweet-er far Thy face to see, And in Thy presence rest.

2 Nor voice can sing, nor heart can frame,
   Nor can the memory find
A sweeter sound than Thy blest name:
   O Saviour of mankind!

3 Oh, hope of every contrite heart,
   Oh, joy of all the meek;
To those who fall, how kind Thou art,
   How good to those who seek!

4 But what to those who find? ah! this
   Nor tongue, nor pen can show:
The love of Jesus, what it is,
   None but His lovers know.

5 Jesus! our only joy be Thou,
   As Thou our prize wilt be;
Jesus! be Thou our glory now,
   And in eternity! Amen.

St. Bernard Tr. Caswall

**308**

1 How sweet the name of Jesus sounds,
   In a believer's ear!
It soothes his sorrows, heals his wounds,
   And drives away his fear.

2 It makes the wounded spirit whole,
   And calms the troubled breast;
'Tis manna to the hungry soul,
   And to the weary, rest.

3 Jesus! my Shepherd, Husband, Friend,
   My Prophet, Priest, and King;
My Lord, my Life, my Way, my End,—
   Accept the praise I bring.

4 Weak is the effort of my heart,
   And cold my warmest thought;
But when I see Thee as Thou art,
   I'll praise Thee as I ought.

    5 Till then, I would Thy love proclaim,
       With every fleeting breath;
    And may the music of Thy name
       Refresh my soul in death. Amen.

John Newton ab.

## THE FORGIVENESS OF SINS

**309 Mear** C.M.     Welsh Air Arr. Aaron Williams

1 Thou dear Re-deem-er, dy-ing Lamb, I love to hear of Thee; No

mus-ic, like Thy charming name, Is half so sweet to me. A-MEN.

2 O may I ever hear Thy voice
  In mercy to me speak;
In Thee, my Priest, will I rejoice,
  And Thy salvation seek.

3 My Jesus shall be still my theme,
  While on this earth I stay:
I'll sing my Jesus' lovely name,
  When all things else decay.

4 When I appear in yonder cloud,
  With all His favored throng,
Then will I sing more sweet, more loud,
  And Christ shall be my song. Amen.

                           JOHN CENNICK *alt.*

**310 Trust** 8s&7s     From Mendelssohn

1 Come, Thou Fount of ev-ery blessing, Tune my heart to sing Thy grace;

## REDEEMING LOVE

Streams of mercy, nev-er ceas-ing, Call for songs of loudest praise.

2 Jesus sought me when a stranger,
Wandering from the fold of God;
He, to rescue me from danger,
Interposed His precious blood.

3 Oh, to grace how great a debtor
Daily I'm constrained to be!
Let Thy grace now like a fetter,
Bind my wandering heart to Thee.

4 Prone to wander, Lord, I feel it;
Prone to leave the God I love;
Here's my heart; oh, take and seal it;
Seal it for Thy courts above. Amen.

ROBERT ROBINSON ab.

## Sicilian Mariner's Hymn 8s&7s.
### SECOND TUNE

♩ = 126

---

See also Hymns under —

JESUS CHRIST
    Ministry and Example . . . . . 61 – 83
    Passion and Crucifixion . . . . . 84 – 96
THE HOLY CATHOLIC CHURCH
    The Lord's Supper . . . . 181 – 187

## THE FORGIVENESS OF SINS

**311 St. Andrew of Crete** 6s&5sD.  J. B. DYKES

1 Christian! dost thou see them On the holy ground? How the powers of darkness

Rage Thy steps a-round? Christian, up, and smite them! Counting gain but

loss; In the strength that cometh By the Ho-ly Cross. A-MEN.

2 Christian! dost thou feel them,
  How they work within,
Striving, tempting, luring,
  Goading into sin?
Christian! never tremble;
  Never be downcast;
Gird thee for the battle,
  Watch and pray and fast.

3 Christian! dost thou hear them,
  How they speak thee fair?
"Always fast and vigil?
  Always watch and prayer?"
Christian! answer boldly:
  "While I breathe I pray!"
Peace shall follow battle,
  Night shall end in day.

4 "Well I know thy trouble,
    O my servant true;
  Thou art very weary,
    I was weary too;
  But that toil shall make thee
    Some day all Mine own,
  And the end of sorrow
    Shall be near My throne." Amen.

ST. ANDREW OF CRETE  Tr. NEALE

*CONFLICT*

## 312 Christmas c.m.
From HANDEL

1 Awake, my soul! stretch every nerve, And press with vigor on; A heavenly race demands thy zeal, And an immortal crown, And an immortal crown.

A-MEN.

2 A crowd of witnesses around
Hold thee in full survey;
Forget the steps already trod,
And onward urge thy way.

3 'T is God's all animating voice
That calls thee from on high;
'T is His own hand presents the prize
To thine aspiring eye;—

4 That prize with peerless glories bright,
Which shall new lustre boast, [gems
When victor's wreaths and monarch's
Shall blend in common dust.

5 Blest Saviour! introduced by Thee,
Have I my race begun;
And, crowned with victory, at Thy feet
I 'll lay my honors down! Amen.

PHILIP DODDRIDGE.

## 313

1 Am I a soldier of the Cross,
A follower of the Lamb,
And shall I fear to own His cause,
Or blush to speak His name?

2 Must I be carried to the skies
On flowery beds of ease,
While others fought to win the prize,
And sailed through bloody seas?

3 Are there no foes for me to face?
Must I not stem the flood?
Is this vile world a friend to grace,
To help me on to God?

4 Sure I must fight, if I would reign;
Increase my courage, Lord!
I 'll bear the toil, endure the pain,
Supported by Thy word.

5 Thy saints, in all this glorious war,
Shall conquer though they die;
They view the triumph from afar,
And seize it with their eye.

6 When that illustrious day shall rise,
And all Thine armies shine
In robes of victory through the skies,
The glory shall be Thine. Amen.

ISAAC WATTS.

## THE FORGIVENESS OF SINS

**314** St. Michael S.M.      Date's Psalter

1 My soul, it is thy God Who calls thee by His grace;
Now loose thee from each cumbering load, And bend thee to the race.

2 Make thy salvation sure;
  All sloth and slumber shun;
Nor dare a moment rest secure,
  Till thou the goal hast won.

3 Thy crown of life hold fast;
  Thy heart with courage stay;
Nor let one trembling glance be cast
  Along the backward way.

4 Thy path ascends the skies,
  With conquering footsteps bright;
And thou shalt win and wear the prize
  In everlasting light. Amen.

LEONARD SWAIN

**315**

1 My soul, weigh not thy life
  Against thy heavenly crown;
Nor suffer Satan's deadliest strife
  To beat thy courage down.

2 With prayer and crying strong,
  Hold on the fearful fight,
And let the breaking day prolong
  The wrestling of the night.

3 The battle soon will yield,
  If thou thy part fulfill;
For strong as is the hostile shield,
  Thy sword is stronger still.

4 Thine armor is divine,
  Thy feet with victory shod;
And on thy head shall quickly shine
  The diadem of God. Amen.

LEONARD SWAIN

## CONFLICT

### 316 Waltham L.M.

J. B. Calkin

1 Stand up, my soul! shake off thy fears, And gird the gos-pel ar-mor on!
March to the gates of endless joy, Where Je-sus, thy great Captain's gone.

2 Hell and thy sins resist thy course;
But hell and sin are vanquished foes,
Thy Jesus nailed them to the cross,
And sung the triumph when He rose.

3 Then let my soul march boldly on;
Press forward to the heavenly gate;
There peace and joy eternal reign,[wait.
And glittering robes for conquerors

4 Then shall I wear a starry crown,
And triumph in almighty grace;
While all the armies of the skies
Join in my glorious Leader's praise. Amen.

ISAAC WATTS

### Mendon L.M.   SECOND TUNE.

Arr. Lowell Mason

## THE FORGIVENESS OF SINS

**317 Welfield** 8.8.6.8.8.6.      H. A. CROSBIE

1 Chil-dren of light, a-rise and shine! Your birth, your hopes, are all divine,
Your home is in the skies, Oh, then, for heav'n-ly glo-ry born, 
Look down on all with ho-ly scorn That earthly spir-its prize. 

2 With Christ, with glory full in view,
Oh, what is all the world to you?
What is it all but loss?
Come on, then, cleave no more to earth,
Nor wrong your high celestial birth,
Ye pilgrims of the Cross.

3 The cross is ours, we bear it now;
But did He not beneath it bow,
And suffer there at last?

4 O blesséd Lord, we yet shall reign,
Redeemed from sorrow, sin, and pain,
And walk with Thee in white.
We suffer now, but oh, at last
We 'll bless Thee, Lord, for all the past,
And own our cross was light. Amen.
                                      EDWARD DENNY

**318 Faith** C.M.      J. B. DYKES

1 Must Je-sus bear the Cross a-lone, And all the world go free?

## CONFLICT

No, there 's a cross for ev-ery one, And there 's a cross for me.

2 How happy are the saints above,
Who once went sorrowing here!
But now they taste unmingled love,
And joy without a tear.

3 The consecrated cross I'll bear,
Till death shall set me free;
And then go home my crown to wear,
For there 's a crown for me.

4 O precious cross! O glorious crown!
O resurrection day!
Ye angels, from the stars come down,
And bear my soul away. Amen.
THOMAS SHEPHERD alt.

ORIGINAL VERSION

1 Shall Simon bear Thy cross alone,
And other saints be free?
Each saint of Thine shall find his own,
And there is one for me.

2 How happy are the saints above,
Who once went sorrowing here!
But now they taste unmingled love,
And joy without a tear.

3 The consecrated cross I'll bear,
Till death shall set me free;
And then go home my crown to wear,
For there 's a crown for me. Amen.
THOMAS SHEPHERD

## 319

1 Oh, speed thee, Christian! on thy way,
And to thine armor cling;
With girded loins the call obey
Which grace and mercy bring.

2 There is a battle to be fought,
An upward race to run,
A crown of glory to be sought,
A victory to be won.

3 O, faint not, Christian! for thy sighs
Are heard before the throne;
The race must come before the prize,
The cross before the crown. Amen.

## Maitland C.M.  SECOND TUNE  G. N. ALLEN

## THE FORGIVENESS OF SINS

### 320 Armes 7.7 7.5.
PHILIP ARMES

1 Chris-tian, seek not yet re-pose, Cast thy dreams of ease a-way;

Thou art in the midst of foes: Watch and pray.

2 Gird thy heavenly armor on,
  Wear it ever, night and day;
  Ambushed lies the evil one:
    Watch and pray.

3 Hear the victors who o'ercame:
  Still they mark each warrior's way;
  All, with warning voice, exclaim,—
    "Watch and pray."

4 Hear, above all, hear thy Lord;
  Him thou lovest to obey;
  Hide within thy heart His word,—
    "Watch and pray."

5 Watch, as if on that alone
  Hung the issue of the day;
  Pray that help may be sent down:
    Watch and pray. Amen.

    CHARLOTTE ELLIOTT *ab.*

### 321 Laban S.M.
LOWELL MASON

1 My soul, be on thy guard, Ten thou-sand foes a-rise;

## CONFLICT

The hosts of sin are press-ing hard   To draw thee from the skies.

2 Oh, watch, and fight, and pray!
 The battle ne'er give o'er;
 Renew it boldly every day,
 And help divine implore.

3 Ne'er think the victory won,
 Nor once at ease sit down;
 Thy arduous work will not be done
 Till thou obtain thy crown.

  4 Fight on, my soul, till death
   Shall bring thee to thy God!
   He'll take thee, at thy parting breath,
   Up to His blest abode.   Amen.
               GEORGE HEATH

## 322 Hymnus 7s

J. B. CALKIN

1 Faint not, Christian! tho' the road, Lead-ing to thy blest a-bode,

Darksome be, and dangerous too, Christ, thy Guide, will bring thee through.

2 Faint not, Christian! though in rage
 Satan would thy soul engage;
 Gird on faith's anointed shield,
 Bear it to the battle-field.

3 Faint not, Christian! tho' the world
 Has its hostile flag unfurled;
 Hold the cross of Jesus fast,
 Thou shalt overcome at last.

4 Faint not, Christian! though within
 There's a heart so prone to sin;
 Christ, the Lord, is over all;
 He'll not suffer thee to fall.

5 Faint not, Christian! Christ is near;
 Soon in glory He'll appear;
 And His love will then bestow
 Power to conquer every foe.   Amen.
               J. H. EVANS

## THE FORGIVENESS OF SINS

**323 Mozart** L.M.      Arr. from MOZART

1. Fight the good fight with all thy might, Christ is thy strength, and Christ thy right;
Lay hold on life, and it shall be Thy joy and crown e-ter-nal-ly.

2 Run the straight race
Through God's good grace,
Lift up thine eyes, and seek His face;
Life with its way before thee lies,
Christ is the path, and Christ the prize.

3 Cast care aside,
Lean on thy Guide;
His boundless mercy will provide;

Lean, and the trusting soul shall prove,
Christ is its life, and Christ its love.

4 Faint not, nor fear,
His arms are near,
He changeth not, and thou art dear;
Only believe, and thou shalt see
That Christ is all in all to thee.

Amen.

J. S. B. MONSELL

**324**

1 Awake, our souls! away, our fears!
Let every trembling thought be gone:
Awake and run the heavenly race,
And put a cheerful courage on!

2 True, 't is a strait and thorny road,
And mortal spirits tire and faint;

But they forget the mighty God, [saint;—
Who feeds the strength of every

3 The mighty God, whose matchless
Is ever new, and ever young, [power
And firm endures, while endless years
Their everlasting circles run. Amen.

ISAAC WATTS *ab.*

**Mendon** L.M.     SECOND TUNE.     Arr. LOWELL MASON

## TRIAL AND TRUST

**325 Portuguese Hymn** 11s     John Reading *alt.*

1 How firm a foun-da-tion, ye saints of the Lord, Is laid for your faith in His

excellent word! What more can He say than to you He hath said, To you who for

refuge to Jesus have fled, To you who for refuge to Jesus have fled?

2 "Fear not, I am with thee, oh, be not dismayed;
For I am thy God, I will still give thee aid:
I'll strengthen thee, help thee, and cause thee to stand,
Upheld by my righteous, omnipotent hand."

3 "When through the deep waters I call thee to go,
The rivers of sorrow shall not overflow;
For I will be near thee thy troubles to bless,
And sanctify to thee thy deepest distress."

4 "When through fiery trials thy pathway shall lie,
My grace all sufficient shall be thy supply;
The flame shall not hurt thee; I only design
Thy dross to consume, and thy gold to refine."

5 "E'en down to old age, all my people shall prove
My sovereign, eternal, unchangeable love;
And then, when gray hairs shall their temples adorn,
Like lambs they shall still in my bosom be borne."

6 "The soul that on Jesus hath leaned for repose,
I will not, I will not desert to his foes:
That soul, though all hell should endeavor to shake,
I'll never,—no, never,—no, never forsake." Amen.

George Keith *ab.*

## THE FORGIVENESS OF SINS

326 Hollingside 7s D.  
J. B. DYKES

1 Jesus! lover of my soul, Let me to Thy bosom fly  
While the nearer waters roll,

While the tempest still is high. Hide me, O my Saviour! hide, Till the storm of

life is past; Safe in-to the haven guide; Oh, receive my soul at last.

2 Other refuge have I none;
   Hangs my helpless soul on Thee;
   Leave, ah, leave me not alone,
     Still support and comfort me.
All my trust on Thee is stayed;
   All my help from Thee I bring;
Cover my defenceless head
   With the shadow of Thy wing.

3 Thou, O Christ, art all I want;
   More than all in Thee I find;
Raise the fallen, cheer the faint,
   Heal the sick, and lead the blind.

Just and holy is Thy name,
   I am all unrighteousness;
False and full of sin I am,
   Thou art full of truth and grace.

4 Plenteous grace with Thee is found,--
   Grace to pardon all my sin;
Let the healing streams abound,
   Make and keep me pure within.
Thou of life the fountain art,
   Freely let me take of Thee;
Spring Thou up within my heart,
   Rise to all eternity. Amen.

CHARLES WESLEY *ad.*

## TRIAL AND TRUST

**Martyn** 7sD.  SECOND TUNE  S. B. Marsh

**327 Humility** L.M.  S. P. Tuckerman

1 He leadeth me: O blessèd thought! O words with heavenly comfort fraught!

Whate'er I do, where'er I be, Still 't is God's hand that leadeth me.

2 Sometimes 'mid scenes of deepest gloom,
Sometimes where Eden's bowers bloom,
By waters still, o'er troubled sea,
Still 't is His hand that leadeth me.

3 Lord, I would clasp Thy hand in mine,
Nor ever murmur nor repine;
Content, whatever lot I see,
Since 't is my God that leadeth me.

4 And when my task on earth is done,
When, by Thy grace, the victory 's won,
E'en death's cold wave I will not flee,
Since God through Jordan leadeth me.  Amen.

J. H. Gilmore  ab.

## THE FORGIVENESS OF SINS

**328 Pascal** 8.8.8.6.  E. J. HOPKINS

1 O Ho-ly Sav-iour, Friend unseen, The faint, the weak, on Thee may lean;

Help me, throughout life's varying scene By faith to cling to Thee.

2 Blest with communion so divine,
Take what Thou wilt, shall I repine,
When as the branches to the vine,
My soul may cling to Thee?

3 Far from her home, fatigued, oppress'd,
Here she has found a place of rest,
An exile still, yet not unblest,
While she can cling to Thee.

4 What tho' the world deceitful prove,
And earthly friends and joys remove,

With patient, uncomplaining love
Still would I cling to Thee.

5 Though faith and hope awhile be tried,
I ask not, need not, aught beside,
How safe, how calm, how satisfied,
The soul that clings to Thee.

6 Blest is my lot, what'er befall;
What can disturb me, who appall,
While as my strength, my rock, my all,
Saviour, I cling to Thee? Amen.

CHARLOTTE ELLIOTT *ab.*

**Flemming** 8.8.8.6.  SECOND TUNE.  Arr. from F. F. FLEMMING

## 329 Bear C.M.
WELSH AIR Arr. AARON WILLIAMS

♩ = 72

1 With joy we med-i-tate the grace Of our High Priest a-bove; His heart is made of ten-der-ness, His bo-som glows with love.

A - MEN.

2 Touched with a sympathy within,
He knows our feeble frame;
He knows what sore temptations mean,
For He hath felt the same.

3 He, in the days of feeble flesh,
Poured out His cries and tears;

And, in His measure, feels afresh
What every member bears.

4 Then let our humble faith address
His mercy and His power;
We shall obtain delivering grace
In the distressing hour. Amen.

ISAAC WATTS ab.

## 330 Angelus L.M.
J. G. W. SCHEFFLER

♩ = 100

1 O Love Divine, that stooped to share Our sharpest pang, our bitterest tear,
On Thee we cast each earth-born care: We smile at pain while Thou art near!

A - MEN.

2 Though long the weary way we tread,
And sorrow crown each lingering year;
No path we shun, no darkness dread,
Our hearts still whispering, Thou art near!

3 On Thee we fling our burdening woe,
O Love Divine, forever dear;
Content to suffer, while we know,
Living and dying, Thou art near! Amen.

O. W. HOLMES ab.

## THE FORGIVENESS OF SINS

### 331 St. Agnes C.M.
J. B. DYKES

1 O help us, Lord, each hour of need Thy heavenly suc-cor give;

Help us in thought, and word, and deed, Each hour on earth we live.

2 O help us when our spirits bleed,
With contrite anguish sore;
And when our hearts are cold and dead,
O help us, Lord, the more.

3 O help us through the prayer of faith,
More firmly to believe;
For still, the more the servant hath,
The more shall he receive.

4 If strangers to Thy fold we call,
Imploring at Thy feet
The crumbs that from Thy table fall,
'T is all we dare entreat.

5 O help us, Jesus, from on high:
We know no help but Thee;
O help us so to live and die,
As Thine in heaven to be.   Amen.

H. H. MILMAN  ab.

### 332 Mason S.M.
E. K. GLEZEN

1 If through un-ruf-fled seas Toward heaven we calm-ly sail,

## TRIAL AND TRUST

With grateful hearts, O God, to Thee, We'll own the fostering gale.

2 But should the surges rise,
And rest delay to come,
Blest be the sorrow, kind the storm,
Which drives us nearer home.

3 Soon shall our doubts and fears
All yield to Thy control;
Thy tender mercies shall illume
The midnight of the soul.

4 Teach us, in every state,
To make Thy will our own;
And, when the joys of sense depart,
To live by faith alone. Amen.

A. M. TOPLADY *ab. and alt.*

### 333 Pax Tecum 10.10.

G. F. CALDBECK

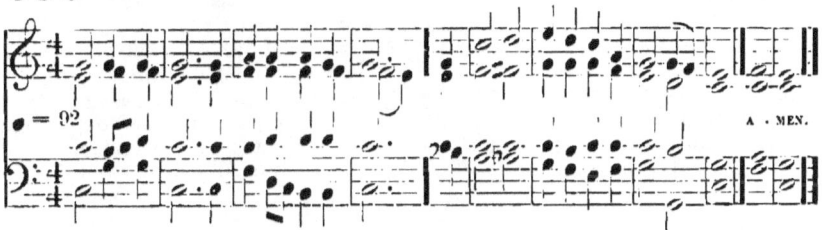

1 Peace, perfect peace, in this dark world of sin:
    The blood of Jesus whispers peace within.

2 Peace, perfect peace, by thronging duties pressed:
To do the will of Jesus,— this is rest.

3 Peace, perfect peace, with sorrows surging round:
On Jesus' bosom nought but calm is found.

4 Peace, perfect peace, with loved ones far away:
In Jesus' keeping we are safe, and they.

5 Peace, perfect peace, our future all unknown:
Jesus we know, and He is on the throne.

6 Peace, perfect peace, death shadowing us and ours:
Jesus has vanquished death and all its powers.

7 It is enough: earth's struggles soon shall cease,
And Jesus call us to heaven's perfect peace. Amen.

E. H. BICKERSTETH

## THE FORGIVENESS OF SINS

**334  St. Mabyn** 8s & 7s  A. H. BROWN

1 Yes, for me, for me He car-eth With a brother's ten-der care;

Yes, with me, with me He shar-eth Ev-ery bur-den, ev-ery fear. A-MEN.

2 Yes, o'er me, o'er me He watcheth,
Ceaseless watcheth, night and day;
Yes, e'en me, e'en me He snatcheth
From the perils of the way.

3 Yes, for me He standeth pleading
At the mercy-seat above;
Ever for me interceding,
Constant in untiring love.

4 Yes, in me abroad He sheddeth
Joys unearthly, love and light;

And to cover me He spreadeth
His paternal wing of might.

5 Yes, in me, in me He dwelleth;
I in Him, and He in me!
And my empty soul He filleth,
Here and through eternity.

6 Thus I wait for His returning,
Singing all the way to heaven;
Such the joyful song of morning,
Such the tranquil song of even. Amen.

HORATIUS BONAR

**335**

1 Always with us, always with us—
Words of cheer and words of love;
Thus the risen Saviour whispers,
From His dwelling-place above.

2 With us when we toil in sadness,
Sowing much, and reaping none;
Telling us that in the future
Golden harvests shall be won.

3 With us when the storm is sweeping
O'er our pathway dark and drear;
Waking hope within our bosoms,
Stilling every anxious fear.

4 With us in the lonely valley,
When we cross the chilling stream;
Lighting up the steps to glory
With salvation's radiant beam. Amen.

E. H. NEVIN  ab.

**Wilmot** 8s & 7s   SECOND TUNE   Arr. from VON WEBER

## TRIAL AND TRUST

### 336 Dulce Carmen 8s & 7s 6l. J. M. HAYDN

♩ = 100

1 Lead us, heavenly Fa - ther! lead us, O'er the world's tempestuous sea;

Guard us, guide us, keep us, feed us, For we have no help but Thee.

Yet possessing ev-ery blessing, If our God our Fa-ther be.

2 Saviour! breathe forgiveness o'er us,
　All our weakness Thou dost know;
Thou didst tread this earth before us,
　Thou didst feel its keenest woe.
Lone and dreary, faint and weary,
　Through the desert Thou didst go.

3 Spirit of our God descending!
　Fill our hearts with heavenly joy;
Love with every passion blending,
　Pleasure that can never cloy.
Thus provided, pardoned, guided,
　Nothing can our peace destroy.
　　　　　　　　Amen.
　　　　　　JAMES EDMESTON

## THE FORGIVENESS OF SINS

### 337 Silver Street S.M.
ISAAC SMITH

♩ =116

1 Give to the winds thy fears; Hope, and be un-dis-mayed; God hears thy

A - MEN.

sighs and counts thy tears; God shall lift up thy head.

2 Through waves and clouds and storms,
He gently clears thy way:
Wait thou His time, so shall this night
Soon end in joyous day.

3 What though thou rulest not,
Yet heaven and earth and hell
Proclaim, God sitteth on the throne,
And ruleth all things well.

4 Far, far above thy thought
His counsel shall appear,
When fully He the work hath wrought
That caused thy needless fear. Amen.

PAUL GERHARDT Tr. WESLEY *ab*.

### 338 St. Mark C.M.
H. J. GAUNTLETT

♩ = 84

1 Oh, for a faith that will not shrink Tho' press'd by every foe; That

## TRIAL AND TRUST

will not trem-ble on the brink Of an-y earth-ly woe;

2 That will not murmur nor complain
 Beneath the chastening rod,
But, in the hour of grief or pain,
 Will lean upon its God;

3 A faith that shines more bright and clear
 When tempests rage without;
That when in danger knows no fear,
 In darkness knows no doubt:

4 A faith that keeps the narrow way
 Till life's last hour is fled,
And with a pure and heavenly ray
 Lights up a dying bed.

5 Lord, give us such a faith as this,
 And then, whate'er may come,
We'll taste, e'en here, the hallowed bliss
 Of an eternal home. Amen.

W. H. BATHURST *ab.*

### 339 St. Ann's C.M.

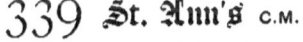

WILLIAM CROFT

1 Un-shak-en as the sa-cred hill, And fixed as moun-tains be,

Firm as a rock the soul shall rest, That leans, O Lord, on Thee.

2 Not walls, nor hills, could guard so well
 Old Salem's happy ground,
As those eternal arms of love,
 That every saint surround.

3 Deal gently, Lord, with souls sincere,
 And lead them safely on
To the bright gates of paradise,
 Where Christ, their Lord, is gone.
 Amen.

ISAAC WATTS

## THE FORGIVENESS OF SINS

### 340 In Memoriam 8.8.8.4.
F. C. Maker

1 My God, my Father, while I stray Far from my home on life's rough way,
Oh, teach me from my heart to say, "Thy will be done."

A - MEN.

2 What though in lonely grief I sigh
For friends beloved no longer nigh;
Submissive still would I reply,
"Thy will be done!"

3 If Thou shouldst call me to resign
What most I prize,—it ne'er was mine;
I only yield Thee what was Thine:
"Thy will be done!"

4 If but my fainting heart be blest
With Thy sweet Spirit for its guest,
My God, to Thee I leave the rest:
"Thy will be done!"

5 Renew my will from day to day;
Blend it with Thine, and take away
Whate'er now makes it hard to say,
"Thy will be done!"

6 Then, when on earth I breathe no more,
The prayer oft mixed with tears before,
I'll sing upon a happier shore:
"Thy will be done!" Amen.

Charlotte Elliott

### 341 Naomi C.M.
H. G. Nägeli

1 Fa-ther, what-e'er of earth-ly bliss Thy sov-'reign will de-nies,

## TRIAL AND TRUST

Ac-cept-ed at Thy throne of grace, Let this pe-ti-tion rise:

2 Give me a calm, a thankful heart,
From every murmur free;
The blessings of Thy grace impart,
And make me live to Thee.

3 Let the sweet hope that Thou art mine
My life and death attend;
Thy presence through my journey shine,
And crown my journey's end. Amen.

ANNE STEELE *ab.*

342 **Dia** 6s

JOSEPH BARNBY

♩ = 92

1 Thy way, not mine, O Lord, How-ev-er dark it be! Lead me by Thine own hand; Choose out the path for me.

2 Smooth let it be or rough,
It will be still the best,
Winding or straight, it leads
Right onward to Thy rest.

3 I dare not choose my lot:
I would not, if I might;
Choose Thou for me, my God,
So shall I walk aright.

4 The kingdom that I seek
Is Thine: so let the way
That leads to it be Thine,
Else I must surely stray.

5 Take Thou my cup, and it
With joy or sorrow fill,
As best to Thee may seem;
Choose Thou my good and ill.

6 Choose Thou for me my friends,
My sickness or my health;
Choose Thou my cares for me,
My poverty or wealth.

7 Not mine, not mine the choice,
In things or great or small;
Be Thou my Guide, my Strength,
My Wisdom and my All. Amen.

HORATIUS BONAR

## THE FORGIVENESS OF SINS

### 343 Sawley C.M.
F. PIGOU

1 Fa-ther of love, our Guide and Friend, O lead us gent-ly on,

Un-til life's tri - al - time shall end, And heavenly peace be won.

2 We know not what the path may be
  As yet by us untrod;
But we can trust our all to Thee,
  Our Father and our God.

3 If called, like Abraham's child, to
  The hill of sacrifice,        [climb
Some angel may be there in time;
  Deliverance shall arise:

4 Or, if some darker lot be good,
  O teach us to endure
The sorrow, pain, or solitude,
  That make the spirit pure.

5 Christ by no flowery pathway came;
  And we, His followers here,
Must do Thy will and praise Thy name,
  In hope, and love, and fear.

6 And, till in heaven we sinless bow,
  And faultless anthems raise,
O Father, Son, and Spirit, now
  Accept our feeble praise. Amen.

W. J. IRONS

### 344 Every Hour 6s & 4s
P. R. SLEEMAN

1 I need Thee ev - 'ry hour, Most gra - cious Lord;

## TRIAL AND TRUST

No ten - der voice like Thine, Can peace af - ford.

2 I need Thee every hour,
　Stay Thou near by;
　Temptations lose their power,
　When Thou art nigh.

3 I need Thee every hour,
　In joy or pain;
　Come quickly and abide,
　Or life is vain.

4 I need Thee every hour,
　Teach me Thy will,
　And Thy rich promises
　In me fulfil.

5 I need Thee every hour,
　Most Holy One;
　Oh, make me Thine indeed,
　Thou blessèd Son. Amen.

ANNIE S. HAWKS

## 345 Avon C.M.

HUGH WILSON

1 There is a safe and se - cret place Be -neath the wings di - vine,

Reserved for all the heirs of grace: Oh, be that ref-uge mine!

2 The least and feeblest there may bide,
　Uninjured and unawed;
　While thousands fall on every side,
　He rests secure in God.

3 He feeds in pastures large and fair
　Of love and truth divine:
　O child of God, O glory's heir,
　How rich a lot is thine!

4 A hand almighty to defend,
　An ear for every call,
　An honored life, a peaceful end,
　And heaven to crown it all! Amen.

H. F. LYTE ab.

## THE FORGIVENESS OF SINS

### 346 Mary Magdalene 6s & 5s D.
J. B. Dykes

1 In the hour of tri - al, Je-sus, pray for me; Lest by base de - ni - al

I depart from Thee; When Thou see'st me waver, With a look re - call,

Nor for fear or fa - vor, Suf - fer me to fall. A - MEN.

2 With forbidden pleasures
Would this vain world charm,
Or its sordid treasures
Spread to work me harm;
Bring to my remembrance
Sad Gethsemane,
Or, in darker semblance,
Cross-crowned Calvary.

3 If, with sore affliction,
Thou in love chastise,
Pour Thy benediction
On the sacrifice;
Then upon Thine altar,
Truly offered up,
Though the flesh may falter,
Faith shall drink the cup.

4 When, in dust and ashes,
To the grave I sink,
While heaven's glory flashes
O'er the shelving brink,
On Thy truth relying,
Through that mortal strife,
Lord, receive me, dying,
To eternal life. Amen.

JAMES MONTGOMERY

## TRIAL AND TRUST

### 347 Lux Benigna. 10.4.10.4.10.10.    J. B. Dykes

1 Lead, kindly Light, amid th' encircling gloom, Lead Thou me on; The night is

dark, and I am far from home,    Lead Thou me on.   Keep Thou my feet; I

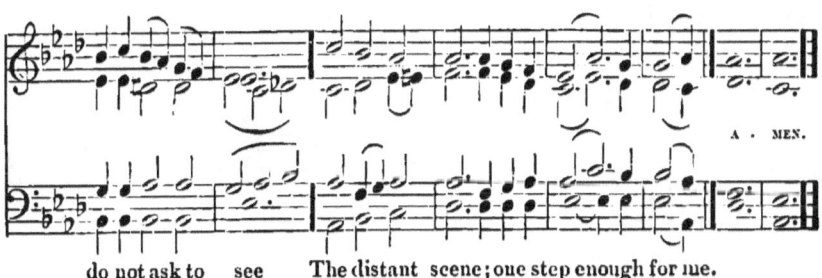

do not ask to   see    The distant scene; one step enough for me.

A · MEN.

2 I was not ever thus, nor prayed that Thou
   Shouldst lead me on;
I loved to choose and see my path: but now
   Lead Thou me on.
I loved the garish day; and, spite of fears,
Pride ruled my will; remember not past years.

3 So long Thy power has blest me, sure it still
   Will lead me on
O'er moor and fen, o'er crag and torrent, till
   The night is gone,
And with the morn those angel faces smile,
Which I have loved long since, and lost awhile. Amen.

J. H. NEWMAN

## THE FORGIVENESS OF SINS

**348 Hebron** 6.4.6.4.6.6.4.    A. B. Spratt

1 More love to Thee, O Christ, More love to Thee! Hear Thou the

prayer I make On bend-ed knee; This is my earn-est plea,—

More love, O Christ, to Thee, More love to Thee!

2 Once earthly joy I craved,
　Sought peace and rest;
Now Thee alone I seek,—
　Give what is best;
This all my prayer shall be,—
More love, O Christ, to Thee,
　More love to Thee!

3 Let sorrow do its work,
　Send grief and pain;
Sweet are Thy messengers,
　Sweet their refrain,
When they can sing with me,
More love, O Christ, to Thee,
　More love to Thee!

4 Then shall my latest breath
　Whisper Thy praise,
This be the parting cry,
　My heart shall raise;
This still its prayer shall be,—
More love, O Christ, to Thee,
　More love to Thee!  Amen.

Mrs. Elizabeth P. Prentiss

## 349 Greenville 8s & 7s D.

J. J. ROSSEAU

1 Gent-ly, Lord, oh, gen-tly lead us, Thro' this lone-ly vale of tears;
2 In the hour of pain and an-guish, In the hour when death draws near,

Through the changes Thou 'st decreed us, Till our last great change ap-pears;
Suf - fer not our hearts to languish,—Suf-fer not our souls to fear;

When tempta-tion's darts as - sail us, When in de-vious paths we stray,
And, when mor-tal life is end - ed, Bid us in Thine arms to rest,

A - MEN.

Let Thy goodness never fail us, Lead us in Thy per - fect way.
Till, by an-gel bands at-tended, We a-wake a-mong the blest. Amen.

THOMAS HASTINGS *ab.*

## THE FORGIVENESS OF SINS

### 350 Merton C.M.
J. P. Jewson alt.

1 O Thou from whom all goodness flows, I lift my heart to Thee;

In all my sor-row, conflict, woes, Dear Lord, remember me.

2 When groaning on my burdened heart
My sins lie heavily,
My pardon speak, new peace impart;
In love remember me.

3 Temptations sore obstruct my way,
And ills I cannot flee,
O, give me strength, Lord, as my day,
For good remember me.

4 Distressed with pain, disease, and grief,
This feeble body see;
Grant patience, rest, and kind relief;
Hear, and remember me.

5 If on my face for Thy dear name,
Shame and reproaches be;
All hail reproach, and welcome shame,
If Thou remember me!

6 The hour is near; consigned to death,
I own the just decree;
Saviour! with my last parting breath,
I'll cry — remember me. Amen.

THOMAS HAWEIS

### 351 Downs C.M.
LOWELL MASON

1 When all Thy mer-cies, O my God, My ris-ing soul sur-veys,

## TRIAL AND TRUST

Trans-port-ed with the view, I 'm lost In wonder, love, and praise.

2 Unnumbered comforts on my soul
Thy tender care bestowed,
Before my infant heart conceived
From whom those comforts flowed.

3 When worn with sickness, oft hast Thou
With health renewed my face;
And, when in sins and sorrows sunk,
Revived my soul with grace.

4 Ten thousand thousand precious gifts
My daily thanks employ;
Nor is the least a cheerful heart
That tastes those gifts with joy.

5 Through every period of my life
Thy goodness I 'll pursue;
And after death, in distant worlds,
The glorious theme renew.

6 Through all eternity to Thee
A joyful song I 'll raise;
For oh, eternity 's too short
To utter all Thy praise. Amen.

JOSEPH ADDISON *ab.*

## 352 Stuttgard 8s & 7s

J. G. C. STÖRL
Arr. by H. J. GAUNTLETT

1 God is love, His mer-cy brightens All the path in which we rove.
Bliss He wakes, and woe He lightens; God is wis-dom, God is love.

2 Chance and change are busy ever;
Man decays, and ages move;
But His mercy waneth never:
God is wisdom, God is love.

3 E'en the hour that darkest seemeth
Will His changeless goodness prove;
From the mist His brightness streameth:
God is wisdom, God is love.

4 He with earthly cares entwineth
Hope and comfort from above;
Everywhere His glory shineth;
God is wisdom, God is love. Amen.

JOHN BOWRING

## THE FORGIVENESS OF SINS

### 353 St. Peter's, Oxford C.M.   A. R. REINAGLE

1 I worship Thee, sweet will of God, And all Thy ways adore;
And every day I live, I seem To love Thee more and more.

A-MEN.

2 I love to kiss each print where Thou
Hast set Thine unseen feet;
I cannot fear Thee, blessèd will!
Thine empire is so sweet.

3 When obstacles and trials seem
Like prison walls to be,
I do the little I can do,
And leave the rest to Thee.

4 I have no cares, O blessèd will!
For all my cares are Thine;
I live in triumph, Lord, for Thou
Hast made Thy triumphs mine.

5 Man's weakness, waiting upon God!
Its end can never miss;
For man on earth no work can do
More angel-like than this.

6 Ride on, ride on triumphantly,
Thou glorious Will! ride on!
Faith's pilgrim sons behind Thee take
The road that Thou hast gone.   Amen.

F. W. FABER  ab.

### 354 Dennis S.M.   H. G. NÄGELI

1 How gentle God's commands! How kind His precepts are!

## TRIAL AND TRUST

Come, cast your burdens on the Lord, And trust His constant care.

2 Beneath His watchful eye  
His saints securely dwell;  
That hand which bears creation up  
Shall guard His children well,

3 Why should this anxious load  
Press down your weary mind?  
Haste to your heavenly Father's throne,  
And sweet refreshment find.

4 His goodness stands approved,  
Unchanged from day to day;  
I'll drop my burden at His feet,  
And bear a song away. Amen.

PHILIP DODDRIDGE

## 355 Waveney C.M.

RICHARD REDHEAD

1 O ver-y God of ver-y God, And ver-y Light of Light, Whose feet this earth's dark val-ley trod, That so it might be bright;

2 Our hopes are weak, our fears are strong,  
Thick darkness blinds our eyes;  
Cold is the night, and oh, we long  
That Thou, our Sun wouldst rise.

3 And even now, though dull and gray,  
The east is brightening fast,  
And kindling to the perfect day,  
That never shall be past.

4 Oh, guide us till our path is done,  
And we have reached the shore  
Where Thou, our Everlasting Sun,  
Art shining evermore.

5 We wait in faith, and turn our face  
To where the daylight springs,  
Till Thou shalt come our gloom to chase,  
With healing on Thy wings.

6 To God the Father, power and might  
Both now and ever be;  
To Him that is the Light of Light,  
And, Holy Ghost, to Thee. Amen.

## THE FORGIVENESS OF SINS

### 356 Olmutz s.m.
Arr. from LOWELL MASON

1 Your harps, ye trembling saints, Down from the wil-lows take;
Loud to the praise of love di-vine Bid ev-'ry string a-wake.

2 Though in a foreign land,
　We are not far from home;
And nearer to our house above
　We every moment come.

3 When we in darkness walk,
　Nor feel the heavenly flame,
Then is the time to trust our God,
　And rest upon His name.

4 His grace will to the end
　Stronger and brighter shine;
Nor present things, nor things to come,
　Shall quench the spark divine.

5 Tarry His leisure, then,
　Although He seem to stay;
A moment's intercourse with Him
　Thy grief will overpay.

6 Blest is the man, O God,
　That stays himself on Thee;
Who wait for Thy salvation, Lord,
　Shall Thy salvation see. Amen.

A. M. TOPLADY *ab.*

### 357 Elvet c.m.
J. B. DYKES

1 Lord, it belongs not to my care Whether I die or live;

## TRIAL AND TRUST

To love and serve Thee is my share, And this Thy grace must give.

2 If life be long, I will be glad
That I may long obey;
If short, yet why should I be sad
To soar to endless day?

3 Christ leads me thro' no darker rooms
Than He went through before:
He that into God's kingdom comes
Must enter by this door.

4 Come, Lord, when grace hath made me meet
Thy blessèd face to see;
For, if Thy work on earth be sweet,
What will Thy glory be?  Amen.

RICHARD BAXTER  ab. and alt.

## 358  Pleyel's Hymn  7s

Arr. from PLEYEL

1 Thine for ev - er! God of love, Hear us from Thy throne a - bove;

Thine for. ev - er may we be Here and in e - ter - ni - ty.

2 Thine for ever! Lord of life,
Shield us through our earthly strife;
Thou, the Life, the Truth, the Way,
Guide us to the realms of day.

3 Thine for ever! oh, how blest
They who find in Thee their rest!
Saviour, Guardian, heavenly Friend,
Oh, defend us to the end!

4 Thine for ever! Saviour, keep
These Thy frail and trembling sheep:
Safe alone beneath Thy care,
Let us all Thy goodness share.

5 Thine for ever! Thou our Guide,
All our wants by Thee supplied,
All our sins by Thee forgiven,
Lead us, Lord, from earth to heaven.
Amen.

Mrs. M. F. MAUDE

## THE FORGIVENESS OF SINS

**359  Wentworth** 8.4.8.4.8.4.  F. C. MAKER

1 My God, I thank Thee, who hast made The earth so bright,

So full of splen-dor and of joy, Beau-ty and light;

So man-y glorious things are here, No-ble and right.

2 I thank Thee too that Thou hast made
    Joy to abound;
So many gentle thoughts and deeds
    Circling us round;
That in the darkest spot of earth
    Some love is found.

3 I thank Thee, Lord, that Thou hast kept
    The best in store;
I have enough, yet not too much
    To long for more,—
A yearning for a deeper peace
    Not known before.

4 I thank Thee, Lord, that here our souls,
    Though amply blest,
Can never find, although they seek,
    A perfect rest,—
Nor ever shall, until they lean
    On Jesus' breast. Amen.

A. A. PROCTER

## TRIAL AND TRUST

### 360 Dir 7s6l.
Conrad Kocher

1 For the beau-ty of the earth, For the beau-ty of the skies,

For the love which from our birth O-ver and a-round us lies:

Lord of all, to Thee we raise This our hymn of grate-ful praise. A-MEN.

2 For the beauty of each hour
   Of the day and of the night,
Hill and vale, and tree and flower,
   Sun and moon and stars of light:
Lord of all, to Thee we raise
This our hymn of grateful praise.

3 For the joy of ear and eye,
   For the heart and mind's delight,
For the mystic harmony
   Linking sense to sound and sight:
Lord of all, to Thee we raise
This our hymn of grateful praise.

4 For the joy of human love,
   Brother, sister, parent, child,
Friends on earth, and friends above,
   For all gentle thoughts and mild:
Lord of all, to Thee we raise
This our hymn of grateful praise.

5 For Thyself, best gift divine!
   To our race so freely given;
For that great, great love of Thine,
   Peace on earth, and joy in heaven:
Lord of all, to Thee we raise
This our hymn of grateful praise.
                        Amen.

F. S. Pierpont *alt.*

## THE FORGIVENESS OF SINS

**361** **Jesus Bone Pastor** 8s7s&4     JOHN H. WILLCOX *alt.*

1 Sav-iour, like a shepherd lead us, Much we need Thy ten-der care;

In Thy pleas-ant pastures feed us; For our use Thy folds pre-pare:

Blessèd Je-sus, Bless-èd Jesus, Thou hast bought us, Thine we are.

2 We are Thine, do Thou befriend us,
  Be the guardian of our way;
Keep Thy flock, from sin defend us,
  Seek us when we go astray;
    Blessèd Jesus,
  Hear the children when they pray.

3 Thou hast promised to receive us,
  Poor and sinful though we be;
Thou hast mercy to relieve us,
  Grace to cleanse, and power to free;
    Blessèd Jesus,
  Let us early turn to Thee.

4 Early let us seek Thy favor,
  Early let us do Thy will;
Holy Lord, our only Saviour,
  With Thy grace our bosoms fill;
    Blessèd Jesus,
  Thou hast loved us, love us still. Amen.

DOROTHY A. THRUPP

## 362 Gounod 8s & 7s 6l.
**CHARLES GOUNOD**

♩ = 100

1 Gracious Saviour, gentle Shepherd, Little ones are dear to Thee; Gathered

with Thine arms, and carried  In Thy bo-som may we  be;  Sweet-ly,

A - MEN.

fond - ly, safe - ly  tend-ed,  From all want and danger  free.

2 Taught to lisp the holy praises
Which on earth Thy children sing,
Both with lips and hearts unfeignéd
May we our thank-offerings bring;
Then with all Thy saints in glory
Join to praise our Lord and King.  Amen.

JANE E. LEESON and J. WHITTEMORE

---

*See also Hymns under —*

GOD, THE FATHER ALMIGHTY . . . . . 25–41
JESUS CHRIST
    Ministry and Example . . . 61–83
THE HOLY CATHOLIC CHURCH
    Consecration and Service . . . . 188–203

## THE FORGIVENESS OF SINS

**363 Aurelia** 7s & 6s D.  S. S. WESLEY

1 In heavenly love a-bid-ing, No change my heart shall fear,

And safe is such con-fid-ing, For noth-ing changes here.

The storm may roar with-out me, My heart may low be laid,

But God is round a-bout me, And can I be dismayed? A-MEN.

2 Wherever He may guide me,
  No want shall turn me back;
My Shepherd is beside me,
  And nothing can I lack.
His wisdom ever waketh;
  His sight is never dim;
He knows the way He taketh,
  And I will walk with Him.

3 Green pastures are before me,
  Which yet I have not seen;
Bright skies will soon be o'er me,
  Where darkest clouds have been.
My hope I cannot measure,
  My path to life is free,
My Saviour has my treasure,
  And He will walk with me. Amen.

ANNA L. WARING

## TRIAL AND TRUST

**364 Ein Feste Burg** Irregular — MARTIN LUTHER

1. A mighty fortress is our God, A bulwark never failing:
Our helper He, amid the flood Of mortal ills prevailing.
For still our ancient foe Doth seek to work us woe: His craft and power are great,
And armed with cruel hate, On earth is not his equal.

A-MEN.

2 Did we in our own strength confide,
  Our striving would be losing;
Were not the right man on our side,
  The man of God's own choosing.
Dost ask who that may be?
Christ Jesus, it is He;
Lord Sabaoth is His name,
From age to age the same,
  And He must win the battle.

3 And though this world, with devils filled,
  Should threaten to undo us;
We will not fear, for God hath willed
  His truth to triumph through us.

The prince of darkness grim,—
We tremble not for him;
His rage we can endure,
For lo! his doom is sure,—
  One little word shall fell him!

4 That word above all earthly powers—
  No thanks to them — abideth;
The Spirit and the gifts are ours
  Through Him who with us sideth.
Let goods and kindred go,
This mortal life also:
The body they may kill:
God's truth abideth still,
  His kingdom is forever.    Amen.

MARTIN LUTHER Tr. HEDGE

## THE FORGIVENESS OF SINS

**365 Alms Giving** 8.8.8.4.   J. B. DYKES

1 My God, is any hour so sweet, From blush of morn to even-ing star,

As that which calls me to Thy feet — The hour of prayer?

2 Blest is that tranquil hour of morn,
And blest that solemn hour of eve,
When, on the wings of prayer up-borne,
   The world I leave.

3 Then is my strength by Thee renewed;
Then are my sins by Thee forgiven;
Then dost Thou cheer my solitude
   With hopes of heaven.

4 No words can tell what sweet relief
Here for my every want I find;
What strength for warfare, balm for [grief,
   What peace of mind.

5 Hushed is each doubt, gone every fear;
My spirit seems in heaven to stay;
And e'en the penitential tear
   Is wiped away.

6 Lord, till I reach that blissful shore,
No privilege so dear shall be
As thus my inmost soul to pour
   In prayer to Thee. Amen.
            CHARLOTTE ELLIOTT *ab.*

**366 Faithful** C.M.   S. P. TUCKERMAN

1 Prayer is the soul's sin-cere de - sire, Ut-tered or un - ex-pressed;

## PRAYER AND ASPIRATION

The mo-tion of a hid-den fire That trembles in the breast.

2 Prayer is the burden of a sigh,
 The falling of a tear,
The upward glancing of an eye,
 When none but God is near.

3 Prayer is the simplest form of speech
 That infant lips can try,
Prayer the sublimest strains that reach
 The Majesty on high.

4 Prayer is the contrite sinner's voice,
 Returning from his ways;
While angels in their songs rejoice,
 And cry—" Behold, he prays!"

5 Prayer is the Christian's vital breath,
 The Christian's native air;
His watchword at the gates of death—
 He enters heaven with prayer.

6 O Thou, by whom we come to God—
 The Life, the Truth, the Way;
The path of prayer Thyself hast trod;
 Lord! teach us how to pray. Amen.

JAMES MONTGOMERY *ab.*

### 367  Mason S.M.

E. K. GLEZEN

1 Come to the morn-ing prayer, Come, let us kneel and pray;
Prayer is the Christian pilgrim's staff To walk with God all day.

2 At noon, beneath the Rock
 Of Ages, rest and pray;
Sweet is that shadow from the heat
 When smites the sun by day.

3 At eve, shut to the door,
 Around its altar pray;

And finding there "the house of God,"
 At "heaven's gate" close the day.

4 When midnight seals our eyes,
 Let each in spirit say,
I sleep, but my heart waketh, Lord!
 With Thee to watch and pray. Amen.

JAMES MONTGOMERY

## THE FORGIVENESS OF SINS

### 368 Tallis' Ordinal C.M.
THOMAS TALLIS

1 Our hearts, O Lord, with grief are rent, O'er vows made all in vain; In anguish dai-ly we re-pent, Each day of-fend a-gain.

2 Now we arise from death to life,
Then sink from good to ill;
Here we begin, there leave our strife,
And work but half Thy will.

3 Oh, help us, Lord, amid all pain,
As warriors true, to stand
Faithful and firm, and thus to gain
Thine own, the better land.

4 Thy land—its gates how bright they
And let no evil in; [shine
Thy boundless land, and all divine,
That hath no room for sin.

5 Thy holy land, where none shall stop
Our souls upon the road,
And win our weak desires to drop
From glory and from God.

6 Oh, rich and priceless is the grace
That we shall there receive!
Nor once Thine image shall deface,
Nor once Thy spirit grieve. Amen.

### 369 St. Agnes C.M.
J. B. DYKES

1 Oh, for a clos-er walk with God, A calm and heavenly frame,—

## PRAYER AND ASPIRATION

A light to shine up- on the road That leads me to the Lamb!

2 Where is the blessédness I knew
  When first I saw the Lord?
  Where is the soul-refreshing view
  Of Jesus and His word?

3 What peaceful hours I once enjoyed!
  How sweet their memory still!
  But they have left an aching void
  The world can never fill.

4 Return, O holy Dove, return.
  Sweet messenger of rest!
  I hate the sins that made Thee mourn,
  And drove Thee from my breast.

5 The dearest idol I have known,
  Whate'er that idol be,
  Help me to tear it from Thy throne,
  And worship only Thee.

6 So shall my walk be close with God,
  Calm and serene my frame;
  So purer light shall mark the road
  That leads me to the Lamb. Amen.

WILLIAM COWPER

### 370 Nox Precessit C.M.

J. B. CALKIN

1 Walk in the light! so shalt thou know That fel-low-ship of love

His Spir-it on - ly can be-stow, Who reigns in light a - bove.

2 Walk in the light! and thou shalt own
  Thy darkness passed away,
  Because that light on thee hath shone
  In which is perfect day.

3 Walk in the light! and ev'n the tomb
  No fearful shade shall wear:
  Glory shall chase away its gloom,
  For Christ hath conquered there!

4 Walk in the light! and thine shall be
  A path, though thorny, bright;
  For God, by grace, shall dwell in thee,
  And God Himself is light! Amen.

BERNARD BARTON

## THE FORGIVENESS OF SINS

### 371 Mary Magdalene 6s&5sD.  J. B. DYKES

1 Pur-er yet and pur-er I would be in mind; Dear-er yet and dear-er,
Ev-ery du-ty find; Hoping still and trust-ing God with-out a fear,

Pa-tient-ly be-liev-ing He will make all clear.

2 Calmer yet and calmer
Trial bear and pain;
Surer yet and surer,
Peace at last to gain;
Suff'ring still and doing,
To His will resigned,
And to God subduing
Heart and will and mind.

3 Higher yet and higher
Out of clouds and night;
Nearer yet and nearer
Rising to the light—
Light serene and holy,
Where my soul may rest,
Purified and lowly,
Sanctified and blest. Amen.
J. W. VON GOETHE

### 372 Via Crucis 6s  S. M. BARKWORTH

1 Go up, go up, my heart! Dwell with thy God a-bove; For

## PRAYER AND ASPIRATION

here thou canst not rest, Nor here give out thy love.

2 Go up, go up, my heart!
 Be not a trifler here;
 Ascend above these clouds,—
 Dwell in a higher sphere.

3 Let not thy love flow out
 To things so soiled and dim;
 Go up to heaven and God;
 Take up Thy love to Him.

4 Waste not thy precious stores
 On creature-love below:
 To God that wealth belongs;
 On Him that wealth bestow.

5 Go up, reluctant heart!
 Take up thy rest above;
 Arise, earth-clinging thoughts;
 Ascend, my lingering love! Amen.

HORATIUS BONAR

### 373 Emmanuel C.M.  From BEETHOVEN

1 O hap-py soul that lives on high While men lie grovelling here! His

hopes are fixed a - bove the sky, And faith for-bids his fear.

2 His conscience knows no secret stings,
 While peace and joy combine
 To form a life, whose holy springs
 Are hidden and divine.

3 He waits in secret on his God;
 His God in secret sees:
 Let earth be all in arms abroad;
 He dwells in heavenly peace.

4 His pleasures rise from things unseen,
 Beyond this world and time,
 Where neither eyes nor ears have been,
 Nor thoughts of mortals climb.

5 He wants no pomp nor royal throne,
 To raise his honor here:
 Content and pleased to live unknown
 Till Christ his life appear. Amen.

ISAAC WATTS ab.

## THE FORGIVENESS OF SINS

**374 Brattle Street** C.M.D.  From PLEYEL

1 While Thee I seek, pro-tect-ing Power, Be my vain wish-es stilled;

And may this con-se-cra-ted hour With bet-ter hopes be filled!

Thy love the pow'r of tho't bestowed; To Thee my tho'ts would soar:

A-MEN.

Thy mer-cy o'er my life has flowed; That mer-cy I a-dore.

2 In each event of life, how clear
   Thy ruling hand I see!
Each blessing to my soul more dear,
   Because conferred by Thee.
In every joy that crowns my days,
   In every pain I bear,
My heart shall find delight in praise,
   Or seek relief in prayer.

3 When gladness wings my favored hour,
   Thy love my thoughts shall fill;
Resigned, when storms of sorrow lower,
   My soul shall meet Thy will.
My lifted eye, without a tear,
   The lowering storm shall see;
My steadfast heart shall know no fear;
   That heart will rest on Thee. Amen.

HELEN M. WILLIAMS

## PRAYER AND ASPIRATION

**St. Peter's, Oxford** C.M. SECOND TUNE — A. R. REINAGLE

**375 Hermann** C.M. — N. HERMANN

1 I know that my Redeemer lives,
  And ever prays for me;
A token of His love He gives,
  A pledge of liberty.

2 I find Him lifting up my head,
  He brings salvation near;
His presence makes me free indeed,
  And He will soon appear.

3 He wills that I should holy be;
  What can withstand His will?
The counsel of His grace in me
  He surely shall fulfil.

4 Jesus, I hang upon Thy word;
  I steadfastly believe
Thou wilt return, and claim me, Lord,
  And to Thyself receive.

5 When God is mine, and I am His,
  Of paradise possessed,
I taste unutterable bliss,
  And everlasting rest. Amen.

CHARLES WESLEY *ab*.

## THE FORGIVENESS OF SINS

**376  St. Edith** 7s & 6s D.    F. Husband

1 To Thee, O dear, dear Saviour, My spirit turns for rest, My peace is in Thy

fa - vor, My pil - low on Thy breast: Tho' all the world de-ceive me, I

know that I am Thine, And Thou wilt never leave me, O blessèd Saviour mine.

2 In Thee my trust abideth,
On Thee my hope relies,
O Thou whose love provideth
For all beneath the skies:
O Thou whose mercy found me,
From bondage set me free,
And then forever bound me
With threefold cords to Thee.

3 My grief is in the dullness
With which this sluggish heart
Doth open to the fullness
Of all Thou wouldst impart:
My joy is in Thy beauty
Of holiness divine,
My comfort in the duty
That binds my life to Thine.

4 Alas, that I should ever
Have fail'd in love to Thee,
The only one who never
Forgot or slighted me!
Oh, for a heart to love Thee
More truly as I ought,
And nothing place above Thee
In deed, or word, or thought.

5 Oh, for that choicest blessing,
Of living in Thy love,
And thus on earth possessing
The peace of heaven above:
Oh, for the bliss that by it
The soul securely knows;
The holy calm and quiet
Of faith's serene repose.  Amen.

J. S. B. MONSELL

*PRAYER AND ASPIRATION*

**377 Marshall** s.m.            G. J. GEER

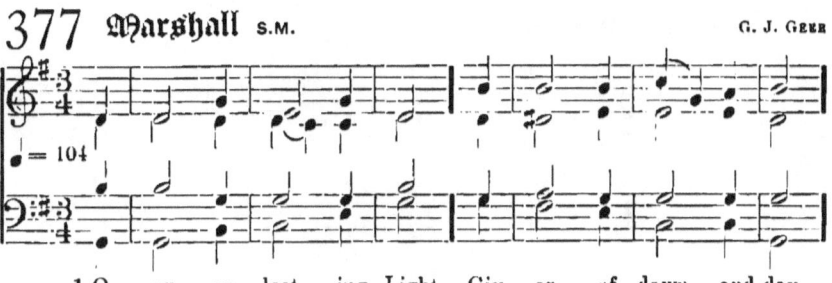

1 O ev-er-last-ing Light, Giv-er of dawn and day,

Dis-pel-ler of the ancient night In which cre-a-tion lay!

2 O everlasting Light,
   Shine graciously within!
Brightest of all on earth that's bright,
   Come, shine away my sin!

3 O everlasting Truth,
   Truest of all that's true,
Sure Guide of erring age and youth,
   Lead me, and teach me too!

4 O everlasting Strength,
   Uphold me in the way;
Bring me, in spite of foes, at length
   To joy, and light, and day.

5 O everlasting Love,
   Wellspring of grace and peace:
Pour down Thy fullness from above,
   Bid doubt and trouble cease!

6 O everlasting Rest,
   Lift off life's load of care:
Relieve, revive this burdened breast,
   And every sorrow bear.

7 Thou art in heaven our all,
   Our all on earth art Thou;
Upon Thy glorious name we call,
   Lord Jesus, bless us now. Amen.

                                     HORATIUS BONAR

---

*See also Hymns under —*

THE CALL TO WORSHIP . . . . . . . . 1–24
THE HOLY GHOST . . . . . . . . 140–152
THE COMMUNION OF SAINTS . . . . . . . . 228–241

## THE RESURRECTION OF THE BODY

**378 Requiem** 4s&6sD.     JOSEPH BARNBY

1 Sleep thy last sleep,
Free from care and sorrow;
Rest, where none weep,
Till th' Eternal Morrow;
Though dark waves roll
O'er the silent river,
Thy fainting soul
Jesus can deliver. A-MEN.

2 Life's dream is past,
  All its sin, its sadness,
Brightly at last,
  Dawns a day of gladness;
Under thy sod,
  Earth, receive our treasure,
To rest in God,
  Waiting all His pleasure.

3 Though we may mourn
  Those in life the dearest,
They shall return,
  Christ, when Thou appearest!
Soon shall Thy Voice
  Comfort those now weeping,
Bidding rejoice,
  All in Jesus sleeping. Amen.

E. A. DAYMAN

# 379 In Christo L.M.

G. M. GARRETT

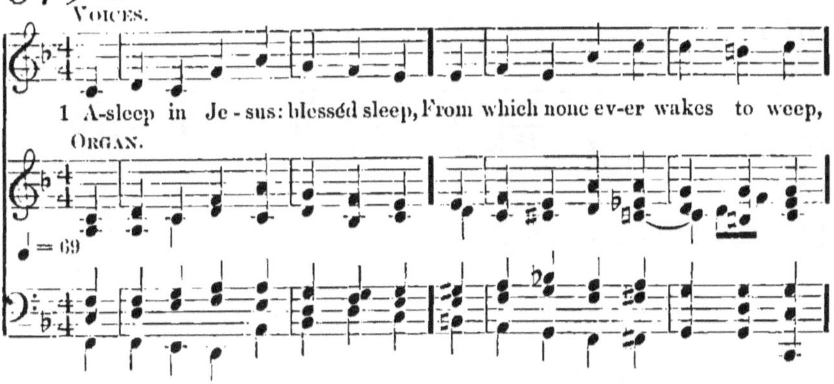

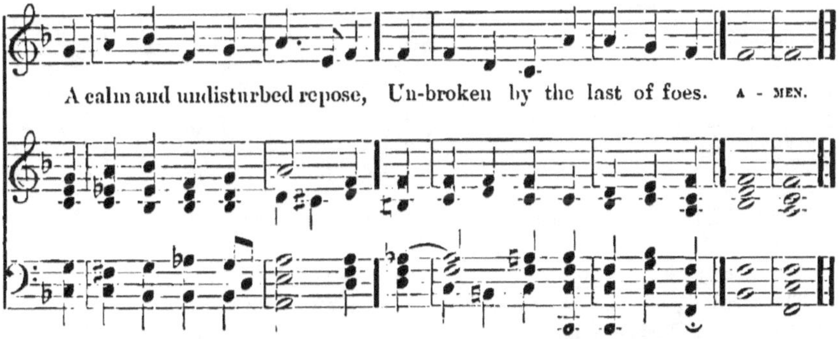

*1 Asleep in Jesus: blessèd sleep, From which none ev-er wakes to weep,*

*A calm and undisturbed repose, Unbroken by the last of foes.* A - MEN.

2 Asleep in Jesus: oh, how sweet
To be for such a slumber meet;
With holy confidence to sing,
That death hath lost his venomed sting.

3 Asleep in Jesus: peaceful rest,
Whose waking is supremely blest;
No fear, no woe, shall dim that hour
That manifests the Saviour's power.

4 Asleep in Jesus: oh, for me
May such a blissful refuge be;
Securely shall my ashes lie,
Waiting the summons from on high.

5 Asleep in Jesus: far from thee
Thy kindred and their graves may be;
But thine is still a blessèd sleep,
From which none ever wakes to weep.
Amen.

Mrs. MARGARET MACKAY *ob.*

**Rest** L.M.  SECOND TUNE  Arr. by W. B. BRADBURY

## THE RESURRECTION OF THE BODY

### 380 Victor S.M.
E. K. Glezen

♩ = 100

1 It is not death to die—To leave this weary road,

A-MEN.

And 'mid the brotherhood on high, To be at home with God.

2 It is not death to close
   The eye long dimmed by tears,
And wake, in glorious repose
   To spend eternal years.

3 It is not death to bear
   The wrench that sets us free
From dungeon chain,—to breathe the air
   Of boundless liberty.

4 It is not death to fling
   Aside this sinful dust,
And rise, on strong exulting wing,
   To live among the just.

5 Jesus, Thou Prince of life!
   Thy chosen cannot die;
Like Thee, they conquer in the strife,
   To reign with Thee on high. Amen.

C. H. A. Malan Tr. Bethune

### 381 Dunn 7.6.7.6.

E. K. Glezen

♩ = 72

1 No, no, it is not dy-ing To go unto our God; This gloomy earth for

## BURIAL OF THE DEAD

saking Our journey homeward taking, A - long the starry road.

2 No, no, it is not dying
Heaven's citizen to be;
A crown immortal wearing,
And rest unbroken sharing,
From care and conflict free.

3 No, no, it is not dying
The Shepherd's voice to know;
His sheep He ever leadeth,
His peaceful flock He feedeth,
Where living pastures grow.

4 No, no, it is not dying
To wear a lordly crown;
Among God's people dwelling,
The glorious triumph swelling
Of Him whose sway we own.

5 O no, this is not dying,
Thou Saviour of mankind!
There, streams of love are flowing,
No hindrance ever knowing;
Here, drops alone we find. Amen.

C. H. A. MALAN Tr. DUNN *ab.*

## 382 Renovation S.M.

From HUMMEL

1 Ser - vant of God, well done! Rest from thy loved em - ploy; The

bat - tle fought, the victory won, En - ter thy Master's joy.

2 The voice at midnight came;
He started up to hear;
A mortal arrow pierced His frame,
He fell, but felt no fear.

3 His spirit, with a bound,
Left its encumbering clay:
His tent, at sunrise, on the ground
A darkened ruin lay.

4 The pains of death are past;
Labor and sorrow cease;
And life's long warfare closed at last,
His soul is found in peace.

5 Soldier of Christ, well done!
Praise be thy new employ;
And, while eternal ages run,
Rest in thy Saviour's joy. Amen.

JAMES MONTGOMERY *ab*

## THE RESURRECTION OF THE BODY

### 383 Requiescat 7.7.7.7.8.8.
J. B. Dykes

1 Now the laborer's task is o'er; Now the bat-tle day is past;

Now up-on the farther shore Lands the voy-a-ger at last. Fa-ther,

in Thy gracious keep-ing Leave we now Thy servant sleep-ing.

2 There the tears of earth are dried;
   There its hidden things are clear;
There the work of life is tried
   By a juster Judge than here.
Father, in Thy gracious keeping
Leave we now Thy servant sleeping.

3 There the sinful souls, that turn
   To the Cross their dying eyes,
The dear love of Christ shall learn
   At His feet in Paradise.
Father, in Thy gracious keeping
Leave we now Thy servant sleeping.

4 There no more the powers of hell
   Can prevail to mar their peace;
Christ the Lord shall guard them well,
   He who died for their release.
Father, in Thy gracious keeping
Leave we now Thy servant sleeping.

5 "Earth to earth, and dust to dust,"
   Calmly now the words we say,
Leaving him to sleep in trust
   Till the resurrection-day.
Father, in Thy gracious keeping
Leave we now Thy servant sleeping.
                Amen.

JOHN ELLERTON

## THE LIFE EVERLASTING

**384** Ḥimmel  6.4.6.4.6.6.4.                                   ARTHUR SULLIVAN

1 We are but stran-gers here, Heaven is our home; Earth is a

des-ert drear, Heaven is our home. Dan- ger and sorrow stand Round us on

ev-ery hand, Heaven is our fa-ther-land, Heaven is our home.   A - MEN.

2 What though the tempests rage?
   Heaven is our home;
Short is our pilgrimage,
   Heaven is our home.
And Time's wild wintry blast
Soon shall be overpast,
We shall reach home at last,
   Heaven is our home.

3 There at our Saviour's side,
   Heaven is our home;
May we be glorified,
   Heaven is our home.
There are the good and blest,
Those we love most and best,
Grant us with them to rest,
   Heaven is our home.

4 Grant us to murmur not,
   Heaven is our home:
Whate'er our earthly lot,
   Heaven is our home.
Grant us at last to stand
There at Thine own right hand,
Jesus, in Fatherland:
   Heaven is our home.  Amen.

T. R. TAYLOR

## 385 Leighton S.M.

H. W. GREATOREX

1 For-ev-er with the Lord; A-men, so let it be, Life from the dead is in that word; 'T is im-mor-tal-i-ty.

2 Here in the body pent,
  Absent from Him I roam,
Yet nightly pitch my moving tent
  A day's march nearer home.

3 My Father's house on high,
  Home of my soul, how near
At times, to faith's foreseeing eye,
  Thy golden gates appear!

4 Ah! then my spirit faints
  To reach the land I love,
The bright inheritance of saints,
  Jerusalem, above!

5 Be Thou at my right hand,
  Then can I never fail;
Uphold Thou me, and I shall stand,
  Fight, and I must prevail.

6 So when my latest breath
  Shall rend the vail in twain,
By death I shall escape from death,
  And life eternal gain. Amen.

JAMES MONTGOMERY *ab.*

## 386 Lyte S.M.

J. P. WILKES

1 Far from my heaven-ly home, Far from my Fa-ther's breast,

## THE LIFE EVERLASTING

Fainting I cry "blest Spir-it, come! And speed me to my rest."

2 Upon the willows long
My harp has silent hung;
How should I sing a cheerful song,
Till Thou inspire my tongue?

3 My spirit homeward turns,
And fain would thither flee;
My heart, O Sion, droops and yearns,
When I remember thee.

4 To thee, to thee I press,
A dark and toilsome road;
When shall I pass the wilderness,
And reach the saint's abode?

5 God of my life, be near!
On Thee my hopes I cast:
O guide me through the desert here
And bring me home at last! Amen.

H. F. LYTE *ab.*

## 387 St. Paul's College s.m.　　　George Lomas

1 One sweet-ly sol-emn thought Comes to me o'er and o'er,—
Nearer my home, to-day, am I Than e'er I've been be-fore;

2 Nearer my Father's house,
Where many mansions be;
Nearer the throne where Jesus reigns,
Nearer the crystal sea;

3 Nearer my going home,
Laying my burden down,
Leaving my cross of heavy grief,
Wearing my starry crown.

4 Nearer that hidden stream,
Winding through shades of night,
Rolling its cold, dark waves between
Me and the world of light.

5 Jesus, to Thee I cling:
Strengthen my arm of faith;
Stay near me while my way-worn feet
Press through the stream of death.
　　　　　　　　Amen.

Phœbe Cary *ab. and alt.*

## THE LIFE EVERLASTING

### 388 Woodland 8.6.8.8.6.
N. D. GOULD

1 There is an hour of peaceful rest, To mourning wanderers given; There is a joy for souls distressed, A balm for every wounded breast: 'T is found alone in Heaven.

2 There is a home for weary souls,
　By sin and sorrow driven,
When tossed on life's tempestuous shoals,
Where storms arise and ocean rolls,
　And all is drear but Heaven.

3 There faith lifts up her cheerful eye,
　To brighter prospects given;
And views the tempest passing by,
The evening shadows quickly fly,
　And all serene—in Heaven.

4 There fragrant flowers immortal bloom,
　And joys supreme are given;
There rays divine disperse the gloom;
Beyond the confines of the tomb
　Appears the dawn of Heaven. Amen.

W. B. TAPPAN *alt.*

### 389 Woolwich S.M.
C. E. KETTLE

1 Come to the land of peace; From shad-ows come a-way;

## THE LIFE EVERLASTING

Where all the sounds of weeping cease, And storms no more have sway.

2 Fear hath no dwelling here;
 But pure repose and love
Breathe through the bright, celestial air
 The spirit of the dove.

3 Come to the bright and blest,
 Gathered from every land;
For here thy soul shall find its rest
 Amid the shining band.

4 In this divine abode
 Change leaves no saddening trace;
Come, trusting spirit, to thy God,
 Thy holy resting-place.

5 "Come to our peaceful home,"
 The saints and angels say,
"Forsake the world, no longer roam;
 O wanderer, come away!" Amen.

Mrs. FELICIA D. HEMANS ab.

## 390 Belmont C.M.    SAMUEL WEBBE

1 When I can read my title clear To mansions in the skies, I bid farewell to ev-'ry fear, And wipe my weeping eyes.

2 Should earth against my soul engage,
 And fiery darts be hurl'd,
Then I can smile at Satan's rage,
 And face a frowning world.

3 Let cares like a wild deluge come,
 And storms of sorrow fall,
May I but safely reach my home,
 My God, my heaven, my all.

4 There shall I bathe my weary soul
 In seas of heavenly rest,
And not a wave of trouble roll
 Across my peaceful breast. Amen.

ISAAC WATTS

## THE LIFE EVERLASTING

**391 Paradise** C.M.D.      JOSEPH BARNBY

1 O Paradise! O Paradise! Who doth not crave for rest? Who would not seek the happy land, Where they that loved are blest?

Where loyal hearts and true Stand ever in the light, All rapture through and through, In God's most holy sight.

A - MEN.

2 O Paradise! O Paradise!
  The world is growing old;
Who would not be at rest and free
  Where love is never cold?
Where loyal hearts and true, etc.

3 O Paradise! O Paradise!
  'T is weary waiting here;
I long to be where Jesus is,
  To feel, to see Him near;
Where loyal hearts and true, etc.

4 O Paradise! O Paradise!
  I want to sin no more;
I want to be as pure on earth,
  As on Thy spotless shore;
Where loyal hearts and true, etc.

5 O Paradise! O Paradise!
  I greatly long to see
The special place my dearest Lord
  Is destining for me;
Where loyal hearts and true, etc.

6 O Paradise! O Paradise!
  I feel 't will not be long;
Patience! I almost think I hear
  Faint fragments of Thy song;
Where loyal hearts and true, etc.    Amen.

F. W. FABER *ab.*

## THE LIFE EVERLASTING

**392 Pilgrims** 11.10.11.10.9.11.   HENRY SMART

1 Hark! hark, my soul! angelic songs are swelling
    O'er earth's green fields and ocean's wave-beat shore,

How sweet the truth those blessèd strains are telling,
    Of that new life when sin shall be no more.

A - MEN.

Angels of Jesus, Angels of light, Singing to welcome the pilgrims of the night.

2 Onward we go, for still we hear them singing,
"Come, weary souls, for Jesus bids you come;"
And, through the dark its echoes sweetly ringing,
    The music of the gospel leads us home.
    Angels of Jesus, Angels of light,
Singing to welcome the pilgrims of the night.

3 Far, far away, like bells at evening pealing,
The voice of Jesus sounds o'er land and sea;
And laden souls by thousands meekly stealing,
    Kind Shepherd, turn their weary steps to Thee.
    Angels of Jesus, Angels of light,
Singing to welcome the pilgrims of the night.

4 Angels, sing on: your faithful watches keeping,
Sing us sweet fragments of the songs above;
Till morning's joy shall end the night of weeping,
    And life's long shadows break in cloudless love.
    Angels of Jesus, Angels of light,
Singing to welcome the pilgrims of the night. Amen.

F. W. FABER *bb.*

## THE LIFE EVERLASTING

### 393 Alford 7.6.8.6.D.
J. B. Dykes

1 Ten thousand times ten thousand, In sparkling raiment bright,
The ar-mies of the

ransomed saints Throng up the steeps of light:'T is finished, all is finished, Their

fight with death and sin: Fling open wide the golden gates, And let the victors in.

2 What rush of alleluias
Fills all the earth and sky!
What ringing of a thousand harps
Bespeaks the triumph nigh!
O day, for which creation
And all its tribes were made!
O joy, for all its former woes,
A thousand fold repaid!

3 Oh, then what raptured greetings
On Canaan's happy shore,
What knitting severed friendships up,
Where partings are no more!

Then eyes with joy shall sparkle,
That brimmed with tears of late,
Orphans no longer fatherless,
Nor widows desolate.

4 Bring near Thy great salvation,
Thou Lamb for sinners slain;
Fill up the roll of Thine elect,
Then take Thy power, and reign;
Appear, Desire of nations —
Thine exiles long for home —
Show in the heaven Thy promised sign,
Thou Prince and Saviour, come!
Amen.

HENRY ALFORD

## THE LIFE EVERLASTING

**394 Sanctuary** 8s & 7s D.　　　　J. B. DYKES

1 Hark! the sound of ho-ly voi-ces, Chanting at the crys-tal sea,—
"Al-le-lu-ia, Al-le-lu-ia, Al-le-lu-ia, Lord, to Thee!"
Mul-ti-tude which none can number, Like the stars in glo-ry stands,
Clad in white ap-par-el, holding Palms of vict'ry in their hands.

A - MEN.

2 Marching with Thy Cross their banner,
　They have triumphed following
Thee, the Captain of salvation,
　Thee, their Saviour and their King;
Gladly, Lord, with Thee they suffered;
　Gladly, Lord, with Thee they died,
And by death to life immortal
　They were born, and glorified.

3 Now they reign in heavenly glory,
　Now they walk in golden light,
Now they drink, as from a river,
　Holy bliss and infinite;
Love and peace they taste forever,
　And all truth and knowledge see
In the Beatific Vision
　Of the Blessèd Trinity. Amen.

　　　　　　CHRISTOPHER WORDSWORTH *ab.*

## THE LIFE EVERLASTING

### 395. Castle Rising. C.M.D.
F. A. J. Hervey

1 The ro-seate hues of ear-ly dawn, The brightness of the day,
The crimson of the sun-set sky, How fast they fade away!
Oh, for the pearl-y gates of heaven, Oh, for the gold-en floor,
Oh, for the Sun of righteousness, That setteth nev-er-more!

A-men.

2 The highest hopes we cherish here,
How fast they tire and faint;
How many a spot defiles the robe
That wraps an earthly saint!
Oh, for a heart that never sins,
Oh, for a soul washed white,
Oh, for a voice to praise our King,
Nor weary day nor night.

3 Here faith is ours, and heavenly hope,
And grace to lead us higher;
But there are perfectness and peace
Beyond our best desire!
Oh, by Thy love and anguish, Lord,
Oh, by Thy life laid down,
Oh, that we fall not from Thy grace,
Nor cast away our crown. Amen.

Mrs. C. F. Alexander

## THE LIFE EVERLASTING

### 396 Children's Praises  C.M. with chorus   Arr. from English Air

1 A-round the throne of God in heaven Thousands of children stand,

Children whose sins are all for-given, A ho-ly, hap-py band.

Singing glo-ry, glo-ry, glo-ry be to God on high.   A-MEN.

2 What brought them to that world above,
That heaven so bright and fair,
Where all is peace, and joy, and love?
How came those children there?
  Singing glory be to God on high.

3 Because the Saviour shed His blood
To wash away their sin;
Bathed in that pure and precious flood,
Behold them white and clean.
  Singing glory be to God on high.

4 On earth they sought their Saviour's grace,
On earth they loved His name;
So now they see His blessèd face,
And stand before the Lamb.
  Singing glory be to God on high.   Amen.

ANNE SHEPHERD

## THE LIFE EVERLASTING

### 397 Homeland  7s & 6s D.
*GREEK MELODY*

1. My Homeland, oh, my Home-land, The land of souls free-born!
   No gloom-y night is known there, But aye the fade-less morn;

I'm sigh-ing for that coun-try, My heart is ach-ing here;

There's no pain in the Homeland To which I'm drawing near.  A-MEN.

2 My Lord is in the Homeland,
  With angels bright and fair;
No sinful thing or evil
  Can ever enter there;
The music of the ransomed
  Is ringing in my ears,
And when I think of Homeland
  My eyes are filled with tears.

3 My loved ones in the Homeland
  Are waiting me to come,
Where neither death nor sorrow
  Invade their holy home:
O dear, dear native country!
  O rest and peace above!
Christ bring us to the Homeland
  Of His eternal love.   Amen.

H. R. HAWEIS

## 398 Emmanuel c.m.

From BEETHOVEN

1 There is a land of pure de-light, Where saints immor-tal reign, In-

fi - nite day ex-cludes the night, And pleas-ures ban - ish pain.

2 There everlasting spring abides,
  And never-withering flowers;
  Death, like a narrow sea, divides
  This heavenly land from ours.

3 Sweet fields beyond the swelling flood
  Stand dressed in living green;
  So to the Jews old Canaan stood,
  While Jordan rolled between.

4 Oh, could we make our doubts remove,
  These gloomy doubts that rise,
  And see the Canaan that we love,
  With unbeclouded eyes.

5 Could we but climb where Moses stood,
  And view the landscape o'er— [flood
  Not Jordan's stream, nor death's cold
  Should fright us from the shore. Amen.

ISAAC WATTS *ab.*

## Varina c.m.d.   SECOND TUNE

Arr. by G. F. ROOT

## THE LIFE EVERLASTING

### 399 Southwell C.M.
H. S. Irons

1 Je-ru-sa-lem, my hap-py home, Name ev-er dear to me,

When shall my la-bors have an end In joy, and peace, and thee?

2 When shall these eyes thy heaven-
And pearly gates behold? [built walls
Thy bulwarks with salvation strong,
And streets of shining gold?

3 There happier bowers than Eden's
Nor sin nor sorrow know: [bloom,
Blest seats! through rude and stormy
I onward press to you. [scenes

4 Why should I shrink from pain and
Or feel at death, dismay? [woe,
I've Canaan's goodly land in view,
And realms of endless day.

5 Apostles, martyrs, prophets, there
Around my Saviour stand;
And soon my friends in Christ below
Will join the glorious band.

6 Jerusalem, my happy home,
My soul still pants for thee;
Then shall my labors have an end,
When I thy joys shall see. Amen

### 400

1 O mother, dear Jerusalem,
When shall I come to thee?
When shall my sorrows have an end?
Thy joys when shall I see?

2 O happy harbor of the saints,
O sweet and pleasant soil,
In thee no sorrow may be found,
No grief, no care, no toil!

3 Thy saints are crowned with glory
They see God face to face; [great,
They triumph still, they still rejoice;
Most happy is their case.

4 We that are here in banishment
Continually do moan;
We sigh and sob, we weep and wail,
Perpetually we groan.

5 But there they live in such delight,
Such pleasure and such play,
As that to them a thousand years
Doth seem as yesterday.

6 Ah, my sweet home Jerusalem,
Would God I were in thee!
Would God my woes were at an end,
Thy joys that I might see. Amen.

Francis Baker ab.

## THE LIFE EVERLASTING

**Rhine** C.M.     SECOND TUNE     Arr. from FRIEDRICH BURGMULLER

**401 St. Alphege** 7s & 6s     H. J. GAUNTLETT

1 Brief life is here our por-tion, Brief sor-row, short-lived care;
The life that knows no end-ing, The tear-less life, is there.

2 O happy retribution!
   Short toil, eternal rest;
For mortals and for sinners
   A mansion with the blest!

3 And now we fight the battle,
   But then shall wear the crown
Of full and everlasting
   And passionless renown.

4 But He whom now we trust in
   Shall then be seen and known;
And they that know and see Him,
   Shall have Him for their own.

5 The morning shall awaken,
   The shadows shall decay,
And each true-hearted servant
   Shall shine as doth the day.

6 There God our King and Portion,
   In fullness of His grace,
Shall we behold forever,
   And worship face to face,

7 Exult, O dust and ashes,
   The Lord shall be thy part;
His only, His for ever,
   Thou shalt be, and thou art! Amen.

BERNARD Tr. NEALE

## THE LIFE EVERLASTING

**402 Christ Church** 6.6.6.6.8.8.  CHARLES STEGGALL

1 Jerusalem on high
My song and city is,
My home whene'er I die,
The centre of my bliss:
O happy place! when shall I be,
My God, with Thee, to see Thy face?

2 There dwells my Lord, my King,
Judged here unfit to live:
There angels to Him sing,
And lowly homage give.
O happy place! when shall I be,
My God, with Thee, to see Thy face?

3 The patriarchs of old
There from their travels cease:
The prophets there behold
Their longed-for Prince of Peace.
O happy place! when shall I be,
My God, with Thee, to see Thy face?

4 The Lord's apostles there
I might with joy behold;
The harpers I might hear
Harping on harps of gold.
O happy place! when shall I be,
My God, with Thee, to see Thy face?

5 The bleeding martyrs, they
Within those courts are found,
Clothed in their white array,
Their scars with glory crowned.
O happy place! when shall I be,
My God, with Thee, to see Thy face?

6 Ah me! ah me! that I
In Kedar's tents here stay!
No place like that on high;
Lord, thither guide my way!
O happy place! when shall I be,
My God, with Thee, to see Thy face?
Amen.

SAMUEL CROSSMAN

403 Pearsall 7s & 6s D.　　　St. Gall. Cath. Gesangbuch

1 The world is ver-y e - vil, The times are waxing late, Be sober and keep

vig - il, The Judge is at the gate; The Judge who comes in mer-cy, The

A - MEN.

Judge who comes with might,
　　Who comes to end the evil, Who comes to crown the right.

2 Arise, arise, good Christian,
　Let right to wrong succeed;
Let penitential sorrow
　To heavenly gladness lead;
To light that has no evening,
　That knows nor moon nor sun,
The light so new and golden,
　The light that is but one.

3 O Home of fadeless splendor,
　Of flowers that fear no thorn,
Where they shall dwell as children
　Who here as exiles mourn;
'Midst power that knows no limit,
　Where wisdom has no bound,
The beatific vision
　Shall glad the saints around.

4 O happy, holy portion,
　Refection for the blest,
True vision of true beauty,
　True cure of the distressed;
Strive, man, to win that glory;
　Toil, man, to gain that light;
Send hope before to grasp it,
　Till hope be lost in sight.

5 O sweet and blessèd country,
　The home of God's elect!
O sweet and blessèd country
　That eager hearts expect!
Jesus, in mercy bring us
　To that dear land of rest;
Who art, with God the Father,
　And Spirit, ever blest. Amen.
　　　　　　Bernard Tr. Neale.

## THE LIFE EVERLASTING

404 St. Anselm 7s & 6s D.  JOSEPH BARNBY

1 For thee, O dear, dear coun-try, Mine eyes their vig-ils keep; For

very love, beholding Thy happy name, they weep. The mention of Thy glo-ry

Is unction to the breast, And medicine in sickness, And love, and life, and rest.

2 With jasper glow Thy bulwarks,
   Thy streets with emeralds blaze;
The sardius and the topaz
   Unite in Thee their rays;
Thine ageless walls are bonded
   With amethyst unpriced;
The saints build up its fabric,
   And the corner-stone is Christ.

3 The Cross is all Thy splendor,
   The Crucified Thy praise;
His land and benediction,
   Thy ransomed people raise:
Jesus, the Crown and Beauty,
   True God and Man, they sing;
The never-failing garden,—
   The garden of their King.

4 Thou hast no shore, fair ocean!
   Thou hast no time, bright day!
Dear fountain of refreshment
   To pilgrims far away!
Upon the Rock of Ages
   They raise Thy holy tower,
Thine is the victor's laurel,
   And Thine the golden dower.

5 O sweet and blessèd country,
   The home of God's elect!
O sweet and blessèd country,
   That eager hearts expect!
Jesus, in mercy bring us
   To that dear land of rest,
Who art, with God the Father,
   And Spirit, ever blest. Amen.

BERNARD Tr. NEALE

## THE LIFE EVERLASTING

**405** **Ewing** 7s&6s D.  ALEXANDER EWING

1 Je-ru-sa-lem the gold-en, With milk and honey blest; Beneath thy contem-

pla-tion Sink heart and voice oppressed: I know not, oh, I know not, What

joys await us there, What radiancy of glory, What bliss beyond compare!

2 They stand, those halls of Sion,
  All jubilant with song,
And bright with many an angel,
  And all the martyr throng:
The Prince is ever in them,
  The daylight is serene,
The pastures of the blessèd
  Are decked in glorious sheen.

3 There is the throne of David,
  And there, from care released,
The song of them that triumph,
  The shout of them that feast;
And they, who with their Leader
  Have conquered in the fight,
For ever and for ever
  Are clad in robes of white.

4 O sweet and blessèd country
  The home of God's elect!
O sweet and blessèd country,
  That eager hearts expect!
Jesus, in mercy bring us
  To that dear land of rest;
Who art, with God the Father,
  And Spirit, ever blest. Amen.

BERNARD Tr. NEALE

## TIMES AND SEASONS

**406 Old Hundred Forty-eighth** 6.6.6.6.8.8.  WILLIAM CROFT

1 For thee we long and pray, O bless-èd Sabbath morn! And all the week we say, Oh, when wilt thou re-turn? Come, come away, day of glad rest, Of days the best, sweet Sabbath day.

A - MEN.

2 Thou tellest us how Christ,
  Arose and left the tomb;
And all the week we say,
  Oh, when will Sabbath come?
    Come, come away, etc.

3 Thou tellest of a rest,
  A peaceful, happy home,
Where all the saints are blest,
  Oh, when will Sabbath come?
    Come, come away, etc.  Amen.

HORATIUS BONAR

## 407

1 Welcome, delightful morn,
    Thou day of sacred rest;
  I hail thy kind return;—
    Lord, make these moments blest:
  From the low train of mortal toys
  I soar to reach immortal joys.

2 Now may the King descend,
    And fill His throne of grace:
  Thy sceptre, Lord, extend,
    While saints address Thy face:
  Let sinners feel Thy quickening word,
  And learn to know and fear the Lord.

3 Descend, celestial Dove,
    With all Thy quickening powers,
  Disclose a Saviour's love,
    And bless these sacred hours;
  Then shall my soul new life obtain,
  Nor Sabbaths e'er be spent in vain.  Amen.

HAYWARD  JOHN DOBELL'S COLL.

## THE LORD'S DAY

**408 Sabbath** 7s6l.  LOWELL MASON *alt.*

1 Safe-ly through an-oth-er week God has brought us on our way;

Let us now a bless-ing seek, Wait-ing in His courts to-day;

Day of all the week the best, Em-blem of e-ter-nal rest. A-MEN.

2 While we pray for pardoning grace
   Through the dear Redeemer's Name,
Show Thy reconcilèd face,
   Take away our sin and shame,
From our worldly cares set free,
May we rest this day in Thee.

3 Here we come Thy Name to praise;
   Let us feel Thy presence near;
May Thy glory meet our eyes
   While we in Thy house appear:
Here afford us, Lord, a taste
Of our everlasting feast.

4 May Thy gospel's joyful sound
   Conquer sinners, comfort saints;
Make the fruits of grace abound;
   Bring relief for all complaints:
Thus let all our Sabbaths prove,
Till we rest in Thee above. Amen.

JOHN NEWTON *ab. and alt.*

## TIMES AND SEASONS

### 409 Bonner 7s & 6s D.   Robert Bonner

1 O day of rest and gladness, O day of joy and light, O balm of care and

sad-ness, Most beautiful, most bright! On Thee the high and low-ly, Bend-

ing before the throne, Sing, Holy, Holy, Holy, To the Great Three in One.   A · MEN.

2 On Thee, at the creation,
　The light first had its birth:
On Thee for our salvation,
　Christ rose from depths of earth,
On Thee, our Lord victorious,
　The Spirit sent from Heaven,
And thus on Thee, most glorious
　A triple light was given.

3 To-day on weary nations
　The heavenly manna falls;
To holy convocations
　The silver trumpet calls,
Where gospel light is glowing
　With pure and radiant beams,
And living water flowing
　With soul-refreshing streams.

4 New graces ever gaining
　From this our day of rest,
We reach the rest remaining
　To spirits of the blest:
To Holy Ghost be praises,
　To Father and to Son:
The church her voice upraises
　To Thee, blest Three in One.   Amen.

CHRISTOPHER WORDSWORTH ab.

## 410

1 The dawn of God's new Sabbath
　Breaks o'er the earth again,
As some sweet summer morning
　After a night of pain.
It comes as cooling showers,
　To cheer a thirsting land,
As shade of clustered palm-trees
　'Mid weary wastes of sand.

2 Lord, we would bring our burden
　Of sinful thought and deed,
In Thy pure presence kneeling,
　From bondage to be freed.
Our heart's most bitter sorrow
　For all our work undone,
So many talents wasted,
　So few true conquests won;

3 Yet still, O Lord long-suff'ring,
　Still grant us in our need
Here in Thy holy presence
　The saving Name to plead;
Until in joy and gladness
　We reach that home at last,
When life's short week of sorrow
　And sin and strife is past.　Amen.

　　　　　　　　　　　Mrs. A. C. Cross

## TIMES AND SEASONS

### 411 York C.M.
SCOTCH PSALTER

♩ = 69

1 This is the day the Lord hath made; He calls the hours His own:

A - MEN.

Let heaven rejoice, let earth be glad, And praise surround the throne.

2 To-day He rose, and left the dead,
And Satan's empire fell,
To-day the saints His triumph spread,
And all His wonders tell.

3 Hosanna to th' anointed King,
To David's holy Son:
Help us, O Lord! descend, and bring
Salvation from Thy throne.

4 Blest be the Lord who comes to men
With messages of grace;
Who comes, in God His Father's name,
To save our sinful race.

5 Hosanna in the highest strains
The Church on earth can raise;
The highest heavens, in which He reigns,
Shall give Him nobler praise. Amen.

ISAAC WATTS

### 412 Wareham L.M.
WILLIAM KNAPP

♩ = 104

1 Lord of the Sabbath, hear our vows, On this Thy day, in this Thy house;

## THE LORD'S DAY

And own as grateful sac-ri-fice The songs which from the desert rise.

2 Thine earthly Sabbaths, Lord, we love;
But there's a nobler rest above:
To that our laboring souls aspire
With ardent hope and strong desire.

3 No more fatigue, no more distress,
Nor sin, nor hell, shall reach the place;
No groans to mingle with the songs
Which warble from immortal tongues.

4 No rude alarms of raging foes;
No cares to break the long repose;
No midnight shade, no clouded sun,
But sacred, high, eternal noon.

5 O long-expected day, begin;
Dawn on these realms of woe and sin:
Fain would we leave this weary road,
And sleep in death, to rest with God.
          Amen.
PHILIP DODDRIDGE *alt.*

### 413 Belmont c.m.
SAMUEL WEBBE

1 Blest day of God, most calm, most bright, The first and best of days; The

la-borer's rest, the saint's delight, A day of mirth and praise.

2 My Saviour's face did make thee shine,
    His rising did thee raise:
This made thee heavenly and divine
    Beyond the common days.

3 The first fruits do a blessing prove
    To all the sheaves behind;
And they that do a Sabbath love
    A happy week shall find.

4 My Lord on thee His name did fix,
    Which makes thee rich and gay:
Amid His golden candlesticks
    My Saviour walks this day.

5 This day must I 'fore God appear,
    For, Lord, the day is Thine:
O let me spend it in Thy fear,
    Then shall the day be mine.   Amen.
JOHN MASON

## TIMES AND SEASONS

**414 Domenica** S.M.  H. S. OAKELEY

1 This is the day of Light! Let there be light to-day!
  O Dayspring, rise up-on our night, And chase its gloom a-way.

2 This is the day of Rest!
   Our failing strength renew:
   On weary brain and troubled breast
   Shed Thou Thy freshening dew.

3 This is the day of Peace!
   Thy Peace our spirits fill!
   Bid Thou the blasts of discord cease:
   The waves of strife be still.

4 This is the day of Prayer!
   Let earth to heaven draw near;
   Lift up our hearts to seek Thee there:
   Come down to meet us here.

5 This is the First of days!
   Send forth Thy quickening breath,
   And wake dead souls to love and praise,
   O Vanquisher of Death! Amen.
   JOHN ELLERTON

**415 Grace Church** L.M.  IGNACE PLEYEL

1 Sweet is the work, my God, my King, To praise Thy name, give thanks, and sing:

## THE LORD'S DAY

To show Thy love by morning light, And talk of all Thy truth at night.

2 Sweet is the day of sacred rest;
No mortal care shall seize my breast;
Oh, may my heart in tune be found,
Like David's harp of solemn sound!

3 My heart shall triumph in my Lord,
And bless His works and bless His word:
Thy works of grace, how bright they shine!
How deep Thy counsels! how divine!

4 Lord, I shall share a glorious part,
When grace hath well refined my heart,
And fresh supplies of joy are shed,
Like holy oil to cheer my head.

5 Then shall I see, and hear, and know,
All I desired or wished below;
And every power find sweet employ,
In that eternal world of joy. Amen.

ISAAC WATTS *ab.*

416 **Mornington** S.M.     LORD MORNINGTON

1 Sweet is the work, O Lord, Thy glo - rious name to sing,

To praise, and pray, to hear Thy word, And grateful offerings bring.

2 Sweet, at the dawning light,
    Thy boundless love to tell;
And when approach the shades of night,
    Still on the theme to dwell.

3 Sweet, on this day of rest,
    To join in heart and voice

With those who love and serve Thee best,
    And in Thy name rejoice.

4 To songs of praise and joy,
    Be every Sabbath given,
That such may be our blest employ
    Eternally in heaven. Amen.

HARRIET AUBER

## TIMES AND SEASONS

### 417  St. George's Chapel 7sD.

G. J. Elvey

♩ = 100

1 Pleas-ant are Thy courts a-bove, In the land of light and love;
Pleas-ant are Thy courts be-low, In this land of sin and woe.
Oh, my spir-it longs and faints For the converse of Thy saints,
For the brightness of Thy face, King of Glo-ry, God of grace.

A-MEN.

2 Happy birds that sing and fly
Round Thy Altars, O Most High;
Happier souls that find a rest
In our Heavenly Father's breast!
Like the wandering dove, that found
No repose on earth around,
They can to their ark repair,
And enjoy it ever there.

3 Happy souls! their praises flow
Even in this vale of woe;
Waters in the desert rise,
Manna feeds them from the skies:
On they go from strength to strength,
Till they reach Thy throne at length,
At Thy feet adoring fall,
Who hast led them safe through all.
Amen.

H. F. Lyte ab.

418 Park Street L.M.5l.  F. M. A. VENUA

1 Before Jehovah's awful throne,
Ye nations bow with sacred joy;
Know that the Lord is God alone,
He can create, and He destroy.

2 His sovereign power, without our aid,
Made us of clay, and formed us men;
And when like wandering sheep we strayed,
He brought us to His fold again.

3 We are His people, we His care,
Our souls, and all our mortal frame;
What lasting honors shall we rear,
Almighty Maker, to Thy name!

4 We'll crowd Thy gates with thankful songs,
High as the heavens our voices raise;
And earth, with her ten thousand tongues
Shall fill Thy courts with sounding praise.

5 Wide as the world is Thy command,
Vast as eternity Thy love;
Firm as a rock Thy truth must stand,
When rolling years shall cease to move. Amen.

ISAAC WATTS  ab.

## TIMES AND SEASONS

### 419 Adoration 6.6.6.6.8.8.
W. H. HAVERGAL

1 Christ is our Cor-ner-stone; On Him a-lone we build; With

His true saints a-lone The courts of heaven are filled: On

His great love our hopes we place, Of present grace and joys above.

2 Oh, then with hymns of praise
　These hallowed courts shall ring!
Our voices we will raise,
　The Three in One to sing;
And thus proclaim in joyful song,
Both loud and long, that glorious Name.

3 Here, gracious God, do Thou
　For evermore draw nigh;
Accept each faithful vow,
　And mark each suppliant sigh:
In copious shower, on all who pray,
Each holy day, Thy blessings pour.

4 Here may we gain from heaven
　The grace which we implore,
And may that grace, once given,
　Be with us evermore,—
Until that day when all the blest
To endless rest are called away. Amen.

LATIN HYMN 8th CENT. Tr. CHANDLER

## 420

1 Lord of the worlds above,
　How pleasant and how fair,
The dwelling of Thy love,
　Thy earthly temples are!
To Thine abode my heart aspires,
With warm desires to see my God.

2 O happy souls, that pray
　Where God appoints to hear!
O happy men, that pay
　Their constant service there!
They praise Thee still: and happy they
That love the way to Zion's hill.

3 They go from strength to strength
　Through this dark vale of tears,
Till each arrives at length,
　Till each in heaven appears:
O glorious seat; where God our King
Shall thither bring our willing feet.

4 The Lord His people loves;
　His hand no good withholds
From those His heart approves,
　From pure and pious souls:
Thrice happy he, O God of hosts,
Whose spirit trusts alone in Thee.
　　　　　　　　　Amen.
　　　　　ISAAC WATTS ab.

## 421 Emmaus C.M.

1 Spir-it Di-vine, at-tend our prayers, And make this house Thy home;

Descend with all Thy gracious powers, O come, Great Spirit, come!

2 Come as the light; to us reveal
　Our emptiness and woe;
And lead us in those paths of life
　Where all the righteous go.

3 Come as the fire, and purge our hearts,
　Like sacrificial flame:
Let our whole soul an offering be
　To our Redeemer's name.

4 Come as the dove, and spread Thy wings,
　The wings of peaceful love;
And let Thy church on earth become
　Bless'd as Thy church above.

5 Come as the wind, with rushing sound,
　With Pentecostal grace;
And make the great salvation known,
　Wide as the human race.　Amen.
　　　　　　　ANDREW REED ab.

## TIMES AND SEASONS

### 422 Innocents 7s
Arr. by W. H. MONK

1 Songs of praise the an-gels sang, Heaven with al-le-lu-ias rang,
When Je-ho-vah's work be-gun, When He spake, and it was done.

2 Songs of praise awoke the morn,
When the Prince of Peace was born;
Songs of praise arose when He
Captive led captivity.

3 Heaven and earth must pass away—
Songs of praise shall crown that day;
God will make new heavens and earth,
Songs of praise shall hail their birth.

4 And shall man alone be dumb,
Till that glorious kingdom come?
No; the Church delights to raise
Psalms and hymns and songs of praise.

5 Saints below, with heart and voice,
Still in songs of praise rejoice;
Learning here, by faith and love,
Songs of praise to sing above.

6 Borne upon their latest breath,
Songs of praise shall conquer death;
Then, amidst eternal joy,
Songs of praise their powers employ. Amen.

JAMES MONTGOMERY

### 423 Silver Street S.M.
ISAAC SMITH

1 Come, sound His praise a-broad, And hymns of glo-ry sing:

## THE LORD'S DAY

A - MEN.

Je - ho - vah is the sov-'reign God, The u - ni - ver - sal King.

2 He formed the deeps unknown;
He gave the seas their bound;
The watery worlds are all His own,
And all the solid ground.

3 Come, worship at His throne,
Come, bow before the Lord;
We are His work and not our own;
He formed us by His word

4 To-day attend His voice,
Nor dare provoke His rod;
Come, like the people of His choice,
And own your gracious God. Amen.

ISAAC WATTS ab.

## 424 Stuttgard 8s&7s.

J. G. C. STÖRL
Arr. by H. J. GAUNTLETT

♩ = 92

1 Praise to Thee, Thou great Cre-a - tor, Praise be Thine from ev - ery tongue;

A - MEN.

Join, my soul, with every creat-ure, Join the u - ni - ver-sal song.

2 Father, Source of all compassion,
Pure, unbounded grace is Thine:
Hail the God of our salvation,
Praise Him for His love divine.

3 For ten thousand blessings given,
For the hope of future joy,
Sound His praise thro' earth and heaven,
Sound Jehovah's praise on high.

4 Joyfully on earth adore Him,
Till in heaven our song we raise;
There, enraptured fall before Him,
Lost in wonder, love, and praise. Amen.

JOHN FAWCETT

## TIMES AND SEASONS

### 425 St. Thomas S.M.
AARON WILLIAMS

1 Come, we who love the Lord! And let our joys be known; Join in a song of sweet ac-cord, And thus surround the throne.

2 Let those refuse to sing
Who never knew our God;
But children of the heavenly King
May speak their joys abroad.

3 The men of grace have found
Glory begun below;
Celestial fruits on earthly ground
From faith and hope may grow.

4 The hill of Zion yields
A thousand sacred sweets
Before we reach the heavenly fields,
Or walk the golden streets.

5 Then let our songs abound,
And every tear be dry:
We're marching through Immanuel's ground
To fairer worlds on high. Amen.

ISAAC WATTS *ab.*

### 426

1 Stand up, and bless the Lord,
Ye people of His choice;
Stand up, and bless the Lord your God,
With heart, and soul, and voice.

2 Though high above all praise,
Above all blessing high,
Who would not fear His holy name,
And laud and magnify?

3 Oh, for the living flame,
From His own altar brought,
To touch our lips, our minds inspire,
And wing to heaven our thought.

4 God is our strength and song,
And His salvation ours;
Then be His love in Christ proclaimed
With all our ransomed powers.

5 Stand up, and bless the Lord,
The Lord your God adore;
Stand up, and bless His glorious name,
Henceforth forevermore. Amen.

JAMES MONTGOMERY *ab.*

## 427 Greenville 8s & 7s D.

J. J. ROUSSEAU

1 Lord, dis-miss us with Thy blessing, Fill our hearts with joy and peace;

Let us each, Thy love pos-sess - ing, Tri - umph in re-deem-ing grace:

O re-fresh us, O re-fresh us, Traveling thro' this wil-der-ness.

2 Thanks we give, and adoration,
For Thy gospel's joyful sound:
May the fruits of Thy salvation
In our hearts and lives abound;
May Thy presence
With us evermore be found.

3 So, whene'er the signal's given,
Us from earth to call away,
Borne on angels' wings to heaven,
Glad the summons to obey,
May we ever
Reign with Christ in endless day.
Amen.

JOHN FAWCETT

*See also Hymns under —*

| | |
|---|---|
| THE CALL TO WORSHIP . . . . . . | 1 – 24 |
| GOD, THE FATHER ALMIGHTY . . . . . | 25 – 41 |
| JESUS CHRIST . . . . . . . | |
| Resurrection . . . . . | 97 – 105 |
| THE HOLY CATHOLIC CHURCH . . . | 157 – 169 |
| THE COMMUNION OF SAINTS . . . | 228 – 241 |

## TIMES AND SEASONS

### 428 Morning Hymn L.M.
F. H. BARTHOLEMON

1 A-wake, my soul, and with the sun Thy dai-ly stage of du-ty run:

Shake off dull sloth, and joyful rise To pay thy morn-ing sac-ri-fice.

2 Wake, and lift up thyself, my heart,
And with the angels bear thy part,
Who all night long unwearied sing
High praise to the Eternal King.

3 All praise to Thee, who safe hast kept,
And hast refresh'd me while I slept;
Grant, Lord, when I from death shall wake,
I may of endless light partake.

4 Lord, I my vows to Thee renew,
Disperse my sins as morning dew;
Guard my first springs of thought and will,
And with Thyself my spirit fill.

5 Direct, control, suggest this day,
All I design, or do, or say;
That all my powers, with all their might,
In Thy sole glory may unite.

6 Praise God, from whom all blessings flow,
Praise Him, all creatures here below;
Praise Him above, ye heavenly host;
Praise Father, Son, and Holy Ghost. Amen.

THOMAS KEN

*MORNING*

### 429 Zephyr L.M.
W. B. BRADBURY

1 O timely happy, timely wise, Hearts that with rising morn a - rise!
Eyes that the beam celestial view, Which evermore makes all things new.

2 New every morning is the love
Our wakening and uprising prove;
Thro' sleep and darkness safely brought,
Restored to life and power and thought.

3 New mercies each returning day,
Hover around us while we pray;
New perils past, new sins forgiven;
New tho'ts of God, new hopes of heaven.

4 If on our daily course our mind
Be set to hallow all we find,
New treasures still, of countless price,
God will provide for sacrifice.

5 Old friends, old scenes will lovelier be,
As more of heaven in each we see:
Some softening gleam of love and prayer
Shall dawn on every cross and care.

6 The trivial round, the common task:
Would furnish all we ought to ask:
Room to deny ourselves; a road
To bring us daily nearer God.

7 Only, O Lord, in Thy dear love,
Fit us for perfect rest above;
And help us, this and every day,
To live more nearly as we pray. Amen.

JOHN KEBLE

### 430

1 O Christ, with each returning morn
Thine image to our hearts be borne;
O may we ever clearly see
Our Saviour and our God in Thee.

2 O hallowed thus be every day;
Let meekness be our morning ray,
And faithful love our noon-day light,
And hope our sunset, calm and bright.

3 May faith, deep-rooted in the soul,
Subdue our flesh, our minds control:
May guile depart, and discord cease,
And all within be joy and peace.

4 May He our actions deign to bless,
And loose the bands of wickedness;
From sudden falls our feet defend,
And guide us safely to the end. Amen.

AMBROSE OF MILAN Tr. CHANDLER *ab. and alt.*

## TIMES AND SEASONS

**431** Haydn 8.4.7.D.   Arr. from HAYDN

1 Come, my soul, thou must be wak-ing! Now is breaking O'er the

earth an-oth-er day: Come to Him who made this splendor,

See thou ren-der All thy fee-ble strength can pay. A-MEN.

2 Gladly hail the sun returning:
　Ready burning
Be the incense of thy powers:
　For the night is safely ended;
　　God hath tended
With His care thy helpless hours.

3 Pray that He may prosper ever
　Each endeavor,
When thine aim is good and true;
But that He may ever thwart thee
　And convert Thee,
When thou evil wouldst pursue.

4 Only God's free gifts abuse not,
　Light refuse not,
But His Spirit's voice obey;
Thou with Him shalt dwell, beholding
　Light enfolding
All things in unclouded day.

5 Glory, honor, exaltation,
　Adoration,
Be to the eternal One:
To the Father, Son, and Spirit,
　Laud and merit,
While unending ages run.  Amen.

F. R. L. VON CANITZ  Tr. BUCKALL

*MORNING*

## 432 Laudes Domini 6s6l.

JOSEPH BARNBY

1 When morning gilds the skies, My heart a-wak-ing cries, May Je-sus Christ be praised. A-like at work and prayer To Je-sus I re-pair; May Je-sus Christ be praised. A-MEN.

2 To Thee, my God above,
I cry with glowing love,
May Jesus Christ be praised:
This song of sacred joy,
It never seems to cloy,
May Jesus Christ be praised.

3 Does sadness fill my mind?
A solace here I find,
May Jesus Christ be praised:
Or fades my earthly bliss?
My comfort still is this,
May Jesus Christ be praised.

4 When evil thoughts molest,
With this I shield my breast,
May Jesus Christ be praised.
The powers of darkness fear,
When this sweet chant they hear,
May Jesus Christ be praised.

5 When sleep her balm denies,
My silent spirit sighs,
May Jesus Christ be praised.
The night becomes as day,
When from the heart we say,
May Jesus Christ be praised.

6 Be this, while life is mine,
My canticle divine,
May Jesus Christ be praised;
Be this th' eternal song
Through all the ages on,
May Jesus Christ be praised. Amen.

GERMAN Tr. CASWALL

## TIMES AND SEASONS

### 433 Angelus L.M.
J. G. W. SCHEFFLER

1 At e-ven ere the sun was set, The sick, O Lord, around Thee lay:
Oh, in what divers pains they met! Oh, with what joy they went away!

2 Once more 't is eventide, and we,
Oppressed with various ills, draw near:
What if Thy form we cannot see?
We know and feel that Thou art here.

3 O Saviour Christ, our woes dispel:
For some are sick and some are sad,
And some have never loved Thee well,
And some have lost the love they had.

4 And some are pressed with worldly care:
And some are tried with sinful doubt:
And some such grievous passions tear,
That only Thou canst cast them out.

5 And some have found the world is vain,
Yet from the world they break not free;
And some have friends who give them pain,
Yet have not sought a friend in Thee;

6 And none, O Lord, have perfect rest,
For none are wholly free from sin;
And they who fain would love Thee best,
Are conscious most of wrong within.

7 O Saviour Christ, Thou too art Man,
Thou hast been troubled, tempted, tried;
Thy kind but searching glance can scan
The very wounds that shame would hide.

8 Thy touch has still its ancient power;
No word from Thee can fruitless fall;
Hear in this solemn evening hour,
And in Thy mercy heal us all. Amen.

HENRY TWELLS

*EVENING*

### 434 St. Matthias L.M.6l.     W. H. MONK

1 Sweet Saviour, bless us ere we go; Thy word in-to our minds in-still;

And make our luke-warm hearts to glow With low-ly love and fervent will;

Through life's long day and death's dark night, O Gentle Jesus! be our Light.

2 The day is done, its hours have run;
   And Thou hast taken count of all,
The scanty triumphs grace hath won,
   The broken vow, the frequent fall.
Through life's long day and death's
   dark night,
O Gentle Jesus! be our Light.

3 Grant us, dear Lord, from evil ways
   True absolution and release;
And bless us, more than in past days,
   With purity and inward peace.
Through life's long day and death's
   dark night,
O Gentle Jesus! be our Light.

4 Do more than pardon; give us joy,
   Sweet fear, and sober liberty,
And loving hearts without alloy
   That only long to be like Thee.
Through life's long day and death's
   dark night,
O Gentle Jesus! be our Light.

5 For all we love, the poor, the sad,
   The sinful, unto Thee we call;
O let Thy mercy make us glad;
   Thou art our Jesus, and our All.
Through life's long day and death's
   dark night,
O Gentle Jesus! be our Light. Amen.

                         F. W. FABER *ab*.

## TIMES AND SEASONS

### 435 Seymour 7s

From VON WEBER

1 Soft-ly now the light of day Fades up-on my sight a-way;
Free from care, from la-bor free, Lord, I would commune with Thee.

2 Thou, whose all-pervading eye
Naught escapes without, within,
Pardon each infirmity,
Open fault, and secret sin.

3 Soon, for me, the light of day
Shall forever pass away;
Then, from sin and sorrow free,
Take me, Lord, to dwell with Thee.

4 Thou, who, sinless, yet hast known
All of man's infirmity;
Then from Thine eternal throne,
Jesus, look with pitying eye. Amen.

G. W. DOANE

### 436 Freude 6s & 4s

E. J. HOPKINS

1 The sun is sink-ing fast, The day-light dies; Let

## EVENING

love a-wake, and pay Her even-ing sac - ri - fice.

2 As Christ upon the Cross
In death inclined,
And to His Father's hands
His parting soul resigned;

3 So now herself my soul
Would wholly give
Into His sacred charge,
In whom all spirits live.

4 So now beneath His eye
Would calmly rest,
Without a wish or thought
Abiding in the breast;

5 Save that His will be done,
Whate'er betide;
Dead to herself, and dead
In Him to all beside.

6 Oh, blessèd Trinity,
One Lord divine!
Thine may I ever be,
And Thou for ever mine. Amen.

LATIN HYMN 18th CENT. Tr. CASWALL *ab.*

### 437 Wickliffe C.M.

THOMAS HASTINGS

♩ = 92

1 I love to steal, a-while, a-way From ev-ery cumbering care,
And spend the hours of set-ting day In humble, grateful prayer.

2 I love, in solitude, to shed
The penitential tear;
And all His promises to plead,
Where none but God can hear.

3 I love to think on mercies past,
And future good implore;
And all my cares and sorrows cast
On Him whom I adore.

4 I love, by faith, to take a view
Of brighter scenes in heaven;
The prospect doth my strength renew
While here by tempests driven.

5 Thus, when life's toilsome day is o'er,
May its departing ray
Be calm as this impressive hour,
And lead to endless day. Amen.

PHEBE H. BROWN *ab*

## TIMES AND SEASONS

### 438 Ignatius S.M.
H. J. GAUNTLETT

1 The day of praise is done;
  The evening shadows fall;
  Yet pass not from us with the sun,
  True Light that light'nest all!

2 Around Thy throne on high,
  Where night can never be,
The white-robed harpers of the sky
  Bring ceaseless hymns to Thee.

3 Too faint our anthems here;
  Too soon of praise we tire;
But oh, the strains how full and clear
  Of that eternal Choir!

4 Yet, Lord! to Thy dear will
  If Thou attune the heart,
We in Thine angels' music still
  May bear our lower part.

5 'T is Thine each soul to calm,
  Each wayward thought reclaim,
And make our daily life a psalm
  Of glory to Thy name.

6 Shine Thou within us, then,
  A day that knows no end,
Till songs of angels and of men
  In perfect praise shall blend. Amen.

JOHN ELLERTON

### 439

1 The day is past and gone,
  Great God, we bow to Thee;
Again as shades of night steal on,
  To Thee for refuge flee.

2 Oh, when shall that day come,
  Ne'er sinking in the west:
That country and that holy home,
  Where none shall break our rest?

3 Where all things shall be peace,
  And pleasure without end,
And golden harps that never cease,
  With joyous hymns shall blend;

4 Where we, preserved beneath
  The shelter of Thy wing,
For evermore Thy praise shall breathe,
  And of Thy mercy sing;

5 And with the angel-host
  Praise, honor, and adore
Thee, Father, Son, and Holy Ghost,
  One God for evermore. Amen.

W. J. BLEW

*EVENING*

## 440 Ellers 10s
E. J. HOPKINS

♩ =100

1 Sav-iour, a-gain to Thy dear Name we raise, With one ac-cord, our

parting hymn of praise; We stand to bless Thee ere our worship cease,

A - MEN.

Then, low-ly kneel-ing, wait Thy word of peace.

2 Grant us Thy peace upon our homeward way;
With Thee began, with Thee shall end the day;
Guard Thou the lips from sin, the hearts from shame,
That in this house have called upon Thy name.

3 Grant us Thy peace, Lord, thro' the coming night,
Turn Thou for us its darkness into light;
From harm and danger keep Thy children free,
For dark and light are both alike to Thee.

4 Grant us Thy peace throughout our earthly life,
Our balm in sorrow, and our stay in strife;
Then, when Thy voice shall bid our conflict cease,
Call us, O Lord, to Thine eternal peace. Amen.

JOHN ELLERTON

## TIMES AND SEASONS

### 441 St. Anatolius 7.6.7.6.8.8.     J. B. DYKES

1 The day is past and o-ver; All thanks, O Lord, to Thee! I

pray Thee that of-fence-less The hours of dark may be: O Jesus, keep me

in Thy sight, And save me through the com - ing night. A - MEN.

2 The joys of day are over;
  I lift my heart to Thee;
And call on Thee, that sinless
  The hours of night may be:
O Jesus, make their darkness light,
And save me through the coming night.

3 The toils of day are over;
  I raise the hymn to Thee;
And ask, that free from peril
  The hours of fear may be:
O Jesus, keep me in Thy sight,
And guard me through the coming night.

4 Be Thou my soul's preserver,
  O God, for Thou dost know
How many are the perils
  Through which I have to go;
O loving Jesus, hear my call,
And guard and save me from them all. Amen.

ANATOLIUS Tr. NEALE

*EVENING*

**442 St. Sylvester** 8s&7s                J. B. DYKES *ab.*

1 Tar-ry with me, O my Sav-iour, For the day is passing by;

See, the shades of evening gath-er, And the night is drawing nigh.

A - MEN.

2 Deeper, deeper grow the shadows,
   Paler now the glowing west;
   Swift the night of death advances;
   Shall it be the night of rest?

3 Feeble, trembling, fainting, dying,
   Lord, I cast myself on Thee;
   Tarry with me through the darkness;
   While I sleep, still watch by me.

4 Tarry with me, O my Saviour;
   Lay my head upon Thy breast
   Till the morning, then awake me,—
   Morning of eternal rest. Amen.

                     CAROLINE S. SMITH *ab.*

**443**

1 Saviour, breathe an evening blessing,
   Ere repose our spirits seal;
   Sin and want we come confessing,
   Thou canst save, and Thou canst heal.

2 Though destruction walk around us,
   Though the arrow past us fly,
   Angel-guards from Thee surround us,
   We are safe, if Thou art nigh.

3 Though the night be dark and dreary,
   Darkness cannot hide from Thee;
   Thou art He who, never weary,
   Watchest where Thy people be.

4 Should swift death this night o'ertake
   And our couch become our tomb, [us,
   May the morn in heaven awake us,
   Clad in light and deathless bloom.
                              Amen.

                     JAMES EDMESTON

## TIMES AND SEASONS

### 444 Tallis' Canon L.M.
Thomas Tallis

♩ = 76

1 All praise to Thee, my God, this night, For all the blessings of the light; Keep

A-MEN.

me, oh, keep me, King of kings! Beneath Thine own Almighty wings.

2 Forgive me, Lord, for Thy dear Son,
The ill that I this day have done;
That with the world, myself, and Thee,
I, ere I sleep, at peace may be.

3 Oh, may my soul on Thee repose,
And may sweet sleep mine eyelids close!
Sleep, that may me more vigorous make,
To serve my God when I awake.

4 When in the night I sleepless lie,
My soul with heavenly thoughts supply;
Let no ill dreams disturb my rest,
No powers of darkness me molest.

5 Oh, when shall I, in endless day,
Forever chase dark sleep away,
And hymns divine with angels sing,
Glory to Thee, eternal King.

6 Praise God, from whom all blessings flow,
Praise Him, all creatures here below;
Praise Him above, ye heavenly host,
Praise Father, Son, and Holy Ghost.   Amen.

THOMAS KEN *ab.*

### 445 Holley 7s
GEORGE HEWS

1 Soft-ly fades the twi-light ray Of the ho-ly Sabbath day;

## EVENING

Gen-tly as life's set-ting sun, When the Christian's course is run.

2 Peace is on the world abroad;
'T is the holy peace of God;
Symbol of the peace within,
When the spirit rests from sin.

3 Still the Spirit lingers near,
Where the evening worshiper
Seeks communion with the skies,
Pressing onward to the prize.

4 Saviour, may our Sabbaths be
Days of peace and joy in Thee!
Till in heaven our souls repose,
Where the Sabbath ne'er shall close. Amen.

S. F. SMITH

## 446 In Memoriam 8.8.8.4.

F. C. MAKER

♩=92

1 The ra-diant morn hath passed away, And spent too soon her golden store;

The shad-ows of de-part-ing day Creep on once more.

2 Our life is but an autumn day,
　Its glorious noon how quickly past;
Lead us, O Christ, Thou living way,
　　Safe home at last.

3 Oh, by Thy soul-inspiring grace
　Uplift our hearts to realms on high;
Help us to look to that bright place
　　Beyond the sky;

4 Where light, and life, and joy, and peace
　In undivided empire reign,
And thronging angels never cease
　　Their deathless strain.

5 Where saints are clothed in spotless
　And evening shadows never fall,[white,
Where Thou, Eternal Light of Light,
　　Art Lord of all. Amen.

GODFREY THRING

*TIMES AND SEASONS*

### 447 Angel Guards  8.4.8.4.8.8.8.4.  CHARLES STEGGALL

1 God that mad-est earth and heav-en, Dark-ness and light;
Who the day for toil hast giv-en, For rest the night;
May Thine angel-guards de-fend us, Slum-ber sweet Thy mer-cy send us,
Ho-ly dreams and hopes at-tend us, This live-long night.

2 Guard us waking, guard us sleeping;
    And when we die,
May we in Thy mighty keeping
    All peaceful lie;
When the last dread call shall wake us,
Do not Thou, O God, forsake us,
But to reign in glory take us
    With Thee on high. Amen.

REGINALD HEBER AND RICHARD WHATELY.

*EVENING*

## 448 Italian Hymn 6.6.4.6.6.6.4.

*Felice Giardini*

1 Fa-ther of love and power, Guard Thou our even-ing hour,

Shield with Thy might; For all Thy care this day Our grate-ful thanks we pay,

And to our Fa-ther pray, Bless us to-night!

2 Jesus Immanuel!
    Come in Thy love to dwell
        In hearts contrite;
    For many sins we grieve,
    But we Thy grace receive,
    And in Thy word believe;
        Bless us to-night!

3 Spirit of Holiness,
    Gently transforming grace,
        Indwelling Light;
    Soothe Thou each weary breast,
    Now let Thy peace possest,
    Calm us to perfect rest,
        Bless us to-night. Amen.

*George Rawson*

*TIMES AND SEASONS*

### 449 Merrial 6s&5s
JOSEPH BARNBY

1 Now the day is o-ver, Night is draw-ing nigh; Shad-ows of the even-ing Steal a-cross the sky.

2 Now the darkness gathers,
Stars begin to peep;
Birds and beasts and flowers
Soon will be asleep.

3 Jesus, give the weary
Calm and sweet repose:
With Thy tenderest blessing
May our eyelids close.

4 Grant to little children
Visions bright of Thee;
Guard the sailors tossing
On the deep blue sea.

5 Comfort every sufferer
Watching late in pain;
Those who plan some evil
From their sin restrain.

6 Through the long night watches
May Thine angels spread
Their white wings above me,
Watching round my bed.

7 When the morning wakens,
Then may I arise,
Pure, and fresh, and sinless
In Thy holy eyes.

8 Glory to the Father,
Glory to the Son,
And to Thee, blest Spirit,
Whilst all ages run. Amen.

S. BARING-GOULD

### 450 Holy Trinity C.M.
JOSEPH BARNBY

1 Dear Je-sus, ev-er at my side, How lov-ing Thou must be,

## EVENING

To leave Thy home in heaven, to guard A lit-tle child like me.

2 I cannot feel Thee touch my hand,
 With pressure light and mild,
To check me as my mother did,
 When I was but a child.

3 But I have felt Thee in my thoughts,
 Rebuking sin for me;
And, when my heart loves God, I know,
 The sweetness is from Thee.

4 And when, dear Saviour, I kneel down,
 Morning and night, to prayer,
Something there is within my heart
 Which tells me Thou art there.

5 Yes, when I pray, Thou prayest too:
 Thy prayer is all for me;
But when I sleep, Thou sleepest not,
 But watchest patiently. Amen.

F. W. FABER *ab.*

### 451 Children's Prayer 8s&7s         SACRED MUSICAL CABINET

1 Je-sus, ten-der Shepherd, hear me: Bless Thy lit-tle lamb to-night;

Through the darkness be Thou near me; Keep me safe till morning light.

2 All this day Thy hand has led me,
 And I thank Thee for Thy care; [me,
Thou hast warmed me, clothed and fed
 Listen to my evening prayer!

3 Let my sins be all forgiven;
 Bless the friends I love so well;
Take us all at last to heaven,
 Happy there with Thee to dwell.
   Amen.

MARY L. DUNCAN

## TIMES AND SEASONS

### 452 Hursley L.M.
Arr. by W. H. MONK

1 Sun of my soul! Thou Sav-iour dear, It is not night if Thou be near:

Oh, may no earth-born cloud arise To hide Thee from Thy servant's eyes!

2 When the soft dews of kindly sleep
My weary eyelids gently steep,
Be my last thought, how sweet to rest
Forever on my Saviour's breast!

3 Abide with me from morn till eve,
For without Thee I cannot live;
Abide with me when night is nigh,
For without Thee I dare not die.

4 If some poor wandering child of Thine
Have spurned to-day the voice divine,
Now, Lord, the gracious work begin,
Let him no more lie down in sin.

5 Watch by the sick; enrich the poor
With blessings from Thy boundless store;
Be every mourner's sleep to-night,
Like infant's slumbers, pure and light.

6 Come near and bless us when we wake,
Ere through the world our way we take;
Till in the ocean of Thy love
We lose ourselves in heaven above. Amen.

JOHN KEBLE *ab.*

### 453 Eventide 10s
W. H. MONK

1 A - bide with me: fast *falls* the | e - ven - tide; The dark-ness

## EVENING

deep-ens; Lord, with | me a - bide: When oth - er help - ers

fail, and comforts flee, Help of the helpless, O a-|bide with me.

2 Swift to its close ebbs *out* life's | little day;
Earth's joys grow dim, its *glories* | pass away,
Change and decay in *all* a- | round I see;
O Thou who changest *not*, a- | bide with me.

3 I need Thy presence *every* | passing hour;
What but Thy grace can *foil* the | tempter's power?
Who, like Thyself, my *guide* and | stay can be?
Through cloud and sunshine, Oh, a- | bide with me.

4 I fear no foe with *Thee* at | hand to bless:
Ills have no weight, and *tears* no | bitterness.
Where is death's sting? where, *grave*, thy | victory?
I triumph still, if *Thou* a- | bide with me.

5 Hold Thou Thy Cross *before* my | closing eyes;
Shine through the gloom, and *point* me | to the skies;
Heaven's morning breaks, and *earth's* vain | shadows flee;
In life, in death, O *Lord*, a- | bide with me.   Amen.

H. F. LYTE

**Trotte's Chant**   SECOND TUNE   A. H. D. TROTTE

## TIMES AND SEASONS

### 454 Benevento 7sD.
SAMUEL WEBBE

1 While with ceaseless course the sun Hast-ed through the for-mer year,

Man-y souls their race have run, Nev-er-more to meet us here:

Fixed in an e-ter-nal state, They have done with all be-low;

A-MEN.

We a lit-tle longer wait, But how lit-tle, none can know.

2 As the wingèd arrow flies
  Speedily the mark to find;
As the lightning from the skies
  Darts, and leaves no trace behind;
Swiftly thus our fleeting days
  Bear us down life's rapid stream:
Upward, Lord, our spirits raise,
  All below is but a dream.

3 Thanks for mercies past receive;
  Pardon of our sins renew;
Teach us henceforth how to live
  With eternity in view:
Bless Thy word to young and old;
  Fill us with a Saviour's love;
And when life's short tale is told,
  May we dwell with Thee above. Amen.

JOHN NEWTON

## THE NEW YEAR

**455** Knight S.M.D.      E. K. Glezen

1 A few more years shall roll, A few more seasons come; And we shall be with those that rest Asleep within the tomb: Then, O my Lord, prepare My soul for that great day; Oh, wash me in Thy precious blood, And take my sins away. A-MEN.

2 A few more suns shall set
  O'er these dark hills of time;
And we shall be where suns are not,
  A far serener clime:
Then, O my Lord, prepare
  My soul for that blest day;
Oh, wash me in Thy precious blood,
  And take my sins away.

3 A few more storms shall beat
  On this wild rocky shore;
And we shall be where tempests cease,
  And surges swell no more:
Then, O my Lord, prepare
  My soul for that calm day;
Oh, wash me in Thy precious blood,
  And take my sins away.

4 A few more struggles here,
  A few more partings o'er,
A few more toils, a few more tears,
  And we shall weep no more:
Then, O my Lord, prepare
  My soul for that bright day;
Oh, wash me in Thy precious blood,
  And take my sins away.

5 'Tis but a little while,
  And He shall come again,
Who died that we might live, who lives
  That we with Him may reign:
Then, O my Lord, prepare
  My soul for that glad day;
Oh, wash me in Thy precious blood,
  And take my sins away. Amen.

HORATIUS BONAR *ab.*

## TIMES AND SEASONS

**456 New Year's Hymn** Irregular — SAMUEL WEBBE

1 Come, let us anew our journey pursue, Roll round with the year, And never stand still till the Master appear. His adorable will let us gladly fulfill, And our talents improve, By the patience of hope, and the labor of love.

2 Our life is a dream; our time, as a stream,
Glides swiftly away,
And the fugitive moment refuses to stay.
The arrow is flown,— the moment is gone;
The millennial year
Rushes on to our view, and eternity's here.

3 Oh, that each in the day of His coming may say,
"I have fought my way through;
I have finished the work Thou didst give me to do!"
Oh, that each from his Lord may receive the glad word,
"Well and faithfully done!
Enter into My joy, and sit down on My throne!" Amen.

CHARLES WESLEY

## THE NEW YEAR

### 457 Amsterdam 7s & 6s D.
JAMES NARES

1 Rise, my soul, and stretch thy wings, Thy better portion trace; Rise from transi-

to-ry things, Towards heaven, thy native place: Sun and moon and stars de-cay;

A - MEN.

Time shall soon this earth remove; Rise, my soul, and haste away
To seats prepared above.

2 Rivers to the ocean run,
  Nor stay in all their course;
Fire, ascending, seeks the sun;
  Both speed them to their source:
So a soul, that's born of God,
  Pants to view His glorious face,
Upward tends to His abode,
  To rest in His embrace.

3 Fly me, riches, fly me, cares,
  Whilst I that coast explore;
Flattering world, with all thy snares
  Solicit me no more!
Pilgrims fix not here their home;
  Strangers tarry but a night;
When the last dear morn is come,
  They'll rise to joyful light.

4 Cease, ye pilgrims, cease to mourn,
  Press onward to the prize;
Soon our Saviour will return
  Triumphant in the skies:
Yet a season, and you know
  Happy entrance will be given,
All our sorrows left below,
  And earth exchanged for heaven. Amen.

ROBERT SEAGRAVE *ab.*

## TIMES AND SEASONS

### 458 Germany L.M.
From BEETHOVEN

♩ = 112

1 Great God! we sing that mighty hand, By which supported still we stand:
The opening year Thy mercy shows; That mercy crowns it till it close.

A-MEN.

2 By day, by night, at home, abroad,
Still are we guarded by our God;
By His incessant bounty fed,
By His unerring counsel led.

3 With grateful hearts the past we own,
The future, all to us unknown,
We to Thy guardian care commit,
And peaceful leave before Thy feet.

4 In scenes exalted or depressed,
Be Thou our joy, and Thou our rest;
Thy goodness all our hopes shall raise,
Adored through all our changing days.

5 When death shall interrupt our songs,
And seal in silence mortal tongues;
Our helper, God, in whom we trust,
In better worlds our souls shall boast.

Amen.
PHILIP DODDRIDGE

### 459 Nuremberg 7s
J. R. AHLE

♩ = 76

1 Praise to God, im-mor-tal praise, For the love that crowns our days!

## THANKSGIVING

Bounteous Source of ev-ery joy, Let Thy praise our tongues employ!

2 All that Spring, with bounteous hand,
Scatters o'er the smiling land;
All that liberal Autumn pours
From her overflowing stores;

3 These, to Thee, my God, we owe,
Source whence all our blessings flow;
And, for these, my soul shall raise
Grateful vows and solemn praise.

4 Should Thine altered hand restrain
Th' early and the later rain;
Blast each opening bud of joy
And the rising ear destroy;

5 Yet to Thee my soul should raise
Grateful vows and solemn praise;
And when every blessing's flown,
Love Thee for Thyself alone.  Amen.

ANNA L. BARBAULD *ab.*

460 **Almsgiving** 8.8.8.4.  J. B. DYKES

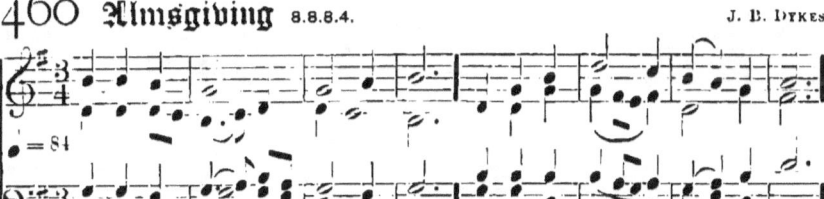

1 O Lord of heaven, and earth, and sea, To Thee all praise and glo-ry be:

How shall we show our love to Thee, Who givest all?

2 The golden sunshine, vernal air,
Sweet flowers and fruit Thy love declare;
When harvests ripen, Thou art there,
  Who givest all?

3 For peaceful homes, and healthful days,
For all the blessings earth displays,
We owe Thee thankfulness and praise,
  Who givest all!

4 Thou didst not spare Thine only Son,
But gav'st Him for a world undone,
And freely with that Blessèd One
  Thou givest all.

5 To Thee, from whom we all derive
Our life, our gifts, our power to give,
O may we ever with Thee live,
  Who givest all.  Amen.

CHRISTOPHER WORDSWORTH

## TIMES AND SEASONS

**461 St. George's Chapel** 7s D.   G. J. ELVEY

1 Come, ye thank-ful peo-ple, come, Raise the song of Harvest-home:
All is safe-ly gathered in, Ere the win-ter storms be-gin;
God, our Ma-ker, doth pro-vide For our wants to be sup-plied:
Come to God's own temple, come, Raise the song of Harvest-home.

2 All the world is God's own field,
Fruit unto His praise to yield;
Wheat and tares together sown,
Unto joy or sorrow grown,
First the blade, and then the ear,
Then the full corn shall appear:
Lord of Harvest, grant that we
Wholesome grain and pure may be.

3 For the Lord our God shall come,
And shall take His harvest home;
From His field shall in that day
All offences purge away;

Give His angels charge at last
In the fire the tares to cast;
But the fruitful ears to store
In His garner evermore.

4 Even so, Lord, quickly come
To Thy final Harvest-home;
Gather Thou Thy people in,
Free from sorrow, free from sin;
There, forever purified,
In Thy presence to abide:
Come, with all Thine angels, come,
Raise the glorious Harvest-home. Amen.

HENRY ALFORD

## THANKSGIVING

**462** Dix 7s6l.    Conrad Kocher

1 God of mer-cy, God of grace! Show the brightness of Thy face;

Shine up - on us, Sav-iour, shine. Fill Thy Church with light di-vine,

And Thy sav-ing health ex-tend Un-to earth's re-motest end. A - MEN.

2 Let the people praise Thee, Lord!
Be by all that live adored:
Let the nations shout and sing,
Glory to their Saviour King;
At Thy feet their tribute pay,
And Thy holy will obey.

3 Let the people praise Thee, Lord!
Earth shall then her fruits afford;
God to man His blessing give;
Man to God devoted live;
All below, and all above,
One in joy and light and love. Amen.

H. F. Lyte

# 463 Melita L.M.6l.

J. B. Dykes

1 E-ter-nal Fa-ther! strong to save, Whose arm doth bind the restless wave, Who bid'st the mighty o-cean deep Its own ap-point-ed lim-its keep: Oh, hear us when we cry to Thee For those in per-il on the sea!

A-MEN.

2 O Christ, whose voice the waters heard,
And hushed their raging at Thy word,
Who walkedst on the foaming deep,
And calm amid the storm didst sleep;
Oh, hear us when we cry to Thee
For those in peril on the sea!

3 O Holy Spirit! who didst brood
Upon the chaos dark and rude,
Who bad'st its angry tumult cease,
And give for wild confusion peace,
Oh, hear us when we cry to Thee
For those in peril on the sea!

4 O Trinity of love and power!
Our brethren shield in danger's hour;
From rock and tempest, fire and foe,
Protect them wheresoe'er they go;
And ever let there rise to Thee
Glad hymns of praise from land and sea. Amen.

WILLIAM WHITING.

464 Gennesaret 12s — ARTHUR SULLIVAN

1 When through the torn sail the wild tempest is streaming, When o'er the dark wave the red lightning is gleaming, Nor hope lends a ray the poor seaman to cherish, We fly to our Saviour:—"Save, Lord, or we perish."

2 O Jesus, once rocked on the breast of the billow,
Aroused by the shriek of despair from Thy pillow,
Now seated in glory, the mariner cherish,
Who cries in his anguish, "Save, Lord, or we perish."

3 And O, when the whirlwind of passion is raging,
When sin in our hearts its wild warfare is waging,
Then send down Thy grace, Thy redeemed to cherish;
Rebuke the destroyer; "Save, Lord, or we perish." Amen.

REGINALD HEBER

## TRAVELLERS' HYMNS

**465 Dundee** C.M. — SCOTCH PSALTER

1 O Lord, be with us when we sail Upon the lonely deep; Our guard when on the silent deck The midnight watch we keep.

2 We need not fear though all around,
'Mid raging wind, we hear
The multitude of waters surge;
For Thou, O God, art near.

3 The calm, the breeze, the gale, the storms,
That pass from land to land,
All, all are Thine,— are held within
The hollow of Thine hand.

4 As when on blue Gennesaret
Rose high the angry wave,
And Thy disciples quailed in dread,
One word of Thine could save:

5 So when the fiercer storms arise
From man's unbridled will,
Be Thou, Lord, present in our hearts
To whisper "Peace, be still."

6 Across this troubled tide of life
Thyself our Pilot be,
Until we reach that better land
The land that knows no sea.

7 To Thee, the Father, Thee, the Son,
Whom land and sea adore;
Thee, Spirit, moving on the deep,
Be praise forevermore. Amen.

E. A. DAYMAN

**466 Waveney** C.M. — RICHARD REDHEAD

1 Je-ho-vah, God, Thy gracious pow'r On ev-ery hand we see; Oh,

## TRAVELLERS' HYMNS

may the blessings of each hour Lead all our thoughts to Thee.

2 If on the wings of morn we speed
To earth's remotest bound,
Thy right hand will our footsteps lead,
Thine arm our path surround.

3 Thy power is in the ocean deeps,
And reaches to the skies;
Thine eye of mercy never sleeps,
Thy goodness never dies.

4 From morn till noon, till latest eve,
Thy hand, O God, we see;
And all the blessings we receive,
Ceaseless proceed from Thee.

5 In all the varying scenes of time,
On Thee our hopes depend;
Through every age, in every clime,
Our Father, and our Friend. Amen.

JOHN THOMSON

### 467 Louvan L.M.
V. C. TAYLOR

1 O Lord, how full of sweet content Our years of pil-grim-age are spent!
Where'er we dwell, we dwell with Thee, In heav'n, in earth, or on the sea.

2 To us remains nor place nor time;
Our country is in every clime:
We can be calm and free from care
On any shore, since God is there.

3 While place we seek, or place we shun,
The soul finds happiness in none;
But with our God to guide our way,
'Tis equal joy to go or stay.

4 Could we be cast where Thou art not,
That were indeed a dreadful lot;
But regions none remote we call,
Secure of finding God in all. Amen.

JEANNE M. B. GUION Tr. COWPER ab. and alt.

## NATIONAL

### 468 America 6.6.4.6.6.6.4.
Adapted by HENRY CAREY

1 My coun-try! 'tis of thee, Sweet land of lib-er-ty,

Of thee I sing; Land where my fa-thers died! Land of the

pilgrims' pride! From ev-ery mountain side Let free-dom ring! A-MEN.

2 My native country, thee,
Land of the noble free,
  Thy name I love;
I love thy rocks and rills,
Thy woods and templed hills:
My heart with rapture thrills
  Like that above.

3 Let music swell the breeze,
And ring from all the trees
  Sweet freedom's song:
Let mortal tongues awake;
Let all that breathe partake;
Let rocks their silence break,—
  The sound prolong.

4 Our fathers' God! to Thee,
Author of liberty,
  To Thee we sing;
Long may our land be bright
With freedom's holy light;
Protect us by Thy might,
  Great God, our King. Amen.

S. F. SMITH

*NATIONAL*

**469 Waverton** 6.6.6.6.8.8.  R. JACKSON

1 To Thee our God we fly For mer-cy and for grace;

Oh! hear our low-ly cry, And hide not Thou Thy face.

O Lord, stretch forth Thy mighty hand, And guard and bless our Fatherland.

2 Arise, O Lord of hosts,
   Be jealous for Thy Name,
And drive from out our coasts
   The sins that put to shame.
O Lord, stretch forth Thy mighty hand,
And guard and bless our Fatherland.

3 The powers ordained by Thee
   With heavenly wisdom bless;
May they Thy servants be,
   And rule in righteousness.
O Lord, stretch forth Thy mighty hand,
And guard and bless our Fatherland.

4 The Church of Thy dear Son
   Inflame with love's pure fire,
Bind her once more in one,
   And life and truth inspire.
O Lord, stretch forth Thy mighty hand,
And guard and bless our Fatherland.

5 Give peace, Lord, in our time;
   Oh, let no foe draw nigh,
Nor lawless deed of crime
   Insult Thy Majesty.
O Lord, stretch forth Thy mighty hand,
And guard and bless our Fatherland.
                    Amen.
                W. W. How

## NATIONAL

### 470 Wareham L.M.
*William Knapp*

1 O God, beneath Thy guiding hand, Our exiled fathers crossed the sea;
And when they trod the wintry strand,
With prayer and psalm they worshipped Thee.

2 Thou heard'st, well-pleased, the song, the prayer,—
Thy blessing came; and still its power
Shall onward, through all ages, bear
The memory of that holy hour.

3 Laws, freedom, truth, and faith in God,
Came with those exiles o'er the waves,
And where their pilgrim feet have trod,
The God they trusted guards their graves.

4 And here Thy Name, O God of love,
Their children's children shall adore,
Till these eternal hills remove,
And spring adorns the earth no more.  Amen.

LEONARD BACON *ab.*

### 471 St. Martins C.M.
*Wm. Tansur*

1 Let children hear the mighty deeds, Which God performed of old,—

NATIONAL

A - MEN.

Which in our youn-ger years we saw, And which our fathers told.

2 He bids us make His glories known,
His works of power and grace;
And we'll convey His wonders down
Through every rising race.

3 Our lips shall tell them to our sons,
And they again to theirs,

That generations yet unborn
May teach them to their heirs.

4 Thus they shall learn, in God alone
Their hope securely stands,
That they may ne'er forget His works,
But practice His commands. Amen.

ISAAC WATTS

472 Dort 6.6.4.6 6 6.4.　　　　　　LOWELL MASON

♩ = 100

1 God bless our na - tive land; Firm may she ev-er stand, Through storm and
2 For her our prayer shall rise To God, a - bove the skies; On Him we

night; When the wild tem - pests rave, Rul - er of wind and wave,
wait; Thou who art ev - er nigh, Guard-ing with watch - ful eye,

A - MEN.

Do Thou our coun - try save By Thy great might.
To Thee a - loud we cry, God save the State. Amen.

C. T. BROOKS and J. S. DWIGHT

# 473 Gloria in Excelsis Deo

OLD CHURCH MELODY

Glory *be* to | God · on | high ‖ and on *earth* | peace · good | will · towards | men.
We praise Thee, we bless *Thee* we | wor · ship | Thee ‖ we glorify Thee, we give *thanks* to | Thee · for | Thy · great | glory.

O Lord *God* heaven · ly | King ‖ *God* the | Fa · ther | Al · — | mighty.
O Lord, the only-begotten *Son* | Je · sus | Christ ‖ O Lord God, Lamb of *God* | Son · — | of · the | Father,

That takest *away* the | sins · of the | world ‖ have *mercy* up | on · — | us.
Thou that takest *away* the | sins · of the | world ‖ have *mercy* up | on · — | us.
Thou that takest *away* the | sins · of the | world ‖ *re* | ceive · our | prayer.
Thou that sittest at the right *hand* of | God · the | Father ‖ have *mercy* up | on · — | us.

A · MEN.

For Thou *only* | art · — | holy ‖ *Thou* | on · ly | art · the | Lord.
Thou only, O *Christ* with the | Ho · ly | Ghost ‖ art most *high* in the | glory · of | God · the | Father ‖ A | men.

# 474 Te Deum Laudamus

From BEETHOVEN

We *praise* | Thee · O | God ‖ we ack*now*ledge | Thee · to | be · the | Lord ‖
All the *earth* doth | wor · ship | Thee ‖ the *Father* | ev · er | last · — | ing.
To Thee all *Angels* | cry · a | loud ‖ the *Heavens* and | all · the | Powers · there | in ‖
To Thee *Cherubim* and | Se · ra | phim ‖ *con* | tin · ual | ly · do | cry ;
*Holy* | Ho · ly | Holy ‖ *Lord* | God · of | Sa · ba | oth ‖
Heaven and earth are *full* of the | Maj · es | ty ‖ *of* | Thy · — | glo · — | ry.
The glorious *company* | of · the A | postles ‖ *praise* | — · — | — · — | Thee ‖
The goodly *fellowship* | of · the | Prophets ‖ *praise* | — · — | — · — | Thee.
The *noble* | army · of | Martyrs ‖ *praise* | — · — | — · — | Thee ‖
The Holy *Church* throughout | all · the | world ‖ *doth* ac | know · — | ledge · — | Thee ;
*The* | Fa · — | ther ‖ *of* an | infi · nite | Maj · es | ty ‖
*Thine* a | dora · ble | true ‖ *and* | on · — | — · ly | Son.
*Also* the | Ho · ly | Ghost ‖ *the* | Com · — | — · fort | er ‖
*Thou* art the | King · of | glory ‖ *O* | — · — | — · — | Christ.
Thou art the *ever* | last · ing | Son ‖ *of* | — · the | Fa · — | ther ‖
When Thou tookest upon *Thee* to de | liv · er | man ‖ Thou didst humble Thy*self* to be | born · — | of · a | virgin.
When Thou hadst over*come* the | sharpness · of | death ‖ Thou didst open the *king*dom of | heaven · to | all · be | lievers ‖
Thou sittest at the *right* | hand · of | God ‖ *in* the | glo · ry | of · the | Father.

T. TALLIS

We be*lieve* that | Thou · shalt | come ‖ *to* | be · — | our · — | Judge.
We therefore *pray* Thee | help · Thy | servants ‖ whom Thou hast re*deemed* | with · Thy | pre · cious | blood.
Make them *to* be *numbered* | with · Thy | Saints ‖ *in* | glo · ry | ev · er | lasting.
O *Lord* | save · Thy | people ‖ *and* | bless · Thine | her · it | age.
*Gov* | — · ern | them ‖ *and* | lift · them | up · for | ever.

(OVER.)

## ANCIENT AND SCRIPTURAL

Day | by · — | day ‖ we | mag · ni ¦ fy · — ¦ Thee ‖
And we | worship · Thy | name ‖ ever ¦ world · with | out · — | end.
Vouch | safe · O | Lord ‖ to *keep* us this ¦ day · with ¦ out · — ¦ sin ‖
O *Lord* have | mercy · up | on us ‖ *have* | mer · — | cy · up | on us.
O Lord let Thy *mercy* | be · up | on us ‖ *as* our | trust · — ¦ is · in ¦ Thee ‖
O Lord in *Thee* | have · I ¦ trusted ‖ *let* me | nev · er | be · con | founded.

## 475 Benedictus

W. CHARD

*From St. Luke I.*

Blessed be the *Lord* | God · of | Israel ‖ for He hath *visited* | and · re | deemed · His | people;
And hath raised up a *mighty* sal | va · tion | for us ‖ in the *house* | of · His | ser · vant | David ;
As He spake by the *mouth* of His ¦ ho · ly | Prophets ‖ which have *been* | since · the ¦ world · be | gan;
That we should be *saved* | from · our | enemies ‖ and *from* the | hand · of | all · that | hate us.
To perform the mercy *promised* to | our · fore | fathers ‖ *and* to re | member · His | ho · ly | Covenant;
To perform the oath which he *sware* to our | fore · father | Abraham ‖ *that* | He · would | give · — | us ;
That we being delivered out of the *hand* | of · our | enemies ‖ might *serve* | Him · with | out · — | fear;
In holiness and righteous*ness* be | fore · — | Him ‖ *all* the | days · — | of · our | life.
And thou, child, shalt be called the *Prophet* | of · the | Highest ‖ for thou shalt go before the face of the *Lord* to pre | pare · — | His · — | ways;
To give knowledge of sal*vation* | unto · His | people ‖ *for* the re | mis · sion | of · their | sins,
Through the tender *mercy* | of · our | God ‖ whereby the day-spring *from* on | high · hath | vis·it·ed | us;
To give light to them that sit in darkness, and *in* the | shadow · of | death ‖ and to guide our *feet* | into · the | way · of | peace.
Glory be to the *Father* | and · to the | Son ‖ *and* | to · the | Ho · ly Ghost;
As it was in the beginning, is *now* and | ev · er | shall be ‖ *world* without | end — | A · — | men.

## 476 Magnificat

W. RUSSELL

*From St. Luke I*

My soul doth *magni* | fy · the | Lord ‖ and my spirit *hath* re | joiced · in | God · my | Saviour ‖
*For* He | hath · re | garded ‖ the *low*li | ness · of | His · hand | maiden.
*For* be | hold · from | henceforth ‖ *all* gener | ations · shall | call · me | blessed ‖
*For* He that is *mighty* hath | magni · fied | me ‖ *and* | ho · ly is · His | Name.
And His *mercy* is on | them · that | fear Him ‖ *throughout* | all · — | gen · er | a- tions ‖
He hath showed *strength* | with · His | arm ‖ He hath scattered the proud in the *imagi* | n · tion | of · their | hearts.
He hath put down the *mighty* | from · their | seat ‖ and *hath* ex | alted · the | humble · and | meek ‖
He hath filled the *hun*gry with | good · — | things ‖ and the *rich* He hath | sent · — | empty · a | way.
*He* re | membering · His | mercy ‖ hath *holpen* His | ser · vant | Is · ra | el ‖
As He *promised* to | our · fore | fathers ‖ *Abraham* | and · his | seed · for | ever.
Glory be to the *Father* | and · to the | Son ‖ *and* | to · the | Ho · ly | Ghost;
As it was in the beginning, is *now* and | ev · er | shall be ‖ *world* without | end · — | A · — | men.

## 477 Nunc Dimittis

JOSEPH BARNBY

*From St. Luke II*

Lord, now lettest Thou Thy *servant* de | part · in | peace ‖ ac | cord · ing | to · Thy | word.
*For* mine | eyes · have | seen ‖ *Thy* | · — sal | va · — | tion;
*Which* | Thou · hast pre | pared ‖ *before* the | face · of | all · — | people;
To be a *light* to | lighten · the | Gentiles ‖ and to be the *glory* | of · Thy | people | Israel.
Glory be to the *Father* | and · to the | Son ‖ *and* | to · the | Ho · ly | Ghost;
As it was in the beginning, is *now* and | ev · er | shall be ‖ *world* without | end · — | A · — | men.

## ANCIENT AND SCRIPTURAL

### 478 Venite Exultemus Domino
WILLIAM BOYCE

*From Psalms XCV and XCVI.*

O come let us *sing* | unto · the | Lord ‖ let us heartily *rejoice* in the | strength ·
of | our · sal | vation ‖
Let us come before His *presence* with | thanks · — | giving ‖ and *show* ourselves
glad · in | Him · with | psalms. ‖
For the *Lord* is a | great · — | God ‖ and a *great* | King · a | bove · all | gods ‖
In His hand are all the *corners* | of · the | earth ‖ and the *strength* of the | hills ·
is | His · — | also. ‖
The *sea* is His | and · He | made it ‖ and His *hands* pre | pared · the | dry · — |
land ‖
O come let us *worship* and | fall · — | down ‖ and *kneel* be | fore · the | Lord ·
our | Maker. ‖
For *He* is the | Lord · our | God ‖ and we are the people of His pasture, *and* the
sheep · of | His · — | hand ‖
O worship the *Lord* in the | beauty · of | holiness ‖ let the whole *earth* | stand · in |
awe · of | Him. ‖
\* For He *cometh*, for He *cometh* to | judge · the | earth ‖ and with righteousness
to judge the *world* and the | peo · ple | with · His | truth. ‖
Glory be to the *Father* | and · to the | Son ‖ *and* | to · the | Ho · ly | Ghost ‖
As it was in the beginning, is *now* and | ev · er | shall be ‖ *world* without |
end · | A · — | men.

### 479 Jubilate Deo
G. J. ELVEY

*From Psalm C.*

O be joyful in the *Lord* | all · ye | lands ‖ serve the Lord with gladness, and come
*before* His | pres · ence | with · a | song. ‖
Be ye sure that the *Lord* | He · is | God ‖ It is He that hath made us, and not we
ourselves; we are His people, *and* the | sheep · of | His · — | pasture. ‖
O go your way into His gates with thanksgiving, and *into* His | courts · with |
praise ‖ be thankful unto *Him* and | speak · good | of · His | name. ‖
For the Lord is gracious, His *mercy* is | ev · er | lasting ‖ and His truth endureth
from *gener* | ation · to | gen · er | ation. ‖
Glory be to the *Father* | and · to the | Son ‖ *and* | to · the | Ho · ly | Ghost ‖
As it was in the beginning, is *now* and | ev · er | shall be ‖ *world* without | end · — |
A · — | men.

## ANCIENT AND SCRIPTURAL

### 480 Deus Misereatur
*J. Barnby*

*From Psalm LXVII.*

God be merciful unto us and | bless · — | us ‖ and show us the light of His counten-
  ance, *and* be merci · ful ' un · to | us;
That Thy way may be *known* up ' on · — | earth ‖ Thy saving *health* a ' mong · —
  | all · — | nations.
Let the people *praise* Thee | O · — | God ‖ yea, let *all* the | peo · ple | praise · — |
  Thee.
O let the nations re*joice* | and · be , glad ‖ for Thou shalt judge the folk righteously,
  and *govern* the | nations · up ' on · — | earth.
Let the people *praise* Thee | O · — | God ‖ yea, let *all* the | peo · ple | praise · —
  | Thee.
Then shall the *earth* bring | forth · her | increase ‖ and God, even our own *God*
  shall | give · us | His · — | blessing.
*God* shall | bless · — | us ‖ and all the ends of the *world* | shall · — | fear · — |
  Him.
Glory be to the *Father* | and · to the | Son ‖ and | to · the | Ho · ly | Ghost:
As it was in the beginning, is *now* and | ev · er | shall be ‖ *world* without | end
  · — | A · — | men.

### 481 Benedic Anima Mea
*W. Lee*

*From Psalm CIII.*

Praise the *Lord* | O · my | soul ‖ and all that is with*in* me | praise · His | ho · ly |
  name.
Praise the *Lord* | O · my | soul ‖ *and* for | get · not | all · His | benefits:
Who for*giveth* | all · thy | sin ‖ and *healeth* all | thine · in | firm · i | ties.
Who saveth thy *life* | from · de | struction ‖ and crowneth thee with *mercy* and |
  lov · ing | kind · — | ness.
O praise the *Lord*, ye angels of His, *ye* that ex | cel · in | strength ‖ ye that fulfill
  His commandment, and *hearken* | unto · the | voice · of His | word.
O praise the *Lord* all | ye · His | hosts ‖ ye servants of *His* that | do · — | His
  · — | pleasure.
O speak good of the Lord, all ye works of His, in all *places* of | His · do | minion ‖
  praise thou the *Lord* | O · — | my · — | soul.
Glory be to the *Father* | and · to the | Son ‖ *and* | to · the | Ho · ly | Ghost:
As it was in the beginning, is *now* and | ev · er | shall be ‖ *world* without | end ·
  — | A · — | men.

## ANCIENT AND SCRIPTURAL

### 482 Cantate Domino
E. K. GLEZEN

*From Psalm XCVIII.*

O sing unto the *Lord* a | new · — | song ‖ for *He* hath | done · — | marvel · lous | things ;
With His own right hand, and *with* His | ho · ly | arm ‖ *hath* He | gotten · Him | self · the | victory.
The Lord *declared* | His · sal | vation ‖ His righteousness hath He openly *shewed* | in · the | sight · of the | heathen.
He hath remembered His mercy and truth *toward* the | house · of | Israel ‖ and all the ends of the world have *seen* the sal | va · tion | of · our | God.
Shew yourselves joyful unto the *Lord* | all · ye | lands ‖ sing re | joice · and | give · — | thanks.
Praise the *Lord* up | on · the | harp ‖ sing to the *harp* with a | psalm · of | thanks · — | giving.
With trumpets *also* | and · — | shawms ‖ O shew yourselves *joy*ful be | fore · the | Lord · the | King.
Let the sea make a noise, and *all* that | there · in | is ‖ the round *world* and | they · that | dwell · there | in.
Let the floods clap their hands, and let the hills be joyful to*geth*er be | fore · the | Lord ‖ *for* He | cometh · to | judge · the | earth.
With righteousness *shall* He | judge · the | world ‖ *and* the | peo · ple | with · — | equity.
Glory be to the *Father* | and · to the | Son ‖ *and* | to · the | Ho · ly | Ghost :
As it was in the beginning, is *now* and | ev · er | shall be ‖ *world* without | end · — | A · — | men.

### 483 Bonum Est Confiteri
J. JONES

*From Psalm XCII.*

It is a good thing to give *thanks* | unto · the | Lord ‖ and to sing praises unto Thy *Name* | O · — | Most · — | Highest;
To tell of Thy loving kindness *early* | in · the | morning ‖ and of Thy *truth* | in · the | night · — | season ;
Upon an instrument of ten *strings*, and up | on · the | lute ‖ upon a loud *instru*ment | and · up | on · the | harp.
For Thou, Lord, hast made me *glad* | through · Thy | works ‖ and I will rejoice in giving *praise* for the oper a · tions | of · Thy | hands.
Glory be to the *Father* | and · to the | Son ‖ *and* | to · the | Ho · ly | Ghost :
As it was in the beginning, is *now*, and | ev · er | shall be ‖ *world* without | end · — | A · — | men.

## ANCIENT AND SCRIPTURAL

### 484  Christ Our Passover
P. HAYES

*From 1 Corinthians V, Romans VI, 1 Corinthians XV.*

Christ our passover is sacri | ficed · for | us ‖ *therefore* | let · us | keep · the | feast;
Not with the old leaven, nor with the *leaven* of | malice · and | wickedness ‖ but with the unleavened *bread* of sin | cer · i | ty · and | truth.
Christ being raised from the *dead* | dieth · no | more‖death hath no *more* do | min · ion | o · ver | Him.
For in that He died, He *died* unto | sin · — | once ‖ but in that He *liveth* He | liv · eth | un · to | God.
Likewise reckon ye also yourselves to be dead in*deed* | un · to | sin ‖ but alive unto *God* through | Je · sus | Christ · our | Lord.
Christ is *risen* | from · the | dead ‖ and become the *first* | fruits · of | them · that | slept.
For *since* by | man · came | death ‖ by man came also the *resur* | rec · tion | of · the | dead.
For as in *Adam* | all · — | die ‖ even so in *Christ* shall | all · be | made · a | live.
Glory be to the *Father* | and · to the | Son ‖ *and* | to · the | Ho · ly | Ghost;
As it was in the beginning, is *now* and | ev · er | shall be‖ *world* without | end · — | A · — | men.

### 485  I am the Resurrection
W. FELTON

I am the resurrection and the *life* | saith · the | Lord ‖ He that believeth in Me, though he were *dead* yet · — | shall · he | live
And whosoever *liveth* and be , lieveth · in | Me ‖ *shall* | nev · — | er · — | die ‖
I *know* that my Re deem · er ' liveth ‖ and that He shall stand at the latter *day* up ' on · — the · — ' earth.
And though after my skin *worms* de | stroy · this | body ‖ yet in my *flesh* | shall · I | see · — | God ‖
Whom I shall *see* | for · my | self ‖ and mine eyes shall be*hold* | and · — | not · an other.
We brought *nothing* | into · this | world ‖ and it is *certain* we can | car · ry | noth · ing | out ‖
The Lord gave and the *Lord* hath | taken · a | way ‖ *blessed* | be · the | name · of · the | Lord.
Glory be to the *Father* | and · to the | Son ‖ *and* | to · the ' Ho · ly | Ghost;
As it was in the beginning, is *now* and | ev · er | shall be ‖ *world* without | end · — | A · — | men.

## 486 Lord, let me know my end

W. CROFT

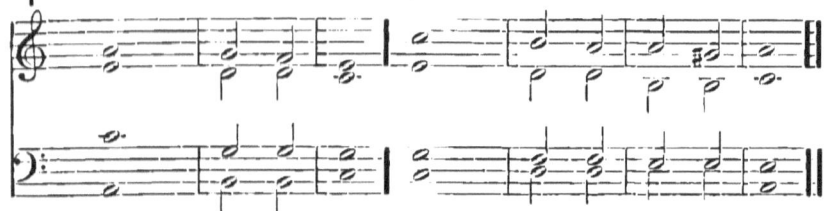

*From Psalm XXXIX.*

Lord, let me know my end, and the *number* | of · my | days‖that I may be certi*fied* how | long · I | have · to | live.
Behold, Thou hast made my days as it *were* a | span · — | long ‖ and mine age is even as | nothing · in re | spect · of | Thee,
And verily every man living is *alto* | geth · er | vanity ‖ For man walketh in a vain shadow, and disquieteth him | self · — | in · — | vain;
He *heapeth* | up · — | riches ‖ and cannot *tell* | who · shall | gath · er | them.
And now, *Lord* | what · is my | hope ‖ *truly* my | hope · is | even · in | Thee.
Deliver me from *all* | mine · of | fences ‖ and make me *not* a re | buke · — | unto · the | foolish.
When Thou with rebukes dost chasten man for sin, Thou makest his beauty to consume away, like as it were a | *moth* | fretting · a | garment ‖ every man *therefore* | is · but | van · i | ty.
Hear my prayer O Lord, and with Thine *ears* con | sider · my | calling ‖ hold *not* Thy | peace · — | at · my | tears.
For I *am* a | stranger · with | Thee ‖ and a *sojourner* as | all · my | fa · thers | were.
O spare me a little, that I *may* re | cover · my | strength ‖ before I go *hence* | and · be | no · more | seen.
Glory be to the *Father* | and · to the | Son ‖ *and* | to · the | Ho · ly | Ghost;
As it was in the beginning, is *now* and | ev · er | shall be ‖ *world* without | end · — | A · — | men.

## 487 Lord, Thou hast been our Dwelling Place

E. K. GLEZEN

*Small notes for organ.*

*From Psalm XC.*

*Lord* Thou hast | been · our | dwelling place ‖ *in* | all · — | gen · er | ations ‖
Before the mountains were brought forth, or ever Thou hadst *formed* the | earth · and the | world ‖ even from everlasting to *everlasting* | Thou · — | art · — | God.
Thou *turn* est | man · to de | struction ‖ and *sayest* Re | turn · ye | children · of | men ‖

For a thousand years in Thy sight are but as *yesterday* | when · it is | past ‖ *and*
as a | watch · — | in · the | night.
Thou carriest them away as with a flood; they *are* | as · a | sleep ‖ in the morning
they are *like* | grass · which | grow · eth | up ‖
In the morning it flourish*eth* and | grow · eth | up ‖ in the evening it is cut *down* |
and · — | with · er | eth.
For we are con*sumed* | by | Thine | anger ‖ and *by* | Thy | wrath · — | are · we |
troubled ‖
Thou hast set our ini*qui*ties be | fore · — | Thee ‖ our secret *sins* in the | light · —
| of · Thy | countenance.
For all our days are passed a*way* | in · Thy | wrath ‖ we spend our *years* as a | tale
· — | that · is | told ‖
The days of our years are *three*score | years · and | ten ‖ and if by reason of
strength they be fourscore years, yet is their strength labor and sorrow; for
it is soon cut *off* | and · we | fly · a | way.
Who knoweth the *power* | of · Thine | anger ‖ even according to Thy *fear* | so · —
| is · Thy | wrath ‖
So teach *us* to | number · our | days ‖ that we may ap*ply* our | hearts · — | un ·
to | wisdom.
Glory be to the *Father* | and · to the | Son ‖ *and* | to · the | Ho · ly | Ghost;
As it was in the beginning, is *now* and | ev · er | shall be ‖ *world* without | end ·
— | A · — | men.

## 488 The Lord is my Shepherd

HART

*Psalm XXIII.*

The *Lord* | is · my | shepherd ‖ *I* shall · — | not · — | want
He maketh me to lie *down* in | green · — | pastures ‖ He leadeth *me* be side · the
| still · — | waters.
He re*stor*eth | my · — | soul ‖ He leadeth me in the paths of *right*eousness | for ·
His | name's · — | sake.
Yea, though I walk through the valley of the shadow of *death* I will | fear · no ·
evil ‖ for Thou art with me; Thy *rod* and Thy | staff · they | com · fort | me.
Thou preparest a table before me in the *presence* | of · mine | enemies ‖ Thou
anointest my head with *oil* my | cup · — | run · neth | over.
Surely goodness and mercy shall follow me all the *days* | of · my life ‖ and I will
*dwell* in the | house · of the | Lord · for | ever.
Glory be to the *Father* | and · to the | Son ‖ *and* | to · the Ho · ly | Ghost;
As it was in the beginning, is *now* and | ev · er | shall be ‖ *world* without end · — |
A · — | men.

## 489 The Beatitudes

Blessed are the poor in spirit: for *theirs* is the | kingdom · of | heaven ‖
Blessed are they that mourn: for *they* | shall · — | be · — | comforted.
Blessed are the meek: for *they* shall in | herit · the | earth ‖
Blessed are they who do hunger and thirst after righteousness: for *they* | shall · —
| be · — | filled.
Blessed are the merciful: for *they* shall ob | tain · — | mercy ‖
Blessed are the pure in heart: for *they* | shall · — | see · — | God.
Blessed are the peace-makers: for they shall be *called* the | children · of | God;
Blessed are they which are persecuted for righteousness' sake: for *theirs* | is · the |
kingdom · of | heaven. Amen.

## 490 Sanctus (May be sung to any Chant.)

*Holy* | ho · ly | holy ‖ *Lord* | — · — | God · of | — hosts ‖
Heaven and earth are *full* | of · Thy | glory ‖ Glory be to *Thee* O | Lord · most |
high · A | men.

# INDEX OF FIRST LINES.

Lines marked † indicate the opening of the hymn as given in some other versions.

| | |
|---|---|
| Abide with me, fast falls the eventide....453 | Christ, above all glory seated..............111 |
| According to Thy gracious word.........184 | Christ for the world we sing..............198 |
| A charge to keep I have..................189 | Christ is our corner-stone................419 |
| A few more years shall roll..............455 | Christ that ever reigneth..................133 |
| A mighty fortress is our God..............364 | Christ, the Lord, is risen to-day..........98 |
| Allelnia! Alleluia! Hearts to heaven....101 | Christian! dost thou see them.............311 |
| Alleluia! Alleluia! The strife is o'er....104 | Christian, seek not yet repose............320 |
| Alleluia! song of gladness................165 | City of God, how broad and far..........160 |
| All glory, laud, and honor................83 | Come, all ye saints of God................114 |
| All hail the power of Jesus' name........113 | Come, every pious heart...................121 |
| All my heart this night rejoices..........51 | Come, Holy Ghost, in love................146 |
| All praise to Thee, eternal Lord..........52 | Come, Holy Spirit, come..................145 |
| All praise to Thee, my God, this night....444 | Come, Holy Spirit, heavenly Dove........143 |
| All that I was, my sin, my guilt..........286 | Come, kingdom of our God................218 |
| Always with us, always with us..........335 | Come, let us anew our journey pursue...456 |
| Am I a soldier of the cross...............313 | Come, let us join our cheerful songs.....119 |
| And canst thou, sinner, slight............256 | Come, let us join our friends above......239 |
| And didst Thou, Lord, our sorrows take..62 | Come, let us sing the Song of songs......21 |
| Angels, from the realms of glory.........60 | Come, Lord, and tarry not................131 |
| Angel voices ever singing..................28 | Come, my soul, thou must be waking....431 |
| Approach, my soul, the mercy-seat......273 | Come, my soul, thy suit prepare..........6 |
| Arise, my soul! my joyful powers.........22 | Come, O Creator Spirit blest..............4 |
| Arise, O King of grace, arise..............167 | Come, quickly come, dread Judge of all..137 |
| Arm thes Thy soldiers, mighty Lord....174 | Come, said Jesus' sacred voice...........250 |
| Around the throne of God in heaven......386 | Come see the place where Jesus lay......97 |
| Art thou weary, art thou languid........247 | Come, sound His praise abroad..........423 |
| Ask ye what great thing I know..........91 | Come, Thou Almighty King..............2 |
| Asleep in Jesus! blessed sleep.............379 | Come, Thou fount of every blessing.....310 |
| As with gladness men of old..............58 | Come, Thou long expected Jesus.........129 |
| At even ere the sun was set................433 | Come to the land of peace................380 |
| At the name of Jesus......................127 | Come to the morning prayer.............367 |
| Awake, and sing the song..................116 | Come to the Saviour now.................264 |
| Awake, my soul, and with the sun........428 | Come, we who love the Lord.............425 |
| Awake, my soul, stretch every nerve....312 | Come, ye faithful, raise the anthem......18 |
| Awake, my soul, to joyful lays............208 | Come, ye thankful people, come........461 |
| Awake, our souls! away our fears........324 | Crown Him with many crowns...........125 |
| | |
| Before Jehovah's awful throne............418 | Dear Jesus, ever at my side...............450 |
| Behold a Stranger at the door............262 | Dear Lord and Master mine.............293 |
| Behold the throne of grace................10 | Dear Saviour, I am Thine................288 |
| Beneath the cross of Jesus.................280 | Depth of mercy! — can there be.........277 |
| Blessed are the sons of God...............295 | Did Christ o'er sinners weep.............255 |
| Blest be the tie that binds.................231 | † Draw nigh, draw nigh, Immanuel......134 |
| Blest day of God, most calm, most bright.413 | |
| Bread of the world, in mercy broken....185 | Eternal Father! strong to save...........463 |
| Brief life is here our portion..............401 | |
| Brightest and best of the sons.............59 | Faint not, Christian, though the road...322 |
| Brightly gleams our banner...............202 | Far down the ages now..................162 |
| By Christ redeemed, in Christ restored..183 | Far from my heavenly home............386 |
| By cool Siloam's shady rill................170 | Father of all, from land and sea..........241 |
| | Father of heaven, whose love profound..271 |
| Calm on the listening ear of night........50 | Father of love and power................448 |
| Children of light, arise and shine........317 | Father of love, our Guide and Friend...343 |
| Children of the heavenly King............230 | Father of mercies! send Thy grace......205 |

# INDEX OF FIRST LINES

Father, whate'er of earthly bliss .........341
Fierce was the wild billow ............. 69
Fight the good fight with all thy might...323
For all the saints who from their labors...233
For all Thy saints, O Lord...............237
Forever with the Lord....................385
For the beauty of the earth..............360
For thee, O dear, dear country...........404
For thee we long and pray................406
Forward be our watchword ................200
From all that dwell below the skies...... 24
From all Thy saints in warfare...........234
From every stormy wind that blows...... 9
From Greenland's icy mountains..........224
From the cross uplifted high.............243
From the eastern mountains............... 57

Gently, Lord, oh, gently lead us.........349
Give me the wings of faith, to rise......236
Give to the winds thy fears..............337
Glorious things of thee are spoken.......158
†Glory to Thee, my God, this night......444
God bless our native land................472
God calling yet! shall I not hear?......263
God eternal, Lord of all................. 23
God is love, His mercy brightens.........352
God moves in a mysterious way .......... 38
God of mercy, God of grace...............462
God that madest earth and heaven ......447
God the Lord a King remaineth.......... 26
Go forward, Christian soldier............195
Go, labor on; spend and be spent........211
Go up, go up, my heart...................372
Go worship at Immanuel's feet...........117
Grace! 't is a charming sound ..........244
Gracious Saviour, gentle Shepherd .......362
Gracious Spirit, Holy Ghost..............147
Great God! how infinite art Thou........ 30
Great God! we sing that mighty hand ...458
Guide me, O Thou great Jehovah ........ 41

Hail the day that sees Him rise .........107
† Hail, Thou long expected Jesus.........129
Hail, Thou once despised Jesus...........124
Hail to the Lord's anointed..............223
Hail to the Prince of life and peace.....115
Happy the man who knows..................190
Happy the souls to Jesus joined..........235
Hark, a thrilling voice is sounding...... 42
Hark, hark, my soul, angelic songs.......302
Hark, hark, the notes of joy............. 46
Hark, my soul, it is the Lord............257
Hark, ten thousand harps and voices...118
Hark, the glad sound, the Saviour comes.. 44
Hark, the herald angels sing............. 48
Hark, the sound of holy voices...........394
Hark! the voice eternal.................. 43
Hark, the voice of love and mercy....... 95
He has come! the Christ of God......... 47
He leadeth me: O blessed thought.......327
Holy Father, hear my cry.................270
Holy Ghost, the Infinite.................148
Holy, Holy, Holy! Lord God Almighty.. 3
Hosanna to the living Lord .. ........... 81
How beauteous are their feet............168
How beauteous were the marks divine.... 65

How firm a foundation, ye saints of the Lord............................325
How gentle God's commands..............354
How precious is the book divine.........155
How sweet, how heavenly is the sight.....232
How sweetly flowed the gospel sound..... 64
How sweet the name of Jesus sounds .....308

I heard the voice of Jesus say...........285
I know that my Redeemer lives..........375
I lay my sins on Jesus...................282
I love Thy kingdom, Lord.................159
I love to steal awhile away..............437
I need Thee every hour...................344
I need Thee, precious Jesus..............275
I say to all men far and near........... 99
I sing th' almighty power of God........ 29
I think, when I read that sweet story of old 71
I was a wandering sheep..................279
I worship Thee, sweet will of God.......353
I 'm not ashamed to own my Lord........177
If Thou impart Thyself to me............292
If through unruffled seas................382
Immortal Love, forever full............. 72
In heavenly love abiding.................363
In the cross of Christ I glory........... 90
In the hour of trial.....................346
It came upon the midnight clear......... 49
It is not death to die...................380

Jehovah God, Thy gracious power........466
Jerusalem, my happy home................399
Jerusalem on high........................402
Jerusalem the golden.....................405
Jesus, and shall it ever be..............180
Jesus calls us; o'er the tumult......... 73
Jesus came, the heavens adoring.........128
Jesus! I love Thy charming name.........305
Jesus, I my cross have taken.............283
Jesus lives! no longer now...............103
Jesus! Lover of my soul..................326
Jesus, meek and gentle...................274
Jesus, my Lord, my God, my all..........291
Jesus shall reign where'er the sun......225
Jesus, tender Shepherd, hear me .......451
Jesus, these eyes have never seen.......306
Jesus! the very thought of Thee.........307
Jesus, Thou joy of loving hearts.........187
Jesus, Thy blood and righteousness......139
Jesus, Thy name I love...................304
Jesus, transporting sound................302
Jesus, where'er Thy people meet......... 8
Joy to the world, the Lord is come ..... 45
Just as I am, without one plea...........267

Kingdoms and thrones to God belong... 226

Lamp of our feet, whereby we trace......156
Lead, kindly light.......................347
Lead on, O King Eternal..................196
Lead us, heavenly Father, lead us.......336
Let children hear the mighty deeds......471
Let our choir new anthems raise.........229
Lift up your heads, ye mighty gates..... 220
Light of the lonely pilgrim's heart.....130
Light of the world, we hail Thee........213

# INDEX OF FIRST LINES

Light of those whose dreary dwelling. ...132
Like Noah's weary dove ................178
Lo, He comes, with clouds descending....136
Look, ye saints, the sight is glorious......112
Lord, dismiss us with Thy blessing......427
Lord, I believe ; Thy power I own......287
Lord, I know Thy grace is nigh me....... 77
Lord, in this Thy mercy's day...........266
Lord, it belongs not to my care..........357
Lord, lead the way the Saviour went.....206
Lord of all being, throned afar.......... 39
Lord of every land and nation............126
Lord of mercy and of might...............272
Lord of our life, and God of our salvation.166
Lord of the Sabbath, hear our vows......412
Lord of the worlds above ................420
Lord, when we bend before Thy throne... 7
Love divine, all love excelling............294

Majestic sweetness sits enthroned.. .....299
Many centuries have fled................181
More love to Thee, O Christ.............348
Must Jesus bear the Cross alone..........318
My country, 't is of thee .................468
My dear Redeemer, and my Lord......... 75
My faith looks up to Thee................ 14
My God, how wonderful Thou art........ 35
My God, I thank Thee ..................359
My God, is any hour so sweet ............365
My God, my Father, while I stray........340
My Homeland, oh, my Homeland........397
My soul, be on thy guard..................321
My soul, it is thy God.....................314
My soul, weigh not thy life................315

Nearer, my God, to Thee ................. 13
No, no, it is not dying.....................381
Now begin the heavenly theme...........296
Now is the accepted time.................260
Now my soul, thy voice upraising........ 87
Now the day is over .....................449
Now the laborer's task is o'er............383

O blessed God, to Thee I raise............ 31
O bread to pilgrims given.................182
O Christ, with each returning morn......430
O day of rest and gladness ..............400
O everlasting light........................377
O Gift of gifts! O Grace of faith..........284
O God, beneath Thy guiding hand.......470
O God of God ! O Light of Light........123
†O God, our help in ages past............ 37
O God, the Rock of ages................. 40
O happy band of pilgrims ................197
O happy soul that lives on high..........373
O holy, holy Lord......................... 33
O holy Saviour, Friend unseen...........328
O Jesus, I have promised.................194
O Jesus, King most wonderful........... 20
O Jesus, Thou art standing..............245
O little town of Bethlehem............... 56
O Lord, be with us when we sail .... ....465
O Lord, how full of sweet content... ....467
O Lord, how good, how great art Thou.... 36
O Lord of heaven, and earth, and sea....460
O Lord our God, arise ...................216

O Lord, turn not Thy face away..... .. 278
O Love divine, that stooped to share.. ....330
O Master, let me walk with Thee......... 76
O Mother dear, Jerusalem .... .........400
O Paradise! O Paradise .................391
O Sacred Head, now wounded............ 88
O Son of man, Thyself hast proved....... 66
O Spirit of the living God.................150
O Thou from whom all goodness flows....350
O very God of very God .................355
O Word of God incarnate.................153
O'er the gloomy hills of darkness.........219
†Oh, cease, my wandering soul...........178
Oh, come, all ye faithful.................. 55
Oh, come and mourn with me awhile..... 85
Oh, come, oh, come, Immanuel..........134
Oh, could I speak the matchless worth....303
Oh, for a closer walk with God...........369
Oh, for a faith that will not shrink.......338
Oh, for a shout of joy..................... 27
Oh, for a thousand tongues to sing........297
Oh help us, Lord, each hour of need.....331
Oh, how shall I receive Thee............. 80
Oh, mean may seem this house of clay... 67
Oh, speed thee, Christian ! on thy way, ..319
Oh, still in accents sweet and strong......212
Oh, sweetly breathe the lyres above ......175
Oh, that my load of sin were gone.......276
Oh, the sweet wonders of that cross...... 86
Oh, timely happy, timely wise............429
Oh, what can little hands do ..... ......203
Oh, where are kings and empires now.....163
Oh, where is He that trod the sea........ 68
Oh, worship the King all glorious above... 25
Once in royal David's city................ 54
One holy Church of God appears ........161
One sweetly solemn thought..............387
One there is, above all others.............120
On Jordan's bank the Baptist's cry....... 61
On our way rejoicing......................193
On the mountain's top appearing.........220
Onward, Christian soldiers................191
Our blest Redeemer ere he breathed.. ...140
Our God, our God, Thou shinest here....142
Our God, our help in ages past.......... 37
Our hearts, O Lord, with grief are rent...368
Our heavenly Father calls................. 5
Our Lord is risen from the dead..........106

Peace, perfect peace, in this dark world ..333
People of the living God .................179
Pleasant are Thy courts above...........417
Praise, my soul, the King of heaven...... 19
Praise to God, immortal praise...........459
Praise to Thee, Thou great Creator.......424
Prayer is the soul's sincere desire........366
Prince of Peace, control my will..........289
Purer yet and purer .....................371

Rejoice, rejoice, believers.................135
Rejoice, the Lord is King ................122
Resting from His work to-day............ 96
Return. O wanderer. to thy home . ......253
Ride on ! ride on in majesty.............. 79
Rise, my soul, and stretch thy wings......457
Rock of Ages, cleft for me ...............269

# INDEX OF FIRST LINES

| | |
|---|---|
| Safely through another week............408 | The sun is sinking fast..................436 |
| Salvation! oh, the joyful sound.........242 | The world is very evil...................403 |
| Saviour, again to Thy dear Name........440 | There is a fountain filled with blood......94 |
| Saviour, blessed Saviour..................301 | There is a green hill far away............89 |
| Saviour, breathe an evening blessing......443 | There is a land of pure delight.........398 |
| Saviour, like a Shepherd lead us.........361 | There is an hour of peaceful rest........388 |
| Saviour, who Thy flock art feeding......172 | There is a safe and secret place.........345 |
| Saviour! who Thy life didst give........209 | Thine arm, O Lord, in days of old........70 |
| See Israel's gentle Shepherd stand.......171 | Thine forever! God of love..............358 |
| Servant of God, well done................382 | Think well how Jesus trusts Himself....249 |
| Shepherd of tender youth.................173 | This is the day of light..................414 |
| Sing of Jesus, sing for ever..............300 | This is the day the Lord hath made......411 |
| Sing we the song of those who stand.....238 | Thou dear Redeemer, dying Lamb........309 |
| Sinner, rouse thee from thy sleep........258 | Thou didst leave Thy throne.............53 |
| Sinners, turn, why will ye die...........254 | Thou sayest, "Take up thy cross........74 |
| Sleep thy last sleep......................378 | Through the night of doubt and sorrow...240 |
| Softly fades the twilight ray............445 | Thy home is with the humble, Lord.....151 |
| Softly now the light of day..............435 | Thy mighty working, mighty God........32 |
| Soldiers of Christ, arise.................192 | Thy way, not mine, O Lord..............342 |
| Soldiers who to Christ belong............201 | "Till He come," oh, let the words.....186 |
| Something every heart is loving.........176 | 'T is midnight, and on Olive's brow......84 |
| Songs of praise the angels sang..........422 | To-day the Saviour calls.................252 |
| Soon may the last glad song arise........227 | To-day Thy mercy calls me...............261 |
| Sovereign of worlds, display Thy power...215 | To Thee, O dear, dear Saviour..........376 |
| Sow in the morn thy seed................207 | To Thee, our God, we fly................469 |
| Spirit Divine, attend our prayers........421 | Triumphant, Christ ascends on high......108 |
| Stand up, and bless the Lord............426 | Triumphant Zion, lift thy head..........164 |
| Stand up, my soul, shake off thy fears....316 | |
| Stand up, stand up for Jesus.............189 | Unshaken as the sacred hill..............339 |
| Still, still with Thee, my God............15 | Uplift the banner! Let it float..........217 |
| Sun of my soul, Thou Saviour dear......452 | |
| Sure the blest Comforter is nigh........149 | Wake the song of jubilee................221 |
| Sweet is the memory of Thy grace........16 | Walk in the light, so shalt thou know....370 |
| Sweet is the work, my God, my King.....415 | Was there ever kindest shepherd........251 |
| Sweet is the work, O Lord...............416 | We are but strangers here...............384 |
| Sweet is Thy mercy, Lord................12 | We bid thee welcome, in the name......169 |
| Sweet Saviour, bless us ere we go........434 | We give Thee but Thine own............204 |
| Sweet the moments, rich in blessing......93 | Weary of earth, and laden with my sin...265 |
| | Welcome, delightful morn................407 |
| Take my heart, O Father, take it.......281 | Welcome, happy morning................105 |
| Talk with me, Lord; Thyself reveal.....11 | What grace, O Lord, and beauty shone...63 |
| Tarry with me, O my Saviour...........442 | When all Thy mercies, O my God........351 |
| Teach me, my God and King.............208 | When God of old came down from heaven.141 |
| Ten thousand times ten thousand........393 | When, His salvation bringing............82 |
| The Church's one foundation............157 | When I can read my title clear..........390 |
| The dawn of God's new Sabbath.........410 | When I survey the wondrous cross......92 |
| The day is past and gone.................439 | When morning gilds the skies............432 |
| The day is past and over.................441 | When this passing world is done........138 |
| The day of praise is done.................438 | When through the torn sail..............464 |
| The day of resurrection..................100 | When wounded sore, the stricken soul...268 |
| The eternal gates lift up their heads....110 | While Thee I seek, protecting Power....374 |
| The glory of the spring how sweet........152 | While with ceaseless course the sun......454 |
| The head that once was crowned with....109 | Why should the children of a King.....144 |
| The King of glory standeth..............246 | With joy we meditate the grace.........329 |
| The King of love my Shepherd is........17 | Workman of God, O lose not heart......210 |
| The Lord is King! Lift up thy voice....34 | |
| The morning light is breaking............222 | Ye choirs of new Jerusalem..............102 |
| The radiant morn hath passed away.....446 | Ye Christian heralds! go, proclaim.....214 |
| The roseate hues of early dawn..........395 | Ye holy angels bright.....................1 |
| The Saviour! — what a noble flame.....78 | Ye servants of the Lord..................188 |
| The Son of God goes forth to war........228 | Yes, for me, for me He careth...........334 |
| The Spirit breathes upon the word......154 | Ye wretched, hungry, starving poor....248 |
| The Spirit, in our hearts..................259 | Your harps, ye trembling saints.........356 |
| † The strife is o'er, the battle done......104 | |

# ANCIENT AND SCRIPTURAL HYMNS.

| | |
|---|---|
| Beatitudes . . . . . . . . . . . 489 | Lord, let me know my end . . . . . 486 |
| Benedic Anima Mea . . . . . . . . 481 | Lord, Thou hast been our Dwelling Place 487 |
| Benedictus . . . . . . . . . . . 475 | |
| Bonum Est Confiteri . . . . . . . 483 | Magnificat . . . . . . . . . . . 476 |
| Cantate Domino . . . . . . . . . 482 | Nunc dimittis . . . . . . . . . . 477 |
| Christ our Passover . . . . . . . 484 | |
| | Sanctus . . . . . . . . . . . 490 |
| Deus Misereatur , . . . . . . . 480 | |
| | Te Deum Laudamus . . . . . . . 474 |
| Gloria in Excelsis Deo . . . . . . 473 | The Lord is my Shepherd . . . . . 488 |
| I am the Resurrection . . . . . . 485 | Venite Exultemus Domino . . . . 478 |
| Jubilate Deo . . . . . . . . . . 479 | |

www.ingramcontent.com/pod-product-compliance
Lightning Source LLC
Chambersburg PA
CBHW022102300426
44117CB00007B/562